NO LAW

NO LAW

*Intellectual Property in the Image of
an Absolute First Amendment*

David L. Lange
and
H. Jefferson Powell

STANFORD LAW BOOKS
An Imprint of Stanford University Press
Stanford, California

Printed in the United States of America on acid-free, archival-quality paper

Library of Congress Cataloging-in-Publication Data

Lange, David, 1938–

No law : intellectual property in the image of an absolute First Amendment / David L. Lange and H. Jefferson Powell.
   p. cm.
  Includes bibliographical references and index.
  ISBN 978-0-8047-4578-9 (cloth : alk. paper)—ISBN 978-0-8047-4579-6 (pbk. : alk. paper)
   1. Intellectual property—United States. 2. United States. Constitution. 1st Amendment. 3. Freedom of expression—United States. I. Powell, Jefferson, 1954– II. Title.

  KF2979.L37   2008
  346.7304'8—dc22   2008011828

Typeset by Westchester Book Group in 10/15 Sabon

*For my wife and companion, Teresa—creative, expressive, and wise,
and always the better writer.*

—D. L.

*For my daughter Sara, whose enthusiastic interest
makes writing a joy.*

—J. P.

Contents

CONTENTS

Preface

OUR BOOK HAD ITS BEGINNINGS in a series of conversations some years ago between its authors, who are friends and colleagues on the faculty of the Law School at Duke University.* Professor Lange, whose professional interests include intellectual property and entertainment law, has long been identified with specialists in these fields who are skeptical of the utility and the impact of the doctrines that limit freedom of expression. Professor Powell has written extensively on subjects centered in the history and theories of interpretation affecting the American Constitution. Meanwhile, each of us has had a particular interest in the First Amendment that antedated the conversations that led to this work.

As our conversations continued, we decided to record our growing conviction that the notions of exclusivity traditionally associated with the intellectual property doctrines of greatest concern in the context of expression (chiefly copyright, but also some aspects of unfair competition, moral rights, trademark law, and even patent law) ought to be constrained in favor of a far wider and more complete susceptibility of that expression to unlicensed appropriation by others. This we thought, in company with many others who had written on the subject, was at least minimally necessary in the interest of creative expression. In truth, however, we were soon convinced that exclusive rights in any expression—whether conventionally creative or not—were simply intolerable in a system of law that prizes the right in individuals to think as they please and to speak as they think—the system of law that Americans (and American courts) like to pride themselves in possessing. As we

---

* The question of voice is a persistent one in coauthored works. We have elected to write in the first person, singular or plural, whenever that is feasible, and in the third person when that voice seems most likely to yield clarity or otherwise appears appropriate. Regrettably nevertheless, some awkwardness is inevitable, for which we apologize.

came to see the matter, the questionable rights arising from exclusivity in expression would likely be constrained in satisfactory measure only if the First Amendment itself were to receive the absolute interpretation its language and formative history might well have justified at large—an interpretation of the sort most often identified with Justice Hugo Black, but an interpretation uniformly rejected by most other Justices through the years, and almost universally dismissed by students of the Constitution. In effect, then, we decided to develop several broad propositions at odds with conventional understandings of the law: first, that the intellectual property doctrines conferring exclusivity in expression, however defensible they may be in themselves, are nevertheless inessential, repressive, and ultimately unacceptable when looked at from the perspective of freedom of expression (propositions again endorsed, at least in part, by many other observers of the field, but not usually carried to the extreme position that we were prepared to embrace); second, both in the service of these insights and as a separate matter of interpretation in its own right, that the speech and press clauses of the First Amendment should be given an absolute reading akin to the one advanced by Justice Black; and finally, that the intellectual property doctrines should be refashioned accordingly. It was not a condition of our undertaking that the results would allow the continuation of any protection of the sort now identified with these doctrines; but in the end we came to believe that legally protected intellectual productivity and freedom of expression could coexist in substantial harmony after all.

The work we initially envisioned was to be relatively brief: this was to be more nearly in the nature of a polemic than a work of scholarship. And we expected to complete it in no more than a few years, perhaps three at most, with each of us writing largely from within the framework of ideas and opinions already formed over the entire period of our professional careers. As time passed, however, the complexity of our undertaking overtook us, with the result that we have now spent some six years in drafting the work, and another year in editing it for final publication. Along the way, brevity has been sacrificed in some part on the altar of footnotes, acknowledgments, and an extensive bibliography, in which we have attempted to acknowledge the important work of oth-

ers whose published writings have preceded ours. Our book is still po-
lemical to a considerable degree, proceeding as it still does mainly from
our a priori convictions. One reviewer of our manuscript has described
it (approvingly) as a "legal fantasy," which may very well capture the
essence of it exactly. But fantasies are sometimes taken very seriously by
those who entertain them, and so it is with us. We do not reject our reviewer's characterization, which seems fair enough on the face of it; but
we would insist that what we have written has been written quite seriously nevertheless, in the thought not only that we are envisioning a legal regime that is consistent with a better interpretation of the American
Constitution, but one that is also entirely plausible when looked at from
within the matrix of American culture.

Is it likely that Congress or the Supreme Court will embrace what we
have suggested? Perhaps not, and almost certainly not in the near term.
Old habits die hard. But then our collective political understanding of
the First Amendment is still relatively young and immature, while the
intellectual property doctrines of concern to us have grown old and
rigid and oppressive. No one can say with complete assurance that the
First Amendment may not yet be understood to mean something like
what Justice Black supposed it ought to mean; certainly no one can
doubt that millions among us are growing tired of paying homage to a
system of intellectual property rights that is increasingly out of touch
with contemporary normative judgments about exclusivity and appropriation in the context of expression. The growing conflict between
freedom of expression and interests protected by the intellectual property doctrines is often characterized as a phenomenon peculiar to the
digital technologies and the Internet; but we think these technologies
have merely made the conflict seem more evident and insistent. The intellectual property doctrines touching upon expression have long presupposed that Congress may make laws abridging expression in order to
encourage it. But the First Amendment has always said that "Congress
shall make no law abridging freedom of speech or of the press." Perhaps
Americans will come to think with Justice Black that "no law" means
no law after all. Perhaps then it will not seem fantastic to refashion intellectual property in the image of an absolute First Amendment.

Acknowledgments

WE BEGIN OUR ACKNOWLEDGMENTS by thanking Deans Katherine Bartlett and David Levi, and the staff and students at the Duke Law School, for support and inspiration. Among many other contributions along the way, we benefitted especially from criticisms of portions of the manuscript in progress offered by the members of a small seminar convened in part for that very purpose. More generally, we have long benefitted greatly from our membership in the community of dedicated scholars and professionals who enliven this superb academic institution.

Professor Lange is additionally grateful to his staff assistants, Dawn Blalock, Dana Norvell, Susan Bates, and Tracey Madrid, and to his numerous research assistants and fellow students of intellectual property. In particular, he is indebted to Matt Block, John Eden, Nita Farahany, and Garrett Levin, who were especially generous with their time and advice. For his initial comprehensive introduction to the doctrinal fields that figure in this work he will always be particularly indebted to Paul Goldstein, whose casebook, *Copyright, Patent, Trademark and Related State Doctrines*, he used many years ago upon his arrival at Duke; and to Melville Bernard Nimmer, whose "great work" (as one court memorably and aptly called his then three-volume copyright treatise), together with a casebook on copyright and the law of ideas, served as additionally intensive tutorials in those subjects, and who augmented the instruction afforded by those works with numerous personal kindnesses, including patient and ungrudging responses to the questions a young teacher found it so very helpful to be allowed to pose from time to time. In the now nearly four decades since Professor Lange began to teach, his early instruction in the field has been augmented by the later colleagueship of many others (practitioners, academics, and judges alike), including among them the present and former members of the regular and adjunct intellectual property faculty at Duke (James Boyle, Lauren Dame, Robert Cooke-Deegan, Wesley Cohen, Troy Dow, Catherine Fisk, Kip Frey, Jennifer Jenkins, Karen Magri, Arti Rai, Jerome Reichman, Kenneth Sibley, and Terri Southwick). To these names must be added those of Mary LaFrance and Gary Myers, his former students and now colleagues and coauthors of a casebook on intellectual property, as well as that of his daughter, Jennifer Anderson, a North Carolina practitioner who has assisted in the several updates and new editions of that casebook through the years. All of their collective wisdom continues to play an organizing role in his own understanding of the relevant doctrines, and thus in his efforts to convey what he takes to be common ground in this book—though for his ultimate apostasy, it must cheerfully be said, they bear no responsibility at all.

Professor Powell adds his profound appreciation for the able research assistance of Wells Bennett, now a practicing lawyer in Washington, D.C., and for many conversations about the First Amendment with his wife Sarah Powell, a principled First Amendment absolutist if ever there was one. His daughter Sara has waited eagerly for this book, not least because David and Terri Lange are her beloved godparents.

We are both indebted beyond words to our friend and colleague David McKenzie, a member of the North Carolina bar, who has acted for much of the past three years as our professional research associate. David has taken the lead in coordinating and completing the myriad and formidable research assignments we have asked him to carry out, including the task of drafting and organizing many of our notes as well as the bibliography. It is both fair and accurate, though no doubt still inadequate, to say that his thorough and untiring efforts have improved the work immeasurably while enabling us to bring it to its conclusion. We are deeply grateful to him.

Finally, to the editors and production staff who have worked with us on behalf of Stanford University Press we offer our sincere thanks; we especially acknowledge the support and encouragement of Amanda Moran and Kate Wahl. Our thanks are due as well to Timothy Seldes, of the distinguished New York City literary agency Russell and Volkening, who at a signal moment in the development of our project kindly read the manuscript and offered invaluable advice and counsel. And to our own professional editor, Elisabeth Lewis Corley, we offer our gratitude and appreciation for her patient, wise, experienced and always good-natured colleagueship as we worked together to complete the final version of the manuscript. It is not Elisabeth's fault if an occasional lapse in diction or infelicity in expression has managed to survive, but rather a consequence of our own sometimes stubborn disinclination to repent our mistakes. Still we shall dare to hope (to borrow an expression from that celebrated film icon of the 1920s, Lina LaMont) that in the end all of Elisabeth's hard work ain't been in vain for nuthin'.

For in the end, of course, we must bear final responsibility for the manuscript in its entirety.

NO LAW

PART I

Intellectual Property in America:
The Idea and Its Merits

CHAPTER I

Unfair Competition and Trademarks

WHAT DO WE MEAN when we speak of intellectual property? What ideas lie behind it? What are its merits?

In the United States, until some thirty years or so ago, the term "intellectual property" was not much used and had no clear meaning. American lawyers (practitioners and academics alike) generally spoke directly of unfair competition, trade secrets, trademarks, copyright, or patent law without supposing that these discrete doctrinal fields should be thought of as part of a larger, overarching subject. Even today, when "intellectual property" is in common usage in this country (and is often employed as though it were a term of art), the fact remains that its clearest function is taxonomical: intellectual property is to copyright, for example, as "family" is to "genus" or "species" to "variety."[1] It is understood to embrace the doctrines that make up its constituent parts, rather than to convey a deeper meaning grounded in theory. To be sure, serious efforts at theory have begun to emerge, some of them engaging indeed,[2] but none can be said to have gained wide acceptance. Instead, the term suggests at most a rough correspondence among the doctrines it embraces—a correspondence derived from the doctrines, however, rather than the other way around.[3]

Yet the term "property" itself traditionally conveys a powerful ideological message in which the right of exclusive and adverse possession plays a central role. Many of us share a common (if tacit) understanding of property that is both atavistic and archetypal; we are thus apt to view it as a kind of ur-right invested with ancient but still essential attributes of our selves in our relationships with others. Property in this not unusual sense typically begins with the recognition of something of value (in legal usage, the res, or, literally, "thing"), around which principles for holding the thing to oneself or sharing it with others are defined and redefined from time to time as circumstances may require. In American life property often appears to define the boundary between that which is private (and mine or yours) and that which is public (and either theirs or everybody's), thereby simultaneously setting us apart from society at large and linking us to it. This is commonly understood to be a function of individual or personal autonomy and dignity arrayed against an aggregation of collective undertakings by and with others, the entirety compounded of entitlements and offsetting obligations both simple and complex.[4] Intellectual property undoubtedly has succeeded to this idea of property in some considerable measure. The deeper theoretical meanings may remain tentative and unsettled, and perhaps even chimerical; but those who embrace intellectual property most ardently find it tempting to suppose that there is an idea behind it nevertheless, which translates (even if, to some degree, by default) into the ancient overarching idea of property at large—again, an idea in which one's personal, exclusive, and adverse possession is offset by complex public obligations. Understood in this way, the concept of intellectual property serves both an ideal and a pragmatic end. We suppose that it is right and decent that a person should possess the fruits of his intellectual labor. We suppose that possession is desirable in practical economic terms as well, for a decent recognition of this central notion of property is widely thought to serve as an incentive to intellectual productivity that might not otherwise be forthcoming, and to the efficient management of the products that are its consequence. And we imagine that, in the end, not merely the individual but society at large will benefit from this state of affairs.[5]

In this part of our book, we begin by responding to the questions we first posed above. In the first two chapters we briefly sketch the doctrines that intellectual property embraces,[6] proceeding in the order in which we have listed them here, while adding or elaborating upon others. We note the rough correspondences among them, as well as their justifications and anomalies. Then, in two additional chapters that complete this part, we will raise the questions that are the occasion for our later efforts in this book: How are we to judge these intellectual property doctrines on their merits? What benefits do they confer upon us? At what cost to freedoms that we value, especially the freedom of thought and speech? What role does the Constitution play in arriving at the balance

4

that now obtains? And is that role adequate to our needs—or amenable to change?

COMPETITION, FAIR AND OTHERWISE

The term "unfair competition" conveys something of its meaning in the words from which the term is formed. Competition is not generally frowned on in American law, of course, nor was it in the late English law from which American law descended. To the contrary, competition has long enjoyed wide approval and a generous latitude.[7] In contemporary American life competition is omnipresent, and is privileged to a degree that may actually strike some observers as indecent if not unfair. A competitor like Wal-Mart may move into a quiet town on the edge of the prairie knowing that any number of small businesses, which may very well have flourished in that place for decades in the hands of pioneers who settled there and their descendants or successors, are now to be driven from the field. This can seem hard, as indeed it is in a perfectly ordinary sense of the word. But the proprietors of a clothing or shoe store, or grocery or hardware or toy store, who can no longer afford to open their doors, have no legal cause of action against Wal-Mart for the misfortune that has befallen them. The superstore's superior purchasing power, which translates into lower prices to consumers as well as gains in efficiency, may bring ruin to these and other smaller storekeepers, but that result is permissible and fair (some would say desirable) when it is the consequence of competition. The law affords no direct remedy. Against the moral considerations that may trouble one or another of us, we posit the economic superiority of competition thus untrammeled. The market will tell us what we want, it is said, and in so doing will enable us to maximize our collective welfare through the efficiencies that result. Efficiency is a choice we make, and if that choice conflicts with morality, so be it. Whether or not the choice involves a conflict is of course a normative question to which more than one answer may be given; many believe the efficient choice is in natural fact the better moral choice as well—for the same aesthetic reasons, conceptually, that form is sometimes said to be at its best when it follows function.[8]

In a narrow range of competitive circumstances, however, the law may intervene on principles that are grounded in deeper considerations of fairness or decency. Lawyers are accustomed to thinking of these principles as having their origins in *equity*, a term of art in Anglo-American law that reflects both a substantive standard and some vestigial remnants of procedure. When the competition involved is seen to be unfair or inequitable, ruinous consequences for competitors (of the sort that Wal-Mart routinely brings in its wake) may become actionable. There are again no clear guidelines here, but it is probably correct to say, for example, that competition engaged in for no purpose other than to ruin another is actionable. Thus, in one well-known case involving a small Minnesota town at the turn of the century, the state's supreme court held that a silent partner in a barbershop who underwrote the opening of that establishment solely for the purpose of driving an earlier barber out of business had committed an act of unfair competition. The inequity in this setting was seen to lie in the deliberate, unadulterated intent or purpose to harm another for no better reason than to achieve that very end.[9]

Somewhere between the two extremes of vigorous competition and ruin for its own sake lies the boundary between fair and unfair competition, a line defined by rules no clearer, but presumably no less worthy, than the economic and moral precepts that give rise to them. Along its way it traverses ground marked off by such proscriptions as are to be found still in the older remedies against fraud, deceit, and misrepresentation, and then meanders on across a sprawling landscape of rights, wrongs, and remedies that we need not explore or map in their entirety.[10] For the purposes of this book it is enough to say only three things more about unfair competition at large: first, that it is older than the other doctrinal fields that make up intellectual property; second, that it is less a creature of statute than are these others, and more a reflection of decisions by judges; and third, that in the matter of remedies (which frequently include injunctive relief) the judges' decisions tend, as we have said, to be grounded in equity (or a perceived sense of fairness), with room for greater procedural flexibility from case to case than is to be expected from the more fixed constellation of money-centered remedies that typically make up the common law.

All of this having been said for the sake of introduction, there are now two parts of the general concept of unfair competition that bear a closer singling out. They function in ways analogous to newer, more parochial doctrines that make up intellectual property law, and they remain influential in that field despite their greater age.

"Passing Off" and the Question of Property

One is the concept called "passing off," which in its original form constrains a merchant against selling his goods as if they were another's. In practice the rule is straightforward enough, and is easily applied and understood. The proprietor of a soda fountain which serves no cola drink but Pepsi-Cola may not sell Pepsi to a customer who has asked for Coca-Cola without first noting that Pepsi is all he has to offer, and then securing the customer's acquiescence in the proposed substitution. The seller may not simply provide Pepsi as if it were Coke. This is a conventional scenario in which passing-off figures; but sometimes a business may prefer to sell another's goods as if they were its own. This too is ordinarily forbidden, under a corollary to the passing off doctrine known as "reverse passing off." For example, a fledgling jeweler may not sell and take credit for a more experienced or better artist's work in order to establish a reputation or to secure custom as yet undeserved.[11]

In each instance these rules belong to the larger field of unfair competition because the practices they prohibit are readily seen to be dishonest and unfair. In what sense, however, do they also belong among the doctrines ascribed to intellectual property? In each instance they protect the originators of goods against the adverse consequences of potential misunderstanding or misrepresentation: a consumer might otherwise conclude, for example, that the "Coke" he thinks he has been served is not up to its usual standards; a person who is misled as to the provenance of a piece of jewelry may continue for at least a while to patronize the lesser jeweler to the detriment of the better artisan. These are consequences of unfairness, but they are also threats to one of the main interests of competitors in maintaining the origins and identity of their goods, services, and the like. Repeated enough times, the experience of substitution may seriously undermine the ability of Coca-Cola or the established jeweler to recoup the investment they have made in bringing their products to market. Disincentives to production are apt to follow. In the case of reverse passing off, meanwhile, something akin to plagiarism can be seen as well. The seller is appropriating credit for another's effort, thereby depriving the true creator of the recognition, and perhaps again the market, to which he is entitled. Beyond these considerations, and in either setting, there is also a wider interest of consumers and the public in avoiding misrepresentation or misunderstanding. When these infect a transaction the public's interest in an efficient marketplace is affronted, as is the consumer's interest in defending his personal integrity against deceit. All of these considerations are said to justify the branch of unfair competition law known as passing off: a sense of decency and fair play; a concern for maintaining the origins, identity, and integrity of goods or services, and thus the market for them; rewarding the original creator with recognition and an ability to recoup his or her investment; and defending the consumer against personal indignities.[12] These may be seen as the particular concerns of this branch of unfair competition; as we will soon see, they are also among the reasons why we recognize interests in trademarks, copyrights, and patents. One can say that there is at least a rough correspondence among them all.[13]

Misappropriation

Meanwhile, a second branch of unfair competition, capable of standing alone but especially noteworthy for the role it has played in the development of other intellectual property doctrines, is sometimes termed "misappropriation." In the United States, the most celebrated example arose in 1918, in *International News Service v. Associated Press*,[14] a decision of the Supreme Court involving an appropriation by International News Service of the content of news dispatches generated by the Associated Press. The raw news events from which these dispatches were compiled could not be copyrighted in themselves, nor had AP taken steps to perfect copyright in its written version of them. To the contrary, AP had posted the dispatches on a public bulletin board accessible to anyone who might pass by. INS copied the dispatches and circulated them to its own client newspapers without acknowledgment or attribution to AP. In these circumstances, Justice Holmes thought that what INS had done amounted to reverse passing off, and should therefore be enjoined unless and until INS acknowledged the provenance of the dispatches it had taken. But a majority of the Court held that the appropriation was a competitive wrong in itself, in that it deprived AP of its ability to recoup the investment it had made in seeking out and reporting the news. Under this view of the matter, AP could claim at least a "quasi property" interest in the news; the injunction against INS would run until the value of the news as news had abated.

Given the theory of the case, and the remedy that followed, this is arguably the most important single decision in the history of intellectual property in America. Certainly it is among the most frequently discussed.[15] We will devote an entire chapter to the case later in our book. For the moment, though, it will suffice to state the central maxim from which the theory and the remedy derived, and for which the case itself stands: namely, that one should not reap where one has not sown. This is, of course, a principle instilled in most of us from earliest childhood. It is the lesson we learn, for example, when we read "The Little Red Hen" and countless other fables grounded in a similar morality. Its corollary, that we are entitled to reap what we have sown, leaving others free to do the same if they have the wit and the will, is at the center of at least one widely accepted and long-held idea of property, an idea that antedates the more particular development of intellectual property doctrines.[16] The principle that underlies the notion of misappropriation as unfair competition is accordingly among the most powerful in the entire field of intellectual property. One senses the wisdom and justice in it, as the Court did in *INS*—or, then again, perhaps one does not, as Holmes did not—but its appeal is not solely that of a common moral precept. The Court's ruling in the case also reflected a conventional economic understanding, then and now, which is that incentives to invest must include an ability to recoup the investment with enough certainty, and in anticipation of enough profit, to justify investing again, meanwhile foregoing other opportunities. The injunction against misappropriation was fashioned with this in mind.

Misappropriation and Exclusivity

Misappropriation, then, is one way to characterize what INS had done. But to speak of the case in this way is to place the emphasis on the wrongdoing of the competitor. To understand the premise of the case fully, we will also want to restate it in terms of an affirmative entitlement belonging to AP. From this perspective we can see that the sine qua non of the (quasi) property interest the Court acknowledged and approved lay in the right of AP to the exclusive possession of the news it had gathered and the dispatches it had prepared, and in its corresponding ability to prevent others from engaging in unauthorized appropriation. Exclusivity and (mis)appropriation were juxtaposed in the majority's view of unfair competition. The one was seen as precluding the other, at least in the absence of a license by the proprietor of the affirmative right. This relationship—again, this juxtaposition between exclusivity and appropriation—is central not only to the doctrine of misappropriation in unfair competition, but to no fewer than six other doctrines at the center of the field of American law we have lately come to call intellectual property. In the federal statutory realms of (1) copyright and (2) patent law, as in the common (or state) law realms of (3) copyright in evanescent works (or common law copyright, as it is often called), (4) trade secrets, and (5) the so-called right of publicity, we will find that the concepts of exclusivity and appropriation are similarly paired. In trademark law, meanwhile, at both the federal and state levels, a growing effort to curtail (6) trademark "dilution" is centered upon the argument that famous marks should be protected against use (or appropriation) by others, even in circumstances in which that usage causes no confusion in the marketplace of the sort that trademarks are traditionally meant to preclude. The thought behind the law of dilution is that the trademark proprietor, having invested in the development of a highly distinctive mark, should be entitled to its exclusive use. Indeed it is accurate, and perhaps even more useful, to say that only in that part of trademark law concerned mainly with confusion does the concept of exclusivity versus appropriation not hold its usual sway; and as we will see, even in that setting the appeal in exclusivity exerts a powerful, if not always transparent, influence on the actual decisions in cases.

The Role of Exclusivity Versus Appropriation

Of course we must delineate these additional areas of substantive law in greater detail if the full import of what we have just said is to be made clear. This we propose to do in the next several pages. But meanwhile it is not premature to observe, as we have, that the idea of exclusivity in a work of the intellect, a commonplace in virtually all of American intellectual property discourse, is also taken by most judges who entertain it to mean that the possessor of the exclusive right is entitled to enjoin others from unauthorized uses of that work—this in order to acknowledge the proprietor's moral claims to recognition, and also to maintain the incentive that the law supposes the producer must have in order to continue to produce the work.[17] When we speak of intellectual property, then, we may well have in mind one or more of the rough correspondences already noted in our treatment of passing off: *a sense of decency and fair play; a concern for maintaining the origins, identity, and integrity of goods or services, and thus the market for them; rewarding the true creator with recognition; and defending the consumer against personal indignities.* What we mean is also likely to be bound up in a juxtaposition of exclusivity and appropriation, offered in the service of moral entitlement, as well as incentives to continued productivity and efficient management.[18]

Misappropriation Extended: Three Doctrines

It is conventional among scholars and judges today to disapprove of misappropriation-as-doctrine on two grounds: first, that the tendentious nature of its jurisprudence renders it excessively protean; and second, that its origins in the *INS* case are suspect as an unwarranted exercise of common law jurisdiction by a federal court.[19] But scholars and judges may propose; in practice experience disposes. And in practice the underlying tenets of misappropriation (the appearance of unfairness and inefficiency in unjust enrichment and free riding—or, in other words, reaping where one has not sown) have come to dominate the thinking in every area of intellectual property in which Congress and federal law have not effectively preempted or largely occupied the field. Three such areas stand out.

Common Law Copyright

The remoter origins of Anglo-American copyright actually lie in the censorship practices of the Tudor monarchy, which sought to regulate the uses of the printing press in the immediate aftermath of Henry VIII's decision to defy the Pope and divorce Catherine of Aragon in order to marry Anne Boleyn.[20] That decision was fraught with difficulties, political and religious, in a day when the one was to a considerable extent the other; and Henry's solution, which was to disavow the Roman Church and declare himself Supreme Head of the Church of England, did nothing to simplify his life or the lives of his subjects, many of whom did not share his obsession with Anne Boleyn or approve his willingness to court excommunication in order to possess her. In the hands of these dissidents the press might have become an even greater nuisance than in fact it did become had nothing at all been done to control it. This was early in the sixteenth century; and insofar as censorship of the press was concerned, it began with the accession of the Tudors, thence to be followed over the next hundred years and more by increasingly elaborate and stringent provisions for licensing, culminating in an enhanced role for the already infamous Star Chamber and the establishment of a Company of Worshipful Stationers whom the Crown invested with royal warrants amounting to monopolies over publications.[21]

By the end of the seventeenth century, however, and in the aftermath of civil war, a regicide Parliament and the Crown's erstwhile subjects had so gained the upper hand that the several Printing Acts that had supported the apparatus of monopoly were allowed to expire. Now the Stationers, deprived of their protection, found themselves upon hard times. At the beginning of the eighteenth century, in the reign of Queen Anne, they managed to persuade Parliament to adopt legislation restoring to them a measure of the control over publications they had formerly enjoyed, this in the form of a new statutory copyright (so called) that was enacted in 1709 and took effect in 1710. One might argue that the underlying reasons for this new right of copy were economic or personal, rather than political, in response to which Sir Thomas More could explain once again how the one is but the other.[22] For our purposes it will do merely to observe that the mechanisms of control and enforcement, from Henry's time to Anne's, remained substantially the same: the statutes conferred exclusive rights to publish upon persons and works favored by the state, to be enforced by both civil and criminal penalties, and this at the expense of persons and works not favored by the state. (This is still an accurate summary of the nature of statutory copyright in our time, of which more later.)

The formal recognition of a statutory right of copy inevitably led to litigation, and thence to the opportunistic proposition that some form of copyright must also inhere in the common law. In truth, that may never have been the case prior to 1709, when the business of copyright in published works was first taken up directly by Parliament; at least the evidence for it is debatable.[23] But by the beginning of the eighteenth century, English courts had concluded nevertheless that some form of copyright in unpublished works could indeed be inferred from the common law—to be displaced or subsumed, however, upon publication, at which point the statutory copyright would vest and the statute itself control. Students of copyright would later sum up the distinction between common law copyright (or the "right of first publication," as it was also sometimes called) and statutory copyright in this way: *When the statutory copyright comes in, the common law right goes out.*[24] Common law copyright came to be recognized formally in American law as well, circa 1834;[25] in that form it survived well into the late twentieth century when the 1976 General Copyright Revision finally incorporated most unpublished works into its scheme, leaving only evanescent works (such as conversations, improvisations, and other unrecorded expression), as well as works formally excluded from federal protection (such as simple ballroom dance steps and possibly data), subject to protection at the common law. Proprietors of works such as these presumably enjoy protection against appropriation by others at least so long as the work remains unpublished. Arguably, they may also enjoy a similar right even after publication. Also arguably, the right or rights they possess may endure in perpetuity. The First Amendment may intervene at some point to curb or curtail these rights, though the cases do not make clear when or whether this is so. In some instances, federal preemption may be effected, either by the terms of the federal copyright statute or by virtue of the implicit conflict between a common law copyright and the federal law; again, neither the statute nor the case law clarifies the issue. This state of nice uncertainty and confusion is the state of common law copyright today.[26]

And whence came its jurisprudence? Well, in truth, the answer to that question is, as we have implied, also uncertain. The earliest English cases on the point are debatable. Samuel Warren and Louis Brandeis actually read some later English common law copyright cases as forerunners of what today we regard as the right of privacy, classically (and still) a matter of tort law.[27] It is probably more accurate to suggest that common law copyright was originally a by-product of exigency, born in the course of litigation when, for a party running out of statute, it became useful to posit an anterior, if hitherto unrecognized, right in the common law. Like other bastard rights, this one may have sprung into life with little in the way of respectable parentage. Increasingly, however, as the notion of misappropriation flourished during the twentieth century despite its detractors, it appeared that common law copyright might be justified most readily by some form of (quasi) property theory as well. In 1994, the American Law Institute's *Restatement (Third) of the Law of Unfair Competition*, with much backing and filling, and while noting that *INS* is justifiably held in wide disfavor, nevertheless appeared to take the reluctant and grudging position that common law copyright may still be understood in American law today as an instance of misappropriation.[28] Though the matter is not free from doubt, it seems to us that the *Restatement*'s hesitant conclusion is defensible, and for our purposes we propose to leave the matter there.

Trade Secrets

A trade secret can be defined as knowledge or information of value in the conduct of a business enterprise by virtue of the fact that it is not generally known by persons outside that business.[29] Trade secrets are of interest to the law chiefly in two settings: when a competitor comes into possession of the secret through "improper means," and when a faithless employee is suborned or otherwise chooses to betray an employer by disclosing the secret improperly.

A trade secret cannot be maintained in knowledge generally known or easily discovered. A biscuit kitchen (of the sort to be found everywhere throughout the American South) can claim no secret in its knowledge that most biscuits are consumed in the morning. This is common ground. Even if an employee were in fact to seize upon that insight for the first time as a result of his employment, he would nevertheless be free to carry the knowledge away with him and use it in his own business later.

The secret must also be secret in fact; once it becomes generally known it is no longer valuable and no longer protectable. This means that the would-be proprietor of a trade secret must exercise care to keep the secret safe. How much care? Reasonable care is enough; one of the recurring issues in this area of law is whether a secret, discovered or uncovered as the case may be, has been the subject of enough care to justify an injunction against its use by the outsider into whose hands the secret has fallen.

The proprietor of a trade secret thus has rights against those who seize it through improper means, or against a faithless employee. But the secret is not held impregnable against all comers. "Reverse engineering" is fully permissible in American law, which means that competitors are free to study the proprietor's business in a deliberate attempt to discern the secrets that make it successful. The competitor is still constrained by the rule against "improper means": industrial espionage is forbidden— including, in one celebrated case, photographs taken during overflights by private aircraft while a chemical plant was under construction.[30] The layout of the plant was apparent from the air, and the secret technology thus lay open to view, but it would have been unreasonably burdensome to take the additional precaution of covering the plant site during the construction phase. The court held that the proprietor had exercised due care in protecting it from discovery. In effect, spycraft were not among the risks the proprietor had to anticipate. ("A schoolboy's trick," the court called the overflights, meanwhile upholding an injunction against subsequent use of the knowledge thereby gained.) Nor is one permitted to make use of secrets that fall into one's hands in circumstances that raise doubt as to whether the secret has been lost through mere innocent inadvertence, as opposed to carelessness. Just where the boundary lines fall, however, among permitted ratiocination, allowable opportunism, and impermissible knavery is often in dispute. One person's morality is not necessarily another's. The standard is clear enough in theory, but its application to particular facts is not always clear at all.[31]

The case of the faithless employee is often a difficult one to judge as well. On the one hand the law is meant to secure employers in good faith against breaches of fiduciary duties. An employee who cold-bloodedly sells out his employer for a handful of silver, or who leaves a situation of employment in order to take unfair advantage of knowledge gained in the course of that employment, may be enjoined against either perfidy. But then, when is blood cold? And when is the departed employee merely acting fairly in his own interests? Dealing with the Judas employee is easiest when the employer has exacted a formal commitment to secrecy in the context of an employment agreement; the well-drafted contract will spell out the circumstances in which a breach of fiduciary obligations will have taken place. Sometimes the employer also exacts a commitment not to compete later; these agreements, though enforceable when limited as to time, place, and the reasonableness of the terms and conditions contained in them, are also strictly construed as a rule, for reasons having to do with the law's unwillingness to see employment converted into indentured servitude. Absent such agreements, however, or their equivalent (as manifested through the employer's enforcement of workplace rules clearly intended to protect secrets), courts tend to side with employees when disputes arise as to the limits of enforceable secrecy.

In American law the trade secret has generally been treated as a matter of tort and contract law, with additional homage to the law of fiduciary obligations. A Uniform Trade Secrets Act, promulgated by the Commissioners on Uniform State Laws, is an effort to wrest the subject matter away from the vagaries of the common law and into the hands of state legislatures. (There is no federal trade secrets law as such.) Can a trade secret be property? Some cases say yes, while others emphasize the question of the defendant's conduct (a dichotomy reminiscent of the Court's discussion in *INS*). The ALI's *Restatement (Third) of Unfair*

Competition, while generally acknowledging everything we have just said, also suggests that violations of trade secrecy can be analyzed as instances of misappropriation. If so, then perhaps it would follow that a trade secret is at least an example of quasi property. On the face of it, at least one of the usual elements of property is to be seen in the case of a trade secret: there is something to be recognized as the object of protection—a thing or entity, in other words, at the center of the right. That entity is the secret itself and the occasional value that it represents in the hands of its proprietor. This much is consistent with the *Restatement*'s usage of terms, in which misappropriation is further translated as "appropriation of trade values" in the illicit circumstances we have just summarized.[32]

Yet in one respect the nature of the exclusive right in a trade secret is notably different from the rights in virtually all other forms of intellectual property. As we have seen, the trade secret is not secure against deliberate efforts by others to discover and replicate it. The exclusivity afforded by most systems of intellectual property is affirmative, formal, plenary, and prescriptive. The exclusivity afforded by trade secret law is also existential. True, all forms of intellectual property have limits on the protection they afford. But in most doctrinal systems the default position is in favor of protection and exclusivity, and against appropriation and use; in the case of trade secrets one can say that the default position is often in equipoise. Trade secret law presupposes the legitimacy of secrecy, but also of discovery and use, while regulating only the manner in which these ends may be pursued. This difference, subtle as it may seem at first, in fact marks trade secret law as a system of protection worthy of particular note. It is consistent, as we will argue at some length later, with an a priori presumption that the lawgiver is to make no law favoring one position above another, or abridging the abilities of the contestants to secure their own ends.

The Right of Publicity

Our subject at this point is publicity, but our narrative begins (as is usual with treatments of this subject) with privacy. Until nearly the end of the nineteenth century American law gave no evidence of recognizing privacy rights of the sort that today we take for granted. In 1890, however, Samuel Warren and Louis Brandeis, once classmates at the Harvard Law School and each now additionally distinguished in his own right, wrote and published an article (in the *Harvard Law Review*) urging that remedies against invasions of privacy be recognized.[33] In the half century or so that followed, a number of courts and legislatures responded to their arguments. By 1960, William Prosser, dean of the law school at the University of California at Berkeley (Boalt Hall), and a distinguished torts scholar, identified four types of privacy that had been recognized widely enough to justify categorization.[34] These "branches" of privacy (as they came to be called) included intrusion (peeping into a private gathering, for example—which as it happens was the sort of breach that had inspired Warren and Brandeis to write); public disclosure of embarrassing private facts (such as the revelation that a person has a loathsome disease); publications having the effect of placing a person in a "false light" (an offense distinguishable from defamation chiefly in that the concern in privacy is with the potential injury to the victim's sensibilities, rather than with harm to reputation); and public appropriation of a person's identity (without consent) for the purposes of commercial advertising or the like. The gravamen of the offense in each of these actions was said (by Prosser) to lie in "outrage"—which led the acerbic Professor Harry Kalven (the University of Chicago Law School's own noted torts scholar) to remark that a standard like this, which offered little in the way of a clear prima facie case, was essentially "a tort without a profile"—how could a party know whether the plaintiff had pleaded facts sufficient to state a prima facie case?[35] Many practitioners would have agreed with Kalven. These privacy actions are all wonderfully entertaining on their facts but, of the four we have sketched, we ourselves have a continuing interest here only in the last, involving misappropriation of identity in commercial settings.

All of us understand that many among us are loath to appear in any public setting, most especially ones in which we are bent to the service of another's commercial undertaking, whether with or without our consent. Jacqueline Kennedy was such a person. To the end of her life she declined to endorse products or, for that matter, public appeals of virtually any sort. On the rare occasion when her wishes were ignored she did not hesitate to pursue a remedy grounded in the fourth branch of privacy.[36] But we understand as well that many public figures do not share Mrs. Kennedy's inclinations toward such matters. Fame itself is celebrated; many believe in its value to the public with a fervor that we ourselves duly note without sharing their enthusiasm.[37] In any event celebrity endorsements are commonplace and have been for a very long while. One must ask, then, how the law should deal with the case of the celebrity who does not seek protection for privacy, but rather for publicity?

As Melville Nimmer observed in the earliest scholarly treatment of the subject, there are advantages to be gained from converting the right of privacy into a right of publicity.[38] A personal right of privacy may be recognized at common law, but that same law will not allow the celebrity to convey his right as such; as we ourselves have also observed in an earlier portion of this chapter, a personal action for damages in tort cannot ordinarily be sold, licensed, or otherwise conveyed.[39] If a conveyance of something amounting to a right of publicity is contemplated, one would expect the transaction to be treated as a matter of property.

Until 1953, however, there was no such property right.[40] American lawyers representing celebrity clients had responded to this doctrinal oversight (as they saw it) with a simple but elegant contractual device: the celebrity would agree to permit his or her identity to be used exclusively in exchange for whatever consideration the parties might agree upon, sealing the bargain and giving it particular legal effect by including in the contract a covenant not to sue in tort for the breach of privacy that would otherwise follow. The covenant was then enforceable under contract law. This was a clever example of the way in which a contract can be used to bargain around a principle or limitation grounded in tort law. More to the point, the surface effect was also much like an outright conveyance of the right of privacy.

Upon closer examination, though, it still amounted to considerably less than that. How much less became clear in 1953, when the Second Circuit Court of Appeals considered the case of *Haelan v. Topps Chewing Gum*,[41] in which a contractual device like the one we have just outlined proved inadequate for reasons grounded in the very limitations on conveyance that we have just discussed. In *Haelan* a baseball player had given an exclusive contractual commitment to a bubble gum manufacturer under which his likeness on trading cards could be included in packages of gum. The usual covenant not to sue for a breach of privacy was included in the agreement. But a third party, debatably innocent as to the existence of the prior agreement, later accepted the player's permission to use his likeness on substantially the same terms and in the same circumstances. Now what had been intended by the first bubble gum manufacturer to be an exclusive arrangement had been converted into one in which a competitor was also claiming like rights with respect to the ballplayer's likeness. Of course each party had a cause of action against the ballplayer for breach of contract. But neither was liable to the other in contract, nor could either enjoin the other, as the later party had no notice of the prior agreement, and neither was guilty of any equitable breach vis-à-vis the other. This meant both were free to continue to use the license, thus nullifying the effect of the covenant of exclusiveness contained in each contract.

In this setting, the court decided, the law should be free to respond by supplying an action better suited to the need.[42] The theory of privacy being clearly inadequate, the law could treat the attempted transaction as one involving a right of publicity—a right that might or might not be thought of as in the nature of property, but in any event one that in the circumstances would justify an injunction in favor of the first party to enter into contract with the player. The second party would continue to have a contract action against the ballplayer; as for the loss of its right to use the player's likeness, meanwhile, the party would be in no worse position than would anyone who might attempt in good faith to acquire a conveyance of property from someone who no longer had the right to make it. Among the hallmarks of property, and a cardinal advantage of property over tort (as Judge Jerome Frank's opinion for the court implied, and as Nimmer elaborated on at length in his subsequent analysis of the case), are the freedom to convey the subject of property, and the resulting clarity and security of that conveyance.

For Nimmer the court's decision was a triumph of legal realism. His essay detailed the points we have summarized here in terms that left no doubt that he approved of Judge Frank's ingenuity in addressing and deciding the matter, as well as the consequences for subsequent transactions in the entertainment marketplace. But he was concerned with the underlying jurisprudence: how should one think about this new right? Surely it should not merely grow like Topsy. And in one especially prescient paragraph he addressed this issue in terms that are both memorable in themselves and directly relevant to our own inquiry here. Citing the decision in *INS*, he noted that some courts had evidenced a willingness to extend the reach of that case to include appropriation where there was neither passing off nor competition between the parties. In one such instance, the New York Court of Appeals had written that "in the complex pattern of modern business relationships, persons in theoretically non-competitive fields may, by unethical business practices, inflict as severe and reprehensible injuries upon others as can direct competitors."[43] Commenting on this statement and others like it, Nimmer observed that the reach of misappropriation thus unbounded was also potentially ungovernable. "If this loose standard were in fact applied by the courts," he wrote, "the already uncertain field of unfair competition would be reduced to a chaos of complete uncertainty, since what lawyer or business man could predict with any degree of certainty where the courts would find that properly aggressive business practices leave off and 'commercial immorality' and 'unethical business practices' begin?"[44]

Between the moment in which Nimmer wrote and the early 1970s, the right of publicity lay mainly dormant. No similarly prescient treatment of *Haelan* was published in the law reviews, nor did another case make its appearance on similar facts. Celebrity endorsements continued to be the subject of transactions, of course, guided by lawyers who may or may not have been tempted by Judge Frank's invitation to treat the right of publicity as if it were property rather than as a waiver of a privacy right. No public record on this point exists one way or another, so far as we can determine. Professor McCarthy, a leading commentator on trademarks and unfair competition, and the author of an additional, separate treatise on the right of publicity, has said that he himself has no evidence that the Second Circuit's opinion had much influence in the fifteen years that followed the decision in *Haelan* and Nimmer's subsequent article applauding the case.[45]

By 1971, however, the right of publicity had made an appearance in two separate cases in California, one filed by the widow and surviving son of Bela Lugosi,[46] and the other filed by the heirs and representatives of Rudolph Guglielmi, known to millions of his fans as the legendary Valentino.[47] In each case the plaintiffs claimed that their decedent's publicity rights were being violated by studios engaged in the practice of "merchandising": that is, the sale of trinkets, such as pictures, statuettes, garments, and the like, derived in theme from motion pictures owed by the studios—but also, in the case of Lugosi and Valentino, bearing the likenesses of the actors who had popularized the roles (as Dracula and the Sheik of Araby) reflected in the merchandise. That the studios owned the copyrights in the pictures was not the issue; they did, and they were accordingly free to exploit the film roles themselves without objection. But use of the actual likenesses of the two actors was another matter. Their contracts had not dealt with the particular merchandising practices engaged in by the studios; had they still been living they might well have enjoined the use of their identities on privacy grounds. But here entered another anomaly arising in the context of privacy. As is true of other personal torts, a claim cannot be brought for an invasion of privacy inflicted after death.[48] A dead person has no privacy to be invaded. Thus, contract or no, the studios were not invading the privacy of Lugosi or Valentino. But what about publicity rights? If they are equivalent to interests in property, surely death does not bring about their end. Property rights generally are not extinguished by the death of a proprietor. Instead, the thing that is the subject of the property right descends to the decedent's heirs and survivors. This was the heart of the claim by the estates of Lugosi and Valentino: that an action for invasion of publicity rights, belonging originally to their decedents, belonged now, by virtue of succession, to them.

Now the game was afoot. The California circuit court judge in the *Lugosi* case held that publicity rights were descendible; the judge in Valentino's case held to the contrary. Not until December of 1979, however, did the California Supreme Court finally hold that in that state no common law right of publicity descended.[49] These actions, and their conflicting outcomes, attracted considerable notice during the decade in which they awaited final decision, inspiring several generations of law review editors to publish scores of articles on the subject of publicity, the majority of them favorable to the right itself, and beyond that, to its survival of the death of the celebrity. (Contrary to popular belief, lawyers love change.) While the cases involving Lugosi and Valentino made their way slowly through the California courts, other cases in other jurisdictions had begun to sprout like fungus in a damp forest floor. The initial results were both confusing and confused. In the Second Circuit, for example, a panel managed to find authority in Tennessee law for recognizing a descendible right of publicity in a diversity setting; the Sixth Circuit held to the contrary, however, on the same facts; the Tennessee legislature then responded with a statutory enactment affirming descendibility; but a Tennessee state court found that legislation to be at least partially invalid.[50]

Despite its uncertain genesis and its halting early development, however, the right of publicity is recognized today in perhaps half the states.[51] In most of them the legislature has overtaken and displaced the efforts of judges, offering instead the seasoned and well-tempered judgments of state legislators. A number of the states allow descendibility, but with some provision for a cutoff date after a period of years have passed following the death of the celebrity in whom the right would have vested.[52] Publicity rights today are commonly characterized as a species of property. And on what theory? Despite Professor Nimmer's misgivings about the cases that had followed *INS*, there is reason to think that the concept of misappropriation reflected there is at the heart of the publicity right after all. As we have seen, the *Restatement (Third) of Unfair Competition* concluded, in 1994, that actionable appropriation of trade values, on a theory of misconduct and consequent economic harm akin to the rationale in *INS*, could be recognized in common law copyright and trade secrets.[53] A third instance of (mis)appropriation was also recognized with respect to "the commercial value of a person's identity."[54] To be sure, as we have also acknowledged, the *Restatement*'s conclusion was hedged about with misgivings as to the protean nature of the right recognized in *INS*.[55] Its discussion of the matter vigorously denounced any notion of a "residual common law tort of misappropriation" on the authority of that decision. In our judgment the *Restatement* was not wrong as to the reservations it offered on the merits.[56] Nevertheless, the proscription against appropriation identified in the three doctrinal fields we have just discussed is in every instance to be seen as equivalent to a matter of entitlement to exclusivity as against a wrongful appropriation. Whether we like it or not, this is ultimately what lay at the heart of *INS*; we think the lingering force of the Supreme Court's decision in that case continues to exert an influence that simply cannot be denied. That influence seems unmistakable in the matter of publicity rights.

Trademark Law
Definition and Examples

In classic contemplation a trademark (or service mark) is a protected symbol of the origin, attributes, and identity of goods (or services) in commerce. The definition is broad: a mark may be recognized in words, phrases, colors, sounds, scents, names, places, designs—in virtually anything at all that may serve to signify the provenance of goods or services in the marketplace while setting them apart from others of like kind.[57] We encounter marks in every aspect of our daily lives. Coca-Cola is perhaps the most famous mark in the world; but others (whether well known or considerably more obscure) will serve if in fact they are understood to be distinctive in the minds of a sufficient segment of the public to make them meaningful. As we write these words, we are surrounded by marks: by Dell, the manufacturer of our laptop; by Timex, the maker of the unpretentious but admirably faithful twenty-dollar steel-case watch that has ordered our life for the past quarter of a century; by the Port leather briefcase in which we carried our manuscript to the mountain cottage where we now work; by the Sony television and DVD player in the living room, which tempt us from our study and the business at hand; by the Crosley Shelvador refrigerator in the kitchen, in which awaits a Sara Lee three-layer chocolate cake—a cake that "nobody doesn't like," least of all us, but which we have sworn a mighty oath not to sample until dinnertime; by the distinctive three-note chime that will signal the arrival of our favored network's evening news; and by the Glenfiddich single-malt whisky waiting in its readily recognizable tricornered green glass bottle, a sip or two of whose contents will restore us and justify our existence at the end of the day. Ah, yes—and (though no longer visible) by the warming presence of the insulation concealed within the newly plastered walls of the cottage: a vivid pink when we approved its installation, the color derived under license from the color of a cartoon panther that figured prominently in the most amusing series of movies Peter Sellers ever made. These are trappings selected more or less at random from the life of an American bourgeois of a certain age and in a certain time and place; they are also marks or marks *manqué*, every one of them possessed of the ability to distinguish the origins and attributes of the goods they signify.

Trade Dress

We are apt to think of marks as words, phrases, logos, or the like. Sometimes, however, the package in which a product is dispensed also proves distinctive enough to set the product apart from others. Distinctiveness in packaging has come to be called "trade dress": the shape of a Coca-Cola bottle is an early example of trade dress with the capacity to function as a mark; our bottle of Glenfiddich is an especially valuable example; the gold box in which Godiva packages its chocolates is another. In American law today the latitude available to trade dress protection is considerable. Even trade dress as attenuated and diffuse as the decor of a restaurant can be protected as though it were a mark if it is sufficiently distinctive—the thought being that distinctiveness is distinctiveness, after all, so why not recognize the distinctive decor of, say, Chili's as functioning in the same way the name of the restaurant and its neon pepper logo do?[58] Still more remarkable, the shape, configuration, or design (or in other words, the appearance) of the product itself—the cut of a child's dress, for example—may be recognized as a mark if the would-be proprietor of that mark succeeds in establishing its distinctiveness.[59] At this point in the development of the law, however, we have left classic definitions behind us and have moved into the realm of applied and legally sanctioned semiotics. Students who come to the subject of trademark law for the first time generally appreciate this at a deep intuitive level, perhaps more fully than their seniors do. Few courses in the law seem as directly related to everyday life as trademark law does. Trademark law tends to reward the student who has spent a lifetime confronting the subtleties of brands and logos. Unnumbered hours at the mall come into their own in the trademarks course, in which mastery of the subject matter ultimately follows only when the student is at home with contemporary commercial iconography. We can easily imagine that Reese Witherspoon's singular success at Harvard Law School may have reached its zenith in her pursuit of trademark law.

Functions versus Functionality

Yet the classic function of a mark today (including trade dress) remains theoretically the same as it was a century ago: to prevent confusion in the marketplace while enabling efficient choices.[60] The man who is sent by his wife to buy Cheerios will not wish to spend undue amounts of time looking for them, nor will he wish to bring home by mistake one of the numerous imitations that compete for his attention at the local grocery.[61] Two distinctive symbols will help him complete the task he has been given: the name of the cereal itself, emblazoned in bold script—which is to say, the classic mark; and the stylized package, rendered in vivid shades of red and yellow, emboldened by a large red heart to indicate the cardiovascular benefits to be found therein—the trade dress in which the product is sold. A handful of rules define and protect these distinctive elements so that the shopper can rely on them. Johnny-come-lately competitors may not use the name (mark) "Cheerios" for their products. Nor may junior competitors so closely imitate the packaging (trade dress) as to sow confusion among shoppers. On the other hand, the configuration of the product itself—the doughnut-shaped bit—probably is functional in its capacity to absorb sugar and milk while retaining its original appearance and taste; it may even be (debatably) generic, in the sense that dry oat cereal in the shape of small "O's" must all look more or less like Cheerios. One can only guess at these conclusions as to the shape of the product, but on either ground—functionality or genericness—trademark law would withhold protection. (In any event, for whatever reasons, competitors do offer cereals that look more or less like Cheerios in the bowl.)

The Cardinal Rules

These rules and the constraints and opportunities they portend for consumers and competitors are relatively straightforward and simple in theory. We have discussed them thus far chiefly in terms of impressions and examples. Let us draw them together somewhat more deliberately at this point by summarizing them with others relevant to the law of trademarks.

Trademarks are recognized and protected under both state and federal law. Distinctiveness in fact is the sine qua non of trademark protection. Distinctiveness is presumed when the mark is suggestive ("Coppertone" for suntan lotion) or arbitrary ("Apple" for computers) or coined or fanciful ("Kodak" or "Exxon"). Marks that are descriptive also may be protected, but only when they have taken on distinctiveness as an additional (or "secondary") meaning in the eyes of an identifiable and reasonably substantial segment of the public ("Vision Center" for an eye clinic). Marks that are fashioned from proper names ("Tiffany" for jewelry, "Mercedes-Benz" for automobiles) or places ("Indian River" for citrus fruits and juices) require proof of secondary meaning as a condition of their recognition for trademark purposes under federal law. Marks that serve utilitarian functions (the absorbent shape and texture of shredded wheat biscuits) are not protected. Neither are marks that have become generic in meaning, which happens when the public uses the mark interchangeably with the goods or services it supposedly distinguishes ("Aspirin" for pain relievers compounded from acetylsalicylic acid). Protection for marks that distinguish goods or services in commerce is conferred upon senior users, as against junior would-be users who propose to offer similar marks with respect to similar goods or services in similar lines of commerce. For as long as the senior user continues to use the mark as a signifier with respect to the goods or services it identifies, the senior user's right of priority continues unabated. Abandonment or misuse of the mark can work a forfeiture of that right, but the right does not otherwise expire of its own accord. The classic test of infringement is whether a junior user's use of the mark is (or is likely to be) confusingly similar to the senior user's use of the mark. There is more, of course, but these are the cardinal principles and some representative examples (taken mainly from the *Restatement (Third) of Unfair Competition*) in a system of law that values practicality in application above elegant theory.[62]

The reader will recognize that the provenance of these rules lies partly in the older field of unfair competition.[63] We do not tolerate misrepresentations by competitors, especially when they are deliberate, dishonest, or unfair; nor do we accept the inefficiencies that follow on the heels of confusion. The former concern is primary in unfair competition (though innocent misrepresentations may also be actionable); the latter concern is ultimate. The principal aim in classic trademark law is to prevent appropriation of marks in circumstances in which confusion will follow or seems likely, whether innocent or otherwise, for confusion will lead to disincentives to productivity and efficient management, as well as affronts to consumers. In its particular concern with confusion, trademark law adds an important focus to the interest we have in a fair and efficient marketplace. Trademark law, when governed by classic rules like the ones we have just summarized, is an essential auxiliary to fair and efficient competition.

Trademarks as Property

The question arises, however: are trademarks the "property" of their proprietors? Is it sensible to think of them as "intellectual property"?

Originally, and perhaps arguably in some lingering sense still today, the answer might well be no. A hallmark of property is that ordinarily its owner may sell, lease, or license it as though the thing to be sold had an independent existence. And indeed, ordinarily it does: we can and do speak of the res (or "thing") at the center of property rights, understanding that a tract of land or an automobile has an existence apart from its function and antecedent to its recognition in law as property. In contrast, one of the immutable rules of classic trademark law is that a mark exists only for so long as it functions as such: the trademark owner who ceases to use the mark is said to abandon it, thereby nullifying its very existence.[64]

Nor is a trademark ever assignable "in gross"—which is to say that it cannot be licensed, sold, or otherwise conveyed as a stand-alone right (an attempt to do so is treated conceptually as abandonment); a mark can only be licensed or otherwise disposed of in association with the goods or services it identifies.[65] In effect, then, a trademark is an auxiliary to these goods or services; it has no separate existence apart from its role as a signifier. Moreover, the trademark functions at least partly on behalf of consumers, whose freedom from confusion is one of the principal justifications for recognizing the mark in the first place, and whose ability to render the mark generic or otherwise useless (through their failure or refusal to recognize it as distinctive) means that they hold the ultimate power to demolish the mark's ability to function, even against the contrary efforts of the would-be proprietor. On these grounds and others like them, some early decisions did suggest that a trademark could not be considered property, but was rather transient in nature, to be recognized and enforced primarily from the perspective of the public interest.[66]

Modern trademark decisions all but invariably hold to the contrary. Judges and commentators today recognize the mark as a species of property—an unusual species, perhaps, but property (or quasi property) nevertheless.[67] The trademark owner invests time, effort, and money in the development of the mark's function in relation to the goods or services in question. In conventional contemplation, investments of this sort deserve recognition as the property of those who have invested in them. The contemporary law of trademarks reflects that judgment in at least a formal (or professed) sense. It is true that a trademark still may not be disposed of apart from the goods or services it identifies. And even in our time, at least in classic theory, an ordinary (as opposed to famous) trademark can be defended against appropriation by a junior user only if and when the appropriation will lead to a likelihood of confusion. This means, again in classic theory, that a mark used to identify an upscale perfume might be appropriated by a junior user for the purpose of identifying an insect repellent. Why? Yet again, because a mark exists, in classic theory, only to the extent that it identifies particular goods or services. The fact that a mark identifies perfume does not mean that it cannot separately identify something else if there is no likelihood of confusion in the separate uses. As to insect repellent, the *de facto* junior user of the mark simply becomes the *de jure* senior user.[68]

But we have been careful in the preceding paragraph to say, "in classic theory." In fact, the law in action is often very much at odds with classic theory. The divergence takes two forms, one indirect and subtle, and the other a straightforward assault upon the theory itself. In this divergence we will encounter and recognize a far more comprehensive concern for exclusive rights of possession and alienation than classic trademark theory would allow.

The indirect divergence is to be seen in the willingness of judges to accept evidence of deliberate or knowing appropriation as evidence of a likelihood of confusion. Under tests widely adopted by state and federal courts alike, knowing appropriation often counts as an indicium of confusion. Of course, in logic, knowing appropriation alone is no such thing. The junior user may simply admire another's mark and conclude, quite sensibly, that it would serve no less admirably to identify his own separate (or very different) goods or services in the marketplace. The test of infringement is confusion or its likelihood, not appropriation. Knowledge of appropriation may be a necessary component of an intent to confuse. But to assume that one can infer confusion from knowing appropriation alone is simply to beg the question.

Why do some judges accept such a rule? Plainly it is because they themselves are either confused as to the theoretical permissibility of appropriation in trademark law, or unwilling to accept the consequences of such a theory. We suggest the latter reason is more often than not the real one. Schooled from earliest childhood in a dozen varieties of the maxim that forbids reaping where one has not sown, these judges imagine that a deliberate appropriation of a senior user's mark is objectionable in itself, and therefore must amount to infringement; and since the test of infringement is likelihood of confusion, they conclude that evidence of knowing appropriation must be evidence of that forbidden consequence. But it is not. Instead, the test represents a degree of inability or unwillingness (sometimes no doubt innocent, but sometimes surely quite deliberate) to accept the classic limitation on trademark infringement to those cases in which there is a likelihood of confusion. As a consequence of this barely concealed concern by judges for the juxtaposition of exclusivity and appropriation, the law of trademarks has come increasingly to resemble the form of unfair competition we encountered in our discussion of *International News Service v. Associated Press*, in which similar concerns played signal roles. But in that case, the appropriation arguably would work a disincentive to production; in the trademark setting in which appropriation poses no likelihood of confusion, it also threatens nothing in the way of corresponding disincentives. Instead, the overlap between misappropriation and trademark theory lies in the bare fact of the appropriation of the mark itself. This is a matter of moral concern, more normative in nature than economic; and in this setting the morality is of anomalous and debatable, if not outright dubious, character.[69]

Dilution

The direct assault on classic theory, meanwhile, is in no sense subtle. Its origins are generally said to have arisen in a seminal article published in 1927 by Harvard Law professor Frank Schechter.[70] In that article, Schechter disputed the underpinnings of the classic theory, arguing instead that "the rational basis of trademarks" lies in the investment made by trademark proprietors in developing marks so highly distinctive that not only will they serve to distinguish goods and their origins in the marketplace but, far more important than that, will actually serve as both geode and repository of the proprietor's good will.[71] Schechter clearly did not have in mind the merely descriptive mark which acquires distinctiveness, or even the inherently distinctive mark that can result when a common word or phrase is used in a suggestive, arbitrary, or fanciful manner. Instead, he mainly imagined the sort of marks that are coined by their proprietors—marks such as "Kodak," which actually figured prominently in his article, to which today we might add such contemporary marks as "Xerox" or "Exxon."[72] Having coined and then developed these marks, Schechter reasoned, proprietors should be protected against appropriation in at least those settings in which uses of the mark by others might diminish or dilute its distinctiveness. Even uses which threaten no confusion in the marketplace—as in the example of insect repellent versus perfume—would be forbidden in Schechter's view if the senior user's mark is highly distinctive, since what ought to count (again under his theory of trademarks) would be dilution rather than confusion.

The dilution theory, as Schechter's argument has come to be called, evolved slowly over the next half century. As recently as twenty-five years ago, dilution was recognized in fewer than half the states, and not at all in federal law. Today, in contrast, dilution has come to be accepted in additional states and, thanks to Congressional action in 1995, and again in 2006, is now a part of the federal Lanham Act.[73] The cause of action under Section 43(c) of the Lanham Act arises in cases in which the commercial use of famous marks by juniors is likely to cause a diminution in the distinctiveness of the mark.[74]

What we can see in the two divergences from classic theory we have just discussed is something of the dynamic and protean nature of contemporary trademark law in response to trademark practice. It is conventional today to build "families of marks," under which numerous goods find a distinctiveness perhaps less individualistic than was once the case, but at the same time more vigorous in the favorable recognition that accrues to them by virtue of their association with other goods and services. Think of Toyota, and its Celica, Corolla, Camry, Avalon, and Lexus models, all of them linked by Toyota's singular reputation for excellent craftsmanship and low maintenance costs. It would be awkward and difficult to achieve these associations (with which we are all familiar, and upon which we undoubtedly have become accustomed to relying) if trademarks were strictly confined to their classic function of identifying particular goods or services alone, or one by one. As global trade has grown, the importance of flexible trademark laws—not merely in the United States, but around the world—has increased accordingly.

Trademarks and Unfair Competition in Summary

We will see in a later chapter that trademark law has its critics; undoubtedly some of their criticisms do hit home. No one, however, can sensibly propose that trademarks do not play a useful and necessary role in the marketplace. Once again, as in the case of passing off, we see a common concern for "a sense of decency and fair play; a concern for maintaining the origins, identity, and integrity of goods or services, and thus the market for them; rewarding the true creator with recognition; and defending the consumer against personal indignities." What we also see, meanwhile, is that, in its contemporary juxtaposition of exclusivity and appropriation, trademark law has come to share a rough correspondence with unfair competition's concern for the disincentives to productivity and efficient management that may follow upon the heels of misappropriation, and with the law's corresponding proscription against reaping where one has not sown.

In this latter aspect of its existence, particularly, trademark law can also be compared with both copyright and patent law, the subjects to which we turn in the next chapter.

CHAPTER 2

Patents, Copyright, and Neighboring Rights

No two legal systems in American intellectual property are more alike in their common origins, nor (at least to a considerable degree) in their common jurisprudence. Yet none are more truly juxtaposed in the details of their existence. Copyright law and patent law are the yin and yang of intellectual property, doctrinal fields whose differing natures serve at least partly to define the boundaries between them. Copyright is the domain chiefly of expressive works, such as those that figure in the arts, entertainment, or the information industries.[1] Patent law offers protection primarily for practicable works of utility, which comprise (in the language of the Patent Act) "any new and useful process, machine, [article of] manufacture or composition of matter, including any new and useful improvement thereof. . . ."[2] Few lawyers presume to practice as specialists across both fields of law. The complexities in each are separately formidable, and the subject matter considerably antithetical. One is a copyright lawyer or a patent lawyer, but ordinarily not both.[3]

We propose to treat copyright and patent law comparatively. Their complexity, however, makes it necessary to adopt a more elaborate system of subclassification than we have thought useful in the case of other intellectual property doctrines. For the tedious burden this may impose on the reader we apologize in advance, trusting (or perhaps merely hoping) that in the end the effort will seem to have been worthwhile.

Constitutional Origins

The common origins of copyright and patent rights in American law are to be found in the Constitution, in Article I, Section 8, Clause 8, which includes among the express powers consigned to Congress the following provision: "To promote the progress of science and the useful arts, by securing for limited times, to authors and inventors, the exclusive right to their writings and discoveries."[4]

In conventional usage the clause was referred to until recently as the "copyright clause" or the "patent clause," according to the subject matter in question. Today it is more often referred to as "the intellectual property clause."[5] This is so, despite the fact that only two among the several fields of doctrinal law under discussion in this part of our book have their origins under this power. Unfair competition, common law copyright, trade secrets, the law of publicity, and trademarks all spring from either state law or (when enacted by Congress) the commerce clause.[6] Professor Lessig has still more recently referred to the "progress clause," a usage we suppose to be original with him,[7] and one that is attractive in calling attention to what appears on the face of the text to be (as the Supreme Court has separately said) "both a grant of power and a limitation."[8] We will employ all of these terms from time to time in our discussion, choosing one as against another mainly in response to our own understanding of the matters in context.

The reader will note that neither copyright nor patent law is expressly mentioned in the clause. But both were widely recognized in the Colonies, which had adapted their laws from English statutes and custom.[9] There is no reason to doubt that the Framers supposed that the language of the clause would empower Congress to introduce these doctrines into federal law essentially as they existed at the time.[10] It also seems probable in retrospect that the Framers were less interested in copyright than they were in patent rights.[11] Patents were at the center of the practical knowledge that a new nation required. Copyright might be respectable enough to share in the aspirations of the enabling clause, but in fact it had played an insignificant role in colonial life and would continue to be eclipsed by patents in both numbers and economic significance until well into the nineteenth century.

Discrete though these rights are, their constitutional provenance is nevertheless thus common; and so is a considerable portion of their underlying jurisprudence. Each is predicated upon some form of originality; each is available for limited times.[12] Each appears to be justified by an assumption, implicit in the clause, that "securing to authors and inventors, the exclusive right to their writings and discoveries" will offer an incentive to productivity that will "promote the progress of science (which meant, in eighteenth century usage, "the field of human knowledge") and the useful arts (in eighteenth century usage, "technology and kindred knowhow")." A decision by the Supreme Court early in the nineteenth century supports this interpretation of the clause. The Court held, in that case and in cases subsequent to it, that copyright and patent rights are to be understood chiefly in terms of what is often described as a quid pro quo: in exchange for the exclusive right to their works, authors and inventors are obliged to dedicate those works to the public domain upon expiration of their limited terms.[13]

Originality

Originality is part of the calculus of rights; the clause appears clearly to contemplate as much. But in this apparently common aspect of their jurisprudence the two rights actually begin to diverge sharply in practice.

Originality is paramount in patent law: a utility patent, now as in the two preceding centuries, issues only if the inventor's discovery is novel—or in other words, without anticipation in the "prior art" (the relevant field of invention).[14] Improvements over the prior art may be judged novel; but mere reinvention (of the wheel, for example) is no invention at all if it is anticipated in the prior art. This is so even if the inventor had no knowledge of that art.[15] The novelty requirement is reinforced by a further standard of invention that precludes the issuance of a patent if the inventor's improvement would have been obvious to one schooled in the art at the time the discovery was made.[16] Thus, to recall the facts of a well-known early decision, it is not enough that a ceramic doorknob be unanticipated (and therefore, literally, novel) if it would nevertheless have been obvious to those who were already familiar with doorknobs fashioned from wood.[17]

In contrast, a copyright is granted on an originality standard that requires no more than that the author not have substantially copied his work from another.[18] In a passage from an opinion by Judge Learned Hand (whose mastery of copyright was so acclaimed in his own time that the holographic manuscript of the opinion has been preserved under glass in the office of the Register of Copyright), we are given perhaps the most widely quoted articulation of this principle: "[I]f by some magic a man who had never known it were to compose anew Keats's Ode on a Grecian Urn, he would be an 'author', and, if he copyrighted it, others might not copy that poem, though they might of course copy Keats."[19]

This is an unlikely scenario, to be sure. David Nimmer (worthy successor author of his father's premier treatise on copyright[20]) reminds us that the first lines of Keats's Ode are these: "Thou still unravish'd bride of quietness, / Thou foster–child of silence and slow time, / Sylvan historian, who canst thus express / A flowery tale more sweetly than our rhyme: / What leaf–fring'd legend haunts about thy shape / Of deities or mortals, or of both, / In Tempe or the dales of Arcady?" Nimmer suggests that anyone who actually believes that a man who had never known it could compose anew Keats's Ode *in haec verba* is in need of a conservator.[21] Adding to the difficulty in understanding Hand's insight in practice is the fact that a second work which is an exact replica of an earlier work may also be found to have been copied from the earlier work on no greater evidence than that fact alone. From such delicious paradoxes is the doctrinal stuff of copyright derived. Nevertheless Hand's observation captures the essence of copyright originality, which requires, as we have said, nothing more than independent creation.[22] In this, copyright and patent law diverge utterly.

Term Limits

Copyright and patent law also diverge sharply in their provisions with respect to "limited times"; this divergence has become more extreme as the two bodies of law have been revised. Patents were issued in 1790 for fourteen years. Even today the most common patent expires twenty years after the filing of the application; other forms of patent rights expire sooner. Copyrights also were granted for a period of fourteen years in 1790, with a provision for renewal for an additional term of similar length. Today, however, the expected average length of a copyright term endures for ninety-five years after the right subsists. In a recent case the Supreme Court held that this extended term of protection does not violate the "limited times" provision of the intellectual property clause—in response to which one can only ask: if not now, then when?[23]

Subject Matter

We have said that copyright protects expressive works; the most important patent right protects works of utility. This distinction is a basic one with which students of copyright and patent law quickly become familiar.

Copyright does not protect ideas, facts, events, concepts, or the like, all of which remain available to everyone.[24] The protected material in an original work of authorship consists only of the expression of these ideas and other similarly expanded or elongated elements of composition. Thus, to offer a frequently cited example, the mere concept of a British spy as a suitable subject for a novel is not protected by copyright.[25] But additional details quickly carry an author across the line from idea to expression where protection begins. Ian Fleming and his successors possess exclusive rights in the character James Bond, a womanizing, martini-swilling ("shaken, not stirred"), Aston-Martin-driving British spy, whose secret identity (007) means that he has been licensed to kill by Her Majesty's Secret Service.[26] But Messrs. Fleming et al. do not own the underlying idea of a British spy itself, which others (John LeCarre, Len Deighton, Jack Higgins, and Alan Furst, to name but a notable few) have exploited with similar success among readers. LeCarre's George Smiley, Deighton's Bernard Samson, Higgins's Sean Regan, as well as Furst's Messrs. Kolb and Brown, all move from unprotected idea to protected expression, exactly as Fleming's James Bond does. This "idea-expression dichotomy," as it is conventionally known, means of course that copyright protection is less comprehensive than it otherwise would be.[27] This is generally thought to be an encouragement to protean efforts at expression, though as we will see in the next chapter this argument is by no means universally conceded.

In patent law, meanwhile, no corresponding distinction is drawn between idea and expression. A novel idea for an improved doorknob is patentable if it is useful and not obvious.[28] The invention includes the idea itself as well as its "reduction to practice," a standard meant to insure that patents issue only to discoveries that are capable of use.[29]

Securing Protection

In the language of the most recent (1976) General Revision, a copyright "subsists . . . in original works of authorship fixed in any tangible medium of expression."[30] Thus, for example, the artist who paints an original work on canvas earns copyright as quickly as his ideas become expression. Formalities were once a prominent feature of copyright law—and a hazardous one for the unwary, whose failure to comply with one or another of the law's complex formal requirements often had the effect of forfeiting the work to the public domain.[31] Vestiges of this system persist even today in works created or published prior to 1989.[32] Since then, however, thanks to the United States' adherence to the Berne Copyright Convention (which forbids signatories to erect or maintain formal barriers of the kind that once figured prominently in American law), formalities have played no role at all in obtaining protection for an eligible work, and only a minor part in maintaining such protection. Still, registration is generally required as a prerequisite to bringing suit for infringement of a United States work in an American court; registration prior to infringement is also a prerequisite to obtaining attorneys' fees and statutory damages.[33] As a result registration practice does continue to figure prominently among those whose works are most valuable or most likely to be infringed. Only rarely does the Copyright Office reject an application for registration outright.[34] The examination process in that Office, while not entirely pro forma, does not ordinarily inquire deeply into the provenance of the work. The application form obliges the applicant to assure the Register under oath that the work is original, but as a rule no attempt is made to search probingly for evidence of prior works that might throw suspicion or doubt upon that assurance. Most copyright applications are ultimately approved as filed. Once issued, the certificate itself is prima facie evidence of originality.[35]

In contrast to the lower profile that formalities now assume in copyright law, patent law continues to require, as it long has done, a rigorous examination of the proposed invention along the lines of inquiry we have suggested above: that is, novelty, nonobviousness (or inventivness), and utility. The Patent Act of 1952 (the last general revision) establishes a number of hurdles that applicants must surmount if the patent is to issue; many applications falter on one or another of these grounds for objection.[36] The applicant is obliged to disclose all instances of "prior art";[37] the examiner reviews this art, and in addition conducts an independent search to determine whether other art may exist that has not been cited. It is common for the examiner to require amendments to the application to narrow the would-be patentee's claim, or to require affirmative disclaimers as to prior or equivalent art.[38] Applications are frequently rejected; patents themselves, even after issuance, are frequently held invalid.

Exclusive Rights and the Nature of Infringement

The Copyright Act confers five particularly important exclusive rights upon proprietors of copyright in original works of authorship. These include: (1) the right to reproduce the work in additional copies (such as successive print runs of a popular book); (2) the right to create derivative works (such as revised editions of books, or sequels or remakes of motion picture films); (3) the right to distribute the work in copies through initial sale, rental, lending, and the like (such as the initial publication of a book or the release of a motion picture film; the distribution right, like the reproduction right, is of particular concern today in the case of peer-to-peer downloading and uploading on the Internet); (4) the right to display a work in public (as when a museum displays a painting or other work of graphic art); and (5) the right to perform a work in public (as when a musical composition is sung by Dolly Parton on stage or is contained in a recording played on the radio).[39] Infringement of these rights occurs when a substantial exercise of one or another of them takes place without the consent of the copyright proprietor and without license to do so under the terms of the Copyright Act itself.[40] Often the infringement is singular and of little real economic effect; yet verdicts of infringement can still follow. In one memorable case a choir director in Iowa was sued for his temerity in having created an alternative vocal arrangement of a musical composition that had been published by the composer in a different arrangement; the later arrangement by the choir director, though almost certainly harmless, nevertheless was held to have violated the derivative works right. In that case the offending arrangement probably would have been better construed as an exercise in fair use, a doctrinal offset against infringement we shall discuss more fully in a moment.[41] Sometimes, however, the claimed infringement, though single in nature, is of undeniable import. For example, a motion picture screenplay that incorporates substantial material from a novel without license may involve considerable damages as well as profits under theories approved by existing law. Meanwhile, the digital technologies and the Internet have led to instances of what can be thought of as "mass infringements" in the context of peer-to-peer file sharing, in which both the reproduction and the distribution rights are likely to be challenged.[42]

Patent law confers upon patentees the right to "exclude others from making, using, offering for sale, or selling the invention."[43] Infringement occurs when an unlicensed party exercises a right that falls within the scope of the patentee's right to exclude.[44] Patent lawyers like to note that these rights do not include the affirmative right to make, use, or sell the invention: it is possible, both in theory and in practice, to obtain a patent which cannot be made, put to use, or sold.[45] Discoveries useful in the fabrication of weapons of mass destruction, for example, may well be patentable and yet not be capable of being practiced by the inventor if the law provides otherwise. In this sense a patent is a form of "blocking right," and is often so described in treatments of the subject.[46]

Copyright infringement is most obvious when one or more exclusive rights are fully exercised in an entire work. Thus, reproducing a work completely, or selling it, or displaying or performing it in its entirety in public is, in the absence of a license or statutory privilege or fair use, an infringement.[47] Similarly in patent law, an infringement is likely to be found when the defendant is making, using, or selling an unlicensed process or structure that corresponds identically to a claim under the protection of a current patent.[48]

In both copyright and patent law, however, an additional area of exclusivity lies in and around the denominated rights. This extended area is not specifically provided for by the respective statutes, but instead has been developed by judges in cases decided over a period of more than two centuries. These interests offer a considerable additional scope of protection for copyright and patent proprietors.

Thus, in copyright, verbatim excerpts of less than an entire work, as well as close paraphrasing and rewording, can amount to infringement; so also can appropriating the plot or outline of a work, even when there is otherwise no word-for-word similarity at all between the protected and the accused works. Learned Hand discussed the most challenging forms of penumbral infringement in *Nichols v. Universal Pictures Corp.*, a case in which one play was alleged to have infringed another:

It is of course essential to the protection of any literary property . . . that the right cannot be limited to the text, else a plagiarist would escape by immaterial variations. That has never been the law, but as soon as literal appropriation ceases to be the test, the whole matter is necessarily at large. [W]hen plays are concerned, the plagiarist may excise a separate scene or he may appropriate part of the dialogue. Then the question is whether the part so taken is "substantial," and therefore not a "fair use" of the copyrighted work. But when the plagiarist does not take out a block in situ, but an abstract of the whole, decision is more troublesome. Upon any work, and especially upon a play, a great number of patterns of increasing generality will fit equally well, as more and more of the incident is left out. The last may perhaps be no more than the most general statement of what the play is about, and at times might consist only of its title; but there is a point in this series of abstractions where they are no longer protected, since otherwise the playwright could prevent the use of his "ideas," to which, apart from their expression, his property is never extended. If Twelfth Night were copyrighted, it is quite possible that a second comer might so closely imitate Sir Toby Belch or Malvolio as to infringe, but it would not be enough that for one of his characters he cast a riotous knight who kept wassail to the discomfort of the household, or a vain and foppish steward who became amorous of his mistress. These would be no more than Shakespeare's "ideas" in the play, as little capable of monopoly as Einstein's Doctrine of Relativity, or Darwin's theory of the Origin of Species.[49]

Nichols was decided in 1931, but the influence of this passage has proved important and enduring. Hand's understanding of the law remains at the center of copyright infringement theory today, and especially so when the issue in a case involves an appropriation of less than an entire work—including, for example, the appropriation of patterns in such contemporary and dynamic works as computer programs.[50]

In patent law, meanwhile, a corresponding theory provides extended protection for patented discoveries. The so-called "doctrine of equivalents" permits a finding of infringement if (echoing the classic formulation of the basic concept of infringement) the accused device performs "the same work, in substantially the same way, to accomplish substantially the same result"—and this is so even if the patent claims do not read on the device:

The doctrine of equivalence casts around a claim a penumbra which also must be avoided if there is to be no infringement. It provides that a structure infringes, without there being literal overlap, if it performs substantially the same function in substantially the same way and for substantially the same purpose as the claims set forth. Equivalence is the obverse of the discounting of literal overlap. The latter is to protect the accused; the former to protect the patentee.[51]

In recent years a substantial dispute has arisen in patent law as to whether the doctrine of equivalents should be maintained or discarded. Established in 1950 in a decision by the Supreme Court,[52] the doctrine of equivalents has never quite enjoyed the degree of acceptance that Hand's patterns test has achieved in copyright. Judges and members of the patent bar have raised the question whether such a doctrine accords with the strict standards of patentability that otherwise obtain in the field. Five of twelve members of the Federal Circuit, sitting *en banc*,[53] actually voted to abolish the doctrine some ten years ago, but the majority's decision to preserve it was subsequently affirmed by the Supreme Court, albeit with substantial modifications.[54] A still more recent decision by the Court appears to have settled on retention of the doctrine for the time being.[55]

The existence of such a dispute within the confines of patent law involves issues to be raised at some length in the next two chapters, but it will not be amiss to anticipate that discussion in summary fashion here. The question is how strictly to construe federal grants of monopolies (or monopoly-like subsidies) awarded pursuant to the intellectual property clause? Proponents of strong intellectual property protection almost always also favor lengthening and widening spheres of protection that are enhanced in turn by more stringent measures against appropriation. That has indeed been the course that copyright and patent laws have taken since the clause was adopted and ratified in 1787; it can also be said to be true of intellectual property at large. In copyright there has been virtually no dissent from within the practicing bar as to this expansion; copyright lawyers now draft most new legislation that is introduced in Congress, drawing upon the expertise of the House and Senate staffs only after the process of drafting is well begun.[56] In patent law, however, lawyers have seen that the expanded right that favors a client today may also harm the same client tomorrow. Trademark lawyers are beginning to recognize the same prospect.

Protectionist Tendencies in Copyright

Why should copyright proprietors appear to be more determinedly protectionist than those in other doctrinal fields? Two answers can be given, the first conceded on every hand, but the second a matter of some conjecture.

The first is that copyrighted materials are by nature more susceptible to widespread unconsented-to appropriation than are the interests protected by other intellectual property doctrines. The public poses little in the way of individual threat to patents; few individuals can hope to make, use, or sell the subject matter of inventions, which typically presuppose a level of skill and access to technology or know-how not widely shared. Trade secrets are subject to reverse engineering, which means that the rules of the game contemplate and approve appropriation in circumstances that do not also involve otherwise inappropriate conduct. The public threat to trademarks is arguably greater: private usage can destroy a trademark by rendering it generic. In fact, however, that happens only rarely, and can be guarded against by an alert trademark proprietor through programs meant to elicit individual recognition of trademarks qua trademarks. If evidence subsequently shows that the public understands the mark to be a mark, then the fact that in careless usage the mark may also assume the properties of the generic (as in,

"Witherspoon, would you kindly 'xerox' this document for me"?) will not ordinarily be enough to invalidate it.

But with the introduction of new and sophisticated copying technologies some fifty years ago (including the Xerox copier, as well as analog tape recording devices and the like), a copyright proprietor became vulnerable to individual appropriations (including private copying for personal use) that had few counterparts in other forms of intellectual property. The digital era has made that vulnerability a matter of even graver concern: unauthorized copies (of movies and recordings in particular) are all but indistinguishable today from authorized copies of a work, so that the end result of private copying can seem substantially more attractive to the copier than was once the case. Still more important, Internet programs designed to facilitate peer-to-peer file sharing mean that individual copies can be downloaded and then widely redistributed to others. The copyright industries estimate that in a single year billions of dollars are lost to peer-to-peer downloading and file sharing. These estimates may be exaggerated, but there is no question from within the perspectives of the industries themselves that the epidemic of individual copying poses a severe challenge. The recording industry speaks of its ultimate extinction, a fear that may be plausible unless the industry succeeds in changing its traditional approach to the market so as to meet the challenge head-on; the motion picture industry is afflicted by the same concerns, and the same necessity for rethinking its approach to the market.[57] The recurrent question in each industry is, "How do you compete with free?" As Professor Lessig has suggested, sellers of bottled spring water might respond by pointing out that successful competition among the purveyors of "free" goods depends on pricing, packaging, assurances of quality, and perhaps above all on "branding."[58] But the copyright industries have responded primarily with programs meant to reinforce the advantages that copyright itself is supposed to afford. These efforts have had only mixed success to date, though attempts to "educate" the public continue, in such venues as movie theaters where trailers warn against "stealing" copyrighted works, and in school classrooms where specialist volunteers lecture students on the importance of extending to copyright the same "yours as opposed to mine" attitude they would bring to other species of property. We see more extreme examples of these efforts in such desperate measures as suits against teenagers and college students, suits intended to intimidate them into submission or, failing that, to punish them with levies and sanctions, both financial and (potentially) criminal in nature.[59] As we have said, all of these concerns and responses spring essentially from the appearance of copying technologies unknown at the midpoint of the twentieth century and still far short of their present capacities a mere twenty-five years ago.

Meanwhile, we think a second explanation for increased vigilance among copyright proprietors may be seen in the so-called fair use doctrine and its indirect effects upon public perceptions of entitlement, as well as on the ethics of copying now that copying is easily achieved. Our thought in essence is that fair use and its close companion, the compulsory license, may well beget increased efforts to limit appropriations, more or less in the way that attempts at progressivity in the course of any endeavor can be expected to provoke reactionary countermeasures. If this is so, it would be natural enough to expect reaction on the part of copyright proprietors proportionately greater than in other doctrinal fields. Other fields have rough counterparts to copyright's fair use doctrine and the compulsory license, but none is as important or as pervasive in its effect upon the proprietor's exclusive rights as is the case in copyright.

Fair Use in Copyright

Much of the intellectually stimulating complexity of copyright law is to be found in the intricate limitations on proprietary rights imposed by the so-called fair use doctrine. The subject is vast, and the history alone an invitation to discursive treatment that we must resist in a book whose aim is largely elsewhere. Yet our larger undertaking would be incomplete without some serious discussion of a doctrine the Supreme Court itself has recognized as essential to the ability of copyright to withstand tests of constitutionality raised by our current understanding of the First Amendment.[60] We will defer consideration of the constitutional dimensions of fair use to subsequent chapters. For the present we will content ourselves (and we hope the reader) with a brief account of the doctrine and how it grew, and some preliminary observations about its significance in the law.

Prior to the adoption of the 1976 General Copyright Revision, fair use fell within the province of judges and judicial opinion. In its origins it appears to have sprung from two discrete concerns, one without doctrinal significance and the other the precursor to the elaborate system of fair use we know and deal with today.[61]

Thus, on the one hand, the term "fair use" was also sometimes employed to mean what today we would be likely to refer to as a de minimis or insubstantial taking. This is not at all doctrinal: lawyers and judges have long relied on the Latin maxim, *de minimis non curat lex*, which means (essentially) that "the law takes no notice of small matters." It is a maxim of general application, whether in copyright or elsewhere.[62] Long after fair use had come to have doctrinal significance, for example, Learned Hand still sometimes employed the term "fair use" as he did in the passage quoted above from *Nichols*, when all that he meant was that the matter was insubstantial—"a trivial pother," as he put it in another case.[63]

Meanwhile, Learned Hand also suggested in *Nichols* that copyright had never been limited to "the literal text," but that is not quite so. Early on, at a time when the federal copyright statute made no provision with respect to derivative works one way or another, fair use was a way of dealing with the public's limited right to appropriate less than the entirety of a work for incorporation into a later work in which original work by another author also appeared.[64] In fact, early in the first century of our experience with it, copyright was sometimes held by the courts not to confer exclusive rights to prepare abridgements or translations of a work, which persons other than the original author might undertake to do as a simple matter of fair use.[65] Of course this particular categorical understanding of the law has long since been altered; today the derivative works right extends to abridgements and translations, as well as to any other alteration of a work in which substantial amounts of previously copyrighted expression appear.[66] But the idea that copyright protection had limitations and boundaries was fundamentally doctrinal. Although altered and enlarged in scope, fair use itself has persisted as a term of art, enabling judges and others to distinguish between exclusive rights in a copyrighted work and rights in the public domain.[67]

In contemporary usage fair use is in the nature of a trump card to be played by an accused infringer against the hand of a copyright proprietor in circumstances in which an appropriation that may appear on its face to be an infringement is nevertheless to be excused. When its recognition still lay entirely within the discretion of judges, the question of fair use was often treated as if it were a matter of equity. Sometimes it might be recognized on grounds consistent with the practice (particularly characteristic of self-conscious American legal realism in the mid-to-late twentieth century) of referring to matters of public interest or concern as though they were categorical imperatives.[68] On still other occasions, fair use was judged according to economic precepts; one of the most intriguing essays on copyright during the late twentieth century was written by Professor Wendy Gordon, who suggested that fair use was copyright's answer to market failure.[69] Sometimes, in the end, fair use could seem essentially arbitrary or, at its worst, no better than a matter of whimsy. Even at its best, given the flexibility inherent in a doctrine that lay entirely within the keeping of judges, the availability of fair use was notoriously difficult to predict in a given case, and undoubtedly was extended or withheld in error from time to time—or would have been, at least, had anyone been able to say with certainty where error might lie.[70] We have suggested, for example, that the result in the case of the Iowa choir director was wrong—that on the facts disclosed there the court would have done better to recognize fair use in the later arrangement.[71] But Professor Nimmer (whom we generally acknowledge to have been the foremost copyright scholar of his time, and our own initial guide to understanding copyright) disagreed with this view; in his opinion, the translation was a straightforward violation of the derivative works right. Is one of us clearly right or wrong in some objective sense? Not even Professor Nimmer would have been likely to make that claim. Fair use is almost always a matter of judgment in which, as he himself suggested, the challenge is akin to practicing the Golden Rule.[72]

In theory none of the exclusive rights in a work of authorship is beyond the reach of a fair use claim. In practice, however, fair use is more likely to be recognized in some circumstances than in others.[73] Sometimes the differences seem intuitively right or natural. Substantial appropriation of commercially valuable work for competitive use is rarely allowed under current law.[74] At the same time, even extensive appropriation for critical or scholarly use in essentially noncompetitive settings is more likely to be recognized as permissible—and still more so when the appropriated work is itself without substantial commercial value.[75] Appropriations from longer or more complex works grounded in fact, such as histories or biographies, are given greater latitude than in the case of poems or musical compositions.[76] Texts are more susceptible to fair use than graphic or pictorial works.[77] Published work is more susceptible than unpublished work.[78] And so on. Sometimes, however, the justifications for differences in fair use treatment are less transparent. Appropriations for the purpose of creating new transformative works[79] are said to deserve the benefit of fair use more often than appropriations for use without additional creativity.[80] Parodies are given considerable protection under the fair use doctrine, on the ground that by definition a parody presupposes a need to "conjure up" the work which it is making light of.[81] That is no doubt so. But one might ask why that is not merely a reason for recognizing that parodies of copyrighted works are more likely to infringe than works which do not depend so heavily on appropriation? The answer given in the cases is that parodies are criticism, and that criticism is important to the public.[82] Again, fair enough (so to speak). But social satire is also important to the public, and yet satire does not enjoy the privileged place that parody does. Why not? Well, again, because satire does not depend upon appropriation as parody does.[83] Ah, then the rule must be this: that socially valuable infringements, when infringement is a necessity, enjoy a favored place within the fair use doctrine, while discretionary infringements, though they may produce work no less socially valuable, are less favored? Yes? In one sense, yes, exactly. But no one really supposes that a principle as existential in nature as this is reliable. Besides, were this the case, the derivative works right would disappear overnight. The explanation must lie elsewhere, as no doubt it does. But where? Alas, not even the Supreme Court, whose jurisprudence lies at the heart of these distinctions, has ever advanced an answer sufficient to the need, not to this very day. In theory fair use may arise in any setting, but in practice its availability is often a mystery, neither clearly sacred nor yet quite profane.

Lawyers take a certain pleasure in obscurity of this sort—copyright lawyers no less so than others.[84] The law of fair use might have gone on indefinitely as a loosely principled judge-made collection of arcana had not a single case appeared in 1973, a case that in a sense marked the end of copyright's long period of innocence and the beginning of its struggle with the copying technologies that plague it (and for that matter plague us all) today. The case was *Williams & Wilkins Co. v. United States*, in which the United States Court of Claims held that fair use protected the National Institutes of Health against liability for infringement in using the newly introduced Xerox copier to reproduce articles from scientific journals for circulation among NIH personnel.[85] Before the advent of the copier, the journals in their entirety were routed to readers one by one, in a fashion then common and unremarkable in offices and institutions, but one that was also slow and for that reason less than satisfactory. Now, in contrast, NIH subscribed to a limited number of the journals from which it reproduced single articles in multiple copies as interest among its workers might dictate. Was this infringement or fair use? No one truly imagined that NIH would increase the number of its subscriptions merely in order to satisfy the appetite of its workers for quicker distribution of individual articles; the new copier did not in fact displace a market for the journals. Or so the Court of Claims reasoned in concluding that fair use protected the Institutes in what they were now doing.[86] Yet the publishers of the journals argued that that was exactly what NIH was doing when it employed the copier. This was neither more nor less than the exercise of the copying or derivative works right in response to an emerging market. Surely this could not be fair use! Disappointed by the result in the case, and alarmed by its implications, the copyright industries mounted a sustained attack on the underlying assumptions indulged in by the court.[87] Today, more than thirty years after the case was decided, we can see that arguments of this sort

PATENTS, COPYRIGHT, AND NEIGHBORING RIGHTS

have not diminished either in frequency or intensity. Indeed, the peer-to-peer file sharing controversy of our time turns on assumptions about displaced markets that are fundamentally like the arguments in *Williams & Wilkins.*

Congress had already determined to codify the fair use doctrine when the decision in *Williams & Wilkins* was announced. But its interest was now heightened by the cries of fear and outrage from the copyright industries, who warned that fair use might play a new and dangerous role as sophisticated copying technologies came into their own. When finally adopted, the 1976 General Copyright Revision responded with measures intended to codify existing doctrine, but also to impose a new procedural discipline upon it, and in particular to prevent findings of fair use that did not take fully into account the economic interests that might be presented by a threat of infringement in a given case. By no means was the Congressional response merely one-sided. Recurring categories of fair use were anticipated and provided for in circumstances that had not appeared in the cases. Today, the Revision provides that a copyright proprietor's rights are "subject to" some fifteen discrete sections elaborating the fair use doctrine through additional exemptions, limitations, or compulsory licenses— provisions hard fought over by interested parties as the Revision neared adoption and in the years since, and ultimately wrought in great detail and at considerable length (running to some seventy densely printed pages in the current copy of the statute that we happen to have at hand as we write).[88] Meanwhile, Section 107, the most general and overarching statement of the principles of fair use itself, provides as follows:

Notwithstanding the provisions of section 106 [setting forth the exclusive rights], the fair use of a copyrighted work, including such use by reproduction in copies or phonorecords or by any other means . . . for purposes such as criticism, comment, news reporting, teaching (including multiple copies for classroom use), scholarship, or research, is not an infringement of copyright. In determining whether the use made of a work in any particular case is a fair use the factors to be considered shall include—

(1) the purpose and character of the use including whether such use is of a commercial nature or is for nonprofit educational purposes;

(2) the nature of the copyrighted work;

(3) the amount and substantiality of the portion used in relation to the copyrighted work as a whole; and

(4) the effect of the use upon the potential market for or value of the copyrighted work.[89]

On the face of the statutory text one might suppose that the exclusive rights are fundamentally subordinate to fair use. In practice, however, and consistent with the legislative history, fair use continues to be treated as an affirmative defense, which means that in an ordinary case the presumption is against the fair use claimant.[90] One might additionally suppose that the "purposes" set forth in Section 107 suggest the parameters of the fair use right, but that too is not the case. Fair use continues to extend potentially to any appropriation or other exercise of the exclusive rights for any purpose and in any setting in which such "use" is "fair."[91] The so-called "mandatory four factors" set forth in Section 107 have succeeded in imposing a formal discipline on fair use, in that every fair use decision since 1978 has dutifully considered the question in terms of the four factors, often at tedious length.[92] In substance, however, the law remains no more certain in result than it was before Section 107 was enacted. In a 2003 law review article summarizing the results in fair use cases, David Nimmer concludes that the doctrine remains largely unpredictable in practice.[93]

In at least one respect, however, the codification of fair use has resulted in a significant, albeit unanticipated, new role for the fair use doctrine. Courts have begun to consider what one might term mass infringement cases, as though they are amenable to resolution within the framework of fair use.[94] There is no warrant for this in the fair use practice prior to 1976, nor in the text of the statute,[95] nor in the legislative history.[96] To the contrary, the history suggests that fair use was to continue to be a matter for decision on a case-by-case basis, as had always been so prior to codification.[97] Yet, once again, pressures on the copyright system resulting from the new copying technologies have seemed to demand a more sweeping mechanism for review than Congress provided in the Revision. In the absence of something explicit, fair use has been summoned to the task. The result has been a two-edged sword. On the one hand courts have been inclined to presuppose direct infringement in cases involving peer-to-peer file sharing, but only for the purpose of judging whether the manufacturer or provider of a given technology is engaged in contributory infringement. In such circumstances, for example, MP3.com, Napster, Aimster, and Grokster were each closed down (in some cases to reemerge later in a copyright proprietor-sanctioned form).[98] Yet in none of these cases was any significant liability assessed on the part of individuals. As a practical matter direct suits against individual defendants remain a daunting and at best uncertain challenge. Even the widely publicized recent actions by the Recording Industry Association of America against a few thousand individual defendants were more in the nature of a gesture (akin to swatting at gnats) than an effective deterrent to peer-to-peer file sharing. In such circumstances, one might conclude that the actual impact of fair use is at best to offer a potential defense to contributory infringers, while affording little in the way of a real assessment of the underlying problem.[99]

Thus, to telescope the history of these developments, in *Sony Corp. v. Universal City Studios, Inc.*, a case filed shortly before the 1976 General Revision took effect, but not decided finally until 1984, the Supreme Court held that home video recording for the purpose of "time shifting" was fair use.[100] The result in *Sony* has since been transmuted into much broader assumptions as to permissible copying—including such new technological generations of industry-sanctioned copying devices as TIVo, which permits digital copying of up to seventy hours of televised copyrighted work. Meanwhile, an additional part of the Court's holding in *Sony* engrafted onto copyright a principle originally (and still) recognized in patent law, to the effect that technologies that have "substantial noninfringing uses" may not be attacked on the ground of contributory infringement.[101] That aspect of the Court's fair use holding in *Sony* has recently been modified in the case of Grokster, a technology provider whose purpose in furnishing the technology was plainly to encourage direct infringements by users engaged in peer-to-peer file sharing.[102] Even so, the industries are still left with the problem of proceeding individually against millions of infringers—in effect a no-win situation.

In summary, then, fair use encourages individual appropriation without effectively defining the point at which it shades into infringement. Meanwhile, the contributory infringement cases against the technology providers have had a mixed outcome at best. On the one hand, it is by now apparent that the providers cannot survive an incautious encouragement to direct infringement. Yet the fundamental holding in *Sony* survives *Grokster*:[103] some forms of appropriation for personal use are still permissible; we are merely unable to say what forms, and when. It is frustration with the practical impact of fair use, engendered by this sort of indeterminacy, that contributes to the industries' urge toward increased and alternative forms of protection.

The Compulsory License

Akin to fair use and intertwined with it in the structure of the 1976 Act, yet distinct in concept and practice, is the so-called "compulsory license,"[104] a device that figures prominently in copyright law.[105] The idea of such a license appeared first in 1909, when Congress enacted an earlier General Revision that for the first time addressed mechanical prefigurations of today's sound recordings. No recognition or protection for sound recordings themselves was made available in the 1909 Act: a decision by the Supreme Court in 1908 had raised the question whether a copyright could inhere in a copy that was not "visible to the naked eye," and Congress chose not to court trouble (so to speak) by extending protection to a medium of embodiment that clearly would not meet that test.[106] But sensing a purpose within the Italian music industry of the time to corner the market in musical compositions worldwide (so it was said),[107] Congress did provide that when a composition was recorded by or with the consent of its proprietor others would have a right to record that composition in similar fashion, upon the payment of a statutory royalty.[108] Whatever threat the Italians may in fact have posed soon passed into the sweet oblivion of scarce-remembered history. The compulsory license lingered on. In time the music industry in the United States accommodated itself to the idea of the license and, as is common in law, devised methods of contracting around it. Thus, in fact, most "covers" of musical compositions were licensed on terms measured against but not by the statutory provision. In other words, the terms of the compulsory license provided a benchmark against which to negotiate, but did not themselves often figure in the actual negotiated license that the musical composition proprietor relied on. With some revisions not important to our narrative, that remains the state of the law and practice with respect to the compulsory license in musical compositions to this day.[109]

Meanwhile, the number of compulsory licenses in copyright law has grown dramatically, even as their complexity has increased by many orders of magnitude. The cable television industry, for example, relies on compulsory licenses with respect to copyrighted works imported via distant signals. Other compulsory licenses (tedious, complex, and considerably diverse in nature) can arise in settings involving such activities, for example, as the satellite carriage of copyrighted content offered by television superstations; certain digital transmissions of sound recordings; and ephemeral recordings intended to facilitate retransmission by the owners of the works so recorded.[110] Of course there is more that could be said about compulsory licenses, but we would be mad were we to delineate these provisions at still greater length in this book, and the reader would be even madder to indulge us. What we have said is enough to frame our original point: the compulsory licenses, like fair use, represent a notable incursion into the property interests that copyright proprietors might otherwise claim.[111] When to these licenses (fairly so called, in that each contemplates upon its exercise some form of prescribed or negotiated payment by licensee to proprietor) are added the many further exemptions and limitations the 1976 Copyright Revision imposes upon the proprietor's exclusive rights with no thought of payment at all, one can see that the nature of the property interest at stake in copyright is substantially different from the more exclusive interest one ordinarily has in a piece of real estate or an automobile—or for that matter in a patent.[112] It is not implausible, then, to suppose that copyright proprietors may be more than ordinarily aggressive in protecting such interests as remain to them. In this, as we have said, they may be acting upon incentives that have no true counterpart in unfair competition, trademark, or even patent law.

The Question of Property in Copyright and Patent Law

Against this lengthy but (we think) necessary background we are ready once again to consider the question that we have posed at the foot of our discussion of each of the doctrinal fields we have previously addressed: in what sense, if any, can copyright and patent rights be considered "intellectual property"? We have seen that unfair competition and trademark doctrines share a community of interests amounting to what we have called "a rough correspondence" among them. As in these fields, so again we can recognize in copyright and patent law a concern for decency and fair play, and for maintaining the origins, identity, and integrity of writings and discoveries, and thus ultimately a coherent market for them. No less so do we reward the original author or inventor with recognition and an ability to recoup his or her investment in productivity through exclusive rights. Indeed, exclusivity is at its zenith in patent and copyright law, where in current law exclusivity is the cardinal incentive to creative productivity and the efficient management of a particular embodiment of creative products—or in other words, the "writings and discoveries" contemplated by the copyright and patent clause.[113] The incentive to be derived from exclusivity may even appear from the text of the copyright and patent clause to have been the very reason for the clause's introduction into the Constitution. In more than one opinion the Supreme Court has affirmed that reading of the clause.[114] Thus it can be said that the hallmarks of property that we encountered earlier in unfair competition and trademarks—exclusivity juxtaposed against the threat of unlicensed appropriation—reappear in the fields of copyright and patents, if anything redoubled in the vigor with which they may be advanced by proprietors. In this, copyright and patent rights may be seen against other forms of intellectual property rights as *primus inter pares*.

It is no less true, meanwhile, that in patent and copyright law we encounter heightened concerns for the interests of others: of individuals as well as the public at large.[115] These are part of the positive law, both statutory and judge-made, as in unfair competition and trademarks; but as is not so in these other doctrinal fields, the concerns for the public domain are bred into copyright and patent law by the decisions of courts construing the language of the clause that justifies them. Thus, the "exclusive rights" that the copyright and patent clause authorizes Congress to confer upon "authors and inventors" may endure for no more than "limited times" in works, and presumably even then only when conferring these rights will "promote the progress of science and the useful arts."[116] As the constitutional provenance of copyright and patent rights is clearer and more obviously justified than is true of other doctrinal fields such as unfair competition and trademarks, so is that provenance limited more directly by the Constitution.[117]

It seems true as well that authors and inventors may have moral claims to recognition that proprietors of rights in other forms of intellectual property share in some measure.[118] In more than one opinion, the Supreme Court has cast doubt upon this proposition, saying in effect that copyright and patent rights are grounded in the Constitution's concern for the intellectual economy that these rights are meant to bring about. Yet recognition of some moral claim as an aspect of an interpretation of the proprietary rights seems intuitively justified. When we speak of "moral rights," however, we must make our meaning clear, for the question of moral rights is inevitably complicated by the even more important question of the public domain.

MORAL RIGHTS AND THE PUBLIC DOMAIN

Moral Rights

The French, who generally figure in any account of *le droit moral*, are said to envision authors as entitled to recognition along four lines of what may be thought of as natural rights: the right to be identified as the creator of a work; the right to decide when and whether to disclose, publish, or otherwise disseminate the work; the right to withdraw from public association with the work, should that association later prove to be embarrassing or otherwise unwelcome; and perhaps most important among the four, the right to prevent others from dishonoring the author

or the work through such offensive assaults upon it as distortion, trunca-
tion, abridgement, alteration or the like. These four rights are widely
recognized in Europe and elsewhere in the world; they are what most
who refer specifically to "moral rights" mean by that term unless they
clearly indicate otherwise.[119]

Moral rights also play a central role among the provisions of the
Berne Convention on Copyright, to which the United States, acting somewhat reluctantly and then only after nearly a century's delay, finally ad-
hered in 1988 (effective March 15, 1989).[120] This reluctance reflected the
United States's long-held insistence that its copyright regime was not
based in natural (or moral) law, but rather in the copyright clause's contemplation of an intellectual economy based on incentives to productivity
provided through limited terms conferred in exchange for eventual dedi-
cation to the public domain.[121] Article 6 *bis* of the Convention requires
that moral rights be recognized "independently of the author's economic
rights," and provides further that "even after the transfer of said rights,
the author shall have the right to claim authorship of the work and to
object to any distortion, mutilation or other modification of, or other
derogatory action in relation to, the said work, which would be prejudi-
cial to his honor or reputation."[122] These provisions could pose a serious
dilemma in the United States where, if not severely limited, they might
lead quickly to a confrontation with the First Amendment, not to mention the copyright law itself.[123] Happily, however, Article 6 *bis* also provides that "the means of redress for safeguarding the rights granted by
this Article shall be governed by the legislation of the country where
protection is claimed." Relying on this provision and a *soupçon* of disingenuousness, the United States professes to see in its legislation provisions sufficient to meet the moral rights requirements reflected in the
Convention.

The reader should understand, meanwhile, that when we refer to
moral rights in the present context we do not mean to endorse the particular moral rights regimes of France or of the signatories to the Berne
Convention. We do not necessarily suppose that moral rights can survive
an expired term of copyright in the United States, nor for that matter
that they can survive a complete transfer of "the author's economic

rights." We have already suggested that the moral entitlement of an author against mutilation of a work must be limited so as to avoid conflict with both the copyright clause and the First Amendment. There is also ample reason to doubt that an author can insist on acquiescence in or acknowledgment of his wish to publicly repudiate a work that he himself has consented to disclose; First Amendment questions surely would arise were a court to attempt to forbid the public from drawing associations between author and work that are in fact there to be seen.

On the other hand, we see no conflict lurking in the proposition that an author or inventor should be entitled to decide whether or not to publish a work or disclose an invention in the first place. That decision is among the exclusive rights granted to an author under the provisions of Section 106 of the 1976 General Copyright Revision; but even in the absence of an explicit provision in the positive law it seems likely as a matter of intuition that most of us would recognize such a right nevertheless, and would think it sensible to speak of it as a matter of moral entitlement. The patent law does not grant any corresponding affirmative right with respect to disclosure, but it clearly presupposes that an inventor may suppress or abandon an invention; the penalty may sometimes result in a forfeiture of the patent claim, but there is no mechanism within the law that obliges the inventor to disclose. Again, positing a right not to disclose in the case of inventions seems intuitively correct.

Similarly, one can easily imagine acquiescing in an author's or inventor's claim to recognition with respect to an original work or discovery. Under current law, patents issue in the name of the inventor. Copyright contains no similar requirement, but there is no reason to suppose that it would be offended by a reasonable provision with respect to recognition, whether or not under separate law, including a provision grounded in moral entitlement. The issue raised by such a provision would seem to have at least as much to do with matters of expedience as of jurisprudence. No serious obstacle grounded in the philosophy of the underlying law should stand in the way. An acknowledgment of provenance is barely more than a matter of truth telling; yet it no doubt cuts to the heart of what is truly at stake in a creator's wish to be recognized. As we will argue in succeeding chapters, an ancient longing to be noted for one's gifts is probably nearer to the true reason why authors and inventors create than is the mere prospect of financial gain.[124] Yet the provenance of a writing or discovery blurs quickly as time and distance, augmented by circumstance, separate it from its author or inventor. At some point the moral claim to recognition must be rejected firmly, more or less as Hand envisioned in the case of the patterns test he posed in *Nichols v. Universal Pictures*.[125] The obligation to acknowledge an author or creator should no doubt be balanced against the practical difficulty in doing so.[126] Scholars may sometimes choose to meet that difficulty head-on, though that is hardly an obligation for all scholars, nor is it necessarily productive of the best scholarship. Sometimes the question of provenance is primarily an obstacle to additional creativity. It is disturbing to imagine Shakespeare or Wittgenstein spending a moment of their precious time on concerns for the origins of the works upon which they built. And obstacles in the path of genius are merely illustrative of the underlying problem and its corollary. No one, great or small, should be warned away from the public domain by the burden of identifying the origins of works that lie within it.

The Public Domain

What do we mean when we speak of "the public domain"? The answer to this is surprisingly complex and indeterminate. Until perhaps twenty-five years ago, one might have responded by saying that the public domain was merely the term to be given to such rights in ideas, discourses, or inventions as might remain after the demands of the intellectual property spheres had been satisfied.[127] Even today that is often what is meant by those who use the term in conventional settings.[128] But the term has taken on additional significance among contemporary students of intellectual property, including judges, practitioners, legislators, and academics, who have come to understand that the public domain also can assume the form of an affirmative entity, as deserving of recognition and entitlement in its own right as any of the discrete doctrines.[129] Seen in this way, the public domain stands as an embodiment of the natural state of being in which ideas and their expression flourish freely prior to their appropriation by persons entitled to claim them by the processes of positive law.[130] Some see the public domain as a commons, a cultivated place akin to a public park, in which all are free to share equally, on common terms.[131] Others see it as a wilderness or frontier, in which ideas and their expression roam free, subject to no rules at all.[132] Still others see the public domain as a status conferring entitlements that are personal, portable, and defining.[133] Under any of these three views, however, and others like them, the role of the public domain vis-à-vis the intellectual property doctrines (trademarks, trade secrets, patents, copyright, and so on) is exactly reversed from conventional understanding: it is the public domain that is the *ur*-right—standing, in order of precedence, first as natural entitlement, then as presumption, and finally in default, while the doctrines themselves are an exception to the rule of free appropriation and expression. Moral rights are not inevitably inconsistent with this concept of the public domain, but neither are they its equivalent; and when they conflict with the public domain, it is they that must step aside.[134] Even the intellectual property clause and the First Amendment, powerful as they are (or ought to be) in the governance of the American Republic, can do no more than partial work in the service of the public domain, where the rights of the American citizen with respect to ideas and their expression ultimately begin and end.

These concepts are at the center of our next two chapters, and we will defer additional discussion accordingly. In the meantime, they bring us to a point of joinder with additional questions addressed to the idea of intellectual property and its merits.

AD INTERIM: A SUMMING UP

Why do we recognize interests in intellectual property? Not for historical reasons; intellectual property has little in the way of history, whether in the United States or elsewhere. In its general usage, the term itself is less than half a century old in this country, and not much older (if as old) in many other parts of the world. Even the discrete doctrines from which intellectual property is derived have had no very considerable past. Copyright in Anglo-American law is barely three centuries old; patent law is scarcely older. Their real development has come mainly in the twentieth century, and in the latter half of the century at that. Trademark proprietors and their lawyers and agents claim a lineage that can be traced to antiquarian practices of marking goods, wares, or services—amphorae inscribed with the names of their owners, for example, or guild practices intended to insure that unlicensed artisans and vendors did not ignore the entitlements conferred upon them by their lords and masters. Even so, contemporary laws governing trademarks and unfair competition bear little resemblance to the practices of antiquity; like copyright and patents they trace their contemporary development largely to contemporary circumstances.

Nor is there any widely accepted progenitive theory to which the origins of these doctrines can be attributed. Natural law or moral rights may justify recognition of copyright and patent law in some quarters of the world—mainly in post-Enlightenment Europe, beginning at the end of the eighteenth century. In America, however, these laws are grounded chiefly in a very different sense of their worth, one in which the justification for laying restraints upon what otherwise would belong to the public domain is said to lie in the "progress" that will follow if originality is rewarded with "exclusive rights" for "limited times." The appearance of a constitutional imprimatur undoubtedly furnishes a significant justification for Americans, who ascribe to the Framers a transcendent wisdom that is its own argument for acceptance. Until late in the twentieth century, however, neither natural rights nor a purpose to encourage creativity was widely recognized elsewhere in the world. With the exception of countries in Western Europe, most sovereign powers did not take copyright or patent law seriously, nor did they accord the sort of respect to trademarks common in the West. In the several Asias, the Near and Middle East, Eastern Europe and Latin and South America, observance of the doctrines was limited or nonexistent; in some countries (among them, notably, India and China, and of course the Soviet states whose collectivist views were antithetical to the notion of private interests in thought and speech) the doctrines were affirmatively ignored or rejected. Repackaged as intellectual property, the doctrines came into their own chiefly in the last three decades of the twentieth century, propelled forward in no small part by the desire for global commerce that fed the trade policies of a handful of so-called "developed nations"—foremost among them the United States, which was determined to lead the rest of the world into the "trade related intellectual property accords" that were engrafted onto the General Agreement on Tariffs and Trade in the course of the Uruguay Round, and ratified at Marrakech in 1994. The result of these developments is the World Trade Organization, a powerful body with considerable political influence around the globe, to be sure, but in no ordinary sense a product of high theory.

Economists, whose prescriptive theories have made their way increasingly into the precincts of legal thought in the last half of the twentieth century, have advanced arguments that justify the doctrines in intellectual property in terms that reflect and augment the Framers' underlying assumptions—that is, as incentives to productivity and efficient management. Economic arguments (especially by lawyer-economists) continue to be the strongest source of theoretical justification for the recognition of these doctrines; but the arguments for them have declined in force as the objects of their attention have gained increasing attention in their own right. The fact is that intellectual property interests lack the finite tangibility characteristic of most forms of property; things protected by copyright and patent are not "rivalrous": once created, they are readily susceptible to replication and subsequent sharing without diminution. Some have argued that the interests provided for by the Framers were never intended to amount to property, but were rather envisioned in terms that today would be seen as regulatory regimes.

In the end, as Justice Holmes might well have observed, the justification of the intellectual property doctrines has come not from theory, but rather from experience. In practice, arguably, they have afforded a great measure of wealth to the nations who acknowledge them and the proprietors who pursue them.

If there were nothing else to consider, then few among us would question the justification for the intellectual property doctrines. But there is another perspective to be taken into account. In recent decades the omnipresence of these doctrines in individual lives, and their convergence with the digital media (including the Internet), have led many to decry what only a few recognized as troublesome before, namely, that we may be recognizing property in ideas and expression only at the expense of thought and speech. This is by no means conceded on every hand. Indeed, the matter is hotly contested. Among the several questions implicit in this debate, three are paramount. One, of course, is whether the original insight is so: whether, in other words, contemporary interests in intellectual property come frequently at the expense of freedom of thought and speech? The second is whether, if that is indeed so, we should continue nevertheless to nurture the growth of the existing doctrines, upon which much of our contemporary culture undeniably is founded and may very well depend? And the third is whether it is possible that the very framework of law and policy from within which these issues spring is itself flawed, so as to suggest the possibility of a resolution of such conflict as there may be along lines not yet widely considered or discussed? These are surely among the most significant public issues of our time. In the chapter that follows we will address them, one by one.

CHAPTER 3

Exclusivity versus Appropriation: Some Questions and Costs

AS WE HAVE SEEN, copyright in America encourages intellectual productivity by protecting the original expression of authors against appropriation by others for a period of time. Patents encourage productivity by inventors in similar fashion. Trade secrets encourage a more modest form of inventive productivity by protecting secret know-how and business practices against improper appropriation. Trademarks and unfair competition encourage confidence and efficiency in the marketplace by protecting trade identity against confusion and appropriation.

Note that intellectual property laws typically do not stop at forbidding unfair, immoral, or otherwise undesirable conduct. They also create or recognize or imply possessory interests that are themselves protected against the forbidden conduct. In copyright this means that expression is typically secured against appropriation as though expression were property—that is to say, with the implied entitlement to exclusivity that the concept of property typically affords. In patent and trade secret law, inventions and know-how become kindred species of property. In trademarks, the law professes to be concerned chiefly with confusion, but in reality often treats trade identity as though it too is property entitled to exclusivity. In unfair competition the law was once concerned mainly with improper conduct such as passing off, but now is concerned more insistently with exclusivity, as is the case with such examples of misappropriation as common law copyright and the right of publicity. The law of intellectual property thus encourages productivity, confidence, and efficiency, or so it is said—but in each instance, of course, an entitlement to exclusivity means that the interests of some persons are protected at the expense of the interests of others.

Questions and costs are implicit in the last sentence. Let us take them each in turn.

SOME QUESTIONS

Does intellectual property encourage productivity, and if it does, is it productivity of a sort that we would not otherwise have? It is sobering to reflect on how little we have in the way of an empirical answer to even the first part of this question. The truth is that we simply do not know in what absolute measure intellectual property encourages productivity. Economists (of the law and economics variety) mostly seem to think it significant. Policy analysts mainly concur. Lawyers and their proprietor clients claim it is. Judges are obliged by law to act as though it is. Lay persons suppose it is. Surely it must be. But where does the evidence really lie? We can ignore for the moment economists, who famously produce beans and can openers on desert islands, while bickering endlessly about how best to do so. Likewise the wonks, who are these days mainly economists manqué. Let us ignore the lawyers and judges, who in matters of this sort are mockingbirds, singing the songs of others. Let us also ignore intellectual property proprietors and their proponents, whose testimony is likely to be tainted by privilege. Ignore them all though we may, however, in the end it is still difficult to deny our own powers of observation. We appear to have, for example, a lot of the stuff the two principal intellectual property regimes supposedly encourage: from copyright (it seems) we have books, movies, songs, recordings, plays, art, architecture, computer programs, and so on; from patents (it seems) we have medicines, new technologies, improvements on old ones, and so many other supposed advances over prior arts that their sheer numbers can mislead the unwary and the optimistic. (A commissioner of patents observed at the end of the nineteenth century that patent law had been so effective that we had by that time invented everything that could be invented.) In an absolute sense it would seem that intellectual property works as it is supposed to.

But then again, how do we know that these things are the net result of intellectual property? Some medicines, yes: it does seem likely that pharmaceuticals are patent-dependent to a notable degree, given the contours of the present marketplace.[1] And some entertainment: it seems obvious enough that copyright or something like it is a necessary ingredient in the production of big movies—works like *Star Wars*, for example, which surely depend on copyright for the financial security that continuing investments in them must have. (In truth this last proposition is debatable; we'll simply concede the point here for the sake of discussion, and return to it later.) But is it accurate to say that all (or most, or *any*) of the products of the intellect that we have listed here are dependent for their very existence on copyright and patent law? If copyright and patent law were abolished would we have these things in equal measure nevertheless? Or fewer of them, or none at all? Or would we, perhaps, simply have as many of them as we actually want and need, and a number of others besides—the latter appearing at the edges of the marketplace from time to time, to test their prospects as new products do when competition is truly free?

Others before us have posed questions like these. There are no certain answers. Let us contemplate them here, for example, in the context of copyright.

Enter the Economists, Pursued by a Breyer

Stephen Breyer (now an Associate Justice of the Supreme Court), while still a young law professor at Harvard some thirty-five years ago, challenged the easy assumptions we make about copyright in an essay that raised questions along just such lines, questions that provoked an uneasy response (mainly silence at the time) from the copyright community.[2] Breyer's argument was that "lead time" (that is to say, getting to market first), augmented by some other corresponding advantages—including, or so a reader might have supposed, the advantage of authenticity that being first often begets in the minds of consumers who associate the product with its first producer—might well furnish most, if not all, of the incentives and protection that copyright affords.[3] The focuses of his study were book publishing, photocopies, and computer programs (then still very new), but the implications in his thinking went considerably further. Most works to which copyright applied at the time seemed to be covered by the thrust of Breyer's arguments. Architectural works were not added to the copyright regime until 1990. But these too would have fallen rather easily within the framework of Breyer's arguments, assuming that such arguments were needed: architects and their works (think Louis Sullivan or Frank Lloyd Wright or Mies van der Rohe) have never been dependent upon the exclusivity afforded by any of the intellectual property regimes.[4]

The weight of opinion has mainly ignored or coopted, rather than refuted, Breyer's arguments, not just then but still today. A common belief is that intellectual property incentives are important to productivity—that the correlation between the products that we see around us, and intellectual property's incentives to their production, is strongly positive, and that the incentives themselves are almost certainly necessary.[5] Further, a common assumption is that investment in new entrepreneurial undertakings is contingent upon the availability of well-established and protected intellectual property regimes. This is most evident in the context of foreign direct investment,[6] which is the focus of the studies, but seems equally plausible in the case of venture capital for start-ups in the United States as well.[7] In this sense, at least, intellectual property and productivity appear to be interdependent.

Yet in the end, the assertion that exclusivity equals productivity is essentially thin or testimonial or theoretical, or some combination of the three, and "believe" is the operative word. We do not know in absolute fact whether intellectual property regimes significantly encourage intellectual productivity, much less whether they are "necessary."[8] A handful of inquiries into the question (mainly in the context of patents) have produced mixed results, as readily supportive of arguments against the necessity of intellectual property regimes as the other way around.[9] Meanwhile, no serious, comprehensive, and elongated inquiry has ever been conducted to determine the answer to either of the questions we have raised at large, nor is one likely to be, for the reason that such an inquiry would require us to experiment in ways we are plainly unwilling to dare—and also for the reason that we are a nation which, given the intellectual property clause, has to a considerable extent presupposed the answers from the beginning of its existence. Believing in intellectual property is like believing in Tinker Bell: we clap our hands, and it is so.

Yet there is also ample anecdotal evidence that intellectual property regimes are in fact often marginal in encouraging the production of many forms of creative productivity, and, at least in terms of exclusivity, may indeed be unnecessary.[10] For the purposes of our book this is especially significant in the case of expression amounting quite clearly to speech—expression of the sort that copyright particularly protects against at-will appropriation.

Breyer was clearly correct, for example, in suggesting that computer programs do not depend for their existence on the sort of exclusivity that copyright confers.[11] Whatever doubt there might once have been about this question, our collective experience in this field is sufficient by now to demonstrate that copyright has been a convenience to some and a burden to others in the field, but by no means a necessity.[12] To be sure, Microsoft has relied heavily on copyright and patent law alike,[13] as have a number of its counterparts; but it is also true that Microsoft's principal competitors today include numerous programs in which protection is either disclaimed altogether or modified so as to eliminate or curtail exclusivity in favor of sharing.[14] In this latter sense, computer programming can be thought of as an extension of American arts and artisanship.[15] Potters, metalsmiths, woodworkers, cabinetmakers, carpenters, blacksmiths, jewelers, and the like have not historically relied on exclusivity, but rather on priority, reputation, and authenticity, as well as other corresponding advantages earned in the marketplace in much the manner suggested by Breyer's analysis.[16] This historic indifference to exclusivity among artisans may well be changing: it is hard not to be aware of intellectual property in our time, and the appeal in it is often strong. But no one can say that the arts and crafts movement in America has been dependent on exclusivity. Much the same thing is true of the fine and applied visual and graphic arts (including photography), which do not appear to have been copyright-dependent in the past, though they are undoubtedly more sensitive to it now that copyright is omnipresent in the culture. Note well the limitations in our claim: we do not say that copyright and exclusivity do not play a role among the arts today, but rather that it is not evident that exclusive rights have been, or are now, essential to such productivity as we have had or may yet desire.

Popular industrial and commercial designs have been similarly independent of intellectual property incentives in the main. Copyright has never extended clear-cut protection to industrial or utilitarian designs as such;[17] trademark law occasionally does,[18] but the protection is problematic and uncertain. Design patents present challenging hurdles and do not in fact reach many popular designs, not even when in theory they might do so.[19] Automobile manufacturers, for example, have never relied on any form of comprehensive protection for their designs, despite the undoubted fact that design can and generally does play a key role in sales. Designs are regularly imitated by competitors, sometimes so closely as to make it difficult to distinguish one car from another at any distance. In this setting, lead time is clearly a source of advantage to the innovator, and a powerful incentive to change in others. Of course automobile makers do depend heavily on their trade identity:[20] the Cadillac mark is a powerful symbol and an undoubted source of advantage in the market. But the design of the Cadillac itself, at any given time, is likely to be one among a number of designs converging upon a common, if constantly evolving, aesthetic, including such notable milestones in design as chromium-plated breasts jutting from the grill, and of course tail fins. In numerous other settings in which design appeals strongly to the public at large, or to some significant segment of it, intellectual property has played no important historic role. Clothing designers, like auto makers, rely heavily on design, but depend chiefly on lead time, authenticity and reputation (or trade identity), as well as price and quality (and sometimes service), for competitive advantage.[21] So do appliance and tool makers.[22] In these last two cases, functionality is to some extent a determinative factor in design, but not entirely: the avocado and copper tints of kitchen appliances, circa 1960, were driven by taste, and not by advantages inherent in exclusivity. Interior designers, meanwhile, like architects, rely on their reputation for aesthetic superiority for such advantage (often very considerable) as they possess in the marketplace. Even when, as in the case of fabric[23] and carpet[24] designs, copyright appears to play a stronger role, the likelihood is that exclusivity does not so much encourage productivity as discourage competition. We would likely have the same multiplicity of designs with or without copyright; exclusivity merely makes them more expensive. In short, despite occasional arguments in favor of design protection in these and similar settings, there is little evidence that such protection has ever been needed, nor does it appear to be needed now.[25]

But what about information and data? The proprietors of data collections relied to some extent on copyright until 1991, when the Supreme Court, in a remarkable departure from its more typical support of copyright in all its manifestations, held that the rationale of the copyright protection claimed by these proprietors was flawed, both in an immediate statutory sense, and still more broadly in terms of the copyright clause itself.[26] The standard rationale for data protection was that the gatherers of this information had expended labor and money (or money's worth) in their collection.[27] Their efforts were often described in the copyright setting as "sweat of the brow"; protection followed on essentially Lockean terms. This had been a well-established doctrine in copyright: by 1991 an extensive line of cases had approved the "sweat of the brow" doctrine, their provenance going well back into the nineteenth century.[28] Yet the Court, in *Feist Publications, Inc. v. Rural Telephone Service Co.*, held that "sweat of the brow" was a concept recognized neither in the definition of the term "compilations" under the 1976 General Copyright Revision, nor in the provisions of Article I, Section 8, Clause 8, which explicitly presuppose "originality" in works of authorship.[29] The result of this turnabout in the law was that data proprietors were stripped of a considerable amount of the protection they supposed they had enjoyed.

Dire warnings followed, of course, in all the usual quarters: in conferences, professional[30] and academic (the latter perhaps better described on the whole as approving, rather than dire); in journals; in Congress;[31] and so on. In Europe a Database Directive followed after some years of study and debate, the effect of which was to secure protection there—not of course as a direct consequence of *Feist* (which had no immediate significance in European nations), but still at least as an indirect response to what data proprietors around the world were lamenting as Armageddon in the United States (where, the center not having held, the Rough Beast was now slouching toward Bethlehem).[32] Despite constant efforts to persuade Congress to offer some alternative form of protection (perhaps under the commerce clause, where "originality" plays no greater role than does the concept of "interstate commerce" itself), none has followed to this day. And yet (*mirabile dictu!*), years after the decision in *Feist*, data go right on being collected and their gatherers continue to flourish in their customary marketplaces and beyond.[33]

Was copyright ever necessary, whether as incentive or as protection? Data proprietors relied on it as a security blanket of sorts, without doubt—but was it necessary? It is not easy to make the case that it was. It is easier to make the case that data will be compiled, whether or not protection follows, for essentially the reasons Breyer contemplated decades ago: those who come to the market first, with reliable information, conveniently packaged and sensibly priced, are likely to go on enjoying the custom of others who prefer to trust the market leaders while leaving the investment in research and development to them.[34]

Meanwhile, with perhaps one notable exception, the press does not depend much today on copyright, and in truth never has done so on any widespread basis. News moves too quickly to make these forms of protection useful. More important than copyright, the ethics of journalism provide alternative sources of incentives, chiefly through aggressive competition augmented by acknowledgment and attribution in cases in which one competitor has managed to "scoop" others. Peer recognition (as in the case of the Pulitzer Prize) also plays an important role in encouraging innovative professional behavior in journalism. Even then, the patterns of competition reemerge quickly; in journalism, one can rest neither on one's laurels nor on the sort of long-term exclusivity afforded by intellectual property. It is not yet entirely fashionable to think of Internet bloggers and their ilk as the next generation of journalists and public intellectuals (though that is plainly what they are), but they are clearly beginning to be an important factor in the so-called "marketplace of ideas"; and it must be said that there is no important evidence that their emergence is a function of copyright or some similar system of exclusivity. If anything, quite the opposite is so. Indeed, when we consider the nature of these and other public discourses in American life, it is difficult to think of a single example that is truly dependent for its very existence upon the availability of exclusive rights in its expression. The Supreme Court has said more than once that "copyright is the engine of free expression,"[35] but, as we will see later, that is mainly ho-kum and blather. Americans are not fundamentally dependent on copy-right exclusivity to generate public discourses. To the contrary, in the relatively rare instances in which such discourses intersect importantly with copyright, the net effect of exclusivity is apt to be suppressive rather than the other way around.

We say "with one notable exception": television news and sports agencies, like their earlier counterparts, the newsreels, and, to a lesser degree, pictorial magazines (now mainly nonexistent, thanks to televi-sion), probably have relied on copyright to generate some portion of their revenues at the margin. This was almost certainly not a significant factor in their origins, however: neither newsreels nor magazines like *Life* or *Look* are likely to have relied on business plans that were truly copyright dependent. Newsreels fed at the same trough as movies; ad-vertising and circulation revenues provided the cornerstones of maga-zines' existence.[36] Such revenues as these media realized from the sale of photos or footage came in the form of windfalls. (This remains true even today in the case of magazines.) The evidence that revenues from licensing have played no greater role in the evolution of the visual media can be seen in this important fact: none of these has established any seri-ous effort at marketing their wares to the public at large beyond the outlets in which they first appear. For example, there are no true coun-terparts among these media to the clearing houses that are commonplace in music where widespread licensing plays a real part in the continuing existence of the music publishing business.[37]

Exclusivity does play a more important role in the entertainment industries—which, significantly, are also often referred to as "the copy-right industries." It is perfectly clear even here, however, that such pro-tection has not always been a necessary incentive to productivity, and may in fact be inessential today. Until the beginning of the twentieth century, the three principal forms of entertainment in America were to be found in books, theater, and music.[38] We shall not repeat Breyer's analysis of "the uneasy case" for copyright in books, except to empha-size that the practice of advances, followed by a well-negotiated publica-tion agreement (between publisher and author), followed by a carefully orchestrated and aggressive marketing plan, have undoubtedly played a considerably stronger role as an incentive to productivity by authors than has copyright itself. Historically, meanwhile, statutory copyright played a minor role in the case of theatrical productions, which also depended instead on incentives like the ones discussed by Breyer. This was especially true in the later medium of vaudeville and burlesque, where wholesale appropriation of the work of others was not only rampant, but also arguably necessary to the evolution of the medium.[39] To be sure, vaudeville and burlesque are now dead, but not for lack of intellectual property protection; they were killed off by the emergence of new media, including motion pictures, radio, and television[40]—the latter two governed by regulatory blue laws that made it impossible to transfer the coarser amusements of vaudeville and burlesque from the stage to the airwaves.[41] The new media have all relied far more heavily on copyright and similar forms of protection since the middle third of the twentieth century; theater learned to do so in that time as well.[42] It is at least debatable, however, whether any of these media have flourished primarily (or significantly) as a consequence of the exclusivity afforded by the intellectual property regimes. Of course we do not doubt that these regimes have been convenient; nor do we doubt that exclusivity has played (and continues to play) a central role in the copyright industries' business plans. We mean merely to question whether in fact the sort of exclusivity that is among intellectual property's most important hallmarks has been essential to their success.

Item: The Music Business

Is copyright exclusivity a necessary incentive to productivity among musicians? Let us begin our response to that question with some anecdotal evidence dear to our hearts.

The Grateful Dead, among the most phenomenal rock bands in the history of the art, did not rely much on intellectual property for their extraordinary success. But then, neither did they object to appropriation of their music and performances.[43] As the now-sainted Jerry Garcia was known to observe, "Once we've played it, it's yours."[44] In every venue the Dead reserved the choicest seats for fans who brought recording equipment to copy the concert from beginning to end. At one hallowed moment in the evolution of the group, before the advent of the digital technologies, the Dead even allowed these tapers to jack their equipment directly into the band's own sound system, the better to suppress the background "noise" that otherwise would have degraded the recordings.[45] It was understood that copies of these recordings would be multiplied a thousand-fold and exchanged for similar recordings of other performances among fans who prized their collections the way the Louvre prizes the *Mona Lisa* (which, by the way, was not produced in response to copyright either). The Dead issued some commercial recordings and participated in some film productions, but these were not the dominant source of the group's revenues, nor were they intended or expected to be.

Copyright incentives thus obviously played a smaller-than-ordinary role in the band's financial success, which was extraordinary nevertheless. Judged entirely in terms of revenues produced,[46] the Dead may have been the single most successful rock band of their time. And how did they succeed? Through the loyalty of their fans (who in reality were something closer to disciples), many of whom followed the group around the country on its frequent tours, camping out at each venue in a caravan that was in its own way a major part of the Dead's appeal.[47] No one who has ever savored a Corona Extra and a grilled cheese sand-wich hastily cooked on a well-crusted one-burner hotplate and served at sundown from the not-all-that-sanitary hands of besandaled sprites in tie-dyed apparel, while wandering amidst the jumbled array of gaily painted one-time school buses and VW Micros (ideally the model with opera windows, like the one Arlo Guthrie drove to the dump in *Alice's Restaurant*), in a pleasant haze of body odor, burning grease, and pa-tchouli, is likely to forget the experience, or what it meant to one's un-derstanding of transcendence. It was easy, in such circumstances, to Expect a Miracle. The Dead themselves meanwhile said nothing to their fans at any of these events. They simply walked onto the stage and began to play, the performance itself enough, and the music all the more deeply satisfying because, already familiar and needing no intro-duction, it also belonged already to the audience as much as to the Dead.[48]

The Dead did not rely on copyright because, as we have said, copies of their music were readily available—but far more than that, because copies were not the true nature of their product, which, as any member of the audience could have told you, was not a product at all, but rather an exercise in community, experience, and authenticity: the communal celebration of the music once again, experienced in the company of others in the authentic presence of the Dead.[49] Perhaps all concerts are religious experiences in some secular sense; if so, the Dead offered something close to a Rapture. Ah, but then, where did the money come from? From the sale of tickets to the concerts, which disappeared by the fistful as soon as they were made available at a signal from the Dead's headquarters, located somewhere north of the Golden Gate and south of Bolinas. And from merchandising—the Dead did sell some paraphernalia—tie-dyed stuff, mainly. These authorized promotional goods were almost certainly copyrighted and trademarked. But then you could buy the same things or their equivalent cheaper outside in the midst of the caravan, where, given their imperfect handmade quality, and their often grimy and sometimes even faintly desperate aspect and character, the authenticity of these items was arguably a notch or two higher than their more expensive and obviously commercial counterparts inside the gated venue itself.

Is copyright an important incentive to productivity among musicians? We have just seen that this isn't necessarily so. The example of the Dead suggests at least that much. To be sure, copyright is a convenience, as well as the norm, for many (let's say most) artists and producers in the contemporary recording industry. Bob Dylan, the Dead's contemporary, friend, and sometime collaborator, has relied on it for a substantial portion of the revenues he has earned over the years. So have countless others. Performers generally count on it, at least indirectly, and the recording industry now swears by it—though in fact this industry had no protection from copyright at all until 1971, and managed to flourish nevertheless. But new recording technologies make all the difference, the recording industry maintains; faced with peer-to-peer file sharing, how can it hope to "compete with free" in the absence of an ever-stronger copyright regime? As numerous contemporary observers of the scene have suggested, the answer to that question is, once again, a function of the business model.[50] If the old model is no longer viable, then the industry may be obliged to find another, the way buggy manufacturers and horse traders did when the automobile came to stay in America. The standard ingredients in successful free-market competition are priority and lead time, quality, price, and service. In the context of the music industry, these can be augmented by authenticity and ambience. Given some combination of these ingredients and others like them, it is always possible to compete with free. There is reason to think the industry is beginning to come to the same judgment. The success of the iPod and its cousins shows that new, lucrative business models are possible, demonstrating at the same time how quality and convenience can be powerful antidotes to simple copying. Copyright and exclusivity may still be a convenience and the norm in that part of the music business devoted to performance and recording. But are they necessary? No. Clearly not.

And what about songwriters and music publishers? Copyright is the norm in many settings here too. Plan to use a musical composition in a theatrical production or a musical or in a television advertisement or motion picture drama, or in a host of other settings like these, in which grand performing rights or synch or master recording rights are involved, and you will need to negotiate a license, which may or may not be granted on terms you like or can afford. Yet negotiated licenses of this sort are not the sine qua non in what is perhaps the most common setting of them all. Recall the compulsory license. When a musical composition has been recorded with the consent of the proprietor, then others who wish to record the music may do so in similar fashion, subject to a statutory obligation to pay for the taking.[51] In this setting, copyright in musical compositions has not depended on exclusivity for most of the past century. Copyright in recorded compositions involves instead what some call a "liability" or "regulatory" regime—in which appropriation by others is a matter of entitlement upon the payment of a rent or fee—rather than a conventional property regime.[52]

Is copyright's more typical exclusivity necessary to the business of song writing and music publishing? Again, no. The compulsory license makes that clear enough. Is at least some form of payment essential as an incentive to the creation of new music? Perhaps not, in some absolute or ultimate sense. Music is an innate form of human expression, and must out whether or not it is bidden. But if music is to be a business, much less an industry, then the answer is yes, of course. Once again the compulsory license offers one model for securing payment. But it is not the only model. In a thoughtful recent book, *Promises to Keep*, Professor William Fisher offers a sensible alternative to copyright and its systems of exclusivity and liability alike.[53] In essence, Fisher's model proposes measuring the value of a composition in the marketplace by tracking its appeal to the public, then compensating the composer accordingly from public funds generated through a special tax designed for the purpose. Not everyone will approve of a scheme that involves government intervention (though the present copyright system is itself a government-centered scheme), much less one envisioning compensation derived from tax revenues.[54] But then it isn't necessary to embrace the details of Fisher's model in order to embrace its deeper wisdom. His proposal clearly demonstrates that it is possible to reimagine incentives to productivity in the entertainment industries—and to do so in a way that does not turn on exclusivity. If copyright were to be displaced and supplanted by something else, Fisher's would be one way to maintain present levels of productivity. Alternatively, as in the case of the recording industry, what may be required, again, are new business models initiated from within the industry itself. In later chapters in this book, we ourselves will endorse another model, not necessarily better than Fisher's in theory, nor superior to models originating within the industry, but also feasible in our opinion, and arguably more responsive in conceptual terms to the other changes we also will propose.

Item: Movies

The motion picture industry actually had its origins in piracy on nearly every level. Would-be producers faced rent-seeking claims and still more oppressive practices arising from the infamous Edison patent trusts, which held patents on essential aspects of motion picture technology.[55] These artists found a measure of relief in escape to the west coast, where not only were the weather and the light more congenial to filmmaking, but where the filmmakers themselves could escape across the border into

Mexico, if need be, one jump ahead of the Pinkerton detectives who bedeviled them on behalf of Edison.[56] (This is, of course, an oft-told tale. Peter Bogdanovich's *Nickelodeon* offers a pleasing version of it in film.) Outlaws that they already were, these producers did not scruple at appropriating the work of others in support of their efforts: early twentieth-century film history is replete with cases in which copyright violations were alleged by authors and their publishers against filmmakers (including, for that matter, Edison) who had produced what today the industry itself would recognize as infringing derivative works.[57] We hasten to add that these early conflicts do not contradict the underlying point we are making here in any fundamental way. In the setting of that time, the plaintiffs in the cases were nothing more than advantage-seeking opportunists, anxious to shore up their place in markets in which they were unwilling simply to compete.[58] Their adversaries were mainly undaunted until the industry reached the point at which advantage-seeking opportunism appealed widely enough to make monopolies the norm. (Film buffs call the period that followed The Golden Age of Hollywood.)[59] Meanwhile, reading the history of the film business, one can be pardoned for concluding that the industry emerged, not as a consequence of copyright and other intellectual property regimes, but rather in spite of the drag on development they represented.

Of course, that was then and this is now. A century later, the motion picture industry can perhaps lay the strongest claim to being copyright dependent. Films in the commercial marketplace range widely in cost of negative, which is to say, the amount of money it takes to develop, produce, and complete a finished picture, ready to reproduce in prints for release and distribution.[60] On the low end, arguably, a creditable feature can be produced for as little as fifty thousand dollars, though that is low indeed;[61] a more typical low-budget feature ranges in cost from perhaps two hundred thousand to something between twelve and twenty million.[62] The typical cost of negative for a modest first-class feature film today comes closer to the fifty-million-dollar mark (give or take twenty million or so); and as every consumer of entertainment news knows full well, budgets well in excess of one hundred million dollars are by no means unknown or, indeed, uncommon.[63] No other form of entertainment varies as widely in cost of production. And this is merely the beginning of the investment. To the cost of negative must be added sums to cover prints and advertising, as well as release and distribution expenses, amounting in all to roughly two to three times the cost of negative. Thus the investment in a fifty-million dollar production really presupposes an investment approaching two hundred million to bring the finished film to market.[64] This is a sum that cannot be recouped from foreign and domestic theatrical distribution alone,[65] but depends as well on subsequent revenue sources, including pay-per-view,[66] video, and DVD sales[67] and rentals,[68] and a number of other so-called "windows,"[69] as well as ancillary (promotional) goods such as toys, games, and the like.[70] (Remember Mel Brooks's discourse on "merchandising, merchandising" in *Spaceballs*.)

The sheer size of the investment typically made in the production, release, and distribution of a feature film invites analogies to the cost of developing new drugs.[71] The economic arguments in favor of patent protection for pharmaceuticals are thus roughly equivalent to the arguments in favor of copyright for the most expensive feature films. Investments of such size are unlikely to be made in the absence of extraordinary market mechanisms enhancing the likelihood of their recovery, at a profit. But the investment in theatrical features is not fixed by objective external considerations to the same degree as is true of drug developments. The cost of the latter is a function of legal standards and testing that must be met and surmounted before the drug can be marketed. Nothing of the sort has ever been so in the case of theatrical film production. Investments at higher levels reflect shifting expectations originating within the industry, rather than the immutable requirements either of law or, for that matter, the marketplace. To put the proposition another way, when investments of gargantuan size are made in such epics as *Waterworld* or *Heaven's Gate* or *Ishtar*,[72] it is because these investments are thought to be justified in the judgment of a relatively small handful of production executives and interested artists, whose reliability in such matters is nicely illustrated by these examples. Even *Star Wars*, a reflection of aesthetic and financial judgment in sharp contrast to the ones just listed, cannot be said absolutely to require the investment that produced it. In fact, an amazingly sophisticated feature-length "episode" in the series has been produced within the past five years by unauthorized independent creators, using digital technologies, for less than fifty thousand dollars.[73] (To his great credit George Lucas has not objected to either the creation or the noncommercial Internet release of this adulatory but plainly derivative work, though it seems clear that he would not approve its theatrical or other commercial release.)[74]

In theory, then, we do not have to have big pictures. Small budget features can be made at levels of investment that do not depend on exclusive rights. In such cases, analysis akin to Breyer's would lead one to expect adequate returns on invested capital, and adequate incentives to continued productivity. Ordinary principles at work in the market would suffice. But big pictures are another matter. Investments in the scores of millions of dollars in a single feature almost certainly cannot sensibly be made in the absence of some form of extramarket sanction that suspends the ordinary rules governing investment, competition, and return, and converts them into rules amounting to a subsidy. (In this dependency filmmakers have come to resemble farmers.)[75] Even then, in the absence of substantial cross-collateralization among theatrical features the industry would collapse. In a nutshell this is the model of the film business today.

Is exclusivity itself a necessary part of that model? In fact the role that copyright and exclusivity have played in the development of the industry has been at best uncertain and uneven. Like the recording industry, movies came late to copyright, and then existed for decades without relying much on copyright's protection against simple copying.[76] There was no need to rely on copyright: films were beyond the copying capabilities of most who saw them; and unauthorized exhibition was similarly impractical.[77] Pirates were a nuisance, but little more. Copyright served mainly as a device for avoiding vigorous competition in the marketplace in the case of derivative works. But then, like the music business, movies began to be more directly threatened by the new copying technologies.[78] By the early 1970s the motion picture industry judged it necessary to fight back. This it did in *Sony Corp. v. Universal City Studios, Inc.*, the case in which the industry attempted to outlaw the

Betamax video recorder.[79] That attempt ended in apparent failure, as the Supreme Court finally decided, in 1984, that recording copyrighted work in a broadcast format for the limited purpose of "time shifting" was not necessarily a violation of copyright;[80] even more important, the Court concluded that the manufacturer of the recording device itself could not be held accountable on a theory of contributory infringement since the recorder was clearly capable of "substantial non-infringing uses."[81] We say apparent failure: in fact the VCR proved to be the biggest boon to revenues the industry had experienced in decades. Video sales and rentals opened a new window for distribution. The motion picture industry itself soared, borne aloft not merely on additional revenues but on the incentives to productivity that new marketing techniques provided.[82]

Then a second shoe dropped. The VCR had been an analog technology, which had inherent limitations: copies of movies on tape suffered from loss of resolution that tempered a potential copier's desire to own them,[83] much less make them a primary source for initial screening. By the end of the 1980s, however, it was clear that the digital technologies offered a threat several orders of magnitude greater than the industry had faced before. Digital copies are all but perfect in the resolution they achieve; in the right circumstances (technically, a matter of compression and bandwidth in the electronic spectrum), copies of two-hour films can be downloaded in a matter of minutes, and shared with others via the Internet.[84] In 2003, Jack Valenti, then president of the Motion Picture Association of America, estimated that 500,000 copies of feature films were being recorded daily without benefit of license.[85] Once again the industry fought back, this time joining the Recording Industry Association of America in efforts to stamp out the successive waves of recording devices that threatened both industries in approximately the same way. The Supreme Court's decision in *Grokster*,[86] in the summer of 2005, though not a decisive victory for the industries, nevertheless made it clear that manufacturers of technologies devised or offered explicitly to facilitate copyright infringement could be held liable on contributory grounds even if the technologies might otherwise be put to noninfringing uses.

Is the sort of exclusivity that copyright affords necessary to the continued existence of the film industry? Despite the Sturm und Drang of the last thirty years, the answer is still clearly, No. Exclusivity is one way to approach the problem of securing revenues sufficient to encourage continued investment in big pictures. Once again, however, other sources of revenue can be envisioned. Professor Fisher's suggestions for direct subsidies presuppose an abandonment of the main structure of exclusivity.[87] Liability regimes (like the ones advanced by our colleague Jerome Reichman) also offer an alternative to the property-centered regime that copyright has become, with its emphasis on exclusivity.[88] Copyright proprietors resist these alternatives, understandably preferring the system they know to ones that might change the rules of the game in unanticipated ways. If nothing were at stake but the question of incentives and rewards, then perhaps it would make sense to close our eyes and pretend that nothing need be done. Copyright proponents could go on believing in the viability of a system of exclusivity which, in the main and despite every effort to defend it, is still unproven as to necessity and apt to go on that way until the end of time.

But something else is at stake. For even if it is true that copyright exclusivity encourages the intellectual productivity its proponents think it does, its very nature forces us to face another stark set of consequences, ones no less important in the scheme of things than copyright itself.

THE COSTS

Copyright quite routinely forbids us to speak or sing or write or draw or paint or dance, or take or exhibit photographs, or read aloud to friends or share music with them, or make or distribute or exhibit films or videos, or for that matter to do a host of other, similar things—if we do them publicly (and sometimes even privately) without license, whether or not for profit, knowing that the expression we choose has already been claimed by others acting under color of law. Copyright is not alone in raising barriers to expression. Patent law forbids us to engage in business practices or to use designs assigned by law to others. Trademarks forbid us to identify ourselves in symbols similarly "belonging" to others. Unfair competition forbids us to imitate or model ourselves after others, lest we engage in "free riding." We have seen, of course, that in each instance there is more to be said in behalf of the rights that forbid us to think and speak as we please. We are earnestly assured that a decent recognition of rights like these will encourage productivity or avoid confusion while securing efficiency. Yet the fact remains that as a consequence of these rights much of our culture is no longer available to be shared freely among us, but is controlled instead by persons other than ourselves, acting in turn under color of law. And the fact is also that more of that culture is thus absorbed by persons other than ourselves with every passing day. Intellectual property rights—rights that make up the several doctrines that we have examined in our first two chapters—are increasingly intrusive and repressive. No ordinary day passes in which we are not confronted by rights supposedly belonging to others, rights meant to constrain us against an exercise of expression that otherwise we would take for granted. The costs we incur in granting these rights are quite literally incalculable, for we can never know what has been foregone in order to indulge them.

Let us consider these costs in terms of creativity and self-expression. When we speak of *creativity* and *self-expression* we mean to use these words in ways that do not presuppose special knowledge. We accept it as given that most of us are born with some innate desire to communicate with others, a desire that seeks its outlet in expression. We suppose that some of us feel this desire more urgently than do others. We understand that sometimes self-expression can amount to an exercise in creativity, and that some of us are more creative in this sense than others. (We take it for granted that Shakespeare was more gifted than Ben Jonson.) We assume that creativity can be cultivated and developed, as can other innate capabilities. We assume as well that it can be encouraged, and we agree that it should be. We assume that it can play a role in any instance of expression, including a spectrum running from the private to the public, and from the personal to the political, which we suppose are sometimes, but not always, the same. But we assume no less firmly that in a free and democratic society we ought not to sanction self-expression in some at the expense of others, the question of creativity notwithstanding.

Whether or not we possess the gifts that Providence assigned to Shakespeare or Jonson, surely in America we are all equal before the law in our entitlement to thought and expression. We accept as true what Justice Louis Brandeis said in *Whitney v. California* about the nature of our mutual compact under the Constitution and the Bill of Rights: that in protecting freedom of speech and press the Founders intended to insure that each of us would be free "to think as you will and to speak as you think."[89] We take that proposition as our mantra throughout this book, for we imagine that in that phrase lies the fullest meaning of what it is to speak of freedom of expression in America. It is the right to self-expression that matters, in our view, and it matters irrespective of the questions of originality and creativity.

We have indicted intellectual property doctrines at large for their constraints against expression. But it is copyright that offends most gravely, and copyright that must bear the brunt of our complaint. Let us be direct: the dark side, and indeed a principal aim, of copyright is to suppress unauthorized expression for a period of time amounting, on average, to almost a century. This may or may not be an encouragement to originality or creativity or some other form of favored productivity in some; it is unquestionably repressive as to others.

Originality

The problem in copyright begins with the originality standard, which (as we have seen) amounts to little more than a requirement that the protected work not have been copied from an antecedent source. Judges have summed up this standard in colorful passages that every copyright lawyer can recite by heart. Here is Holmes, for example, in *Bleistein v. Donaldson Lithographing Co.*, a case in which one question was whether a poster advertising circus acts could be protected by copyright, despite the fact that the acts, as depicted, were essentially faithful representations of performances one might actually see under the Big Top itself:

It is obvious that the . . . case is not affected by the fact, if it is one, that the pictures represent actual groups—visible things. They seem from the testimony to have been composed from hints or description, not from sight of a performance. But even if they had been drawn from the life, that fact would not deprive them of protection. The opposite proposition would mean that a portrait by Velasquez or Whistler was common property because others might try their hand on the same face. Others are free to copy the original. They are not free to copy the copy. . . . The copy is the personal reaction of an individual upon nature. Personality always contains something unique. It expresses its singularity even in handwriting, and a very modest grade of art has in it something irreducible, which is one man's alone. That something he may copyright unless there is a restriction in the words of the [copyright] act.[90]

This is akin to the standard that Learned Hand had in mind when he said, in *Sheldon v. Metro-Goldwyn Pictures Corp.*, that "if by some magic a man who had never known it were to compose anew Keats's Ode on a Grecian Urn, he would be an 'author,' and, if he copyrighted it, others might not copy that poem, though they might of course copy Keats's."[91] Of course we are as susceptible as the next law professor to the Delphic and the unimaginable. Justice Story said once that copyright "comes nearer to the metaphysical" than any other branch of law.[92] We ourselves have no doubt that a well-taught course in copyright obliges the initiate to master even more in the way of pleasurable arcana than does admission to the highest order of Odd Fellows or the ultimate degree of the Masonic Lodge. The fact remains, however, that a threshold as low as copyright's originality standard is bound to produce absurd results and egregious overprotection. We see it at its nadir in a passage from yet another oft-cited and much remarked-on opinion, this one written by Judge Jerome Frank in *Alfred Bell & Co. v. Catalda Fine Arts*, in which mezzotint engravings derived from well-known paintings in the public domain were held entitled to protection, as against arguments grounded in the copyright clause and its supposed requirement of "originality":

It is clear . . . that nothing in the Constitution commands that copyrighted matter be strikingly unique or novel. . . . All that is needed to satisfy both the Constitution and the statute is that the "author" contributed something more than a "merely trivial" variation, something recognizably "his own." Originality in this context "means little more than a prohibition of actual copying." No matter how poor artistically the "author's" addition, it is enough if it be his own. . . . There is evidence that [the engravings] were not intended to, and did not, imitate the paintings they reproduced. But even if their substantial departures from the paintings were inadvertent, the copyright would be valid. A copyist's bad eyesight or defective musculature, or a shock caused by a clap of thunder, may yield sufficiently distinguishable variations. Having hit upon a variation unintentionally, the "author" may adopt it as his and copyright it.[93]

Bad eyesight, defective musculature, a clap of thunder, followed in each instance by a claim of entitlement—upon such poppycock as this is originality in copyright constructed.

The underlying justification for a standard that is no standard at all is to be understood in terms of the threat that bourgeois Philistinism might represent were the originality standard to be more demanding. This concern is suggested in the passage from Holmes we have quoted above, and is made more explicit still in another part of the same opinion: "It would be a dangerous undertaking for persons trained only to the law to constitute themselves final judges of the worth of pictorial illustrations, outside of the narrowest and most obvious limits."[94] This is not in itself a silly thought, to be sure. And if granting protection were all that were at stake, one could afford to be sympathetic toward the degraded standard that has evolved from thinking like this. But in the end, despite Hand's fanciful image, copyright is essentially a zero-sum game. To recognize originality in one work is generally to confer an entitlement to exclusivity that precludes appropriation of the protected subject matter of that work in yet another work. In each of the cases we have cited, and in scores of others like them, the ultimate outcome is that one person's defective musculature (or clap of thunder or whatever) provides the basis upon which another person may be silenced by law. This is more than ad hoc; it is arbitrary to an unconscionable degree. The Red Queen herself would be pleased.

We see that these outcomes apparently do not violate the copyright clause. But how can a regime like this be defended against obvious claims that it violates the First Amendment? Why is it not the rule that judges "trained only to the law" should be obliged to decline altogether to pass judgment on which works are entitled to expression and which not?

There are essentially two such defenses, each of them internal to the copyright doctrine itself: one is that the idea-expression dichotomy allows ideas to remain free to all even if the expression of the ideas may be held exclusively by only a few; the other is that the fair use doctrine insures that exclusivity will be waived in favor of appropriation in circumstances in which, on balance, a waiver is justified. These defenses are greatly prized and much cited by copyright protectionists and their allies in adjacent fields of intellectual property. A majority of the Supreme Court has appeared to approve them in passing, most recently in *Eldred v. Ashcroft*, the last case before the Court in which an opportunity to do so was presented.[95] Yet this purported resolution of the First Amendment question is surely far from settled law; no case has ever been decided in which the question was squarely presented and addressed at respectable length, and the authority for this position is scant. Nor is either defense an adequate safeguard against the essentially repressive nature of copyright and its prevailing system of propertied exclusivity.[96]

The Idea-Expression Dichotomy

We are told that copyright constraints mean merely that we must choose another form of expression.[97] The idea remains free; only the protected expression of that idea is forbidden to those who have no license to make use of it.[98] This is at best a hollow distinction, however, and one that is essentially whimsical in practice.[99] Ideas and their expression are frequently inseparable. Learned Hand acknowledged as much when he said, in one of the last opinions he was to write: "The test for infringement is of necessity vague . . . [N]o principle can be stated as to when an imitator has gone beyond copying the 'idea,' and has borrowed its 'expression.' Decisions must therefore inevitably be ad hoc."[100] This was admirable candor from a judge nearing the end of a professional lifetime considerably devoted to an effort to make sense of copyright. Copyright specialists in our own time have reason to know how truly Judge Hand wrote. The distinction between idea and expression cannot be predicted in advance with any degree of certainty. Given a dispute between a copyright proprietor and Hand's "imitator," and barring early settlement or capitulation, only litigation offers hope of final resolution as to the distinction between idea and expression,[101] and then the outcome is the result of a judicial coup de main: the parties in dispute propose; the court disposes. This is nice work if one happens to be a copyright lawyer or a judge. It is expensive agony and dangerous for the litigants, however, who find themselves caught up in a potentially ruinous winner-take-all contest, one that will be decided (they learn sooner or later, often to their horror) on the basis of a judgment that is, as Hand conceded, "inevitably ad hoc."[102]

Meanwhile, the central assumption embodied in the idea-expression dichotomy is itself deeply flawed. It simply is not the case that ideas ordinarily can find an adequate outlet in independent and original expression.[103] As courts have recognized, this is clearly not so when multiple forms of expression are inefficient, or when expression is dictated by circumstances or expectations external to the speaker.[104] Peter Pan's instructions to Wendy Darling as to the best route to Neverland ("Follow the first star, then turn to the right, and fly straight on until morning") cannot be improved upon as an efficient guide. Nor is there any way to produce a comprehensive theatrical feature film treatment of the Battle of Gettysburg that does not pose Blue against Gray and friend against friend, or contemplate Lee's troubled relationship with the faithful but recalcitrant Longstreet, or reenact Pickett's charge against the Federal cannon waiting among the trees just beyond the meadow. The filmmaker in each production must have similar common recourse to the underlying history and circumstances of both time and place. Indeed, copyright does not always pretend otherwise: recurring problems like these sometimes find their resolution in one or another of copyright's subordinate internal doctrines, such as merger and *scenes à faire*, under which copyright protection is set aside in favor of the public domain.

Merger is recognized in theory when an insistence on separating idea and expression will lead beyond the ad hoc to the inefficient, the impossible, or the absurd. When merger makes its appearance in a case, the entirety of the expression is treated as if it is no more than the idea, and protection is forfeited accordingly.[105] Simple directions (such as instructions for entering a contest, written on the side of a package of cereal) are the classic example; but the doctrine lends itself to cases that go well beyond that. Merger is appropriate in any case in which idea and expression cannot be separated sensibly.[106] Meanwhile, the concept of *scenes à faire* similarly acknowledges the necessity of rendering certain settings according to custom or prevailing expectation (as in the appearance of the Eiffel Tower in a film whose *mise en scène* is Paris). Like merger, *scenes à faire* represents an exception to protection.[107] The latter doctrine works reasonably well, though not always: Judge Hand himself may have failed to take *scenes à faire* adequately into account in deciding *Sheldon v. Metro-Goldwyn Pictures Corp.*,[108] involving the film *Letty Lynton* (starring Joan Crawford and Robert Montgomery, directed by Clarence Brown, and released by MGM in 1932), in which widespread public fascination with South American settings and scenarios in that time may have played a more important role than Hand allowed in the development and production of what he found to be an infringing work in part because of its setting in Rio. The consequences of his opinion for the film were dire. Though critically well reviewed and considerably well received by filmgoers upon release, it has been generally unavailable to the public since the decision against it in 1936. But then that is an entirely acceptable consequence of copyright, if not indeed its purpose, is it not: to silence or darken unlicensed expression in the interest of expression that has the imprimatur of monopolists licensed by the state?

Meanwhile, merger is often overlooked or avoided by judges who cannot quite bear the thought that the inseparability of idea and expression will mean repudiating protection in a work that seems to them (intuitively) to be worthy of it. Photographs and other visual or graphic works, particularly works reflecting natural settings (like the one in *Bleistein*), often benefit from this avoidance of responsibility.[109] By now, judges have invented an entire vocabulary of illicit conceptualization, such as the absurd notion that a work's original expression can be detected in its "total concept and feel."[110] Never mind that this is a measure even more ungovernable than is the idea-expression dichotomy itself.[111] A "concept" is explicitly excluded from copyright originality under Section 102(b) of the Act. Half of the standard is thus forbidden to begin with. The other half cannot even be discussed, much less debated, beyond the precincts of the judge's breast.

But these are small potatoes. Let us suppose that doctrinal exceptions to protection, such as merger and *scenes à faire*, are enough sometimes to dispose of some concerns in some recurring settings, whether considered under copyright or from the perspective of a nascent First Amendment. The central proposition in the idea-expression dichotomy—that an idea ordinarily may find adequate expression in infinitely variable forms—remains no less deeply flawed.[112]

The idea-expression dichotomy generally presupposes that an idea precedes or follows from expression, as prologue or précis; but very often it is closer to the mark to say that the idea itself is the product of a particular instance of expression, apart from which it has no relevant existence at all. It is one thing to say "I regret that I have but one life to give for my country," and quite another to say that "I'm a Yankee Doodle Dandy / Yankee Doodle, Do or Die." One may at first imagine that the idea is approximately the same in each of these instances of expression, but that is not really so unless we retreat to a level of generalization at which it becomes meaningless to speak of "freeing" the idea.[113] The important idea in each instance is not merely different from the other, but is in fact produced by its own expression, rather than the other way around.[114] To speak meaningfully of ideas, then, is generally to speak of them in contexts in which their expression has given them meaning.[115] It is little more than blather to speak of a dichotomy between idea and expression. The careful thinker, the precise speaker, the truly imaginative creative artist, will not like to be told that he or she must find still a third way to express an idea, when it is already clear that two will sometimes be two too many.[116]

Sometimes we must be able to speak in the words of others for reasons grounded in the very fabric of our culture. We know, for example, that the ideas behind Martin Luther King's "I Have a Dream" speech cannot truly be understood apart from the expression in which he conveyed them at the foot of the Lincoln Memorial in the summer of 1963. The speech gripped our imagination then, as it does now, precisely because of the language in which it was expressed. King himself arguably appropriated significant portions of the speech from various sources of inspiration, among them the Bible and spirituals which no doubt he had known all his life, and from sermons he had heard or delivered himself.[117] These were sources we would have expected him to revisit, and to use as he saw fit, without hesitating for a moment out of fear that he might trespass on someone else's claim.[118] In appropriating what he took from them, and joining them with what he thought to add himself, he fashioned inspiration of his own. Our lives are enriched by King's words and even by the very manner in which he gave them voice. And let us brook no argument about it: these were King's words, for the speech he gave that day made them in the truest sense his own. The ideas in that speech alone, though noble and aspiring beyond all doubt, cannot truly be comprehended in that setting apart from the language and the delivery in which he gave them thought and form and feeling. No less so, his words are ours as well. Our sensibilities fairly urge us to express them in identical terms, so far as we are able, as if in communion with him and his auditors in that moment. In a sense it is even disrespectful to propose that we do otherwise.

Just so, the remarkable film that Abraham Zapruder took in Dallas later in that same year, as President Kennedy's motorcade approached and then passed by Dealey Plaza, is priceless today, not because of the ideas that lay behind it but because of the moments of agony and loss it captured and expressed—and beyond these, because of the information potentially conveyed within the individual frames from that film: How many shots were fired? From which direction? By one assailant or more? Copyright's claims upon us in these circumstances are insignificant and absurd, as are the purported distinctions between idea and expression. Copyright surely played no role at all in the original decision by Zapruder to station himself on the grassy knoll; other incentives, no doubt largely personal, led him there.[119] He chose the place from which to film, and the film itself, and the camera and the lens and the technical settings—yes, all of these things he chose, to be sure; but these have nothing at all to do with originality in copyright, properly understood, much less with the distinction between idea and expression. The techniques by which he "rendered" his work belong to everyone, as did the "timing" which brought him there.[120] He had nothing to do with composing the subject of his work (God forbid!); it was serendipity and nothing more that enabled him to record the actual moment in which the president was slain. His perspective on the scene arguably gave him some slight claim to copyright in the work, though only of the thinnest imaginable sort, for idea (or subject) and expression merge in this film, as they often do in photographic works in which images themselves are appropriated from reality.[121] But then suppose that copyright had played a larger role—what of it? In the end the justifications for exclusivity in copyright all fall in upon one central insight, evident to all but the most ardent and insensitive proponents of protection: it is monstrous to think that the expression in this film should or could belong exclusively to anyone. In decency, if not in law, idea and expression in this setting cannot be separated. The supposed dichotomy between them is altogether meaningless.[122]

These examples, each well known to copyright specialists, and endlessly discussed and debated, serve as vivid illustrations of our point about the essential impossibility in the supposed distinction between idea and expression. But they stand apart merely in the transcendence of the moments they convey. No less important to our rejection of the idea-expression dichotomy are those instances of less dramatic import, which are legion.[123]

Novels go unwritten and unpublished, or are published under threat of liability, injunction, seizure, and destruction. Why? Because they depend in some measure on work under claim of exclusive entitlement (to characters, for example, and other elements of expression) by an earlier author or proprietor who will not license their creation. In such cases, observing the distinction between idea and expression, and treating the latter as the exclusive property of the earlier author, can threaten or even foredoom a later work.[124]

Alice Randall's *The Wind Done Gone* is a recent example.[125] Intended as a parody of Margaret Mitchell's *Gone With the Wind*,[126] Randall's novel was written from the perspective of the slaves at Tara whose interpretation of the events created by Mitchell was not at all as Mitchell herself would have imagined or approved.[127] Her estate sought an injunction on the ground that characters and plot from the original novel had been infringed,[128] and prevailed in that effort despite arguments on behalf of Randall's work to the effect that no substantial part of Mitchell's actual expression had been appropriated.[129] The injunction stood until set aside by the Eleventh Circuit: the court ruled initially from the bench at the conclusion of oral argument on First Amendment grounds (for the first and only time in copyright history)—pending an opinion on a fair use defense,[130] which eventually sent the case back to the district court for further hearings.[131] The case was then settled without an ultimate determination on the fair use ground.[132] In many respects, Randall and her publisher, Houghton Mifflin (whose determination to stand up for the novel was as admirable as it was unusual), can be seen to have obtained a victory in the affair. But at what cost? The novel itself was under injunction for weeks; in another federal circuit the outcome might have been very different. The parties meanwhile can reasonably be calculated to have spent sums approaching half a million dollars in order to bring the matter to a point at which it could be resolved—all of this in a case in which copyright was interposed as a bar to expression by an African-American author who sought to reimagine and then relate an alternative and untold slave narrative in an era central to the nation's history and its culture.[133]

Sometimes personal sentiment of a more benign sort plays a role. During his lifetime the popular author John D. MacDonald published scores of novels, one series comprising twenty-two books featuring the character Travis McGee.[134] McGee was an amiable self-described boat bum, who made his home aboard the *Busted Flush*, a houseboat he had won in the course of a poker game, and which he now kept more or less permanently moored in Slip F-18 at Fort Lauderdale's fictional Bahia Mar. A worthy counterpart to such other rugged adventurers as his contemporary James Bond, with whom he shared a taste for gin and women, McGee made his living as a "salvage expert," who recovered things that had been lost (always as a result of malign human forces) by unfortunates less physically and mentally capable than he (and considerably less daring), to whom he extended his assistance in exchange for fifty percent of the value of the salvage (a real bargain when you knew the circumstances, and not infrequently a maiden's only hope for survival to boot), meanwhile occasionally finding time to reflect at large on the wondrous nature of human existence.[135] The series was among the most popular and financially successful of its time—and in our view justifiably so.[136] Even now, some twenty years after the last work in that series was published (MacDonald died in 1986),[137] Travis McGee novels remain much sought after in secondhand bookstores, which seldom manage to keep more than a few in stock for longer than a few weeks. First editions are rare and very expensive. MacDonald's work in this series was, in short, nothing less than a masterpiece in the estimation of his many readers.

More than one would-be successor author[138] has applied for permission to write and publish additional novels derived from the series. But MacDonald's son has refused a license to all comers, saying that he does not wish to see his father's achievement and memory sullied by imitations. A number of things can be said of the son's position in a setting like this. On the one hand it is an understandable and even admirable demonstration of filial loyalty and devotion. Yet these are not traditionally among the principal interests to be protected by copyright. Recall that copyright in American law is protected for reasons aimed at promoting the progress of human knowledge, rather than for reasons of moral or sentimental entitlement. Would it not suffice, in circumstances such as these, to require an attribution to the senior MacDonald, acknowledging him as the originator of Travis McGee, accompanied perhaps by a further acknowledgment to the effect that later novels employing the character are derived from the earlier ones, but are not the work of the original author, and that they have not been "authorized" by his heirs or representatives? Would these attributions and acknowledgments not faithfully reflect the facts of the matter, while doing no harm to the legitimate aspirations of a successor author?

For otherwise consider the consequences of indulging the author or his heir in simple exclusivity: legions of admirers, not merely of the father's achievements, but of Travis McGee's as well, are to be deprived of further news of the latter's adventures for another half century. Eventually, to be sure, in the year 2056, when copyright in the last Travis McGee novel will presumably expire under current law, additional novels by admiring imitators may be written and published, with or without the approval of MacDonald's son.[139] But that thought is in the nature of a stork's dinner, for by that time the series will no doubt seem as dated as the Hardy Boys do now (not to mention all those once-enthralling but now-forgotten novels about the daring lads who flew Spads and Sopwith Camels against the ravening Hun in the Great War). And those among us who today would read (and write) additional novels in the Travis McGee series, with an appetite still stronger than our failing pulse rate, will, by that time, be as dead as MacDonald père is now.

Novels make useful examples of what copyright costs in terms of expression threatened or foregone, besides being especially dear to our hearts. But they are joined by countless other examples in other mediums. Biographies and other works of the public intellect are enjoined or abandoned, and the research in anticipation of their appearance forfeited. Why? Because their completion depends on access to expression in the subject's earlier work that is now forbidden. Films go unproduced, or are released in truncated or distorted versions. Why? Because rights to the earlier expression they incorporate cannot be cleared, or can be cleared only at costs in excess of the filmmaker's resources.[140] Dramatic works are darkened, comedy squelched, and music silenced, in response to claims to exclusive rights by earlier composers: recall, again for the sake of example, the fate of the hapless choir master in Clarinda, Iowa, who sought only to create an arrangement that would match the limited capacities of his singers, and who then sought only to share what he had done with the composer of the original song, whose thanks took the form of a suit for infringement.[141] In each of these settings, and again in hundreds of others like them, the effect of recognizing exclusivity in copyright is to silence the expression in a later work. And note that this is so even when the later work is created by an author who has no conscious recollection of the earlier work at all.[142] Why? The answer according to copyright orthodoxy, in this setting, as in all other cases of infringement, is that appropriation must be seen as an actionable offense (akin to trespass) against exclusive interests in property, without regard to motive or intent if the taking is substantial.

Fair Use

Copyright sometimes recognizes the inadequacy of the idea-expression dichotomy, in circumstances like the ones just discussed, as well as others. In such cases, sometimes, the Copyright Act itself may offer some relief, always limited in scope, however, and tailored to fairly specific circumstances in which Congress has decided, on balance, to make no law abridging freedom of expression.[143] In other settings, more generally, the Act provides, as we have seen, that fair use of a work under copyright is not an infringement of a proprietor's exclusive rights if the later work, on balance, is viewed favorably according to four mandatory "factors."[144] Taken together, these provisions do represent a formal concession to what the copyright industries like to call "users' rights."[145] (This is a term that reflects an underlying conception of creativity we will say more about in due course.) Perhaps at one time fair use might even have served as an adequate accommodation of the conflict between rights generated under the copyright clause and rights protected against abridgment by the First Amendment. Professors Patterson and Joyce have suggested as much.[146] But the fair use doctrine today is altogether inadequate.[147] An all but indecipherable hodgepodge of precedents and statutory mandates, fair use in our time (measured in light of the decided cases) often amounts to little more than caprice heaped upon caprice, with no one in the end but judges to decide when and whether exclusivity or appropriation is to have the upper hand in a given setting.[148] (David Nimmer correctly suggests that "reliance on the four statutory factors to reach fair use decisions often seems naught but a fairy tale.")[149] We do not propose to make sense of fair use here, or to prescribe a better approach to its employment. In our judgment, the very concept of fair use is misplaced when questions of this kind appear.

EXCLUSIVITY VERSUS APPROPRIATION

By now it should be clear that the central issue to be confronted in cases like these is not originality, nor the idea-expression dichotomy, nor yet again, fair use; the issue, rather, is what it costs when exclusivity is juxtaposed against appropriation. We have said that the full costs cannot be reckoned; there is no way to calculate them. We cannot know what opportunities have been missed when copyright stands in the way of subsequent expression. We are surely not wrong to suspect that the loss is likely to be substantial. Much of what is valuable in Shakespeare's works was appropriated by him without license or payment.[150] If we imagine merely that one among his many works might have been precluded under our own system of exclusivity, fees, and licensing, we can begin to sense the dimensions of what we ourselves forego—and still we cannot calculate the loss with any certainty, whether in economic, cultural, or other terms.[151] Yet we can be sure that the accommodations we are obliged to make to exclusivity demand more of us than it is either sensible to expect or possible for us to give without grave sacrifice.[152]

Why, then, do we make them? Is it that we prize independence and originality in thought and expression so strongly that all else must be sacrificed? Self-expression does not depend on them, though they are sometimes thought to be attributes of the creative mind; and even then they are rarely enough by themselves. We do not subscribe to everything that has been uttered in the past twenty years or so about the Death of the Author[153] and the Myth of the Romantic Creator.[154] But creativity of any sort surely presupposes freedom to imagine, and (as Yale law professor Jed Rubenfeld has suggested) freedom of imagination must presuppose an ability to remember, to imitate, and to appropriate.[155] Zechariah Chafee said (years ago, to be sure, and against a background of very different sensibilities) that the dwarf who stands on the shoulders of a giant can see farther than the giant standing alone.[156] No doubt that is true. It is truer still of the giant who stands on the shoulders of a dwarf. (Shakespeare's achievements were of the latter variety.) In either case, the underlying thought is undoubtedly correct: imitation and appropriation can be fully as important as originality to freedom of expression.[157] True independence of thought and expression means being free to choose one or the other or both, at will.[158] In most cases, moreover, it is unnecessary to elevate or deprecate one creator in order to understand and appreciate another. That may be the task of critics, but critics must not be suffered as censors. Most of us know the difference.

One understands that Bob Dylan created himself by immersing himself in the works of earlier artists like Woody Guthrie and Pete Seeger, and then emerging from them again as if reborn.[159] Groucho Marx wrote of coming into his own as a performer through a process of "trial and error," in which creativity began with appropriation amounting to outright theft. "If the comic was inventive," Groucho added, "he would gradually discard the stolen jokes and the ones that died and try out some of his own. In time, if he was any good, he would emerge from the routine character he had started with and evolve into a distinct personality of his own."[160] Freedom to appropriate in the service of creativity is among the more important interests at stake when we confront any doctrine grounded in the sort of exclusivity that copyright takes for granted.[161] Groucho's conditions ("if the comic was inventive; if he was any good") reflect critical judgments that come naturally to mind in settings in which creativity is on display. Groucho was not wrong to think in these terms, nor are we.[162] But does it follow that these are the sorts of judgments that should find their resolution in the law? Surely it ought not lie within the province of critics or Congress or the courts to decide these questions for us. They are decisions that lie, for better or for worse, within the sensibilities of each and every one among us.[163] Holmes said, in essence, that "judges trained to the law" should not be counted on to act as arbiters of creativity, and of course he was right.[164] Creativity is a supremely individual affair. Hand conceded, in effect, that no principle can guide us in our recognition of it; the decisions we make must be "inevitably ad hoc."[165] Neither Holmes nor Hand appears to have seen where admissions like these must lead, however. These are, or so we might have imagined, ultimately among the more important reasons why Congress is to "make no law" abridging freedom of expression. In the end it is expression that counts, not originality or creativity.

Proponents of exclusivity often speak of the property interests at stake, as if thereby to make it plain that property should prevail in any contest with interests in expression.[166] But why should propertied exclusivity ever trump free expression? In truth, the law has no principled answer to this most obvious of questions. It may make perfect sense to speak of copyright and other similar interests as though they are property; let them be property if property they are. But surely they are also expression—or "speech" (and sometimes "press"), within a perfectly ordinary meaning of these terms as they appear in the First Amendment. To be sure, it can seem a bit odd to think of property as if it were also expression. After all, we do not ordinarily think of houses and lawnmowers as expressive—though the house in the gated community can speak volumes about its owners, as can the battered pickup truck and riding mowers that belong to the proprietors of their lawn service. But expression is exactly what springs to mind when we think of novels or poems or sermons or songs or films or choreography or the like, which in every case we recognize as central to the purposes and function of the First Amendment. Why should we think otherwise when works such as these also assume some of the dimensions of property?

Interests in property are often subordinated to more important interests, whether public or private. The homeowner whose neighbors command his obedience to restrictive covenants, or whose community enforces historic zoning regulations, will have no difficulty understanding what we mean. If interests in exclusivity are at odds with interests protected by the First Amendment, surely more is needed than a simple assertion of "property rights!" to resolve the dispute. Exclusivity may be a natural attribute of traditional interests in property; but in the context of intellectual property it is heavily counterintuitive. This is so for at least three reasons that precede, and are independent of, arguments arising from the First Amendment.

Thomas Jefferson and the Nature of Property

In the first place, as we have seen, the thing that is the subject of most traditional interests in property is also ordinarily tangible, and therefore (in the language favored by our colleagues elsewhere in the academy) rivalrous.[167] This is to say that if you have a can of beans and an opener (meanwhile presupposing the absence of an economist) you can share the beans only so far before the contents of the can are entirely depleted. If you build your house on a pretty piece of land, others who might wish to build there will be precluded from doing so to the extent that the property will sustain only one house. If you own a car or a lawnmower you are likely to lend them to others only to the extent that your use of them is not thereby precluded. Note that these are constraints *ex naturae*—imposed by their very nature. They are not the consequence of property law, but rather presage what the law is likely to recognize and provide.[168] Most traditional property laws reflect this underlying natural state of affairs; exclusivity is thus a common (though not inevitable nor unmoderated) response.

But the thing at the heart of an interest in intellectual property is not bounded by its inherent physical nature, nor is it scarce in this physical sense.[169] Sharing it with others does not diminish or deplete it, either, for as Thomas Jefferson observed almost two hundred years ago (in a passage well known to every contemporary student of intellectual property):

> If nature has made any one thing less susceptible than all others of exclusive property, it is the action of the thinking power called an idea, which an individual may exclusively possess as long as he keeps it to himself; but the moment it is divulged, it forces itself into the possession of every one, and the receiver cannot dispossess himself of it. Its peculiar character, too, is that no one possesses the less, because every other possesses the whole of it. He who receives an idea from me, receives instruction himself without lessening mine; as he who lights his taper at mine, receives light without darkening me. That ideas should freely spread from one to another over the globe, for the moral and mutual instruction of man, and improvement of his condition, seems to have been peculiarly and benevolently designed by nature, when she made them, like fire, expansible over all space, without lessening their density in any point, and like the air in which we breathe, move, and have our physical being, incapable of confinement or exclusive appropriation.[170]

Of course Jefferson was not speaking of "ideas" in the peculiar and forced sense in which copyright now attempts to distinguish them from "expression." It appears that he actually had patents in mind when he wrote, though the fundamental insights in this passage are no less consistent with copyright than with any other species of intellectual property in which exclusivity is under contemplation.[171] The burden of his comment went much deeper than mere doctrine. What Jefferson challenged was the logic of exclusivity in the context of intangible expression of every sort, once published.[172] Exclusivity is at odds with the very nature of ideas and their expression. This has always been so: Jefferson wrote in 1813, when no one spoke of "communications" or "convergence"; yet what he said would do credit to a contemporary critic. Today we say that "information wants to be free"[173]—or, in Brandeis's celebrated phrase from *Whitney v. California*, "free as the air to common use."[174]

What was true for Jefferson is no less so for us in a second respect as well. The creative mind, in our time no less than in his own, is alive to the possibilities in ideas and expression alike, and is quickened by their presence in the air. It is in the nature of expression, moreover, exactly as he observed, that it should "force itself" upon us, and that we should be unable to "dispossess ourselves of it." If there is a difference across the ages in this respect, it is merely that with every passing decade the cumulative weight of the ideas and expression that bear upon us grows progressively heavier. We do not suppose that Jefferson's was a "simpler" time; it is sophomoric and narcissistic to imagine so. But even he would no doubt concede today that the "age of symbols" Justice Frankfurter observed some half a century ago has become still more intense as we have entered upon the digital era.[175] Ideas and expression, like the interests in property they supposedly reflect, confront us everywhere. It is a commonplace in our time that we cannot escape them. In our judgment, this encroachment is not new; how could we think so, knowing what Jefferson wrote? But its progress can be thought of as phenomenal, and in that sense the very omnipresence of what has always been an occasion for comment can be seen as having assumed proportions that oblige us now to act as well. If expression is to force itself upon us, and take up lodging with or without our leave, surely it cannot simultaneously reside exclusively with others, subject only to their control. If the Tinker Bell we and our children know is sent by Hollywood rather than by Peter Pan, surely we must have something to say about when she comes and goes, and how she spends her time with us, and we with her.

In these two respects, Jefferson armed us with arguments that undercut the logic of exclusivity. In a third, he suggested the shape of an alternative response:

Stable ownership is the gift of social law, and is given late in the progress of society. It would be curious then, if an idea, the fugitive fermentation of an individual brain, could, of natural

right, be claimed in exclusive and stable property. . . . Society may give an exclusive right to
the profits arising from them, as an encouragement to men to pursue ideas which may produce utility, but this may or may not be done, according to the will of the society, without
claim or complaint from any body.[176]

Note that in this passage Jefferson offers an implicit interpretation of the
"exclusive rights" referred to in the intellectual property clause, an interpretation that does not envision exclusivity of the sort that both copyright and patent law have featured since the beginning of the Republic.
There is no hint in his letter that he was conscious of having done so; it
appears rather that he was innocently interpreting the clause in the only
way that made sense of his larger view of rights in ideas and expression.[177] Exclusivity in a work (as against a right in others to appropriate
it) is the wrong entitlement, for the reasons he suggested, but an exclusive
right to profits may be another matter altogether. Of course one must not
confuse a right to profits with a right to rents: the former presupposes
that there are net revenues; the latter, on the other hand, envisions payment whether or not funds are available. Profits may make perfectly good
sense, as an alternative to exclusivity; presumably nothing need be paid
unless a source of payment is forthcoming. If rents are to be exacted
without concern as to the availability of such a source, however, then the
ability of others to appropriate a work will be jeopardized and may in
fact be precluded. It follows, then, that a compulsory license (of the sort
we have seen in copyright) would not suffice as a response to Jefferson's
concerns.[178] Only a system that recognizes an unconditional right of appropriation for the sake of expression will suffice.

Insights More Important Than We Can Use?

What are the larger implications in Jefferson's letter?[179] His insights call
into question the sufficiency of doctrinal responses to the conflict between
exclusivity and appropriation. And they suggest in turn the urgency in
calls for a more considered response from the First Amendment.

One of the most prominent policy issues of our time, of course, is
posed by the phenomenon of peer-to-peer file sharing via the Internet.
This is where the greater part of the energy now being expended on all

sides of the larger issue of appropriation and expression is actually centered. Most of us understand the phenomenon itself. Someone (and let
us face it: that someone is usually a young person, and often a student)
downloads a recording of a song or movie protected by copyright, using
one of a host of increasingly sophisticated Internet search engines to find
and record it, and then sends it on to others using the same engine. This
means in theory that the recording and film industries are deprived of a
sale.[180] They say that if such copying is not stopped they will decline and
eventually perish. It is usual to discuss these points in economic terms;
but this also usually loads the discussion, for an economics-centered
analysis means that the playing field is likely to be tilted in favor of protection and away from appropriation.[181] The copyright perspective itself
is relatively simple; unlicensed copying and distribution are generally
forbidden.[182]

The fact remains, however, that using the new technologies to make
copies of recorded works is also generally an exercise in creative expression. Even the simplest form of direct copying generally involves selec-
tion, an indisputably creative act; file sharing involves self-expression,
and is also indisputably creative.[183] Copyright proponents will not like
for us to say these things, but that does not mean we are wrong. Copyright rules do not prescribe the boundaries of creativity, merely because
their usual function is to limit it or forbid its exercise. In the case of file
sharing, the supposed miscreants are doing essentially what record and
film producers themselves do when they decide what and whom to produce and release. Record producers invest more time and money, but
then that is merely where the problem begins: the new technologies now
make it possible for creative appropriation and sharing to cost less.
Peer-to-peer file sharing reflects a major shift in the way the culture is
transmitted from one person or entity to another.[184]

Or consider the proposal by Google to scan the collections of major
libraries, the better to make them searchable on the net. The plan raises
obvious, if unusually sophisticated, questions under three of copyright's
exclusive proprietary rights: reproduction; derivative works; and distribution. In some cases, display and even performance rights may be implicated.[185] It is even conceivable that rights in one-of-a-kind works of

visual art may be involved.[186] Google does not actually contemplate an ongoing violation of these rights; in its view of the matter, it will merely offer limited access to the works so that searchers can more easily identify and then reach the works that they may wish to examine. That will be well within the reach of fair use in Google's interpretation of that doctrine. But copyright proprietors observe that Google will have to make at least one full copy of each work in order to afford the sort of access it has in mind. And this, the proprietors say, will violate at least the reproduction right, if nothing else. (As of this writing the Authors' Guild and a consortium of French copyright proprietors have filed suit, demanding an injunction against the proposed activity.)[187] We do not propose to pursue the issues raised by this dispute at length. For our purposes it is enough to observe that here again is evidence of a potential cultural shift occasioned by digital technologies and the Internet that make the underlying questions of exclusivity and appropriation a phenomenon deserving of more measured attention than it has had.

The question is whether we can bring ourselves to recognize Jefferson's insights, now that they are no longer merely prescient?

Recognizing the Public Domain

At one time it might have seemed enough to address the problems posed by copyright and other forms of intellectual property from within the parameters of the doctrines themselves. We wrote some twenty-five years ago, along lines like the ones we are revisiting here, an essay in which we proposed an affirmative recognition of the public domain, one that would restore, or so we hoped, a diminishing balance within intellectual property doctrines between protection and the free availability of works.[188] Our concern, then as now, was with the threat to creativity and a shared culture posed by increasing encroachments upon the public domain. It seemed at the time that copyright and patent law were not the main threats—that other upstart doctrines, such as the right of publicity or the notion of dilution in trademark law (both then still relatively undeveloped in the law), were the more serious potential obstacles to our ability to share the culture as we imagined we had done since the days of the Founders. Our thought was that an affirmative recognition of the public domain should serve to remind us that there were interests at stake going well beyond the justifications that are said to underlie the intellectual property doctrines. We suggested that Congress and the courts adopt deliberate measures to balance all proposals for new legislation (legislation that would expand the reach of intellectual property) against their resulting encroachment upon no less important interests affirmatively provided for by the public domain. And (for a time) a test derived from our proposal did indeed play at least a modest role in the course of legislation under consideration in the House subcommittee that oversaw new legislation.[189] But no test as fragile as the one we suggested could withstand the forces that time and circumstances raised against it. The copyright industries, like their counterparts in other fields that make up intellectual property, have succeeded in persuading Congress that without new laws to combat the new technologies, the industries themselves are doomed to decline, decay, and eventual failure. The Digital Millennium Copyright Act of 1998[190]—an extraordinarily complex piece of legislation, drafted primarily by the industries themselves, and especially intended to permit copyright proprietors to establish virtual venues,[191] secured by digitally encoded gates and fences and protected against trespass (or hacking) by severe civil and criminal penalties—is but one of numerous responses to these pleas, with others waiting in the wings as we write these words.[192]

Many observers of this scene have written or spoken since our essay on the public domain appeared, with the result that the public domain movement in American law today is thriving well beyond the limits of our own vision.[193] Yet the last quarter century has seen the lines drawn more clearly and with greater opposing force between intellectual property proponents and the proponents of what Professor Lessig calls "Free Culture."[194] It no longer seems enough to suggest that reform can come from within the intellectual property fields and the industries they support. A conflict has erupted between the notions of exclusivity in intellectual property law and the sense of entitlement to expression the First Amendment appears to have been intended to assure. The underlying issues are not new, but the extent of the conflict and its role in our everyday existence press upon us as never before. A public domain in which we are free to think and remember and speak as we please remains a viable and central goal. But the means for attaining that goal is now in doubt.

One might have expected the Constitution to chart the path toward the public domain. But the intellectual property clause continues to lie silent as to the most pressing issues. And the First Amendment has yet to turn its full attention to the challenge. In the chapter that follows we will examine some of the reasons why the Constitution in our time is unequal to the task before it.

CONFLICT AND THE CONSTITUTION

We have meant meanwhile to sketch, in admittedly impressionistic terms, a field of conflict between exclusive rights generated and protected by copyright and its companion doctrines in the field of intellectual property, and the very different, often antithetical rights that are recognized and protected by the First Amendment. We have suggested in this chapter that intellectual property rights amounting to exclusivity are probably less certain as to necessity than we are accustomed to supposing, but entirely certain in the encroachments they make into the public domain. We have argued that this is not, in truth, a new problem, but rather one that has been slow in gaining recognition. And we have acknowledged that in our time the conflict is recognized on every hand.

Now the question is, why has the Constitution offered neither a satisfactory response nor an adequate resolution?

CHAPTER 4

"Exclusive Rights" and the Constitution

WE HAVE TRIED to make it clear that a central focus of our inquiry in this book is on the limitations imposed on expression by the concept and practice of exclusivity under current intellectual property regimes— regimes that routinely forbid appropriation of expressive works in the absence of a license. We have suggested (in company with many others) that these limitations have led to a conflict between the regimes and the Constitution, a conflict in multiple dimensions, in which interests in property are pitted against freedom of expression. In the first three chapters of our book we have examined the regimes themselves. Now we turn our attention toward a more deliberate examination of the regimes from within the perspective offered by the Constitution, and ask why it is that a conflict as obvious as the one we have been discussing has not yet been the subject of more deliberate efforts by Congress and the courts to resolve it? In this setting, we think it will be useful if we elaborate a bit on our earlier effort to set the limits of our understanding and discussion of expression. Here again, we employ the term "expression" conventionally, but also as a synonym for those aspects of speech and press that are within the province of the First Amendment.

We do not accept for the purposes of this book the distinction that sometimes has been drawn between speech and press under that amendment. Specifically, we reject the notion that either interest is superior or inferior to (or greater or lesser, or more or less important than) the other. Whatever may be said of such notions in other settings, we think they have never been made the basis of settled law, and we do not accept them here.[1] Instead we treat both speech and press as complementary equivalents, in the nature of fraternal twins, embracing a continuum of expression that begins with imagination and thought, and that may (though it need not always) end in some publication or disclosure going beyond the limits of a merely personal, private, or otherwise constrained utterance.[2] As we use it in this context, then, expression is both a conventional term and one that encodes the particular meaning of speech and press within the limits of the First Amendment that we have suggested here.

Nor do we intend to be caught up in the intriguing but essentially distracting question of when expression is also to be seen more fundamentally as action (or some other thing), thereby arguably taking us beyond the reach of the First Amendment.[3] Justice Black, who believed (correctly, or so we will argue) that the First Amendment laid absolute constraints upon the power of Congress to abridge freedom of expression, nevertheless concluded that some of what might very broadly be considered expressive acts did not fall fairly within the meaningful embrace of the amendment. So do we conclude—though not necessarily in exact accordance with Justice Black's own understanding.[4] We do accept the proposition that the meaning of expression under the First Amendment encounters limitations in the more obvious conventional settings. Thus, for example, perjury, fraud, and acts of violence (such as looting), all of which may in some sense be expressive, are beyond the reach of the First Amendment for our purposes.[5]

We also accept conventional limitations from within the intellectual property doctrines, limitations that serve functions essentially apart from a primary constraint upon expression itself. When (for example) trademark law limits the use of symbols in order to avoid confusion in the marketplace, we do not understand these limits to offend against the Constitution, though of course more draconian (or disingenuous) limits (such as interpretations of "confusion" that emphasize knowing appropriation, as well as those encoded within the notion of dilution) may indeed give offense.[6] We do not need to define these limits more closely or comprehensively at present, however. It will be enough to say that our discussion throughout this book generally envisions and addresses those instances of expression, otherwise readily cognizable as such under the First Amendment, that are also the subject of exclusivity, whether according to copyright or under another doctrine within the field of intellectual property at large.

Against this necessary background, we are ready once again to resume our discussion.

CONSIDER THE FOLLOWING

(CALL IT THE ORTHODOX ACCOUNT)

The United States is a society in which freedom of expression is central. We Americans define ourselves as American in part by the role that free expression plays in our common life. We are, or so we tell ourselves, committed to and characterized by the broadest possible range of expression, all of it essentially free of the deadening hand of governmental supervision and control.[7]

Nor can there be any doubt that the culture of the United States is indeed characterized by a remarkably wide-ranging symphony (cacophony, some would have it) of expression. In every medium possible to our technology and our imagination, Americans are besieged by the products of this culture of free expression. Novelists, poets, painters, musicians, photographers, moviemakers, politicians, pundits and journalists, multinationals with products to sell, psychics with fortunes to tell, defenders of moral majorities and immoral minorities, proponents of prophetic dissent, cranks and crackpots, interest groups and religious groups, and ordinary, individual citizens—all participate. All contribute to a realm of freedom to say what one thinks, or feels, or wishes to communicate for whatever reason (selfless or blatantly commercial, it matters not), that we take pride in imagining is unsurpassed in human history for its richness and its diversity, and for its tolerance, in the interests of the few, of that which deviates from the sensibilities of the many.[8]

The reality of free expression is matched, moreover, by America's commitment to safeguard it by legal means, above all by enshrining the principle of free expression in the Constitution of the United States where it is ordinarily beyond the reach of censorship by the organs of any American governmental institution, federal, state or local. The law of the First Amendment, as we usually think of it (the reality is more complicated, and we will touch on that in a later section, but for now we will use the term as shorthand) is of a breadth and complexity that rivals even the most detailed of regulatory schemes. Its preeminent theme is the preservation of expression *from* regulation. Among other things this has led to an unprecedented legal crusade to maximize the number of ways in which expression can escape the inevitable desire of functionaries and their masters to manipulate the world of ideas and their expression in the interests of government.[9] Against the interests, wishes, claims, and protests of government—even those that have the imprimatur of a political majority acting through democratic means—the American law of free expression protects academics and public intellectuals, journalists, critics and dissenters, advertisers and purveyors, and creators of high art and low, as well as individuals of every hue and stripe, including those assorted misanthropes who do not wish to speak but who rather wish very much the opposite, including, for example, those who wish not to participate in a civic ritual contrary to their convictions or beliefs,[10] or not to sport a license plate with a slogan contrary to their politics or their taste.[11] Taxes on newspapers[12] and regulations about utility company mailings[13] can raise high questions of First Amendment law; so can statutes limiting contributions to electoral campaigns,[14] administrative decisions about what can be broadcast and when,[15] and public efforts to prevent hate-filled demonstrations[16] and intrusive solicitations.[17] The authority of a public school to regulate what its students wear,[18] and what they say in the school assembly,[19] and what they find in the school library[20]—that authority as to each and every such issue is one of constitutional moment within the scope and reach of the First Amendment.

This is but a handful of examples. A comprehensive list of such issues would be lengthy indeed: in the last fifteen years federal courts alone have mentioned the First Amendment in more than ten thousand cases. In many of these cases, of course, the First Amendment claim was trivial or the reference tangential; but that must be balanced against the fact that the states' courts invoked the First Amendment in an equal number of cases in the same period—and the fact as well that judicial enforcement of First Amendment freedoms dates back not fifteen but almost ninety years, not to mention the significant body of decisions that have considered claims of free expression under state constitutions or federal statutes. Many of these decisions, to be sure, have rejected the particular claim of free expression before the court. But the exact number of successful free expression legal claims, even if we could determine it, would mean little. The basic point is beyond quibble: courts in America have developed a complex and fundamentally libertarian case law of free expression, one that applies as its chief presumption the validity of unfettered freedom of expression, and the invalidity of government attempts to decide what may or may not be said.[21]

A number of years ago, the great constitutional lawyer Charles L. Black, Jr., wrote that "We Americans have up to this point, within human limits and with some bad passages, made good on our promise of freedom of expression—both of expression explicitly political and of expression only implicitly political, if it is political at all—freedom of opinion and freedom in way of life."[22] Black's words suggest the deep connections between freedom of expression as a cultural norm and freedom of expression as a constitutional value. The legal norm encourages and informs the culture, while the libertarian assumptions of the culture mold the thought and action of those entrusted with legal authority. Culture and commitment are mutually reinforcing, in ways that undergird the claim that the United States has "made good on our promise."

BUT NOW CONSIDER THIS
(CALL IT THE WAY THINGS ARE)

In 1897, Mark Twain observed that "it is by the goodness of God that in our country we have those three unspeakably precious things: freedom of speech, freedom of conscience, and the prudence never to practice either of them."[23] Twain of course had in mind the existence of social constraints on freedom of expression, not the possibility of limitations or defects in the law's protection of expression. It could hardly have been otherwise: in Twain's day judicial enforcement of what we now call "First Amendment freedoms" was essentially nonexistent in any direct or explicit form. In this book, in contrast, our concern is precisely with the existence (as a matter of hard reality, rather than mere possibility) of a body of law that has come to serve not the American "promise of free expression" but rather an ill-judged social experiment—one intended to encourage intellectual productivity, but in fact designed and administered so as frequently to narrow the ultimate range of expression while fencing off broad areas of discourse, art, and opinion from the First Amendment's libertarian principles. In this undertaking, we speak of the law of intellectual property and, still more often and more specifically, of the federal statutes and judicial doctrines that make up the American system of copyright protection.

As we have seen, under the laws of the United States relating to copyright, the mere utterance of a certain form of words can lead to criminal prosecution.[24] Yale law professor Jed Rubenfeld has made the point this way: "In some parts of the world, you can go to jail for reciting a poem in public without permission from state-licensed authorities. Where is this true? One place is the United States of America."[25] In the enforcement of those same laws, federal courts regularly issue injunctive orders, enforceable by fine or imprisonment, forbidding actions that in any other legal context would be shielded, self-evidently, from official interference by the First Amendment. After the fact, those same courts regularly award money damages in judgment against defendants for what they have said, written, or expressed in written, visual, aural, or graphic form. In addition, running throughout this body of law is the assumption that judges (who are governmental officials, let us remember) can and should make close findings of fact and conclusions of law about which instances of expression should or should not lead to prosecution, invoke injunctions, and impose financial liability. As we have also seen, acting under the guise of protecting intellectual property rights, government officials decide what may be said (printed, broadcast, and so on); they make decisions that are, in essence, value judgments about the social utility of expression; they direct the compulsory force of the state against speakers because they have spoken in ways that do not accord with public law and policy. In all of these respects, much of intellectual property law affords a perfect example of a legal scheme for the regulation of expression—precisely what the First Amendment prohibits, or so one might suppose.[26]

The coexistence of the First Amendment and contemporary American intellectual property is on its face a puzzle: both practically and conceptually the two legal regimes plainly address overlapping areas of conduct and do so with antithetical methods and results. The First Amendment guarantees expressive liberty and intellectual property restricts it; the First Amendment bars government from making choices about what is said and heard, while intellectual property empowers government to empower others to make such choices. Of course no complex legal system will be without its tensions and, perhaps, localized inconsistencies; but the antagonism between the First Amendment and intellectual property goes beyond the unavoidable consequences of complexity. The promise of freedom of expression and the enforcement of contemporary intellectual property rights—again, copyright is the preeminent example—appear to be in stark contradiction to one another. How can this be?

COPYRIGHT AND THE QUESTION OF ITS FIRST AMENDMENT IMMUNITY

Such apparent contradictions should not escape notice, and of course they have not. The federal judiciary, charged with primary responsibility for arbitrating the law of intellectual property, and equally preeminent in making a legal fact of the First Amendment's promise, has an answer. Perhaps the bluntest formulation of that answer was supplied by the United States Court of Appeals for the District of Columbia Circuit in its decision upholding the 1998 Copyright Term Extension Act. According to a panel of that court, "the regime of copyright itself respects and adequately safeguards the freedom of speech protected by the First Amendment."[27] The apparent contradiction, in short, does not exist, and "copyrights are categorically immune from challenges under the First Amendment."[28] The statutory and doctrinal tools by which the judiciary administers copyright law, involving as they do the exercise of judgment about which expression to permit, and which to suppress, themselves "give adequate protection to free expression."[29]

As a rhetorical matter, the D.C. appeals court went too far: reviewing the court's decision, the Supreme Court of the United States disavowed the lower court's incautious language. "We recognize," a seven-justice majority on the high court remarked, "that the D.C. Circuit spoke too broadly when it declared copyrights 'categorically immune.' "[30] But the justices uttered this comment, surely a mild rebuke at most, in an opinion that approved the essential thrust of the appeals court's reasoning even as it affirmed the court's decision. The Supreme Court's decision in that case, styled *Eldred v. Ashcroft* before the Court, confirms the unsurprising fact that the First Amendment/intellectual property contradiction has not gone unnoticed. But *Eldred* makes it equally clear that judicial awareness need not lead to an adequate judicial resolution of the contradiction. To see that this is so, and how, let us now examine how the Supreme Court itself explains the compatibility of free expression and copyright protection.

Under the statutory scheme in place from 1976 until 1998, copyright protection for works of individual authorship lasted from the work's creation until fifty years after the author's death. The statute the Court sustained in *Eldred* (the so-called Sonny Bono Copyright Term Extension Act of 1998)[31] extended this period: under the Act copyright in most individually authored works now runs from creation of the copyrighted work until seventy years after the death of the author.[32] Other published works are protected, on average, for only slightly less than a century.[33] The Act applies to copyrights existing at the time of enactment as well as to those created after its effective date. Before the Supreme Court, the plaintiffs argued that Congress lacks the power to apply the Act to existing copyrights, and that doing so violates the First Amendment's guarantee of freedom of expression. (The Court actually agreed to review a broader First Amendment claim, that the extension of future copyrights also violated the amendment, but the plaintiffs did not pursue this claim.)[34] As we have noted, the Court rejected both arguments by a lopsided majority.

The Court reached the same (negative) conclusion about each of the *Eldred* plaintiffs' claims. In doing so, however, the Court made it quite clear that for the justices it was the copyright clause argument that deserved serious attention, while the First Amendment claim needed no more than pro forma examination. The Court's disparate treatment of the two arguments is self-evident. In her opinion for the Court, Justice Ginsburg devoted almost twenty-one pages to the copyright clause issue;

she disposed of the First Amendment in fewer than three. Her copyright clause discussion was correspondingly detailed and coherent, if ultimately unpersuasive. As we will see, however, Justice Ginsburg's treatment of the First Amendment was not only telegraphic, it was affirmatively unconvincing—unless one starts (as the majority plainly did) with the presumption that the First Amendment is of little relevance to issues of intellectual property.

We shall have more to say presently about the copyright clause discussion in the opinion of the Court in *Eldred v. Ashcroft*. Our present concern, however, is with the *Eldred* Court's handling of the First Amendment claim, and with what it reveals about the contemporary understanding (or, more precisely, lack of understanding) of the relationship between freedom of expression and intellectual property. To do so, we must ask the reader to engage in a close and critical examination of the Court's reasoning.

COPYRIGHT VERSUS THE FIRST AMENDMENT, ACCORDING TO *ELDRED*

The First Amendment discussion begins with a one-sentence summary of the plaintiffs' legal argument, followed immediately by a summary rejection of that argument and a series of assertions intended to support that rejection. (Because the plaintiffs were the losing party below, they were the party seeking review by the Court, which therefore referred to them as the "petitioners.") The two summaries are deceptively simple. "Petitioners separately argue that the [Act] is a content-neutral regulation of speech that fails heightened judicial review under the First Amendment. We reject petitioners' plea for imposition of uncommonly strict scrutiny on a copyright scheme that incorporates its own speech-protective purposes and safeguards."[35]

The Court's restatement of the plaintiff's argument—again, that the Act is a "content-neutral" regulation of speech subject to "heightened judicial scrutiny"[36]—refers to a concept often employed in free speech cases. Contemporary First Amendment doctrine distinguishes regulations of expression in which the burden on expression is related to its content from regulations in which the burden on expression is unrelated to content.[37] The former "content-based" regulations are, the Supreme Court has said repeatedly, "presumptively invalid":[38] in reviewing them a court must use "the most exacting scrutiny" to ensure that it upholds only those regulations that are "narrowly tailored" in order to serve a compelling governmental interest.[39] In contrast, "content-neutral" regulations that impose "an incidental burden" on expression are reviewed for their compatibility with the First Amendment under what the Court has termed an "intermediate level of scrutiny": in this case the regulation is valid if "it furthers an important or substantial governmental interest; if the governmental interest is unrelated to the suppression of free expression; and if the incidental restriction on alleged First Amendment freedoms is no greater than is essential to the furtherance of that interest."[40]

There is no need in this context to work out the arcane, not to say baroque, distinctions the Supreme Court's decisions have drawn in attempting to explain the differences between compelling interests and important ones, or to recognize a regulation that is "narrowly tailored" as opposed to one that is "no greater than is essential." The Court's main point is clear enough: what it calls content-based regulations of speech are, in the vast majority of cases, presumptively invalid; content-neutral regulations require a more fine-tuned balancing between the constitutional right and the government's actions. But in both categories, the Court expressly requires "heightened judicial scrutiny" in order to protect freedom of expression, while limiting any restriction on that freedom to situations posing a clear governmental need. To reject the application of either form of heightened scrutiny, whether "strict" or "intermediate," to a claim that government is infringing First Amendment freedoms is to deny, explicitly or by necessary implication, that the government is interfering with free speech in a constitutionally significant manner.

Against this background, Justice Ginsburg's treatment of the plaintiffs' threshold claim, that the Court should apply some sort of heightened scrutiny, is nothing less than bizarre.[41] Unless she (and the other members of the majority) failed to see the Act as having *any* cognizable impact on *any* constitutionally protected expression at all, a student of the First Amendment cases would expect that the Court's initial response would be to determine which level or form of heightened scrutiny was appropriate, and then apply the proper scrutiny. The opinion takes a different approach, however—one that appears essentially indifferent as to the reasoning the Court customarily uses in deciding First Amendment claims.[42] Despite acknowledging (a bit later on in the opinion) the plaintiffs' reliance on a case, *Turner Broadcasting System, Inc. v. FCC*,[43] which did employ intermediate level scrutiny, Ginsburg restates their argument as a "plea for imposition of uncommonly strict scrutiny" to the Act, implying (incorrectly) that there is something "uncommonly strict" about the use of intermediate scrutiny in reviewing content-neutral laws.[44] (We presume she was not, more simply but even more strangely, mischaracterizing, as "strict scrutiny" in the doctrinal sense, the plaintiffs' argument that *Turner*—thus, intermediate scrutiny—was the appropriate mode of analysis. If we are wrong about this, it would reenforce, in a different way, the air of inattention that hangs over the First Amendment discussion in *Eldred*.)

Having set up, however inaccurately, the threshold inquiry into the proper level of scrutiny, Justice Ginsburg then immediately drops the issue. Instead, she continues with a number of observations amounting to assertions, each apparently meant to undermine the need for any sort of judicial scrutiny of the Act. (We shall enumerate these assertions, and our discussion of them, for clarity.)

(1) *The first assertion purports to invoke the "original" understanding of the two constitutional provisions at issue.*

"The Copyright Clause and First Amendment were adopted close in time. This proximity indicates that, in the Framers' view, copyright's limited monopolies are compatible with free speech principles."[45] It is true, of course, that the copyright clause, which is part of the original Constitution, adopted in 1788, and the First Amendment, ratified by the requisite number of states by 1791, were adopted "close in time." But what is supposed to follow from this observation? The Court sometimes says that the founding generation's practice under the Constitution can shed light on the proper interpretation of the requirements of the founding constitutional text.[46] Justice Ginsburg's suggestion that the original text sheds light on the meaning of a subsequent constitutional provision amending the text is rather different, and not at all convincing.[47] By definition, the copyright clause cannot be seen as an intentional gloss on the First Amendment; neither the First Congress's consideration of the First Amendment nor its passage of the first copyright act led to any recorded discussion of the relationship between copyright monopolies and free speech. The absence of debate over a potential constitutional issue is a flimsy basis for drawing a conclusion about the Founders' views on that issue. Perhaps they saw no relationship; perhaps they simply overlooked the issue. In any event, the most that one could plausibly say is that the First Congress appears to have seen no incongruity between copyright protection of the sort it knew and approved and "free speech principles." Perhaps the argument can be made that the modest copyright scheme set up by the first copyright act should be treated as constitutionally identical to copyright after the 1998 Act. But that is an argument to be made, not assumed, and the opinion for the majority in *Eldred* makes no effort to go beyond assumption.

Nor can mere chronological proximity take the place of actual evidence in making claims about the Founders' views. The infamous Sedition Act of 1798 was enacted "close in time" to the First Amendment's adoption, but it has long been settled that the Sedition Act, rather than being a valuable early interpretation of the First Amendment, was a violation of the amendment. As the Court observed many years ago, "[a]lthough the Sedition Act was never tested in this Court, the attack upon its validity has carried the day in the court of history."[48] In other words, the founding generation, or many members of it, were capable of making a mistake about the implications and application of the First Amendment and, in the case of the Sedition Act, actually did so, even after a full debate on the constitutional issues. In the First Amendment context, it is clear that the "free speech principles" that the Founders constitutionalized cannot be narrowly defined in terms of the Founders' practices.

(2) *The opinion for the majority in* Eldred *goes on to make an additional point ostensibly about the original understanding of copyright and free speech.*

Indeed, copyright's purpose is to promote the creation and publication of free expression. As *Harper & Row* [a case decided in 1985] observed: '[T]he Framers intended copyright itself to be the engine of free expression. By establishing a marketable right to the use of one's expression, copyright supplies the economic incentive to create and disseminate ideas.' "[49] Let us lay aside for the moment an argument about historical accuracy in this passage. Considered merely as part of an argument that a given statute is constitutional under the First Amendment, the insight in it is a non sequitur. Assuming the Court to be right about the original purpose of the copyright clause, this still says nothing about whether *in fact* the Copyright Term Extension Act can fairly be said to promote or provide incentives for free expression. First Amendment law regularly inquires into the actual impact of regulation on expression, not the goals of the constitutional grant of power that Congress invokes in enacting the regulation.

(3) *Neither of the first two supposedly historical points is compelling in itself, nor is either a part of any established pattern of First Amendment analysis.*

Having offered them, however, Justice Ginsburg then turns to a consideration that is relevant in ordinary First Amendment debate—the extent to which the regulation limits its intrusion on expression—but does so entirely without reference to any particular First Amendment doctrine. "[C]opyright law," her opinion for the majority continues, "contains built-in First Amendment accommodations," the first of which is that copyright "distinguishes between ideas and expression and makes only the latter eligible for copyright protection." Citing only the insight itself as authority, the opinion assures the reader that "this 'idea/expression dichotomy strike[s] a definitional balance between the First Amendment and the Copyright Act.' "[50] But First Amendment law long ago rejected the idea that government can justify a restriction on expression simply on the ground that it has no objection to the same *idea* being expressed in a different manner. Under the First Amendment, "the usual rule [is] that governmental bodies may not prescribe the form or content of individual expression" any more than they may prescribe its cognitive content.[51]

In addition, Justice Ginsburg's opinion invokes copyright's concept of fair use, which (as we have seen) privileges the actual reproduction of copyrighted expression in certain situations: "The fair use doctrine affords considerable 'latitude for scholarship and comment,' and even for parody. . . ." The opinion does not acknowledge, however, that the case law to which it refers also reveals a central attribute of the fair use doctrine, which is that it entrusts the decision about what counts as fair use (and thus may be included in expression) not to the individual (which is the norm ordained by the First Amendment), but to the courts.[52] Finally, Ginsburg's opinion claims that the Act "itself supplements these traditional First Amendment safeguards" by exempting certain entities from the strictures of copyright in limited circumstances.[53] Once again, what she sees (and, it appears, the majority also see) as "speech-protective" safeguards make no sense as a justification for infringement of free expression under First Amendment case law. The fact that government allows some speakers, sometimes, to engage in speech which is forbidden to other speakers all of the time in no way alleviates the First Amendment problem. If anything, such discrimination exacerbates the constitutional problem, creating a category of favored speakers and thus, inevitably, a category of disfavored speakers as well.

(4) *The penultimate step in the majority opinion's rejection of the First Amendment claim in* Eldred *addresses the plaintiffs' reliance on* Turner Broadcasting System.[54]

That case involved a federal statute requiring cable operators to transmit broadcast stations through their own cable systems; the majority in *Eldred* stresses the factual dissimilarity between that statute and the 1998 Copyright Term Extension Act. *Turner* "bears little on copyright," Justice Ginsburg writes, because unlike the statute in *Turner*, the 1998 Act "does not oblige anyone to reproduce another's speech against the carrier's will."[55] Nothing is said, meanwhile, of *Turner*'s actual (and clear) relevance to *Eldred* as a recent articulation of the standard of review to be applied if an Act is to be seen as a content-neutral regulation of expression. Instead the majority opinion simply informs its readers that the First Amendment "bears less heavily when speakers assert the right to make other people's speeches."[56] No cases support this proposition in a considered way, however. As was true of the majority's opening summary of the plaintiffs' First Amendment argument, this is simply a tendentious and even misleading description of their claim. In short, Ginsburg offers neither reason nor precedent for the majority's conclusion that the factual differences between the two cases make *Turner* legally irrelevant.

(5) *As we noted earlier, the Supreme Court in* Eldred *gently disavows the lower appellate court's statement that all copyright law is "categorically immune from challenges under the First Amendment."*[57] The final step in the Court's discussion of the First Amendment issue, however, concludes with a pronouncement that is only marginally less sweeping. "[W]hen, as in this case, Congress has not altered the traditional contours of copyright protection, further First Amendment scrutiny is unnecessary."[58] Thus, without ever confronting the fact that the 1998 Act applies directly and incontrovertibly to expression that in any other context would be protected by the First Amendment, and without any effort to show how copyright's "built-in free speech safeguards" actually parallel the protection to expression afforded by heightened judicial scrutiny, Justice Ginsburg's opinion for the majority simply dismisses the relevance of any existing First Amendment doctrine to a claim like that in *Eldred*. Against the claims of copyright, the First Amendment has no independent voice.

ORTHODOXY AND HERESY REVISITED

The orthodox account of free expression's centrality in the United States is radically at odds with the Court's treatment of free expression in *Eldred v. Ashcroft*. *Eldred* is more than a regrettable opinion that happens also to have been poorly (or cavalierly) reasoned: *Eldred* is a deliberate and conscious denial that the First Amendment puts any external limitation on copyright law, or at any rate copyright law which follows "traditional contours."[59] The Court's discussion of the First Amendment is slipshod and unconvincing, but it is slipshod and unconvincing on principle, as it were. As seven, perhaps eight,[60] members of the Supreme Court saw the world, copyright law inverts the ordinary presumptions of First Amendment analysis. Governmental regulation, which everywhere else is what threatens freedom of expression, actually becomes expression's protector when it is "traditional" copyright law, and the justices know this not because a principled argument has been made that it is so, but rather by defining it as so. In the world of *Eldred*, it is the intrusion of the First Amendment into a vast regulatory scheme against which the Court must be on guard, not government's invasion of the domain of free expression.

The opinion in *Eldred* would be remarkable were it not for the fact that the Court has never been willing to acknowledge the obvious conflict between copyright and the First Amendment.[61] Yet fact it is: in this categorical departure from orthodoxy the Court has never offered so much as a single opinion confronting this conflict directly (much less deliberately and thoughtfully) and resolving it in a measured way. Justice Ginsburg's opinion in *Eldred* is thus remarkable (despite all our fulminating) neither for what it says nor for what it does not say. She is simply dissembling as the Court has always done. But if it is no longer possible to be surprised by the Court's disingenuous reliance on invented history and cavalier rhetoric, it is still appropriate to be deeply affronted. The idea-expression dichotomy is no justification for the Court's preferential treatment of copyright; neither is fair use. As we have seen, the one is conceptually flawed; the other is capricious to the point at which it is no more principled than whimsy. The entire point of copyright is to suppress unauthorized expression by many in favor of a privileged few in the pursuit of what is believed to be a justifiable end. The result is clear. The relevant dichotomy is not idea against expression; it is copyright against the First Amendment in a game the First Amendment is slated to lose.

Something is clearly wrong, then. What we have called the heretical rebuttal—the claim that freedom of expression is a glittering but empty boast, unmasked by intellectual property's increasing dominance over expression—is disturbingly accurate. If *Eldred* were itself a sport, the important question would be how to enable (and persuade) the Court to undo its mistake. But *Eldred* is in fact the predictable and express end point of an attitude toward intellectual property and the First Amendment that runs through the cases and much of the secondary literature as well.[62] *Eldred* is not a mistake, as most of the justices and many others see the world, and at the same time it is a dreadful error if there is any fundamental truth to the claim that the United States is dedicated to the freedoms of thought and speech. The task is not to correct a discrete blunder in a single case, or even in a line of cases, but rather to reimagine the legal universe, so that the incompatibility between such regimes as copyright, in which exclusivity is the centerpiece (and of which *Eldred* is the natural culmination), and the promise of the First Amendment can be seen and understood. Only then will the American legal system find appropriate means for making intellectual property accommodate itself to freedom of expression rather than the reverse. But we are anticipating what can only come later: first comes the question of origins. How did the law of the First Amendment and the law of intellectual property come together to beget *Eldred*? Something is wrong. How did it get that way?

THE COPYRIGHT AND PATENT CLAUSE VERSUS THE FIRST AMENDMENT

We are not originalists, but still there is something to be said for inquiring into the question of what the Framers might have thought about these matters.[63] It appears to us most likely that they simply did not anticipate the conflict between intellectual property and the First Amendment that we have just outlined. There was no "intellectual property" in 1791. As we have said, intellectual property is a construct peculiar to our time—and, in the United States, peculiar to a relatively recent moment in that time. What the Framers knew and presumably anticipated in the context of the Constitution were copyright and patents. These were mere foreshadowings of the complex and extended doctrinal fields to follow. Unlike the elaborate property-centered regimes we know and understand today, copyrights and patents appear to have been affirmations of more rudimentary notions of monopoly, grounded in the thought that intellectual productivity might be encouraged more fully (to the ultimate benefit of the public domain) if the profits of that productivity were allowed to accrue "exclusively" to authors and inventors "for limited times."[64] The copyright and patent clause did not specify what exclusivity was to mean; but then it did not specify the actual regimes that would follow either—whether copyright or patent law, or perhaps some sui generis regime envisioned by a Congress acting under the powers conferred upon it by the clause. The clause was added late in the summer of 1787, and, so far as can be ascertained from the records of the convention, made its way into the original draft of the Constitution without debate. It is likely that the Framers did not dwell long on the matter; to the extent that they envisioned anything specific, it was probably that copyright and patent laws would follow, as indeed they did.

Copyright subsisted in books, maps, and charts, and lasted for no more than fourteen years, with the possibility of a renewal term of equal length.[65] Though sometimes explained or defended in terms of authors and their writings, copyright actually protected against little more than outright appropriation of one publisher's work by another.[66] Patents were available for useful inventions, again for a term of fourteen years, but without provision for a renewal term.[67] But relatively few of either "writings" or "inventions" actually appeared until well into the early nineteenth century;[68] and though authorized in common by Article I, Section 8, Clause 8, the two were distinct.[69] The subject matter of each right was conceptually quite separate. Though the clause referred to neither, what linked them most obviously in the Constitution were, as we have said, a common concern for monopolies in general, and a common willingness on the part of the Framers to strike a compromise with that concern in the interest of encouraging a certain form of welcome productivity.[70] That the subjects contemplated in the clause might be linked most dangerously in their underlying relationship to ideas and expression is unlikely to have suggested itself to those who approved the adoption of the clause. Certainly there is no substantial affirmative evidence that it did.[71]

Nor should we be much surprised by that oversight. Neither copyright nor patent law yet resembled the exclusive regimes we must contend with in our time. As several scholars have noted in varying contexts, injunctive relief, the chief enabling implement of propertied exclusivity, did not find widespread use in America until well into the nineteenth century, long after all but the hardiest of the Framers had gone to his eternal reward. Not until 1819 did the first affirmative provision for injunctive relief appear in either the Copyright or Patent Act. Even then injunctions were granted sparingly until later in the century. Damages were awarded in cases of infringement; but infringers were seldom enjoined. In effect, then, the copyright and patent rights were granted under regimes of entitlement that were closer to compulsory licenses than to the regimes devoted to exclusivity that we know today. As we will say presently, we do not think the Framers are likely to have taken particular note of this limitation in their time, and of course they could not in ours. But the limitation is significant in either setting nevertheless. It is frequently said in our time that the nearly simultaneous adoption of the copyright and patent clause and the First Amendment suggests that the Framers saw no potential for conflict between them.[72] That is probably true enough. But it can hardly be argued that they actually weighed the potential for conflict as we are obliged to do. How could they? The copyright and patent regimes they might have known were notably unlike the regimes we face today.

Professors Patterson and Joyce have suggested that the Framers actually saw those regimes as harmonious with the First Amendment; the conflict between them now arises because we have forgotten the Framers' understanding of their relationship.[73] This is an elegant and appealing thesis. It depends heavily, however, on an understanding of the history and jurisprudence of copyright and patent law that we think it unlikely the Framers actually possessed. Certainly, again, they left no record of such an understanding in the context of the copyright and patent clause. As for the First Amendment, meanwhile, the most that can be said generally of the Framers in connection with its adoption appears to have been said best by the great First Amendment scholar, Zechariah Chafee, who suggested that "the framers had no very clear idea what they meant."[74] This is not to say that they had no notion of the Amendment's implications. As we will say at some length later in this book, they were likely to have had some sense that it would proscribe prior censorship of the press, as did the law of England. But they might very well have rejected the English "Catch-22," which was that freedom to publish might be punished thereafter. The Crown and Parliament were in many respects essentially antithetical to the new Federal Government of the United States, not merely in structure but in the underlying sense of what freedom meant as well. Moreover, the amendment was not limited to freedom for the press; speech also was to be free, and was in fact listed before the press. In our judgment, it is not too bold to imagine that the Framers may have intuited a wider latitude for freedom of expression than did the English. We will argue that this latitude was meant to be the consequence of a limitation in the power of Congress to abridge expression, rather than in an affirmative provision for freedom of expression in itself. But if so, the jurisprudence still lay far ahead in 1791. There was indeed no extended First Amendment jurisprudence in the United States at all until 1919, when issues of domestic censorship arising from American participation in the Great War at last reached the Supreme Court in circumstances inviting the resolution of those issues against an as-yet-unarticulated standard under that amendment. Even then, in those early days of the twentieth century, the courts went no further than to propose entry-level definitions aimed at regulations abridging speech in ways more obviously coercive than copyright or patent rights were then understood to be.

THOMAS JEFFERSON ON EXCLUSIVITY AND "EXCLUSIVE RIGHTS"

The copyright and patent clause of the Constitution had been opposed initially by Jefferson, who went so far as to write to Madison in 1788 to suggest that a provision affirmatively restraining monopolies be included among the Bill of Rights then under consideration. "The benefit of even limited monopolies," Jefferson wrote, "is too doubtful to be opposed to that of their general suppression." Though his position on the matter did not carry, he continued to the end of his days to entertain and articulate the reservations that had moved him while the constitutional debates were still underway.[75] As we have suggested in the preceding chapter, his letter to Isaac McPherson, written in 1813, reflected the considered judgment of a mature public intellectual with respect to ideas and their expression. Consider again the three most important thoughts in that missive (edited here):

[1] If nature has made any one thing less susceptible than all others of exclusive property, it is the action of the thinking power called an idea, which an individual may exclusively possess as long as he keeps it to himself; but the moment it is divulged, it forces itself into the possession of every one, and the receiver cannot dispossess himself of it. [2] That ideas should freely spread from one to another over the globe, for the moral and mutual instruction of man, and improvement of his condition, seems to have been peculiarly and benevolently designed by nature, when she made them, like fire, expansible over all space, without lessening their density in any point, and like the air in which we breathe, move, and have our physical being, incapable of confinement or exclusive appropriation. [3] Society may give an exclusive right to the profits arising from them, as an encouragement to men to pursue ideas which may produce utility, but this may or may not be done, according to the will of the society, without claim or complaint from any body.[76]

No court has given full effect to the insights expressed by Jefferson— not even the Court in *Graham v. John Deere Co.*, which (in mid-twentieth century) did acknowledge them deliberately, and gave them place as an articulation of a constitutional standard imposed by Article I, Section 8, Clause 8, but which then ended its decision by acquiescing formally in the limits imposed by yet another amendment to the Patent Act.[77] Indeed, as of this writing, on only one occasion has the Court ever relied on the intellectual property clause as a constraint sufficiently weighty in itself to invalidate an explicit enactment by Congress. On that occasion (in the *Trade-Mark Cases*,[78] in 1879) the Court held that an attempted enactment of comprehensive trademark legislation failed as an exercise of power under this clause because trademarks do not necessarily presuppose any degree of originality or creativity.[79] The decision in *Eldred v. Ashcroft* suggests that no such occasion is additionally in the offing insofar as the traditional doctrinal fields (copyright and patent law) are concerned.

Yet we can see today the deeper import of Jefferson's insight. What he said in his letter to McPherson would have done no violence to the legitimate interests of authors and inventors under the copyright and patent clause. The language of the clause is aimed more obviously at productivity than at exclusivity; the latter is merely a means to achieve the former, and even then it is not self-defining. "Exclusive rights" did not inevitably mean a right to oppose appropriation of works by others; again, as Professor Walterscheid has noted, affirmative provisions for injunctive relief were introduced into American copyright and patent law for the first time in 1819.[80] Jefferson's elaboration on the phrase (an "exclusive right to the profits") is an altogether plausible interpretation of its meaning. His is arguably the closest thing we have to an understanding of what the Framers themselves may actually have thought, for though he was not among their number in Philadelphia, still he was their contemporary, and more than that, he wrote from within the matrix of his experience, which was also theirs.

We have acknowledged that Jefferson was thinking specifically of patents, which, as an inventor himself (and having acted ex officio as patent administrator while serving as secretary of state), he had reason to understand in a practical sense. Were his thoughts about patent law equally applicable to copyright? Despite occasional efforts by copyright protectionists to distinguish the one from the other in the context of this passage, no persuasive distinction can be drawn. Copyright is not more readily susceptible to exclusive possession than are patents. Let us also understand, again, that Jefferson surely did not mean to separate ideas from expression in the way we do now. The idea-expression dichotomy we know was essentially undeveloped in the copyright law of his time; and in any event the supposed distinction between them has never played a role in patent law, whether then or now.

Meanwhile, what he wrote would have done no violence to any adequate theory of freedom of expression either, whether under the First Amendment or the copyright and patent clause. For what he wrote suggested the nature of the things to be taken account of in fashioning and limiting the systems of protection in copyright and patent law from perspectives well beyond the parochial interests of proprietors under those regimes. First, there was the nature of the interest to be encouraged and, to the extent necessary to that end, protected: in Jefferson's view, its evanescence and its significance alike oblige us to acknowledge that it cannot be transmuted into exclusive property rights without threatening the natural, inescapable, and desirable transmigration of ideas and their expression among those who encounter them. Second, and as a corollary to the first, such "exclusive rights" as may (or may not) be appropriate should be limited to "the profits arising" from the protected ideas and their expression. Note that this is not the equivalent of a conventional proposal for a compulsory license, nor would it lead to a so-called "liability regime" of that sort. While profits arising from an appropriation might be made the subject of an entitlement, an appropriation for purposes not leading to the generation of net revenues would not.[81]

METASTASIS AND THE LIMITS OF CONSTRAINT

Would that Jefferson's thinking had prevailed in his own time, with everything that might have meant for intellectual property and the First Amendment today! Instead, a century and more would pass, from 1791 until the early 1920s, in which the First Amendment would go essentially without definition—this too is part of the explanation of how we came to be where we are today. For in that same period, while the First Amendment still slumbered, copyright and patent law grew apace.[82]

To maps, charts, and books, the subject matter of the first copyright act of 1790, Congress added fine arts in the form of paintings, designs, etchings, engravings, and prints in 1802, musical compositions in 1831, dramatic works in 1856, photography in 1865, and sculpture as well as models or designs intended for perfection as works of fine art in 1870. By 1909 the subject matter of copyright was said to include "all the writings of an author," and while this was not entirely true (motion pictures were not included until the Townsend Amendment of 1912, and sound recordings were excluded until the Sound Recording Amendment of 1971), still the fact was that copyright was no longer the relatively modest monopoly it had been a century before.[83]

In the course of these amendments, certain issues affecting the nature of copyright had been addressed and defined, in part of course by

Congress, but no less so, as to the underlying jurisprudence, by the courts. By 1909, one could say the following things about copyright, which were true then and which (with some modifications in terminology and some additions of rights) remain true today: that copyright was conventionally recognized as a right in intangible property;[84] that the right was grounded in the Constitution's intended encouragement of original works of authorship; that the production of these works was meant to enrich the public domain; and that meanwhile, as an inducement to the production of these works, authors could claim certain rights of exclusivity (as against freedom of appropriation by others), for limited periods, in the original works they had created.

There is no real question that by 1909 the principal justification for copyright was—as judges and scholars alike often implied, then and now—a kind of "quid pro quo," in which a limited monopoly was granted to authors in their writings in order to encourage the production of works of authorship that would ultimately enrich the public domain.[85] This was the fundamental theory of the law, a theory which reflected the standard of the Constitution as expressed in the copyright clause. The statute itself was an exercise in positive, rather than natural, law. Copyright was defended chiefly as an instrument for fashioning an intellectual economy.[86] The author's moral rights, when they were recognized at all, were distinctly less important.[87]

To the extent that the Constitution could claim a role in copyright's development, that part was played by the copyright clause, which presupposed the fundamental legitimacy of the regime. The First Amendment was not yet so much as an understudy. Having come first to the stage, so to speak, copyright was free to portray itself without limitation, except as limits might be suggested from within the matrix of copyright itself, augmented by its interaction with the clause. To be sure, one cannot say that copyright was unconstrained; but neither can one claim that such constraints as there may have been were prompted by any widely shared thought of limits or responsibilities beyond the dimensions of copyright itself and the constitutional provisions from which it had evolved.

The growth of patent law, meanwhile, was similarly marked in this same period by rapid expansion, offset by concerns for the consequences

of excess that might follow were the expansion to go altogether unchecked. As we have seen, the law came to be limited in three classic
ways: first, patents could issue only as to inventions that offered true
novelty, a standard that precluded patenting where the inventor's claim
was anticipated in the prior art; second, the invention must be "inventive" (or "nonobvious") as well as novel, a standard that was meant to
avoid patents for what were merely modest advances over the prior art;
and third, the invention had to be useful, which of course precluded recognition for those discoveries that were harmful, but which also meant
that claims as to discoveries that were merely promising could not be
acknowledged either.[88] Taken together, the limitations imposed by the
patent law were undoubtedly more substantial than were those imposed
by copyright. The same conceptual observation may be made in the
case of patents that we have made about copyright: in each instance,
such limits as there were sprang into existence from the center of each
field itself. Neither field held itself out as responsive in this sense to any
concerns but its own. But of the two it was patent law, and not copyright, that was the more effectively constrained.[89]

One may wonder why this should have been so, particularly given
the fact that patent terms also were sharply limited in duration as
against the longer terms of protection recognized by the law of copyright. There is no clear answer to this question. In some sense, the specific differences appear to have been adventitious in nature. Copyright
and patent law grew separately, were derived from discrete antecedent
systems in English and Continental law, and were meant to respond to
disparate concerns for productivity. But we think that is not the entirety
of the story. It seems to us in retrospect that patent law may have offered
the more apparent danger in the early years of the Republic. In truth,
though Americans entertained the notion of copyright in works of authorship, we did not think such works altogether central to our progress
as a nation. These were the things that authors toyed with; they probably did not figure widely in our early reckoning of progress.[90] In contrast, advances in the useful arts were the very stuff of progress, and we
counted ourselves the richer for every invention or discovery the new
century brought. Steam engines, railroads, harvesters and plows, revolv-

ers and repeating rifles, electricity and the telegraph, telephones, motion pictures and the wireless: we were intoxicated by the products of the patent system throughout the nineteenth century, and proud of our collective achievements—so much so that (as we have previously noted) the commissioner of patents was inspired to announce at the St. Louis World's Fair that we had reached nearly the end of such discoveries as were ever apt to be patentable. Like Kansas City, we had gone about as far as we could go. Somewhere in the midst of all this patent hubris, we think, lies the answer to the question we have posed as to why patents were more constrained than were copyrights. Perhaps it was simply the case that, valuing inventions more highly than we did authorship, we also took them more seriously as threats.

But what was it, more precisely, that we feared, whether from copyrights or patents? Not collisions with the values still to be articulated in the course of thousands of opinions in First Amendment cases still to be decided—this was never the case in the nineteenth century for the reasons we have advanced; but rather collisions with the right to self-determination and the economic imperatives central to the self-assessment of a raw young nation. We had begun the century by understanding monopolies as former colonists understood them, as artifacts of privilege, as fetters to be avoided whenever possible, to be accorded primacy in law only sparingly. Seen now in retrospect, it was the great work of copyright and patent law in that century to fashion apparent responses to these concerns, while transmuting the form of the monopolies themselves so utterly and yet so subtly that it is sometimes difficult to realize how limited these constraints actually were.

Today, in contrast, the transformation is apparent. As we have noted, some threat to freedom of expression is encoded in all of the intellectual property regimes, and may be encountered from time to time. But it is copyright that we must take most seriously in our time, for it is copyright, more so than any of the other regimes, that has taken as its central attribute an entitlement on the part of copyright proprietors to the exclusive possession of expression that otherwise would belong to us all. Today the principal challenge to freedom of expression is to be seen in copyright exclusivity.

DOES COPYRIGHT VIOLATE
THE FIRST AMENDMENT?

Readers who are already familiar with the field will know that this question was posed first by Professor Nimmer, in a lecture delivered to the Copyright Society of the United States in March 1970, and then published in a slightly revised version in the *UCLA Law Review* later in that same year.[91] By the time his work appeared, he had established himself as the nation's foremost scholar of copyright, and was achieving a growing reputation as a scholar of the First Amendment as well. One may well ask what it was that prompted him to write?

The First Amendment had emerged during the 1960s as a central force in American life. The Supreme Court's 1964 decision in *New York Times Co. v. Sullivan*, though formally limited in scope to libels involving public officials, spoke in broader terms of the need to ensure that public discussion would be "uninhibited, robust and wide-open."[92] In a dozen key decisions that followed between 1964 and the summer of 1971, the Court succeeded in transforming a once relatively quiet, if arcane, corner of tort law into a new field having profound First Amendment significance; but more than that the Court's decisions managed to bring the First Amendment itself to the attention of thoughtful Americans at large.[93] Among the more intriguing issues debated in the course of that metamorphosis was whether the amendment was "absolute"—whether "no law" truly meant *no law*, as Justice Black insisted[94] (usually with the concurrence of Justice Douglas)[95]—or whether its application in given circumstances was subject to exercises in "balancing" individual interests against public interests, as seven other members of the Warren Court variously supposed instead.[96] In the context of *New York Times* and the cases that followed closely behind it in this period, the answer to that question meant the difference between an absolute privilege to publish a defamatory statement, and a privilege that was "qualified" or balanced in terms of other interests.[97] When the Court decided, in 1967, that the *New York Times* privilege also extended to invasions of privacy in certain settings, Professor Nimmer published an article that defended the qualified privilege in libel settings, but sharply criticized it in the context of invasions of privacy.[98]

Meanwhile, in circumstances that also captured Nimmer's attention, Justice Black had written important opinions in two cases (decided on the same day as *New York Times*, March 9, 1964) involving the copyright and patent clause—opinions in which Black's absolutist views were thought by some observers to have found expression in a setting not immediately related to the First Amendment, and yet one that offered unmistakable parallels to it in constitutional terms.[99] And in this setting, in which the formal question in each case was whether the copyright and patent clause preempted the states in their efforts to enforce misappropriation claims that mirrored to some extent claims cognizable under the federal patent regime, the entire membership of the Court had concurred with Black in holding that preemption was absolute.[100] The Court's holdings in these two companion cases greatly alarmed members of the nascent intellectual property bar, for whom the availability of state doctrines to augment federal protection had seemed a valuable supplement, especially when the more rigorous standards established under the federal regimes could not be met; and to whom, meanwhile, the prospect of a new link between intellectual property and an absolute First Amendment was decidedly unwelcome. We cannot know what Professor Nimmer thought of these cases when they were first decided, in 1964; his treatise on the law of copyright had been published in its first edition in 1963, and did not include an extended treatment of them until some time after they appeared. In subsequent editions, however, he incorporated the apparent teachings of *Sears* and *Compco* (as the two cases were known) in full measure, contemplating, on their authority, that record piracy—which had yet to be addressed in the federal copyright act, and therefore could only be prohibited by the states, presumably on some theory amounting to misappropriation—was now effectively beyond reach.[101] What this meant, among other things, was that Professor Nimmer saw no significant distinction to be drawn between patents and copyrights, insofar as the implications for preemption in Black's opinions were concerned.[102]

Perhaps these simultaneous transformations in the two fields of law that most engaged him prompted Nimmer to ask his question about copyright and the First Amendment. And then again, perhaps it was one or more among a number of cases he discussed in the essay itself that had first drawn his attention. Whatever the answer to this preliminary inquiry may be, the fact is that for the first time in the history of American law this vital question had been squarely posed and then addressed at some length by a scholar whose views were entitled to be taken seriously: *Does copyright abridge the First Amendment guarantees of free speech and press?*

In the years since Nimmer wrote, scores of essays have revisited the question. Yet no one has managed to put the case for recognition of a conflict better than did Nimmer himself in three paragraphs at the outset of his essay:

The first amendment tells us that "Congress shall make no law . . . abridging the freedom of speech, or of the press." Does not the Copyright Act fly directly in the face of that command? Is it not precisely a "law" made by Congress which abridges the "freedom of speech" and "of the press" in that it punishes expressions by speech and press when such expressions consist of the unauthorized use of material protected by copyright? But surely, many will conclude, the first amendment does not apply to copyright infringers. Yet, is such a conclusion justified? The language of the first amendment does not limit its protection to speech which is original with the speaker, but rather states that Congress shall make "no law" abridging freedom of speech; and Mr. Justice Black has said that this reference to "no law" means no law, "without any 'ifs' or 'buts' or 'whereases.'" If one adopts Justice Black's absolutist approach to the First Amendment it is difficult to see how any copyright law can be regarded as constitutional.

It might be contended that copyright laws fall within a built-in exception to first amendment protection, not by the words of the first amendment, but by reason of another passage of the Constitution, namely the copyright clause, expressly authorizing Congress to grant to authors "the exclusive right" to their "writings." However, there are several reasons why refuge for copyright may not be found in this manner. First, if a completely literal reading of the first amendment is to be made, then we must likewise recognize that the first amendment is an amendment, hence superseding anything inconsistent with it which may be found in the main body of the Constitution. This, of course, includes the copyright clause. In any event, even were the original Constitution and the Bill of Rights to be viewed as a single instrument, the copyright clause may not be read as independent of and uncontrolled by the first amendment. Because Congress is granted authority to legislate in a given field, it does not follow that such a grant immunizes Congress from the limitations of the Bill of Rights, including the first amendment. As illuminated in Reed v. Covert (per

Mr. Justice Black, incidentally): "The United States is entirely a creature of the Constitution. Its power and authority have no other source. It can only act in accordance with all the limitations imposed by the Constitution." Any other conclusion would, of course, render the first amendment, as well as the remainder of the Bill of Rights, meaningless. If the constitutional grants of power to the Congress were not subject to the limitations imposed by the Bill of Rights, then such limitations would have no meaning at all to a government whose only powers are derived from such grants.

But if the copyright clause does not render the first amendment inoperative, why does not the contrary conclusion follow? Doesn't the first amendment obliterate the copyright clause and any laws passed pursuant thereto? This returns us to Mr. Justice Black's absolutist approach. It cannot be denied that the copyright laws do in some degree abridge freedom of speech, and if the first amendment were literally construed, copyright would be unconstitutional.[103]

In Nimmer's essay, to be sure, these arguments were in the nature of devil's advocacy, which he then undertook to refute at some length, employing balances that were predecessors to the sort that we have recounted in previous discussion. The idea-expression dichotomy figured prominently in his conclusion that no general conflict between copyright and the First Amendment existed, as did the elaborate apparatus of fair use.[104]

For us, however, Nimmer's arguments nicely anticipate our own views—except for the last sentence we have quoted from the third paragraph, which we think goes too far. Like Nimmer, we understand the subject matter of copyright to amount to just such speech as the First Amendment ordinarily protects. Like Justice Black, we think no provision abridging freedom of speech or press can be defended: "no law" means *no law*—and no balancing, either, for once a threshold decision has been made as to whether an interest in question amounts to expression within the reach of the amendment, we think Congress is entirely without additional power to abridge it. Like Jefferson, however, we think that a "stable society" may nevertheless set aside "profits arising" from an exploitation of an original work. What is forbidden by the First Amendment is exclusivity of the sort that arises, for example, when copyright, acting on behalf of a proprietor, opposes appropriation of an original work by others for the purposes of further expression, or when it conditions such an appropriation upon the payment of rents in excess of profits accruing from such an appropriation. In either case copyright abridges freedom of expression. Against this understanding of "exclusive rights," we think (as we imagine both Jefferson and Black might have thought) that much of the present copyright act is otherwise unobjectionable, or at least unobjectionable from the perspective of the First Amendment.

THE LITERATURE, ALBEIT IN PASSING

As we have said, in the nearly forty years that have followed since Nimmer's essay appeared, numerous works, many of them elegant indeed, have elaborated upon the question he posed in his seminal essay. Many others have contributed indirectly to our collective understanding of the underlying issues. We cannot hope to do justice to this rich literature in the time and space available to us in this book, but we can at least identify some recurring themes among them. Some writers, like Professors Denicola and Goldstein, who published early essays, resolved the question Nimmer propounded essentially as he did, by concluding that the balances between the interests served by copyright and the First Amendment are fundamentally sound, and need no elaborate restructuring.[105] Some, like Professors Patterson and Joyce, and Judge Stanley Birch, to name but a few, have emphasized the importance of fair use as an additional response to the First Amendment, while offering a way to envision an understanding on the part of the Framers that would harmonize the copyright clause with the First Amendment.[106] Others, more numerous, suggest that new balances need to be established in order to offset the encroachments into protected expression that are the consequence of new technologies and increased protectionism; the DMCA figures prominently among the causes for alarm. A growing number, like Professors Aoki, Benkler, Boyle, Lessig, Litman, and Samuelson, emphasize the increasing omnipresence of the new technologies, and the effect upon the culture of their convergence with the intellectual property regimes.[107] As time has passed, the literature has deepened in intensity and scope; Professor Netanel's discursive essays of a few years ago have been elaborated still more recently, and are now destined for elaboration at book length.[108] A number of articles have dealt with issues that may seem at first to be essentially parochial, but that, upon reflection, add significantly to the larger First Amendment literature: among these, for example, Professor Yen's essay on the relationship between the First Amendment and the idea/expression dichotomy in copyright (as well as the questionable business of recognizing copyright in a work's so-called "look and feel") offers a sensitive additional inquiry into the initial issues raised earlier by Nimmer, Goldstein, and Denicola, while suggesting greater deference to freedom of expression;[109] meanwhile, Professors Lemley and Volokh offer a fresh perspective on injunctive relief as a potential violation of otherwise well-established First Amendment standards.[110] Increasingly, the question Nimmer addressed in the context of copyright has been expanded to take in the other intellectual regimes as well. Lemley and Volokh anticipate our own conviction that violations of the First Amendment are not limited to copyright; others have joined in addressing adjacent doctrines.[111]

In the beginning, those who wrote in response to Professor Nimmer's question were chiefly to be found among the intellectual property faculties in American law schools. (For obvious reasons, international scholars have not had much to say about intellectual property and the First Amendment.) But scholars whose primary interest originally lay in fields other than intellectual property have joined in the discussion at large, to decidedly useful effect. Professors Baker, Rubenfeld, and Van Alstyne, for example, each a constitutional scholar of note, have published valuable essays written primarily from the perspective of the First Amendment, rather than copyright or intellectual property.[112] In some cases, the discussion has led to a shift in scholarly emphasis. Professors Boyle and Lessig whose primary interests originally lay in critical studies and constitutional law are now among the most prominent intellectual property scholars in the country; each has written books, as well as numerous essays, aimed directly or indirectly at finding new common ground between intellectual property and freedom of expression.[113] Finally, some writers have published works on the copyright and patent clauses that in some sense augment works aimed at the First Amendment. These include important essays by Professors Heald and Sherry, Professor Pollack, and Judge Kosinski.[114]

EXCLUSIVE RIGHTS" AND THE CONSTITUTION

Fair use has emerged as a central study in the past thirty-five years, though in truth it has been taken seriously for a considerably longer period. Alan Latman, a distinguished New York practitioner, adjunct professor at New York University until his death in 1984, and coauthor of casebooks and treatises in the area of copyright, submitted the first comprehensive study of fair use in 1961;[115] it appeared among some twenty Copyright Office Studies, commissioned by the then register of copyright, Abraham Kaminstein, as part of the Office's preparation of materials for Congress in connection with what became the General Copyright Revision of 1976. An outpouring of works have appeared since then, including important contributions by Professors Patterson, Joyce, Gordon, and Fisher.[116] An especially influential essay written by Judge Leval appeared in the *Harvard Law Review* in 1990; Leval argued that fair use ordinarily should be recognized only in those settings in which the antecedent work was transformed in the derivative work.[117] An equally plausible essay, by Professor Weinreb, argued that Leval's suggestions were more restrictive than Section 107 of the Copyright Act contemplated; in the end, Weinreb concluded, "fair is simply fair."[118] A more recent essay by David Nimmer suggests that fair use is essentially governed by the copyright equivalent of the Golden Rule; in this suggestion he follows in the footsteps of his father.[119]

Meanwhile, questions as to the legitimacy of numerous other policies and practices internal to the various intellectual property regimes have led to a considerable body of literature aimed at reforms that do not necessarily spring from a formal concern for the First Amendment, but that, if implemented, would nevertheless confer a beneficial, if indirect, effect upon interests in free expression. Among many others, Professors Dreyfuss, Jaszi, Lemley and Lichtman, Menell, Merges, O'Rourke, Rai and Eisenberg, Reichman and Uhlir, and Reese, as well as Paul Geller, have offered works of particular value.[120]

A considerable body of literature addressing the public domain has appeared in the past twenty-five years, including an early essay by Professor Lange, with subsequent valuable works by Professors Benkler, Boyle, Chandler and Sunder, Cohen, Jaszi, Litman, Samuelson, and

Zimmerman, among others; still additional works by these and other authors were written in anticipation of the first Duke Law School conference on the public domain, and subsequently published in *Law and Contemporary Problems*.[121] Concerns for the public domain have led to the establishment of a Center for the Study of the Public Domain at the Duke Law School; the law school at Stanford is host to the Creative Commons, a not-for-profit organization offering a less restrictive alternative to copyright protection, whose primary founders were Professors Lessig and Boyle, acting in collaboration with numerous others. Pioneering efforts along similar lines appeared still earlier at Berkeley and American University, in the form of the Samuelson-Glushko clinics, which fund interventions in litigation of signal importance to the field. At Harvard, the Berkman Center has long served to focus scholarly and professional attention on the importance of the new technologies.[122]

Economic policy has also figured in the literature, commandingly so: despite our occasional gibes at economists, we must not fail to acknowledge that law and economics sometimes appear all but synonymous in our time. Judge Posner, with his University of Chicago colleague, William Landes, published a benchmark essay on the economic justification for intellectual property some twenty years ago.[123] Since then, essays by scores of scholars, including most of those whom we have already identified in other, more specific settings, have added importantly to this central area of focus and concern in connection with intellectual property. Professor Wendy Gordon, whose essay on fair use as a response to market failure is a well-recognized classic in the field, also has offered what we think to be one of the best economic justifications for the intellectual property regimes.[124] A recent collection of essays by leading scholars appears in a symposium published by the *Vanderbilt Law Journal*, edited by our colleague Professor Reichman.[125]

Computer and cyberspace law have formed yet another essentially discrete field for study in recent years. Among the most notable contributions to the literature in this area are those written over a twenty-year period by Professor Samuelson, whose efforts have shaped the field to a considerable degree, while earning her a MacArthur fellowship.[126] She has been joined in these efforts by a number of scholars of note, who have produced works of lasting significance; among them Professor Julie Cohen's *"Lochner* in Cyberspace" is essential reading in this setting, and well beyond.[127]

Our brief survey of the literature began with the appearance of Professor Nimmer's essay in 1970.[128] Of course important work of very real relevance appeared still earlier. Among works of lasting significance are essays by Professor (later Judge) Benjamin Kaplan of the Harvard Law School faculty, whose *An Unhurried View of Copyright,* published as a collection of three lectures in 1967, continues to influence thinking in the field today,[129] and a considerable body of law review articles published by the late Professor Ralph Brown, of the Yale Law School faculty.[130] Professor Zechariah Chafee authored a still-earlier article on the nature of copyright that remains a classic in the field.[131]

A ROAD LESS TRAVELED BY

Given the literature we have just acknowledged (all too briefly and, no doubt, with unintended omissions grounded in ignorance or oversight), it is difficult to imagine an unanticipated suggestion for improvement in the interplay between the intellectual property regimes and the First Amendment. It is true that Congress and the courts have proved largely unresponsive. But this is not to say that we should fail to give our continuing attention to the many thoughtful proposals that have been made. The very effort by so many to address these issues lends useful credibility to the sense of urgency that is at the heart of the literature. Continuing efforts should be welcomed by all who believe, as we do, that it may yet prove possible to imagine the circumstances in which the regimes could find a way to coexist with the freedom of every individual to think and speak and publish at will.

Yet much of what has been suggested presupposes that in the end some form of intellectual property is necessary. The result is an inclination to accept compromise as inevitable. We think, to the contrary, that intellectual property as we know it could be abandoned altogether without permanent damage to the economy, and without serious harm to our culture. Professor Fisher's *Promises to Keep* offers an alternative to the present regimes in the field of entertainment; Professor Rubenfeld has suggested a form of profits-centered copyright that Jefferson might have accepted, and that we ourselves can endorse.[132] Were alternatives altogether unimaginable, however, it would not follow that we must accept what we have. The Framers authorized Congress to enact laws with respect to writings and discoveries; they did not command Congress to do so, however, nor did they imagine, much less prescribe, the regimes we now have. Progress was a goal, but it was also obviously an experiment. Nothing obliges us to continue that experiment if our experience teaches us that what we have done to date is a mistake.

Much of what has been written also presupposes that the First Amendment cannot sensibly be understood in absolute terms. The First Amendment may speak in absolute terms, as it does, but we are widely encouraged nevertheless to understand that the Framers did not mean *no law*—they meant *only commendable law* or something of the sort. It is said that Congress must be free to abridge speech and press alike if the reasons for doing so seem important enough. Judges must be counted on in turn to decide, on balance, where the limits of free expression lie. In this view Congressional action in the presence of an acquiescent First Amendment is a given; Congress can only be persuaded or obliged to act (or not act) wisely. We think, however, that Congressional action, whether wise or not, is precisely what the First Amendment forbids when the resulting enactments abridge expression. Of course it is true that not every expressive utterance or act falls within the embrace of the amendment. Whether it does or does not is a question that cannot be avoided—though the answer to the question, properly addressed, is more a function of definition than of balance. Beyond such unavoidable questions, we will argue at length later in this book, the First Amendment leaves Congress no room to act, and the judiciary nothing to balance.

If we approach the issues addressed in the literature to date from the perspectives suggested in the two preceding paragraphs, we think five consequences follow. First, there can be no more thought of inevitable compromise. Copyright, like the other expressive doctrines we have examined, will survive or not, according to a First Amendment analysis that leaves no room for a priori determinism of that sort. Second, the amendment itself will be understood to lie beyond the reach of balances like the ones Professor Nimmer thought inevitable. Third, accepting (as he also thought inevitable) that the expressive interests reflected in the intellectual property regimes lie well within the meaning of expression embraced by the First Amendment, we will also conclude that these interests are fully protected against Congressional efforts to abridge them. It will not matter whether we have thought of them as property or not; nor will doctrinal principles affect the outcome. Congress will be seen to be without power to confer monopolies in expression that otherwise would belong to the universe of discourses. Fourth, we will be free to model the exclusive rights authorized by the copyright and patent clause in ways that will accommodate their legitimate but subordinate role to the paramount interests reflected in the First Amendment. And finally, it is Congress that must lead the way toward any such accommodation, for it is Congress that bears the first obligation to recognize and act within the constraints imposed upon it by the First Amendment. The results, we think, will accord with what we can imagine the Framers might have expected and understood. No less important, our own understanding of these results will bridge the distance that now separates our time from theirs.

LOOKING AHEAD, IN RETROSPECT

We began the four chapters that make up the first part of our book by examining the idea of intellectual property and its merits from within the matrix of doctrines it comprises. We have tried to give full measure to the arguments for these doctrines: incentives to productivity, efficiency in the marketplace, and concern for the individual dignity of consumers count heavily among the justifications most often cited. Though moral rights have played a less prominent role among the justifications in American copyright and patent law, there is no doubt that they have made an appearance. "Sacrificial days devoted to such creative activities deserve rewards commensurate with the services rendered," the Supreme Court has said;[133] similar sentiments can be found in the jurisprudence governing other doctrines as well. Suitable acknowledgment is one aspect of moral entitlement; a related but separate aspect is to be seen in the commandment that forbids "reaping where one has not sown." The power in this commandment derives from our deepest and most personal sense of property; it is at the heart of Locke's argument as to why we justly recognize entitlements to exclusivity in others when their labor has produced a crop. It is no less a cousin to our own more intimate understanding of the moral weight in laws against fraud and theft. That it may run as a deep and often unacknowledged seam through the substrate of laws governing intellectual property should therefore not surprise us. Indeed, we will argue that it is among the most significant and intractable influences in the jurisprudence of that field.

We might also expect, however, that this moral commandment lies close to the heart of our objections in principle to exclusivity in copyright and other doctrines. And so it does, at least to the extent that it reinforces the notion of expressive misappropriation, whether in unfair competition or trademark law, or patent and copyright law, or in one of the newer doctrinal fields such as the right of publicity. When thoughts of misappropriation are grounded in this commandment, the consequences are likely to weigh heavily against freedom of expression. The indictments against propertied exclusivity in expression that we have advanced in this part of our book stem primarily from the law's willingness to grant injunctive relief against "reaping where one has not sown." But we have also seen that exclusivity need not mean exclusivity in possession. It is possible to imagine exclusive rights that are limited, as Jefferson suggested, to the "profits arising" from creative endeavor. From this perspective, we will argue in the second part of our book that "misappropriation" is a misnomer: an act of appropriation need imply nothing more than an obligation on the part of one who has appropriated original expressive work from another to acknowledge the taking, and to share ratably with that creator in the apportionable profits, if any, that may result. Misappropriation and unfair competition in expression can thus be reimagined as appropriation in the service of fair competition.

In this fashion, we believe, it is possible to imagine the conditions for coexistence between the intellectual property doctrines and an absolute First Amendment. It is toward that end that we now turn our attention in the second part of our book.

PART II

Intellectual Productivity and Freedom of Expression

CHAPTER 5

Foreshadowings: *International News Service v. Associated Press*

THE YEAR WAS 1918. For the purposes of our study, no more significant moment had appeared since the founding of the Republic. As a practical matter the early twentieth century was a time of growing appreciation for the values reflected in both intellectual commerce and freedom of expression; it was also a time when the expectations and entitlements each might have of the other remained ill defined and formally immature. Within the year, however, a single decision in the United States Supreme Court, touching upon the subject of unfair competition in the newspaper business, but decided against the backdrop of a world at war, would suggest the conditions of their coexistence in the century ahead. That decision is the subject of this chapter.[1]

The First Amendment had yet to be construed by the Supreme Court as 1918 arrived. Freedom of speech and press were realities of a sort. Americans enjoyed them both with a conscious and often exuberant sense of entitlement. Indeed, these freedoms were deeply embedded in the American experience, as more than one editor, tarred and feathered for his failure to gauge the contrary temper of his readership, and more than one malefactor hounded into prison by the baying of the press, had learned to their dismay.[2] Yet, in law, freedom of speech and press remained abstractions. One could not speak of them in terms either of philosophy or of theory, at least not upon the basis of any authority grounded in judicial precedent. The Court would consider the amendment for the first time within the next year,[3] but the development of philosophy and theory in this field would proceed only gradually.[4] More than one wrong turn would be taken before the nature of the uneasy relationship between freedom of expression and intellectual commerce finally began to appear.

Meanwhile, a century and more had passed since the ratification of the Constitution, and with the passing years had come a transformation in the dimensions of copyright and patent law, from systems meant to be confined by limited grants of Congressional monopolies (authorized in Article I, Section 8, Clause 8), to ones grounded far more generously, not to say aggressively, in the supposed tenets of affirmative property rights.[5] This transformation in the fortunes of copyright and patent rights had not come about, however, as a result of any serious attempt at policy-making. It was rather the product of sustained and successful efforts by copyright and patent lobbies to persuade Congress to enlarge, enhance, and shore up the dimensions of the limited monopolies. Congress itself was not the architect of change, but rather a largely acquiescent instrument in the hands of those proprietors and their lobbyists who sought it. The truest agent of transformation was exigency enlisted in the service of limited competition, and its straightforward aim was to secure an advantage in the marketplace, to be conferred upon copyright proprietors and patentees at the expense of upstart competitors. No legal philosophy worthy of the name drove these changes, though some theoretical debates did figure in the background.[6] Philosophy and theory would come later in the guise of mainly formal arguments to justify what had already been done.[7]

And yet, vast areas of what today we recognize as intellectual property remained essentially uncharted in 1918. Trademark law was among them. No truly significant federal presence in this field would appear until after the close of World War II.[8] Such law as there was lay chiefly in the hands of state courts and legislatures, or within the province of federal courts which, as yet unconstrained by *Erie Railroad Co. v. Tompkins*,[9] were free to fashion rules of common law application essentially as they saw fit in actions founded upon diversity of citizenship.[10] Unfair competition, meanwhile—still an ill-sorted area of rights and obligations, half tort and half property, from which trademarks traced their lineage—remained another, potentially larger, piece of terra incognita, whose dimensions and boundaries lay unfixed and largely unexplored.[11] We have seen that competitors were forbidden to pass off their goods as the goods of another, or the goods of another as their own, this as a result of rules fashioned according to restraints imposed by unfair competition. Competitors were also forbidden to compete simply for the sake of ruining an adversary—at least this was probably the rule.[12] There may have been still more to unfair competition along these lines, though it would be hard to say so with certainty, or with any assurance as to the underlying reason for the constraint, other than the rule of law itself, which was imposed mainly according to the conscience of the court. Sometimes these were rules that might resemble the constraints derived from a property regime. But courts did not ordinarily think it necessary to say so. In fact the rules of unfair competition were probably more in the nature of restraints upon misconduct, imposed for the sake of the general welfare as tort rules are, with liability to be fashioned accordingly, than they were restraints against trespass or conversion, in deference to exclusive possessory rights, as rules of property typically are.[13]

And then it happened that International News Service and The Associated Press went to war, not once but twice over: first literally, as each sent legions of reporters to Europe to gather news of the Great War; and then figuratively, with each other, in consequence of their conflicting efforts in that theater, the result of which was the lawsuit that is the subject of our interest here. We have already introduced the case in an earlier chapter; and we have noted that its place in contemporary legal theory is, in the view of many students of the case, dubious and perhaps even threatening. Yet the case remains a vital part of any serious inquiry into the nature of intellectual property. Its central tenet, not reaping where one has not sown, continues to fascinate and even compel our collective attention. More than one elegant study of the case has thus resulted, with insights into its provenance that take us well beyond the opinions filed there.[14] But our own interest in the case just now is centered entirely within the limits of what the justices who decided it had to say. More precisely still, the limits of what they had to say are the very reason for our own renewed attention to it now. Our discussion, then, begins with the facts as they are revealed in the opinions.

These were two of the great news-gathering agencies of their time. Together they reached about half of the 2,500 newspapers in America. Of the two, AP was the older and the larger, with associated daily newspapers numbering some eight or nine hundred, or a little more than twice the four hundred newspapers served by INS. Each service spent millions of dollars annually in its efforts to report the news. AP's effort was the larger in money's worth, with expenditures amounting to about $3.5 million; INS spent some $2 million on its efforts. By virtue of its longevity in the field AP appears also to have enjoyed an advantage not merely to be measured in numbers, but in the very availability of the news itself. For as the capitals and frontiers of Europe closed in the wake of widening hostilities after August 1914, or so the pleadings in the lawsuit suggested, AP continued to enjoy residual access to events and means of transmission (including cables and telegraph lines) that were no longer available to the more junior INS. In consequence INS was no longer able to serve its newspaper subscribers or their readers as AP still could do.[15] To put the proposition another way, for some fifteen percent of American readers, news of the Great War (into which Americans would be drawn as active combatants) was now beyond the reach of their accustomed source.[16]

But it was the habit in that time for Associated Press to post its news each day on a bulletin board outside its offices in lower Manhattan. News as such enjoyed no copyright, then or now; and for practical reasons AP claimed none in its expression.[17] And so it happened, over time, that agents of International News Service began to copy the AP's posted news and carry it away, sometimes in summary versions but sometimes verbatim, for rewriting or retransmission to INS's subscribers. INS paid nothing for its appropriations, though there is no reason to suppose that AP would have licensed them willingly in any event.[18] To add insult to injury, INS often succeeded in transmitting the news it had appropriated to subscribers in the western United States more quickly than AP could do to its own affiliates, with the result that AP would occasionally find itself "scooped" by its own news. These were the circumstances that brought the resulting lawsuit to the Supreme Court.[19]

In its complaint Associated Press claimed that International News Service's actions amounted to misappropriation of the news, a wrong characterized as an act of unfair competition, against which AP demanded an injunction to prevent further appropriation.[20] Misappropriation was not altogether unknown to the law before this litigation arose, but even so this was not a conventional unfair competition case, given the nature of the subject matter and the circumstances of its appropriation.[21] In at least that sense, the action was novel.[22] Likewise, though injunctions against further wrongdoing were readily granted in cases of unfair competition, few instances could be found in which an injunction had been directed against the further publication of a communication whose provenance was not plainly unlawful in itself and whose content was neither inaccurate nor otherwise the subject of liability.[23] The action was important as well as novel, moreover, for in American law this was the first time that concerns for the obligations and constraints embodied in intellectual commerce had come into open, direct, and acknowledged conflict with concerns for the dissemination of expression of matters obviously vital to the interests of the public at large.[24]

Three notable opinions were filed in the Supreme Court. A fourth might have been, though in fact it was not. It is not our practice in this book to read the law quite this closely in every setting; but in this instance we shall pay some extended attention to each opinion (including the opinion that went unwritten), for each suggests an approach to the underlying conflict between intellectual property and freedom of expression that bears directly upon our own thinking. The case is a paradigm and perhaps something more. The reader who understands the issues in *International News Service v. Associated Press* already understands much of the tension in our larger agenda, and much of the direction we propose to take as well.

Mr. Justice Pitney wrote for the majority. It has not been Justice Pitney's fate to be especially well remembered for the contributions he made during his tenure on the Court, nor indeed to be much remembered for anything at all. But on this occasion the opinion he offered was powerful; it has survived as a seductive, if problematic, way of measuring the conflicting claims in cases of misappropriation in which copyright or patent rights do not take precedence. Though lamented by most (not all) contemporary students of intellectual property, it has unquestionably shaped the law in the decades since it was delivered.[25] It warrants our attention, as much for what Pitney did not say as for what he did.

Three questions were presented, Pitney said: (1) whether there was any property in news; (2) whether such property, if any, as there might be could survive its initial publication; and (3) whether INS's appropriation of the news amounted to "unfair competition in trade."[26]

To the first inquiry, Pitney actually devoted little attention,

since [he said] it seems to us the case must turn upon the question of unfair competition in business. And, in our opinion, this does not depend upon any general right of property analogous to the common-law right of the proprietor of an unpublished work to prevent its publication without his consent; nor is it foreclosed by showing that the benefits of the copyright act have been waived. We are dealing here not with restrictions upon publication but with the very facilities and processes of publication.[27]

In fact, of course, the Court would have had no choice but to address the question of "restrictions upon publication" if the Associated Press had had its way. But perhaps it was accurate to say that the Court was not "dealing with" that issue. Pitney continued:

Obviously, the question of what is unfair competition in business must be determined with particular reference to the character and circumstances of the business. The question here is not so much the rights of either party as against the public but their rights as between themselves. And, although we may and do assume that neither party has any remaining property interest as against the public in uncopyrighted news matter after the moment of its first publication, it by no means follows that there is no remaining property interest in it as between themselves. For, to both of them alike, news matter, however little susceptible of ownership or dominion in the absolute sense, is stock in trade, to be gathered at the cost of enterprise, organization, skill, labor, and money, and to be distributed and sold to those who will pay money for it, as for any other merchandise. Regarding the news, therefore, as but the material out of which both parties are seeking to make profits at the same time and in the same field, we hardly can fail to recognize that for this purpose, and as between them, it must be regarded as *quasi* property, irrespective of the rights of either of them as against the public.[28]

But if the news was not to be held in secret (as of course it could not be if those who gathered it had any thought either of profit or of service), then how was INS to be faulted for appropriating it? After all, the news that AP gathered was posted every morning on its own bulletin board in plain view of everyone who should pass by. Passersby were meant to appropriate it. And if, having appropriated it, the public's right in turn to disseminate it was not in question, then how was INS to be enjoined against doing what everyone else was free to do? The answer was that no one was free to do what INS had done:

The fault in the reasoning lies in applying as a test the right of the complainant against the public, instead of considering the rights of complainant and defendant, competitors in business, as between themselves. The right of the purchaser of a single newspaper to spread knowledge of its contents gratuitously, for any legitimate purpose not unreasonably interfering with complainant's right to make merchandise of it, may be admitted; but to transmit that news for commercial use, in competition with complainant—which is what defendant has done and seeks to justify—is a very different matter. In doing this defendant, by its very act, admits that it is taking material that has been acquired by complainant as the result of organization and the expenditure of labor, skill, and money, and which is salable by complainant for money, and that defendant in appropriating it and selling it as its own is endeavoring to reap where it has not sown, and by disposing of it to newspapers that are competitors of complainant's members is appropriating to itself the harvest of those who have sown. Stripped of all disguises, the process amounts to an unauthorized interference with the normal operation of complainant's legitimate business precisely at the point where the profit is to be reaped, in order to divert a material portion of the profit from those who have earned it to those who have not; with special advantage to defendant in the competition because of the fact that it is not burdened with any part of the expense of gathering the news. The transaction speaks for itself and a court of equity ought not to hesitate long in characterizing it as unfair competition in business.[29]

"To reap where it has not sown": perhaps (as we have already suggested) no metaphor in any case touching upon intellectual commerce resonates as powerfully as does this one—it runs as a leitmotif through virtually all intellectual property doctrines today, serving as a reason for decision even when it is not articulated as such.[30] Clearly Pitney and the majority were not destined to remain alone in responding to the thought. But why should the notion of reaping where one has not sown be so seductive in circumstances such as these? It is a commonplace, of course, that under Locke's conception of property one ought to be entitled to reap the benefit of one's own labors in converting or improving what one finds at hand. Yet this is true, according to Locke's own third proviso, only when what remains available for others "is enough, and as good."[31] And surely what was available to INS (never mind the public) was neither. If, in these circumstances, the result of INS's appropriation was the destruction of AP's investment, then what of it? Was that not exactly what AP was obliged to expect, according to the nature of the interest at stake—indeed, according to the rules of the game?

Here was perhaps the only place in his opinion in which Pitney's conviction turned slippery. Consider this response to the arguments (which were INS's arguments, the reader will understand) just stated:

> It is no answer to say that complainant spends its money for that which is too fugitive or evanescent to be the subject of property. That might, and for the purposes of the discussion we are assuming that it would, furnish an answer in a common law controversy. But in a court of equity, where the question is one of unfair competition, if that which complainant has acquired fairly at substantial cost may be sold fairly at substantial profit, a competitor who is misappropriating it for the purpose of disposing of it to his own profit and to the disadvantage of complainant cannot be heard to say that it is too fugitive or evanescent to be regarded as property. It has all the attributes of property necessary for determining that a misappropriation of it by a competitor is unfair competition because contrary to good conscience.[32]

Property. Quasi property. Property again. The subject of the appropriation in the case changes character as required from passage to passage in Pitney's opinion. Yet it is fair to conclude, taking all in all, that he did not conceptualize the news as property in the fuller (and certainly not the fullest) sense of the term.[33] Locke be damned, then, with his notions of commingled labor and his inconvenient third proviso. What moved Pitney (and the Court) was a felt sense of impropriety in conduct that called for a remedy rather than a theory. The impropriety by INS did not lie in the conversion of property as such, but rather in what economists today would call "free riding."[34] And the remedy was to be found not in forbidding appropriation altogether, but rather forbidding it for so long as might be necessary to allow the Associated Press to recoup the investment it had made from such value as its investment might create:

It is to be observed that the view we adopt does not result in giving to complainant the right to monopolize either the gathering or the distribution of the news, or, without complying with the copyright act, to prevent the reproduction of its news articles, but only postpones participation by complainant's competitor in the processes of distribution and reproduction of news that it has not gathered, and only to the extent necessary to prevent that competitor from reaping the fruits of complainant's efforts and expenditure, to the partial exclusion of complainant, and in violation of the principle that underlies the maxim "sic utere tuo," etc.[35]

* * *

There is some criticism of the injunction that was directed by the District Court upon the going down of the mandate from the Circuit Court of Appeals. In brief, it restrains any taking or gainfully using of the complainant's news, either bodily or in substance from bulletins issued by the complainant or any of its members, or from editions of their newspapers, *"until its commercial value as news to the complainant and all of its members has passed away."* The part complained of is the clause we have italicized; but if this be indefinite, it is no more so than the criticism.[36]

No one would call this a victory for freedom of expression. The news is reserved to one party against appropriation or publication by another; readers are to be inconvenienced and even left in ignorance to the extent necessary; there is no apology for this encroachment upon the freedom of the press nor even any acknowledgment of it—worse, it is said that the remedy is equitable and that the public's interest in the matter is irrelevant or merely negligible. The excuse is competition and profit, reinforced by a vague sense of fairness. This is no victory for expression. It is rather a paradigm of intellectual property at work in the service of commerce, and more so even today than in that time.[37]

Yet there may still be something to follow and even to admire in Pitney's example, something to draw upon in our contemporary thinking about how to reconcile the conflicts that arise between intellectual property and freedom of expression. For if, as he suggested, we do not assign the fullest status of property to works of expression; if we recognize them as the source of nothing more permanent than revenue streams limited in time and nature to whatever may be required to achieve the recoupment of an investment—then, as we shall presently suggest at greater length, with but a single amendment to Pitney's

opinion and a corresponding amendment to the injunction affirmed in
the case, it is possible to imagine a degree of harmony between the
monetary interest and the public interest that does justice to such exclusivity as may be defensible in intellectual commerce while doing
justice simultaneously to the limitations we think imposed by the First
Amendment.

More of this in good time. For the moment, however, let us consider
the second opinion filed in the case, this one (admirably brief, brilliantly
realized, but ultimately disappointing and unsatisfactory) by Justice
Holmes, with Justice McKenna concurring.

In Holmes's view, to begin with, the case was not about property, at
least not in either of the senses that Pitney had suggested:

When an uncopyrighted combination of words is published there is no general right to forbid other people from repeating them—in other words there is no property right in the combination or in the thoughts or facts that the words express. Property, a creation of law, does
not arise from value, although exchangeable—a matter of fact. Many exchangeable values
may be destroyed intentionally without compensation. Property depends upon exclusion by
law from interference, and a person is not excluded from using any combination of words
merely because some one has used it before, even if it took labor and genius to make it. If
a given person is to be prohibited from making the use of words that his neighbors are free
to make some other ground must be found.[38]

In Pitney's view, of course, it was the (mis)appropriation itself that
furnished that ground.[39] And in one conventional reading of his opinion he may even be thought to have inverted his reasoning so as to conclude (in opposition to Holmes) that "if there was value there must be
property," rather than "if there was property there may be value." Indeed, from a contemporary perspective, this would not necessarily
amount to an inversion at all. Judges, legal scholars, and economists
today often conclude something very much to this effect in analogous
settings.[40] The contemporary doctrinal analyses underlying trade secrets
and the right of publicity rest precisely upon such reasoning. It is another matter altogether to decide whether such analysis is defensible—this
is an issue we can lay aside; but there is no question that even if Pitney

did reason to this effect he would not necessarily be thought wrong to-day for having done so.

In fairness, though, this is not exactly what Pitney said. From his perspective it appears rather to have been the case that the concept of property was (as we have implied) something of an inconvenience. What counted was misconduct, albeit misconduct by misappropriation, in which the subject of the misappropriation was variously described as property or quasi property. Yet this misappropriation was not quite the same as the conversion one understands conventionally to touch upon or presuppose an exclusive estate in property.[41] The remedy Pitney approved appears to have been limited in effect to recoupment and perhaps a bit more. Certainly there is no suggestion of anything like a permanent estate in the news to be inferred from his final comments upon "the going down of the mandate" and the terms of the injunction.

But Holmes declined to acknowledge this larger aspect of the case, at least in the absence of legislation establishing the action directly. For students of the law in our time, of course, it may seem odd, a little, to suppose that a court should wait for legislative action before fashioning a rule or a remedy. In 1918 it did not seem odd at all. The question had to do with jurisdiction or power to act, and (Pitney's opinion notwithstanding) its absence was often thought to be constraining. In Holmes's view, no property right could be recognized in the Associated Press for just this reason: no legislature had acted to that effect.[42]

Instead, finding no estate in property at all, and no analogous reason for forbidding an appropriation of the news by INS, he called upon the more conventional understanding of unfair competition in which "passing off" (or "palming off," as he termed it, after the usage in British law) figured.[43] This form of misrepresentation was commonly reckoned to be a wrong against the public who were deceived, though Holmes himself did not say so. It could also be seen as a wrong against the person whose goods were the subject of the misrepresentation and whose entitlement to recognition was thereby misappropriated, and it was in this latter sense that Holmes supposed the Associated Press's complaint lay grounded:

The ordinary case is a representation by device, appearance, or other indirection that the defendant's goods come from the plaintiff. But the only reason why it is actionable to make such a representation is that it tends to give the defendant an advantage in his competition with the plaintiff and that it is thought undesirable that an advantage should be gained in that way. Apart from that the defendant may use such unpatented devices and uncopyrighted combinations of words as he likes. The ordinary case, I say, is palming off the defendant's product as the plaintiff's but the same evil may follow from the opposite falsehood—from saying whether in words or by implication that the plaintiff's product is the defendant's, and that, it seems to me, is what has happened here.

Fresh news is got only by enterprise and expense. To produce such news as it is produced by the defendant represents by implication that it has been acquired by the defendant's enterprise and at its expense. When it comes from one of the great news collecting agencies like the Associated Press, the source generally is indicated, plainly importing that credit; and that such a representation is implied may be inferred with some confidence from the unwillingness of the defendant to give the credit and tell the truth. If the plaintiff produces the news at the same time that the defendant does, the defendant's presentation impliedly denies to the plaintiff the credit of collecting the facts and assumes that credit to the defendant. If the plaintiff is later in Western cities it naturally will be supposed to have obtained its information from the defendant. The falsehood is a little more subtle, the injury a little more indirect, than in the ordinary cases of unfair trade, but I think that the principle that condemns the one condemns the other. It is a question of how strong an infusion of fraud is necessary to turn a flavor into a poison. The dose seems to me strong enough here to need a remedy from the law. But as, in my view, the only ground of complaint that can be recognized without legislation is the implied misstatement, it can be corrected by stating the truth; and a suitable acknowledgment of the source is all that the plaintiff can require. I think that within the limits recognized by the decision of the Court the defendant should be enjoined from publishing news obtained from the Associated Press for [blank] hours after publication by the plaintiff unless it gives express credit to the Associated Press; the number of hours and the form of acknowledgment to be settled by the District Court.[44]

The distance between Holmes and Pitney cannot be determined merely from the tenor of their opinions. Formal questions having to do with property divided them, at least to a degree. But a close reading of the two texts suggests that in fact they were troubled by much the same thing as they considered the Associated Press's complaint: the appropriation or misrepresentation by INS gave it an advantage in the marketplace that it ought not have. What divided them was not truly the cause but rather the remedy. And here is an opportunity to examine one of the great (and still inadequately explored) divides in intellectual property law.

Let us begin by acknowledging and then setting to one side the formal question of damages, which figured not at all in either opinion. There is scarcely any doubt that damages to the interest to be protected could (and probably would) be calculated today. To the extent that AP had lost revenues or good will from INS's actions, a contemporary court would include the loss as a measure of the remedy. Property or no, the loss, if cognizable, would also be compensable. But as the case came to the Court from the entry of a preliminary injunction, no question of damages had yet been raised.

But money itself assuredly was in issue. The Associated Press had spent millions gathering the news. International News Service, in the position of a free rider, was gaining the benefit of that investment without commensurate risk to its own capital. And here is the cardinal difference between the remedies approved by the two opinions we have examined. Pitney's injunction was meant to allow the Associated Press to recoup its investment. Holmes, though acknowledging the investment and conceding that "fresh news is got only by enterprise and expense," would allow AP nothing more than an attribution as the source of the news, and an acknowledgment by INS as to the circumstances of its taking. We are bound to ask: Why the difference between them? Whose is the better position? And where in the matrix of these conflicting opinions does freedom of expression figure, if at all?

The difference between them is in imagination and detachment: Pitney's the former; Holmes's the latter. Pitney's opinion is powerful, and has endured, thanks to his willingness to stretch the boundaries of unfair competition, to see in misappropriation a misconduct objectionable in terms (again, free riding) not yet commonly spoken of or even acknowledged at the time he wrote, and to approve a remedy (all but) suited to the need. Holmes—well, let us say that Holmes was Holmes. Elliptical, incisive, above all disinterested, his opinion begins where it begins (in the common law of Massachusetts, probably, a very long time earlier) and ends where it ends, without apology or, one supposes, much inclination to dwell further on the matter.

One could have wished for both imagination and engagement, for then the outcome in the case might easily have been worthy of approbation. As it is, neither opinion commands our assent. Pitney assumes too much on behalf of the Associated Press in approving the lower courts' injunction. Holmes assumes too little. Pitney's opinion upholds a prior restraint against the press. Holmes's opinion is willing to approve such a restraint as well, though in practical terms it is clear that he does not suppose that the injunction he has in mind will remain in force for very long. After all, what is it to INS to acknowledge AP if the effect is to free the news for appropriation and there is no additional consequence? It is the taking followed by the subsequent exploitation that is in issue, not the attribution or acknowledgment. One can conclude, then, from the perspective of the public and its interest in having access to the news, that Holmes's opinion drives quickly toward the better outcome. But if this is so, still it is the result of nothing deliberate or caring in Holmes's approach. This is Darwinian law, a mere matter of stimulus and response, with no investment in the consequences, no thought for the public, no interest in the plaintiff's case beyond an application of the law itself, nor even any serious concern for the defendant's default. The opinion is sanguine, lofty, cool. One is reminded of Daumier's *avocat*, haughty in his dismissal of his widowed client's tearful remonstrances: "You have lost your case, it is true, *chère madame*, but then you have had the pleasure of hearing me plead it."

Are these criticisms too harsh? We think not. For as we have suggested, the opinions must be measured not only in terms of each other but in their relationship to freedom of expression, the one issue that gave the matter its novelty on the facts, and yet the one issue not truly addressed by the Court. And here, we will argue, neither of the opinions we have considered withstands the test of time. Commerce cannot justify even as tempered an encroachment upon the dissemination of the news as Pitney and the Court supposed. Advantages and disadvantages in competition must be addressed and considered more deliberately in terms of free expression than either Pitney or Holmes proved willing to do if we are to be satisfied with the result either of them envisioned.

For an essay that expresses something of what is missing in these two, we must turn instead to the third opinion in the case, in which Justice Brandeis dissented alone. For Brandeis, as for Holmes, there was no property to be recognized in news. Like Holmes, Brandeis reacted in part to the fact that no legislative action could be pointed to that would colorably support such a claim. But unlike Holmes, or for that matter Pitney, Brandeis clearly read the implications in the case in terms of the news and its distribution, and beyond that as an exercise in weighing commerce against expression:

News is a report of recent occurrences. The business of the news agency is to gather systematically knowledge of such occurrences of interest and to distribute reports thereof. The Associated Press contended that knowledge so acquired is property, because it costs money and labor to produce and because it has value for which those who have it not are ready to pay; that it remains property and is entitled to protection as long as it has commercial value as news; and that to protect it effectively, the defendant must be enjoined from making, or causing to be made, any gainful use of it while it retains such value. An essential element of individual property is the legal right to exclude others from enjoying it. If the property is private, the right of exclusion may be absolute; if the property is affected with a public interest, the right of exclusion is qualified. But the fact that a product of the mind has cost its producer money and labor, and has a value for which others are willing to pay, is not sufficient to ensure to it this legal attribute of property. The general rule of law is, that the noblest of human productions—knowledge, truths ascertained, conceptions, and ideas—become, after voluntary communication to others, free as the air to common use. Upon these incorporeal productions the attribute of property is continued after such communication only in certain classes of cases where public policy has seemed to demand it.

* * *

The rule for which the plaintiff contends would effect an important extension of property rights and a corresponding curtailment of the free use of knowledge and of ideas; and the facts of this case admonish us of the danger involved in recognizing such a property right in news, without imposing upon news-gatherers corresponding obligations.[45]

Brandeis acknowledged "the obvious injustice involved in such appropriation" as INS had engaged in, but observed that a legislature, weighing the matter, would surely consider circumstances beyond the competence of any court to judge.[46] How might a legislature, thus informed, respond? In at least three ways, he thought. Legislators might refuse to extend a remedy altogether, concluding that to do so "[would] open the door to other evils, greater than that sought to be remedied."[47] Alternatively, legislators might extend the fullest remedies, including provisions for both damages and injunctive relief, but only upon condition that the beneficiary of the remedy would also act in effect as trustee for the public, correspondingly burdened by an obligation to supply the news "at reasonable rates and without discrimination, to all papers which applied therefor. If legislators reached that conclusion, they would probably go further, and prescribe the conditions under which and the extent to which the protection should be afforded; and they might also provide the administrative machinery necessary for insuring to the public, the press, and the news agencies, full enjoyment of the rights so conferred."[48]

The first of these two suggestions recalled action in fact taken before 1911 in the United States Senate which rejected a proposal to protect news during the first few hours after it had been gathered; the simple rejection of that proposal might have suggested something of at least one legislative body's reaction to the issues, though it would not bind Pitney and the majority in a subsequent action in equity. The second suggestion acknowledged or anticipated the apparatus of the several communications acts adopted by Congress, particularly the Communications Act of 1934, which, until amendments enacted in 1996, imposed upon broadcast news gatherers fiduciary obligations roughly parallel to the ones Brandeis may have had in mind.

But it is the third suggestion that commands our fullest attention:

[L]egislators dealing with the subject might conclude, that the right to news values should be protected to the extent of permitting recovery of damages for any unauthorized use, but that protection by injunction should be denied, just as courts of equity ordinarily refuse (perhaps in the interest of free speech) to restrain actionable libels, and for other reasons decline to protect by injunction mere political rights; and as Congress has prohibited courts from enjoining the illegal assessment or collection of federal taxes. If a legislature concluded to recognize property in published news to the extent of permitting recovery at law, it might, with a view to making the remedy more certain and adequate, provide a fixed measure of damages, as in the case of copyright infringement.[49]

And here, the reader will see, is the germ of an intriguing idea indeed.

Suppose that a fourth opinion had been filed in the case, one incorporating this suggestion in Brandeis's third hypothetical legislative enactment. (Let us lay aside the demand for legislation in order to deal with the merit in the proposal as the Court might have done, while remaining mindful of the fact that ultimately this is, as Holmes and Brandeis both supposed, work better suited to the temper of a legislative body than to the judgment of a court.) Suppose that Pitney's opinion were modified to reflect at least a portion of the thinking advanced here by Brandeis: thus, no injunction against appropriation as such, but rather a provision for the distribution of net revenues (revenues, mind you; not damages) resulting from a competitive appropriation by INS. Imagine the injunction thus modified running until the Associated Press's investment had been recouped, with some additional measure of profit; or perhaps until the "value" in the result of its investment had been exhausted; but in any event for no longer than a period amounting to a "limited time." And then to this scheme add Holmes's insistence on an acknowledgment of the provenance of the work. Surely this would have done no disservice to the position favored by Pitney and the majority. Consider the consequences of an opinion thus configured from the perspective of any similar action involving commerce in products of the intellect: a continuing incentive to invest in desirable intellectual productivity, but an incentive augmented by a mechanism for sharing in the revenues resulting from any competitive appropriation and exploitation, rather than by an injunction against the appropriation itself, or by a presupposition grounded in the notion of a priori damage resulting from appropriation.

One can imagine objections to the scheme. The transaction costs associated with an injunction modified along these lines might prove troublesome, though in point of fact they should not prove more so than the task of tracking injunctions administered routinely by courts in other complex matters. Nor is there anything inherently unworkable in such a system, or destructive to the core value of the interests now acknowledged by the intellectual property regimes. To the extent that copyright recognizes compulsory licenses one can find partial analogs in the law for such a system, then and now. Brandeis, who clearly saw as much himself, presumably had in mind Section 1(e) of the Act of 1909, which subjected musical compositions to a compulsory license once the work was recorded with the permission of its author or proprietor.[50] Additional licenses have been added to the law under the 1976 General Copyright Revision and subsequent enactments.[51]

Of course we must understand clearly that damages could not serve as an appropriate measure of recovery in quite the way Brandeis imagined. An award of damages unconnected to a subsequent competitive exploitation would do little more than fix the value of an interest that would thus still remain a matter of property, and unacceptably so from the perspective of any adequate First Amendment theory. But net revenues arising from a competitive exploitation, and measured by the contribution of the appropriation in the production of such revenues, might pose no similar issue.[52] We need not expand on the distinction between damages and net revenues just now. The point here is not to suggest that copyright compulsory license systems are or are not in compliance with the First Amendment, but rather that analogs to a compulsory license are not in any sense foreign to the law of intellectual property. Nor is the compulsory license the only analogy to be drawn. Infringement theory in copyright practice, then and now, routinely results in recoveries measured in part by net profits. Meanwhile, against protests grounded in the moral rights or sensibilities of proprietors, Holmes's remedy against misrepresentation might be added to the modified injunction, so that attribution and acknowledgment could be required as well.

Is it plausible to imagine that provisions of this sort also would withstand a suitable First Amendment scrutiny? Brandeis, whose influential opinions would take on a virtually iconic status in later First Amendment settings, appeared to think so in this case, and (as we have modified his thinking) it seems to us with good reason. Again consider the consequences: no restriction against appropriation or further dissemination, and thus no impediment to the free exercise of expression; no concern for motives; indeed, no interest in the circumstances of the appropriation at all, really—the taking itself is no longer to be seen as wrong or wrongful. Viewed in this way, the appropriation is a simple matter of entitlement. To be sure, Brandeis did not invoke the First Amendment quite this directly in his opinion, but that is hardly surprising. He may not have recognized then what we now know: that doctrines internal to the field of intellectual property cannot be counted on to limit the impulse to maintain and prolong exclusivity at all costs. In any event, there was as yet no doctrine he could have invoked. As we have said, the First Amendment in 1918 was still an empty vessel waiting to be filled.

Brandeis's opinion in *International News Service v. Associated Press*, like the opinions written by Pitney and by Holmes, cannot fail to leave us with a keener sense of the task that lay ahead. The case suggested, as no other case before it had, how protean interests arising in the course of commerce in products of the intellect, if left unchecked, can conflict with still more important interests touching upon freedom of speech and press. The challenge then was to imagine the terms upon which these interests could coexist, taking into account the paramount place the First Amendment presumably must hold in any reconciliation that might follow. The challenge ultimately would be to imagine a First Amendment capable of constraining intellectual property without destroying it.

CHAPTER 6

Intellectual Productivity and Freedom of Expression: The Conditions of Their Coexistence

AMONG THE THINGS that we have seen thus far is that intellectual property is unlike other forms of property. To begin with, the thing at the center of intellectual property is in fact no thing at all in the ordinary sense of being tangible, but is rather an idea, a concept, a feeling, a perception, an understanding, an expectation, an insight, an identity, a discovery, a practice, an invention, a writing, an expression, or something of the sort. In every instance it is an entity lacking in corporeal substance, and thus dependent for its existence upon nothing more substantial than an intellectual accord—an accord that arguably confers the only sense in which the term "intellectual" property can be understood as having meaning. In Jefferson's charming simile, as candles may be lit one from another infinitely with nothing in result but added light, so the ideas from which intellectual property is spun can be shared endlessly without loss of their identity. In ordinary experience, as Jefferson plainly thought and as Brandeis (echoing Jefferson) himself observed in *INS*, an idea, "once loosed upon the earth, is free as the air to common use."[1] Nor is this the entirety of the matter, or even the more important insight; for as Jefferson additionally observed in his reflections on the essential nature of an idea, "the moment it is divulged, it forces itself into the possession of every one, and the receiver cannot dispossess himself of it."[2] Thus the stuff of intellectual property, once it has been made public, not only need not be exclusively possessed—in fact it cannot be. And this is so whether we will have it so or not.

What we can see as well, then, is that the stuff of intellectual property, once public, is in every instance neither more nor less than the very experience of thought and speech and culture alike—endlessly, reciprocally, unavoidably, and inescapably at large among us, separately and at once. And here is the source of our dilemma when law attempts to intervene with traditional notions of property in the face of traditional notions of freedom of expression. Discoveries, expression, and the like cannot be exclusively possessed by some persons acting under color of law, and remain free at the same time for all to experience and in turn express again. Our old friend and colleague, George Gillmor, makes this point from time to time: one cannot knit a vest with sleeves.

But what is to be done? Like Brandeis, we can identify three obvious responses. One is to say, as generally speaking we have said for more than two centuries, that the interests identified and protected in intellectual property shall continue to be protected for some at the expense of others. We may continue to insist on this, never mind the clarity with which we now see that these interests are in conflict with interests identified and supposedly protected on behalf of others under the First Amendment. This is essentially the position now taken by most federal courts in most settings, including the Supreme Court in *Eldred*.[3] A second is to say, as we have not done but still might one day do, that the First Amendment touches upon interests more important than the interests embraced by intellectual property, and so must be held paramount whenever and wherever the two appear to be in conflict. A third is to say, as we are beginning to say sometimes, but only rarely and then irresolutely, that the interests associated with intellectual property and the First Amendment are both of such vital significance to our culture that we must seek to find the terms upon which they can coexist. Each response deserves to be acknowledged, for each has something to recommend it.

We have previously acknowledged the importance of intellectual property to the contemporary economy and culture. The prevailing justifications are to be found in the incentives to productivity and efficient management that intellectual property is said to furnish, and in the acknowledgment of the moral entitlements of authors and inventors that its doctrines may afford.[4] These justifications are not beyond criticism and dissent.[5] The idea of intellectual property does not accord with the idea of more traditional forms of property, and not merely in the particular respect that we have just summarized above. Unlike the more traditional forms of property, which respond to ancient impulses and are themselves in some sense archetypal, intellectual property is (as Jefferson supposed it must be) merely a recent cultural invention, and one that is by no means universal in its appeal or acceptance beyond the provinces of the West.[6] From an economic perspective the idea of intellectual property appears to be less about property than about the sort of privilege and subvention that we recognize as problematic or indefensible when we encounter it in farm subsidies and other kinds of pork-barrel provender. It is, at best, still fundamentally antithetical to the main tenets of a free market or an unregulated economy.[7] In cultural terms, again properly understood, it is increasingly not about the protection of property, but rather about the moral principle recognized in *INS*, namely that one should not reap where one has not sown[8]—which is to suggest that intellectual property is more about concerns for unfair competition or moral rights than about exclusivity *ex necessitate*.[9]

Yet conceding all of these objections as we do, we must nevertheless allow as well that in fact the principal intellectual property industries in America have gradually become embedded in both the economy and the culture. Our economy has come to presuppose the centrality of monopolies or privileges, as well as other principles of fair competition, including the privileges and principles reflected among the intellectual property doctrines. Our contemporary culture is virtually defined by the products of the entertainment and communications industries.[10] The legitimacy and utility of intellectual property regimes are now widely accepted in global commerce too, this often (seemingly) to our own particular national advantage.[11] Intellectual property exports (principally by the entertainment and communications industries) contribute importantly to the American balance of trade.[12] Among nations with wealth to invest (the United States is one), adequate enforcement of intellectual property interests is sometimes thought to be a prerequisite to the sort of foreign direct investment that other emerging nations require.[13] There is no escaping the conclusion: intellectual property is central to the way we think now about America and its productivity, at home and abroad.

But of course it does not follow that even interests as important as these must continue to be enforced at the expense of disparate interests of still greater value. Can First Amendment interests be said to be of that latter character? The difficulty in responding to this question from within the framework of contemporary economic parameters is that intellectual property and First Amendment interests are at least disparate in character, and may well be inescapably antithetical. This may at first appear to be a paradox, since we have just observed that the stuff from which intellectual property interests are spun is also the stuff of First Amendment interests. But there is no paradox here. An entity may assume more than one identity; a question as to comparative economic value often arises when one identity is incompatible with another, so that comparative value must be measured in terms of opportunity costs. It is easy enough to say what it would cost to withhold protection from intellectual property; it would cost whatever affirmative economic value we now assign to the interests whose recognition would thus be foregone. But opportunity is all but impossible to assess: we know of no measure upon which an affirmative economic value of First Amendment interests can be established.

Yet few who have lived within its shelter would deny that the First Amendment has real value, intangible and inexpressible though it may be. In a celebrated concurring opinion filed in *Whitney v. California*,[14] an early and important decision in the development of First Amendment theory and practice,[15] Justice Brandeis captured something of the importance of the First Amendment to the success of the American Republic. Recalling (without attribution) the words of the Roman historian Tacitus (himself writing of the reign of the popular and benevolent Emperor Trajan) Brandeis observed that the First Amendment secured to Americans the same degree of contentment and fulfillment Roman citizens had known in their moment of deliverance: "that freedom to think as you will and to speak as you think."[16] It has been the burden of courts in the twentieth century to give meaning to these words, and in doing so to assign value to the First Amendment. No one can doubt that (aside from the questions raised by intellectual property) they have taken this challenge seriously. As we have suggested, no part of the Constitution has grown more dramatically or played a greater role in defining the American experience than has the First Amendment. In the decades since 1918—the year in which *INS* was decided as well as the year immediately preceding the Supreme Court's first important decision touching upon the meaning of the First Amendment—the value of the Amendment has grown by measures that are beyond our ability to account for here. Perhaps no complete assessment of the First Amendment's place in American life is possible. Certainly it seems likely that for most Americans the cultural value of the First Amendment exceeds by severalfold the value assigned to the interests protected by intellectual property. From a cultural perspective it is entirely plausible to suggest that First Amendment interests are beyond price.

Which interest weighs most in the balance? Were we free (or forced) to choose, would we favor intellectual property, with its economic and cultural benefits, or would we prefer instead the less tangible but surely more essential benefits conferred by freedom of expression under the First Amendment? In the balance struck by the courts to date, the preference has gone to intellectual property. This is in part a reflection of the relative immaturity of First Amendment jurisprudence at critical early moments in the development of intellectual property, an immaturity that we have noted in earlier chapters. We in turn appear until lately to have become accustomed, collectively, to the status quo. (As our friend and colleague Walter Dellinger reminds us from time to time, there is no gainsaying the normative force of the actual.) It is also true that the courts' preference for intellectual property has been augmented and enabled by a combination of blindness and disingenuousness: a blindness (seemingly willful) to the reality of the conflict between the interests at stake; a disingenuousness in disguising that blindness, typified by such nonsense as the Supreme Court's insistence that the Framers intended copyright to serve as "the engine of free expression."[17]

The fact is, but for the long dormancy of the First Amendment, the need to reconcile the conflict in values between intellectual property and freedom of expression might have pressed itself upon us a century or more ago—might indeed have altered the outcome in *INS*. Had that happened it seems unlikely that intellectual property would have gained the clear ascendancy that it has enjoyed in our time. What is far more likely, given the way in which the First Amendment has grown in other quarters, is that at the very least we would long since have sought to find the terms upon which intellectual productivity and the First Amendment can coexist, each in the fullest measure of harmony consistent with its separate prospects, but with the firm understanding that such conflict as might still remain would inevitably require an acknowledgment of the primacy of the First Amendment.[18]

What might those terms be? In summary we suggest these: continuing incentives to invest in the productivity of expressive works we have come to associate with intellectual property; freedom meanwhile for others to appropriate those works in the service of both competition and self-expression; mechanisms for sharing in the revenues resulting from competitive appropriation; acceptable transaction costs; a clear recognition of limited moral rights, with room as well for limited management of competition and expression in the service of the public good; and not least among them, a carefully limited but primary role under the Constitution for legislatures rather than judges, with transparency in the process, and clarity in result. In the next several pages we shall elaborate upon each of these in turn.

CONTINUING INCENTIVES

We accept for the sake of argument that continuing incentives to invest are essential if we are not to forego such advantages, economic and cultural alike, as the intellectual property system has afforded us. In truth we may suppose that the world would not falter in its progress if the present incentives (or as we think them to be, subsidies) for encouraging intellectual productivity were abandoned in favor of more nearly laissez-faire alternatives.[19] But we have posited a commitment to coexistence for the sake of our inquiry here, and we shall presume that continuing incentives are, as if by definition and prescription alike, sine qua non. In the history of intellectual property in America, certainly, encouragements to invest in the production of writings, discoveries, trade and personal identities, and the like, have been given primacy of place among the justifications for the continuing existence of the system.[20] Concern for incentives played a prominent role in the decision in *INS*, which we have presented as a metaphor for intellectual property at large; and while we think that the moral imperatives reflected in the injunction in that case may in fact have played the greater role in Pitney's opinion, still the importance of incentives cannot be discounted, whether as rhetoric or as one perception of reality.[21]

But there is no necessary relationship between incentives and exclusivity. Rational investors, in whose interest presumably we should seek an accommodation, will not care where their money comes from so long as they can count reasonably on recouping their investment with profits equivalent to the profits that would have resulted from exclusivity. It is the stability of their investment that is of primary concern, that and of course the potential for gain. The mechanisms for ensuring them are of lesser consequence. Or so at least it ought to be. In fact markets and investors alike may prefer exclusivity for a number of reasons. Markets and investors do not always respond favorably to change. There is always the normative force of the actual to be taken into account, which in this setting would presumably argue for the superiority of the status quo; and there are other reasons for resistance as well. Markets and investors depend on information, which in turn requires an understanding of the way things work; change can threaten know-how. Investors prefer control, which they sometimes mistake for efficiency, and exclusivity is undoubtedly an instrument of control. And markets function best, it is said, when regulated least.[22]

These are not irrational grounds for preferring exclusivity, but neither are they sufficient to elevate it from preference to imperative. They are arguments mainly for the sake of the comfort and convenience of those who favor business as usual. A change in the way we regard intellectual property interests would require new insights, new habits of thought, and in some instances new business models, but these are transient concerns that would abate with time. Given an assurance that investment can be recouped with profit, exclusivity is simply not an essential function of intellectual productivity. Competitive appropriation of the sort that figured in *INS* is by no means inconsistent with such continuing incentives. We have seen in our earlier discussion, for example, that compulsory licenses in copyright do not materially affect the continued vitality of the music business, which has long since learned to accommodate them. It may even be said that the music business has benefited from the practices in the marketplace that such licenses have encouraged. Nothing essential would be lost should exclusivity be abandoned elsewhere. To be sure, we do not propose the continuation of liability regimes of the sort represented by the compulsory license, which as we and others have suggested would not in the end suit the needs of an adequate system of free expression. But even a change to the revenue-sharing model we have previously endorsed—or to the quite different model proposed by Professor Fisher—would not work havoc in the marketplace. Even if continuing incentives to invest are assumed to be a necessary condition for continued intellectual productivity, exclusivity itself can be sacrificed without important loss.[23]

FREEDOM TO APPROPRIATE

From the perspective of the First Amendment, meanwhile, freedom to appropriate works of the intellect is the essential condition for the coexistence that we envision. In the evolution of the First Amendment to date, multiple theories addressing and defining freedom of expression have been advanced by scholars and courts alike.[24] These we have touched upon in an earlier chapter; we will elaborate upon them as need be in subsequent portions of our book. It is enough for the moment to note that at the center of them all is a common concern for the question of freedom from suppression, a concern aimed at realizing the well-being that follows when citizens are free not only to "to think as they will" but also to "speak as they think."[25] Our contention here is that the exclusivity commonly recognized and protected among the principal intellectual property doctrines is antithetical to the realization of that freedom.

The reasons for this we have also summarized in earlier chapters, but it will be useful to recall them briefly here, with particular emphasis upon copyright, the field in which the discord seems perhaps most obvious, comprehensive, and intractable.[26] Since Professor Nimmer first acknowledged the possibility of an adversarial relationship between copyright and the First Amendment more than thirty years ago, others have wrestled with the issue at length.[27] Among a number of leading copyright scholars a rough consensus has emerged to the effect that a potential conflict does exist.[28] The conflict they have recognized is essentially as we have described it here: it inheres in a fundamental inconsistency between the aims of exclusivity and freedom of expression. There is dissent from this proposition, to be sure. Some equally respected scholars say that copyright contains within its own doctrines adequate safeguards to insure that the essential aims of the First Amendment cannot be abridged.[29] This has also been the position of most practitioners, as well as most (though not all) judges who have had occasion to consider the issue. Professor Nimmer himself concluded that copyright's well-known dichotomy between idea and expression (pursuant to which copyright protection vests in expression while leaving the idea within that expression untouched) usually is sufficient to ensure that a fair balance will be achieved between the interests it protects and the interests protected by the First Amendment. Where that balance is insufficient, Nimmer added, copyright's fair use doctrine means that even some portions of the author's protected expression may be appropriated as of right, particularly in the service of a new creative work.[30] In rare cases the First Amendment may be called upon to protect rights in expression that copyright may threaten.[31] Others who have written since Nimmer, however, have noted that the balance struck in his approach means that copyright concedes essentially nothing; such sacrifice as there may be is largely on the side of the First Amendment. This is at least arguably an opportunistic balance, or one that mistakenly sees compromise where there is only illusion.[32] For when questions of infringement or entitlement are settled in favor of a copyright proprietor, the fact remains that only the proprietor is free to speak as he thinks. Others may think as they please, and they may even echo the proprietor's ideas, but they may not speak them in the language in which he first framed them. In some cases, perhaps, that may not matter, but in many others it will, and in the latter group the commonality of the idea is plainly insufficient. Under the First Amendment, copyright should not stand in the way of our ability to speak as we please, and this is so whether or not what we have to say takes the form of expression first uttered by others.

The embrace of copyright is broad and deep, and its impact upon expressive endeavors heavy. Under the 1976 General Revision its subject matter includes literary, musical, and dramatic works; pantomimes and choreography; pictorial, graphic, and sculptural works; motion pictures and other audiovisual works; sound recordings; and architectural works.[33] Yet these are the very elements of expression that one would expect to see most readily protected by the First Amendment. Similarly, copyright touches upon creative activities that are most obviously expressive. By the very nature of their work, writers, musicians, filmmakers, photographers, actors, dancers, artists, and architects are all particularly subject to the effects of copyright and its doctrines. Copyright claims to offer incentives to creative productivity, but in its commitment to exclusivity copyright also offers barriers to creativity, and often enough these more than offset such incentives as there are. The copyright industries (motion pictures, television, music, recording, publishing) are notoriously closed to outsiders and newcomers. The harsh reality is that for most creative artists these industries offer neither prospects nor incentives. There are multiple and complex reasons for this reality, but among them is the inescapable fact that no one can create freely without building upon the creativity that has gone before. Yet copyright stands in the way of creative appropriation.[34]

We have emphasized copyright and its concern for kindred forms of creativity in this passage, but the reader will kindly bear in mind that what has been reemphasized here is no less true of expression at large; it has its analogs in the other intellectual property fields as well. In patent law, for example, the reach of protection has lately been extended to business methods, so that a fundamental aspect of personal expression, the manner of earning a living, is now a subject of patentable entitlement and exclusivity.[35] The result is that we live increasingly as medieval vassals lived, able to work only at the pleasure of the sovereign and its privileged lords, who in our own time are exemplified in this setting by the whim of the patent office and the Federal Circuit. In trademark law we are told that phrases and symbols common to the language may not be used in common business settings if the effect of that usage will be to "dilute" the distinctiveness of those phrases or symbols in the hands of a few whose use preceded ours—whose fundamental claim to entitlement, in other words, lies in nothing more than the raw fact of priority.[36] In the field of publicity rights, a law of recent vintage established mainly for the benefit of celebrities and public figures, we are warned against any usage of their names, likenesses, or identities, this despite the fact that in every instance these have meaning only as a consequence of public participation in their development.

From the perspective of the First Amendment we think that intellectual property's insistence upon exclusive possession by proprietors is no longer tolerable in expressive settings. Defenders of the status quo will claim either that the problems we have identified here as well as earlier in this book are exaggerated or nonexistent, or that the solutions to them should come from within the fields in which they appear.[37] But nothing could be clearer in our time than that the doctrinal fields cannot be counted on for adequate self-discipline. When freedom of expression is thought to be in conflict with the property rights that intellectual property doctrines presume to recognize and protect, the latter will always prevail unless constrained. Increasingly it appears that effective constraint must come from the First Amendment, for by now it is evident that it will not come from any other source.[38]

In the considerable literature that has appeared in the past thirty years numerous (and probably innumerable) suggestions have been advanced for achieving harmony between intellectual property and the First Amendment. Given the First Amendment doctrines that we have inherited from the work of courts in the century just ended, it is inevitable that these suggestions have assumed similar complexity. At the heart of the matter, however, is the recurring friction between disparate interests in intellectual productivity and expression. On the one hand, as Pitney thought in *INS*, intellectual productivity of the sort we value in America presupposes a continuing ability to recoup the investment made in securing that productivity, with at least enough gain accruing to the investor to make the effort and the risk worthwhile. On the other, as Brandeis was to imply in *INS* and later say in *Whitney*, the First Amendment presupposes a common ability to think as we please and speak as we think.[39] Viewed in this way, it is remarkable how slight an accommodation need be made to supply the needed parity between them and so correct the imbalance that now prevails. For nothing more is required in the end than that intellectual productivity be assured of continuing incentives to produce, while freedom of expression is secured by the ability to appropriate freely that which is produced.

Let us suppose, then, that the accommodations we have suggested thus far are to be brought into reality. We must touch next upon the remaining conditions for coexistence outlined earlier: a plan for revenue sharing in the wake of competitive appropriations; provisions for moral rights and the public interest; and a preference for transparent legislative action.

REVENUE SHARING

We have concluded (in company with others[40]) that the right of appropriation must extend not merely to private appropriation for personal use, but also to competitive or commercial uses. This will of course have a profound impact on the intellectual property industries. Critics and opponents of our proposal will suggest that the economic effects of a change like this are bound to be decidedly adverse if not disastrous, and the cultural effects clearly unwelcome. We ourselves have no doubt that some alarm will follow in the near term. In time, however, the reality will surely be otherwise. There is no question that allowing appropriations for competitive or commercial purposes would bring about major changes in the marketplace. In copyright, derivative works (such as sequels and remakes in the motion picture industry and publishing industries) will no longer belong exclusively to the originators of the works in question. But then, in terms of possessory interests, the copyrighted work, once published, will never belong exclusively to the creator. That is the purpose of the transformation we have in mind. Patentees would no longer enjoy the exclusive right to make, sell, and use the subject matter of the patent, at least to the extent that subject matter touched upon speech or press interests. Not all patentable subject matter does: chemical processes, for example, presumably do not; nor would pharmaceuticals; probably, most of the subject matter of utility patents would escape the reach of the First Amendment. But we have previously suggested some of the subject matter that we think would be affected (many aspects of business method patents), and others no doubt would be as well, design patents most obvious among them. Trademark proprietors presumably could claim continuing rights against confusion in the marketplace on grounds now familiar in the law—there is almost certainly no serious First Amendment argument to be made in favor of fraud, deceit, confusion, or the like; but the de facto possessory interests that now figure in (and disfigure) much of trademark law would have to go. Similarly, unfair competition could continue to observe the distinctions advanced by Holmes in *INS*: passing off would continue to be forbidden, as he proposed in that case. But injunctive relief against misappropriation of the sort recognized by Pitney would pass from existence.[41] We will not pursue these consequences at length just now; a subsequent chapter in this book is devoted to them, and we will leave additional discussion to that place. For the moment we mean merely to acknowledge fully, without hesitation or hedging, that the regime we envision here would transform our experience of intellectual property, as it would transform our understanding of rights in expression.

We presume it follows that much value would be lost were no offsetting provision possible. But we have begun our discussion of the conditions for coexistence by hyphothesizing that the original investor's incentive to engage in intellectual productivity will have to be maintained if we are not to lose the benefits of that productivity. The models for such an accommodation are many. Brandeis proposed three in *INS*. While he contemplated legislation (which, as we shall say now, and then expand on presently, we think the better course), courts have it within their power to respond adequately.[42] In *INS*, the Court might have ordered periodic accounting and payments by the defendant based upon revenues resulting from its use of the Associated Press's work, less expenses generated by *INS* in the course of that use. This would have posed no conceptual or practical difficulties not already familiar to courts of the time in other settings, nor would it have been unfamiliar in then-contemporary infringement practice, where such calculations were also well established. Infringers (then and now) are customarily allowed the benefit of a comparison of their own original work with the amount of the work they have appropriated. For example, in the case of a motion picture starring Julia Roberts, with a finding of copyright infringement in the underlying screenplay, the producers' liability for profits resulting from the infringement would be offset against the value added by Roberts' presence in the picture.[43] In *INS*, of course, the defendant's publications apparently offered nothing but the Associated Press's work; INS would have been entitled to offset its own investment in distributing the work, but there would have been no occasion to discount its obligation further as in the case involving Roberts.

A cautionary note must be sounded once again, however, along lines we have expressed before. The point is vital and must be emphasized, even at the risk of taxing the reader's patience.

As we have noted, contemporary literature has tended to focus on proposals conceptually attributable to Guido Calabresi and Douglas Melamed, whose coauthored essay on "liability regimes" some thirty years ago contemplated a legislative approach to compensation akin to the compulsory licenses in copyright and patent law.[44] Our colleague Jerome Reichman, for example, has offered an attractive and sophisticated interpretation of Calabresi's liability regime intended to encourage follow-on innovation in utilitarian settings.[45] A recent book-length proposal by William Fisher suggests a more radical alternative regulatory scheme that would eliminate exclusive possessory interests in favor of compensation to creators from federal funds.[46] Other suggestions could be added to this abbreviated list. Subject to the reservation expressed in the next paragraph, we need not prefer one to another. What is acceptable, we would say, can never be more restrictive than this: a provision for apportioning revenues resulting from competitive appropriation, one that is calculated to preserve incentives to create the original work without impairing the absolute freedom of others to bend that work to the service of their own further expression.

It is important to understand that, whatever proposal may be settled on for sharing revenues, it cannot amount to a "liability regime" in the original sense of the term.[47] As Calabresi and Melamed envisioned it, the concept of liability reflected an understanding in which the presumed relationship between the parties was one of disparity, akin to the relationship between victim and wrongdoer.[48] That may have been appropriate in the settings they had in mind when they wrote; it may still be appropriate in essentially utilitarian settings. But it will not do in the context of our discussion, in which expression of the sort embraced by the First Amendment is central. Between an original creator of such expression and those who come to the creation later, there is room for neither a dominant nor a subordinate role; they are simply equals in the entitlement experience of expression. The creation is privileged but so is the encounter, for the one leads inevitably to the other, exactly as Jefferson understood. They are paired in nature; and thus we must prize them both in law. As between them there is neither right nor wrong. There is only equality augmented by equity, and from the latter a sense of fairness in the apportionment of such net revenues, if any, as subsequent exploitations of the work may generate.

TRANSACTION COSTS

We have presumed in this connection that the transaction costs associated with whatever provision is adopted should be proportional to the undertaking. Here a brief additional elaboration is in order. We do not imagine that the costs of the transaction can or should be measured solely in terms of efficiency. Efficiency is but one concern when issues beyond the realm of economics arise, and this is such a case. First Amendment interests must not be cabined in such a way as to make them turn on the sort of calculations suited to transactions in pork bellies, retail trade, or arbitrage. To the contrary, as we have suggested previously in this chapter, First Amendment interests can only be valued sensibly in terms that do not depend on our ability to quantify them. This means that the question of transaction costs in this context must be assessed against judgments that are modified accordingly. Judgments of this sort cannot be prescribed; they can only be derived from experience. Nothing more can be expected or required.

MORAL RIGHTS AND THE PUBLIC INTEREST

Judgment of an even more complex sort will be needed to deal with the very different issues raised by moral rights. Creators of expressive works, accustomed by the habits of our culture to a wide experience of exclusivity and control over works that will no longer belong exclusively to them, are likely to smart under the burden of their loss. If so, this is an unavoidable consequence, for appropriation by others is central to the undertaking we propose. We must understand that some resistance is likely to be inevitable, for the act of creation often evokes a sense in the creator of an identity with the work that cannot be compensated in money or money's worth. The issue here is not necessarily compensation, but rather sensibilities and feelings: appropriation is often experienced as a threat to the creator's amour propre. Though these are concerns whose intensity can be expected to abate somewhat in time as cultural norms conform to a new reality, still the passage of time alone is unlikely to displace the effect upon feelings entirely. While it cannot be said that the concept of intellectual property in itself springs from some chthonic impulse, a creator's identification with his or her work almost certainly does.[49] This does not mean that a creator may forbid appropriation, which is itself now to be seen as the norm. But the creator's sense of loss must be taken seriously and addressed, for it would be a callous thing to treat it with indifference or contempt.

As we have noted in an earlier chapter, the classic *droit moral* originated in the French cultural understanding and experience of creative productivity, and is perhaps still associated first with the law of France.[50] The *droit moral* conventionally includes four discrete rights, initially personal to the author of a work, but descendible and protectable in the hands of a deceased author's heirs: the right to decide when and whether to disseminate the work; the right to be identified as the creator of the work; the right to withdraw from association with the work; and perhaps most significant among the four, the right to prevent others from subjecting the work to distortions, truncations, mutilations, or the like.[51] In France, moreover, the State also may claim what is in essence a separate right of national patrimony with respect to work of significant cultural worth.[52]

In the American experience of intellectual property little room has been made for moral rights. As we have seen, copyright and patent rights have historically been justified in terms of a classic quid pro quo thought to be implicit in the Constitution. In exchange for rights in writings and discoveries for limited terms, the author or inventor is obliged ultimately to dedicate the work to the public domain.[53] This is essentially an economic bargain, rather than a reflection of moral sentiment or entitlements. Trademark rights, likewise, are justified by the role they play in the marketplace. The Copyright Act includes a limited array of provisions affecting works of visual arts and digital recordings which are fairly to be understood as having originated in concerns for moral rights.[54] The Lanham (Trademark) Act contains provisions that deal with false advertising and misrepresentations as to the provenance of works.[55] Since the United States's adherence to the Berne Convention in 1989, an obligation to respect the author's moral right against mutilation supposedly binds us under the terms of Article 6 *bis*, though in fact we still have relatively little in the form of legislation or practice to match the recognition of moral entitlements for creators elsewhere in the world.[56]

In our discussion here we do not mean to endorse the *droit moral* as such, much less in its entirety. To speak of moral rights is to draw upon a useful analogy, but one must not go too far. As we have said, the right affecting abridgement, for example, would be entirely antithetical to the terms of our proposal. Even under current law, such a right, if taken seriously, would preclude much of what Americans have long supposed to be their own entitlement with respect to works in the public domain. Aesthetic issues of importance to the public, like a creator's concerns for affronts to his or her sensibilities, are of course equally beside the point. The very essence of our proposal lies in the understanding that each of us must be free to think as he pleases about matters of this sort, and free as well to express himself accordingly. In law this must leave no room for debating the merits of that thought or the expression that follows.

But we take it that the more intimate personal rights pose little or no corresponding threat. The right to be identified as the creator of an original work (a right that copyright itself does not directly afford at present) need not interfere with the ability of another to make subsequent use of that work. An obligation to acknowledge the announced wish of a creator to disassociate himself from the work also would pose no necessary threat. In either instance a subsequent user could appropriately be required to exhibit a decent respect for the provenance of a work when provenance is clear or readily discoverable. Excessive requirements to either effect could impose a burden on appropriation and subsequent use that the First Amendment should not tolerate, but that problem would not inevitably arise.[57]

Meanwhile, there is no suggestion here that a creator who elects not to share the work with the world may be forced to do so. The First Amendment as we envision it would not sanction trespass or invasions of privacy. The unpublished poems of an Emily Dickinson could not be wrested away should she wish to keep them secreted in her bedroom. Once published, however, they would belong to the ages. It is a nice question whether they would be subject to appropriation should they be released to the world as a result of trespass or subterfuge. We might have supposed not in an earlier, simpler time before the digital technologies and the appearance of the Internet. Now we think the better judgment would run to the contrary. An intruder could be forbidden the pleasure of his theft for so long as the theft itself remained undisclosed, but others into whose hands the work might later fall should not suffer as a result, and this would be so though they might well know or have reason to know that the work had been made public against its creator's express wishes. It is probably not merely futile and unwise, but contrary to our understanding of the principle that forbids Congress to abridge freedom of speech or press, to attempt to impose sanctions against those who have come to knowledge of the work through no original, precipitating act of their own.

Likewise, in the view we take, legislation and other efforts aimed at digital rights management for closely held works would not inevitably contravene the First Amendment.[58] Contracts imposing conditions upon the further dissemination or disclosure of an unpublished work could be given effect if fairly bargained for and suitably limited. Equitable principles governing fiduciary obligations would continue to have effect as between the parties. And so on. Thus, an author could disclose an unpublished work to the members of her writing group or to an agent or prospective publisher or producer in confidence, assured that the work could not be appropriated by them, or by others immediately complicit with them. In such circumstances, for so long as a work remained a matter of confidence in fact, no First Amendment right would be implicated. Once public, however, neither law nor contract nor principle of equity could forbid the further dissemination of the work by others who played no initial part in the violation of the confidence. The right to appropriate that we propose finds its authority in the First Amendment, and springs from the impropriety of any attempt to abridge the ability of a citizen to reflect upon or publicly share the contents of his or her mind.

What we are suggesting in this passage is a regime loosely akin to the law of trade secrets we discussed in an earlier chapter, but modified according to the First Amendment principles at stake here. Recall that under conventional analysis a trade secret may be protected against unauthorized use by persons who have privileged access to it only for so long as the secret otherwise remains a secret.[59] When the secret is publicly disclosed, whether through inadvertence or through the sort of inductive analysis and discovery called "reverse engineering," the secret becomes available for all to use.[60] A question often arises as to whether the proprietor was merely indifferent or even negligent in allowing a secret to become public, or whether the secret was stolen or obtained through improper means, such as trespass or breach of confidence.[61] Indifference and neglect resulting in public disclosure work a forfeiture of the trade secret rights, but against those who have acquired the secret through improper means injunctions may forbid the use of the purloined work.[62] Under current law, an innocent third party is obliged to take note of what is probable with respect to the disclosure: that is, whether the secret appears to have come to light as a result of something reasonably beyond the proprietor's control. If so, even the third party must stay its hand in making use of the secret. In the regime we propose with respect to expression and the First Amendment, however, the last principle would be reversed. A third party member of the public, having taken no affirmative step to steal or betray a confidence, would be free to act upon knowledge otherwise gained, even knowing (or suspecting) its provenance. The reason again is that the First Amendment generally should leave no room for the law to impose constraints upon public knowledge, however it may have come into view.

We will return to these issues and others like them in a concluding chapter addressed more squarely to the practical consequences of the First Amendment regime we propose. For the moment it will suffice to have sketched in the image we envision. Finer lines will inevitably need drawing, and time and space extending well beyond the confines of this book will be necessary. What we are proposing is a plenary reconsideration of the principles and tenets of intellectual property in light of a First Amendment interpretation that is itself unlike the regime we have fashioned to date. Reform of this magnitude cannot be entirely sketched in advance. It must be wrought, again, from judgment and experience.

LEGISLATIVE INITIATIVE

These notes bring us finally to the central role that legislative action must play in achieving this reform. Legislatures seem best suited to the task of fashioning such a system and are probably favored by the Constitution. State legislatures have had little to contribute to the development of copyright and patent law since the ratification of the Constitution, but they have played a substantial role in the development of trademark doctrines and principles of unfair competition, and can go on doing so. Nothing in what we have in mind supposes otherwise. Meanwhile, the copyright and patent clause affirmatively provides for Congressional power to act in the interest of "science and the useful arts."[63] The commerce clause,[64] once interpreted narrowly by the Supreme Court, with resulting limits to its utility in intellectual property settings, has long since been freed from most such restrictions by the Court's more expansive view of the clause's meaning and compass.[65] Against this constitutional background Congress has had two centuries of experience in fashioning the copyright and patent systems, and more than half a century with trademarks. These regimes, flawed as they are in certain fundamental respects, have otherwise worked reasonably well in practice. They have led to the economic benefits we have summarized here and in an earlier chapter, and have contributed importantly to the development of the culture. Were it not for the unresolved conflict with the First Amendment that is the subject of our concern in this book, one would be hard put to advance persuasive reasons for shifting the responsibility for fashioning the intellectual property regimes to a coordinate branch of government, even if the Constitution were amenable to such a move. Congress may have failed to see the First Amendment issues in the earliest years of the Republic; but courts must bear the responsibility for perpetuating that early oversight and for much of the continuing error, for it is courts that have claimed the principal role in interpreting the Constitution since *Marbury v. Madison*.[66] The Court's decision in *Eldred* was only its most recent opportunity to address the issue and its most recent failure to do so.[67]

The moment has arrived when Congress can no longer avoid its responsibility. Of course our arguments here are addressed to the Court as well, for we do not dispute the ultimate role it has assumed in interpreting the Constitution, nor do we doubt the supporting role it must play if the ideas we advocate are to bear fruit. But it is Congress whom the First Amendment addresses, and Congress whose obligation it is to impose no abridgement upon freedom of speech or of the press.[68] The rest of the government is bound to abide by this commandment, but Congress must provide the ways and the means through legislation that accepts the reality that courts are unwilling to face. It may seem odd in our time to address Congress concerning a matter of constitutional interpretation, and certainly it is unconventional to do so. But the reality is that the Constitution has always contemplated an independent, and we would say primary, role for Congress in understanding the meaning of its provisions. Courts have assumed the role of arbiter as to such matters, and no doubt it is too late in the history of the Republic to expect a change as to that. But Congress nevertheless plays the part of provisioner, and it is in the latter role that the proposals we are advancing here must take shape. What we envision and propose is a political response to the constitutional issues we have raised, rather than a judicial one. This is wholly appropriate, and almost certainly consistent with what the Framers would have thought suitable had they thought about this matter at all. (We have said they did not; we make no claim of originalism here.) The time has come for these issues to be resolved through legislative recognition in the course of legislative processes and enactments, rather than through intervention by the courts or by the Court. Case-by-case adjudication has failed and seems likely to go on failing in the absence of Congressional initiative: reform must now come bill by bill.

In our judgment this is not only an appropriate course, but the preferable one as well. The judicial process, constrained as it is by issues raised in actual cases and controversies, cannot be expected to take the lead in comprehensive constitutional or institutional reform. We have grown accustomed to supposing otherwise, perhaps, as a result of judicial initiatives taken in the latter half of the twentieth century—including initiatives with respect to the First Amendment. But our collective experience has shown us that four results follow when courts set out to make law: first, that the decision-making process is unacceptably ad hoc and opaque; second, that the consequences of the process cannot be adequately calculated or measured in advance; third, that no practical recourse is available when the consequences are improvident or adverse; and fourth, that errors in judgment, insight, understanding, or opinion are consequently perpetuated long past the time when, in the hands of a more responsive body, they might have been recognized and acted upon.[69] So it has been, we would say, in the case of the conflict between intellectual property and the First Amendment.

In its present state of being, the First Amendment the Court has fashioned in the last century offers little of consequence and nothing of value in establishing the terms of coexistence for intellectual productivity and freedom of expression. The Court's First Amendment is better understood as an obstacle to attaining such an end. As we shall presently explain at greater length, a theory of constitutional interpretation propounded by Holmes and accepted (albeit with some misgivings) by most of the justices who have followed him, has led by fits and starts to this state of affairs. The theory—or more properly the heuristic, for what Holmes advocated was an approach to experimental interpretation rather than a theory in itself—proposes that the Constitution should be interpreted generally through the application of a series of attenuated balances, each exquisitely contrived to enable the Court, acting in the role of deferential arbiter, to review Congressional acts as to their sufficiency within an otherwise evolving framework of the Constitution.[70] There is little room for constitutional absolutes in this approach, nor is there meant to be: Congress proposes; the Court, rather than the Constitution, disposes. Of course many provisions of the Constitution cannot be read in absolute terms; they can only be read as Holmes proposed.[71] In the case of the First Amendment, however, the practical effect of Holmes's approach to interpretation has been to undermine a provision best understood as an absolute constraint upon Congressional power to act, producing instead an instrument allowing judicial review of the propriety of that power when exercised. In the First Amendment setting, as in others, the Court plays out its role with considerable deference to Congressional will; in cases of doubt, Congressional legislation is usually upheld. But what this means in the case of intellectual property is that judicial deference inures to the benefit of proprietors and the measure of exclusive rights they prefer, for as we have said the idea of intellectual property has long held sway in Congress over whatever inconsistencies with the First Amendment might otherwise be sensed or seen. This is a cycle that perpetuates the conflict and ensures that it is unlikely to be broken unless Congress itself takes the lead in doing so.

In this chapter, we have identified the terms upon which creative productivity and freedom of expression can coexist. In discussing these conditions we have presented them as if the essential presupposition—a sacrifice of exclusivity in favor of an absolute right of appropriation—is itself a matter to be newly weighed in the balance. This is consistent with the Court's interpretation of the First Amendment to date. In fact, however, we propose an interpretation of the First Amendment that leaves no room for drawing such a balance. In the approach we take the right to appropriate is not to be seen as a matter for election, but rather as an inevitable consequence of a better understanding of the amendment than Holmes and the Court have given us. In the end the result can be equivalent to the compromise we have spelled out here. Intellectual productivity can continue to have its incentives, while expressive appropriation will be unburdened by the idea of property. But this equivalence will be the result of a new legislative response to a new constitutional reality, one in which intellectual property will be refashioned in the image of an absolute First Amendment.

PART III

The First Amendment in America: Some Chapters in a History of Debate

CHAPTER 7

The Origins of the First Amendment
and the Question of Original Meaning

ON SEPTEMBER 14, 1787, the Friday before the Philadelphia convention adjourned forever, two of its members, Charles Cotesworth Pinckney and Elbridge Gerry, moved to add a provision to what is now Article I, Section 9 of the Constitution. The provision would have required "that the liberty of the Press should be inviolably observed." Although Pinckney was later to claim that the issue was "fully debated" by the Framers, James Madison's notes record only a single comment, by Roger Sherman—"It is not necessary—The power of Congress does not extend to the Press"—and the laconic observation that the motion "passed in the negative."[1] Thus the Constitution which the Framers proposed contained no language generally addressing individual freedom of expression, although they did include a provision guaranteeing to Congress's members the traditional parliamentary privileges of the House of Commons, one of which is that "for any Speech or Debate in either House, they shall not be questioned in any other Place."

The omission did not pass unnoticed. Opponents of ratification complained that the failure to include a declaration of individual rights was a fatal defect, and muttered darkly about the baleful significance of the Framers' indifference, or hostility, to liberty of speech and press. In response, the advocates of ratification insisted repeatedly that by enumerating what the federal government may do, the Constitution necessarily implies what the government may not do. The Constitution's delegations of power would provide the mechanism by which the Constitution would safeguard liberty, and in particular the liberty of the press. Alexander Hamilton, for example, wrote in *Federalist* 84 that "The truth is, after all the declamation we have heard, that the Constitution is itself in every rational sense, and to every useful purpose, A BILL OF RIGHTS." There can be no need to protect, say, liberty of the press under a Constitution that delegates to government no power over the press in the first instance.

"For why declare that things shall not be done which there is no power to do?" Individual liberty would be secure under the proposed Constitution by virtue of the fact that in it the people would grant no power to the instrumentalities of government to interfere with the press.[2]

Among the leading proponents of the Constitution, James Wilson was the most insistent on this point—that the fundamental principle that Congress's powers are enumerated by the Constitution is in itself a sufficient protection for liberty—but some of Wilson's allies, while making the argument, were uneasy about how far to push its logic. This was in part a product of the fact that the proposed Constitution included provisions, chiefly in Section 9 of Article I, which forbade the exercise by Congress of powers not on their face delegated to Congress, a fact which appeared to show that the Framers themselves had not been willing to rely solely on the principle of enumeration. Along with his contemptuous dismissal in *Federalist* 84 of the arguments of the "intemperate partizans of a bill of rights," in number 78 Hamilton actually invoked the existence of Section 9's restrictions as a reason why it was necessary to ensure the "complete independence of the courts of justice." An independent judiciary, he asserted, "is peculiarly essential in a limited Constitution," by which (Hamilton explained) "I understand one which contains certain specified exceptions to the legislative authority."[3] Judicial independence is vital, Hamilton argued, if courts are to possess the ability to invalidate statutes transgressing these "exceptions to the legislative authority" without fear of legislative retribution: "Limitations of this kind can be preserved in practice no other way than through the medium of the courts of justice; whose duty it must be to declare all acts contrary to the manifest tenor of the Constitution void. Without this, all the reservations of particular rights or privileges would amount to nothing."[4]

Like Wilson and Hamilton, Madison originally saw little value in the sort of declaration or bill of rights attached to many state constitutions. As with state constitutional provisions announcing the principle of separation of powers, Madison thought such "parchment barriers" to governmental overreaching ineffective.[5] However, in 1788, in the midst of the struggle over ratification, Madison engaged in a polite debate by correspondence with his friend Thomas Jefferson (then minister to France) during the course of which Madison's position apparently began to shift. In the course of their discussion, Jefferson echoed Hamilton's association of constitutional provisions guaranteeing personal liberties with enforcement by the judiciary: he noted that in "the arguments in favor of a declaration of rights," Madison had omitted "one which has great weight with me, the legal check which it puts into the hands of the judiciary."[6] By the following year, Madison was prepared to take the initiative in proposing to the First Congress that provisions amounting to a federal Bill of Rights should be submitted to the states for ratification as part of the Constitution.

Madison's motives were doubtless political for the most part: he wanted both to conciliate those honestly troubled by what they saw as a gap in the Constitution and to head off the proposal of amendments that would actually weaken the new federal government. But at the same time, Madison articulated, in the speech in which he presented what ultimately became the first ten amendments, a rationale for the amendments that clearly rejected the idea that constitutional powers and constitutional liberties do not overlap: "It is true that the powers of the general government are circumscribed; they are directed to particular objects; but even if government keeps within those limits, it has certain discretionary powers with respect to the means, which may admit of abuse to a certain extent." Within the affirmative scope of Congress's delegated authority, in short, it is possible to imagine legislation that would invade freedoms commonly believed to belong to the individual. To prevent such "abuses," Madison now conceded, the inclusion of provisions expressly protecting such freedoms would be salutary. "The great object in view is to limit and qualify the powers of Government, by excepting out of the grant of power those cases in which the government ought not to act, or to act only in a particular mode."

In explaining how constitutional texts protecting individual liberty could play this role, Madison now adopted the reasoning Hamilton and Jefferson both articulated: "If [Madison's proposed amendments protecting aspects of individual liberty] are incorporated into the Constitution, independent tribunals of justice will consider themselves in a peculiar manner the guardians of these rights; they will be an impenetrable bulwark against every assumption of power in the Legislative or Executive; they will be naturally led to resist every encroachment upon rights expressly stipulated for in the Constitution by the declaration of rights." In this speech, Madison thus drew a tight connection between the express recognition of those freedoms in the Constitution and the provision of an incentive for the judiciary to use its constitutional independence to enable it to protect those freedoms against legislative (or executive) infringement. *If* the vital aspects of liberty are "incorporated" into the Constitution, "expressly stipulated for" in the text, they become law, not just a set of political objectives but a set of legal rules lying within the courts' special competence and interest as the constitutional interpreters of the law. The judges would then ("naturally") have particular reasons—we assume Madison had in mind their amour propre and their natural inclination to defend the prerogatives of their institution, in addition to the implicit appeal to professionalism and the ideal of independent decision making—to "consider themselves in a peculiar manner the guardians of these rights."[7]

Madison succeeded: a version of his suggested amendments, although not including one that would have protected liberty of the press against state infringement, was endorsed by Congress, and by 1791 enough states had ratified what we now know as the first ten amendments to make them part of the Constitution, known then and later as the (originally missing) federal Bill of Rights. As of that date, the Constitution commanded that "Congress shall make no law . . . abridging the freedom of speech or of the press." But what, exactly, did that commandment *mean*? Neither Madison nor any other participant in the process that led to the adoption of the First Amendment is recorded as giving a definition or explanation. To be sure, except for Madison's great speech introducing the amendments, our records are scanty, but what we have does not indicate any concern over the meaning of "freedom of speech or of the press," which the Republic decided to include among those "rights expressly stipulated for in the Constitution."

One possible answer was that the words of the First Amendment's speech and press clauses encoded a determinate, fixed meaning, that the absence of debate over their interpretation was the product of a consensus based on language. There was (and is), furthermore, an obvious candidate for this encoded and determinate meaning, that supplied by Sir William Blackstone in his *Commentaries on the Laws of England*, published between 1765 and 1769. Blackstone was the first lawyer to hold a university chair in the English common law (the judge-made law "common" to the realm), and the book was his attempt to synthesize and present a comprehensive view of the entirety of the common law, from its fundamental constitutional principles through what we would now call the law of property, tort, and crime. Blackstone had a happy gift for expression, and the four volumes of the *Commentaries* were a runaway success on both sides of the Atlantic. Despite Blackstone's rather Tory sensitivities, the Revolution and Independence did little to slow his rapid ascent to the status of the oracle of that law which Americans, by and large, viewed themselves as sharing with the English. Blackstone, in short, was an Authority, and treated as such. And Blackstone, as it happened, had discussed "liberty of the press" in the fourth volume of the *Commentaries*.[8]

Volume four was subtitled "Of Public Wrongs," and Blackstone's discussion of the press, found in a chapter on offenses "against the Public Peace," was a sort of rhetorical appendix to his explication of the crime of libel. Libels, as Blackstone defined them, were "malicious defamations of any person, and especially a magistrate, made public by either printing, writing, signs, or pictures, in order to provoke him to wrath, or expose him to public hatred, contempt and ridicule." Recalling his discussion of the civil tort of libel (in his third volume, "Of Private Wrongs"), Blackstone used a procedural distinction to underline the unique significance of the crime: whereas in a civil suit by an individual, the defendant could plead the truth of his defamatory statement in bar of the action, in a criminal prosecution, truth was no defense: "the tendency which all libels have to create animosities, and to disturb the public peace, is the whole that the law considers." The criminal law of libel thus controlled the very form of writing or other expression, without regard to the defendant's purposes or, indeed, the consequences if any of his expression.

In exercising this sort of control over expression, Blackstone went on to write, "the *liberty of the press*, properly understood, is by no means infringed or violated."

The liberty of the press is indeed essential to the nature of a free state: but this consists in laying no *previous* restraints upon publications, and not in freedom from censure for criminal matter when published. Every freeman has an undoubted right to lay what sentiments he pleases before the public: to forbid this, is to destroy the freedom of the press; but if he publishes what is improper, mischievous, or illegal, he must take the consequences of his temerity. To subject the press to the restrictive power of a licenser . . . is to subject all freedom of sentiment to the prejudices of one man, and make him the arbitrary and infallible judge of all controverted points in learning, religion, and government . . . . Thus the will of individuals is still left free; the abuse only of that free will is the object of legal punishment.

Upon the expiration of the last British statute providing for governmental licensing of printing in 1694, Blackstone concluded, "the press became properly free . . . and has ever since so continued."

In light of later developments, as well as of the argument that Blackstone's definition of liberty of the press provides the original meaning of the free speech and press clauses, it will be valuable to pause briefly to consider the long passage just quoted. Blackstone is regularly invoked in modern literature, and indeed in 1798 by critics of the federal Sedition Act (on which more later), as evidence of the crabbed and narrow view English (and American) law took of press freedom at the time the First Amendment was written: as long as there is no censorship in advance—no "prior restraint" in the language of contemporary constitutional law—the press is free. The imposition of subsequent liability is simply irrelevant, by definition. This is, of course, in one sense a much narrower view than modern First Amendment law generally takes, although as the reader also knows, where intellectual property is concerned modern American law regularly permits the use of prior restraints. But note two other features of Blackstone's discussion. Blackstone located the core of the liberty at issue in the "free will" of "individuals," and he identified the governmental evil to be avoided as the subjection of that freedom to publish whatever any freeman thinks and wishes to express to the "prejudices" or the "arbitrary and infallible" will of a governmental official. Blackstone explained his narrow definition of liberty of the press, in other words, by a broader and strongly libertarian rationale. Later American discussion would raise the question whether the definition satisfied the rationale.[9]

If it were proper to see the First Amendment as originally encoding a specific and determinate meaning, Blackstone's discussion would supply an obvious possibility—the only possibility, it has sometimes been argued. The distinguished constitutional historian Leonard Levy, for example, published in 1960 a well-known study entitled *Legacy of Suppression*, in which he argued that a narrow, Blackstonian, no-prior-restraint rule was clearly the interpretation the creators of the First Amendment assumed would be given to the speech and press clauses, and that the subsequent development of a broader view of the First Amendment was the imposition on the amendment of a new (if, from Levy's personal perspective, more desirable) meaning. But Levy's and similar arguments, are, we think, mistaken for several reasons.

The first and in some ways most fundamental problem with such arguments is that they rest on an assumption that founding-era Americans understood constitutional or (more generally) legal interpretation as the extraction from the written instrument of a determinate meaning that is, as we said above, encoded in the words of the document. It is quite clear, however, that this was not a settled and generally shared assumption at the time.[10] One entirely orthodox argument about the proper interpretation of a legal instrument was to assert that it used words with a settled legal meaning, and that its words were to be given that meaning. When the Sedition Act's defenders made this argument about Blackstone and liberty of the press, the logic of their argument was professionally plausible (assuming one agreed that Blackstone's definition *was* the settled legal meaning) but it was not conclusive. Other arguments, employing different logic, were equally orthodox. In particular, founding-era legal interpreters often assumed that the full meaning of a law could not even in principle be known at the point in time the text was drafted because the experience of particular controversies over the law was necessary to a complete understanding of the implications and applications of its words. As Madison put the point in *Federalist* 37, "[a]ll new laws, though penned with the greatest technical skill, and passed on the fullest and most mature deliberation, are considered as more or less obscure until their meaning be liquidated and ascertained by a series of particular discussions and adjudications." The founders, to be sure, were not deconstructionists: the point, in their mind, was not that words are infinitely manipulable but that precisely because words *are* meaningful, there is a basis for reasoned debate over their meaning as words, as a text, and not simply as a code for some other, extratextual meaning.[11]

A second problem with Levy's argument is one that, admirably, he himself raised at length in his 1985 revision of *Legacy of Suppression*, significantly retitled *Emergence of a Free Press*. Without abandoning his earlier claim that the First Amendment's original meaning was Blackstonian, Levy documented the coexistence of a remarkably free press in colonial America with the occasional prosecution for seditious libel. But even in 1985 Levy insisted that, however much American practice provided the seedbed for a broader view of free expression, the Blackstonian legal understanding of press freedom at the time of the First Amendment's origin was unchanged because he could find no evidence before 1798 of any reconsideration of the legal meaning of the idea. As we shall see shortly, there *is* such evidence (which Levy was aware of but inexplicably discounted); our point at the moment is that there existed, at the time the First Amendment was created, a competing possibility for the meaning of freedom of speech and press—the generally libertarian practices of the American press. It was, once again, a perfectly orthodox legal argument by the standards of the late eighteenth century to argue that a public instrument's words ought to be interpreted in the light of their shared common understanding rather than according to some "precise technical sense" when the two conflict. As Hamilton wrote in *Federalist* 83, "the natural and obvious sense of [a constitution's] provisions, apart from any technical rule, is the true criterion of construction."[12] If Americans (rather than American lawyers) generally understood and acted on freedom of expression along lines broader than Blackstone's definition, it was professionally plausible to argue that "the common acceptation of the words," and not their "professional meaning," was controlling.[13] Arguments from technical meaning and from popular understanding were competing *legal* possibilities at the time, and an a priori assumption that one or the other can be used to explain the *historical* evidence is unwarranted.

In any event, and in final response to arguments like Levy's, there is direct evidence, predating the struggle over the Sedition Act, that sophisticated American legal interpreters did not necessarily believe that "liberty of the press" was an expression with a fixed legal meaning or that its interpretation in a constitutional provision could be settled by a simple resort to Blackstone.[14] In rebutting attacks on the Constitution for its failure to mention liberty of the press, Hamilton suggested that a provision on that subject would be objectionable precisely because its meaning would be too uncertain to provide any real protection for press freedom.

"What signifies a declaration that 'the liberty of the press shall be inviolably preserved?' What is the liberty of the press? Who can give it any definition which would not leave the utmost latitude for evasion? I hold it to be impracticable."[15] Hamilton's comment shows that there was nothing self-evident about the idea that a constitutional provision safeguarding liberty of the press would encode Blackstone's definition.[16]

Hamilton's dismissal of worry over the absence of a free press provision could be attributed to the exigencies of partisan advocacy: he was making a case for the Constitution against a serious and potentially damaging objection. This does not render his argument meaningless: at a minimum, we know that a shrewd and highly skilled controversialist believed that his argument about the indeterminacy of "liberty of the press" would be persuasive to many of his readers. But an even more telling example of founders refusing to treat Blackstone as a final authority can be found in a private 1789 exchange of letters between William Cushing, then chief justice of the Massachusetts high court, and John Adams, shortly before the latter took office as the first vice president. Cushing, who went on to become one of the original associate justices of the United States Supreme Court, wrote Adams about "a difficulty" he felt about the proper construction of Article 16 of the Massachusetts Declaration of Rights, which states that "[t]he liberty of the press is essential to the security of freedom in a State and . . . ought not, therefore, to be restrained within this Commonwealth." Unlike the critics of the Sedition Act a few years later, Cushing did not question the overall constitutionality of criminal prosecutions for seditious libel under a provision safeguarding freedom of the press. He did raise the question, however, whether Article 16 required the admission of truth as a defense in such a case, even though (as Blackstone taught) at English common law "truth cannot be pleaded in bar of an indictment." But unlike the defenders of the Sedition Act, Cushing did not believe that the common law definition of "liberty of the press" found in Blackstone controlled the interpretation of Massachusetts's constitutional guarantee. "The question is—whether [the English rule] is law now *here* . . . If therefore that point has never been adjudged here (and I don't know that it has been), perhaps we are at liberty to judge upon it *de novo* upon the reason of the thing and from what may appear most beneficial to society."

Cushing's letter then proceeded to lay out a series of considerations supporting the conclusion that Article 16 required that "falsity . . . be a necessary element in a libel." Cushing anticipated the critics of the Sedition Act in rejecting a definitional limitation of liberty of the press to a prohibition on prior restraints, on the ground that the provision's words "understood according to English, make no such distinction" and that the effect of subsequent punishment is similar to that of previous censorship. He invoked a famous English case, and the position taken by the one judge in the case remembered as a friend to liberty, to argue that Article 16 ought to be read as a correction of the common law, implicitly invoking a well-known canon of construction that a new law should be interpreted to address the "mischief" which provoked it. In turn, society's obligation to protect the name and reputation of the citizen disallowed, in Cushing's judgment, any argument that Article 16 prohibited libel prosecutions altogether, although the importance of Article 16's goals required that such prosecutions be circumscribed. The task, then, was to develop an operational rule that would address these considerations in the light of "the reason" of Article 16.

What is that liberty of the press, which is essential to the security of freedom? The propagating literature and knowledge by printing or otherwise tends to illuminate men's minds and to establish them in principles of freedom. But it cannot be denied also, that a free scanning of the conduct of administration and shewing the tendency of it . . . tends to the *security of freedom in a State*; even more directly and essentially than the liberty of printing upon literary and speculative subjects in general.

Cushing suggested, therefore, that Article 16 ought to be interpreted to require that truth be admitted as a defense in criminal prosecutions, notwithstanding any prior English or American practice to the contrary. "By the spirit and implication of this article, laws of England, not usually practiced on here, are not to have force with us, and laws actually practiced on, but repugnant to the Constitution, are set aside." In his response, Adams endorsed Cushing's reasoning and his conclusion.[17]

Note what Cushing (and Adams) did and did not do. Neither regarded English common law (or Blackstone) as dispositive. The task of construing the state's free press provision, while informed by the past, required the interpreter to interpret the words of the provision in the light of "the reason of the thing" (the meaning of a free press examined from first principles) and the needs of a society dependent on an enlightened and freedom-loving citizenry. Article 16, properly construed, therefore would require the modification or rejection of the English rule and also of Massachusetts law on the subject to the extent that any of these were contradictory to the purposes—in the Massachusetts context—of a guarantee of a free press. In suggesting an answer to the specific question he had raised, Cushing did just that: he created a new rule of law based on his judgment about what would make the most sense of the Massachusetts provision. In substance, to be sure, Cushing's specific answer departed only modestly from Blackstone: Article 16 required a particular modification in the law governing criminal libel. But to say that was to overthrow altogether the authority of Blackstone, except as one voice in a debate over the meaning of free speech, for Cushing's modest answer was a wholesale rejection of Blackstone's equation of a free press with the absence of a censor. Even more important, if possible, is the fact that two prominent and experienced American lawyers, engaged in a discussion of a free press provision in a context where they had no motive except a sincere wish to interpret it rightly, shared the belief that in order to be faithful interpreters of the constitutional text they would have to ask questions not just about the past but even more importantly about what legal rules would achieve the constitutional goal of ensuring the "propagation [of] literature and knowledge by printing or otherwise" in order to "illuminate men's minds and to establish them in principles of freedom." Cushing's formulation of Article 16's goal is also interesting: like Blackstone he identified the purpose of a free press in terms of freedom both individual and societal, although Cushing put it from the perspective of the recipient rather than that of the person wishing to publish his sentiments.

Another example of the nonexistence in the period between 1789 and 1798 of a Blackstonian consensus on the meaning of a free press comes from the infamous XYZ affair in early 1798. After months of unsuccessful negotiation with the government of Revolutionary France, during which French officials, including the foreign minister Talleyrand, alternately harangued and attempted to extort money from the three American special envoys, the envoys prepared a formal vindication of their conduct, addressed to Talleyrand and signed by all three but primarily drafted by future chief justice John Marshall. One of the many complaints which the French had alleged against the American government was its failure to "repress" "invectives and calumnies against the [French] Republic." The centerpiece of Marshall's response was a statement of constitutional principle.

The Genius of the Constitution & the opinions of the people of the United States cannot be overruled by those who administer the government. Among those principles deemed sacred in America, among those precious rights considered as forming the bulwark of their liberties, which the Government contemplates with awful reverence; and would approach only with the most cautious circumspection, there is no one, of which the importance is more deeply impressed on the public mind, than the liberty of the press.

For Marshall, no matter how harmful and unjustified a libelous publication might be, no response that would involve "enslaving the press" was acceptable in the United States.

Picking up on Blackstone's dichotomy between the liberty and the licentiousness of the press, Marshall conceded that "this liberty is often

carried to excess [and] has sometimes degenerated into licentiousness";
at the same time, he implicitly but clearly corrected Blackstone's assertion that criminal libel prosecutions are an appropriate means of dealing with licentious expression without impairing the press's freedom.
"[T]he remedy has not yet been discovered. Perhaps [such expression] is
an evil inseparable from the good to which it is allied, perhaps it is a
shoot which cannot be stripped from the stalk, without wounding vi-
tally the plant from which it is torn." The federal government was therefore without any institutional means of responding to calumny against
France or, indeed, against itself, although American courts, Marshall
observed, "are alike open to all who consider themselves as injured."
Speech harmful to society, Marshall concluded, "is a calamity incident
to the nature of liberty."[18]

Unlike Cushing in his letter to Adams, in drafting the reply to Talleyrand, Marshall was not engaged in dispassionate constitutional
analysis, and in addition he was writing under extreme time pressure.[19] As a consequence the exact constitutional implications of his
discussion of press freedom, a discussion which never explicitly invoked the First Amendment, are unclear. Marshall did not assert the
blanket unconstitutionality of all "remedies" for the misuse of the
press, but only that "they have never yet been devised in America,"[20]
and his remarks about the impossibility of separating liberty and licentiousness without enslaving the press were, except in the final instance,
given as possibilities rather than constitutional certainties. That said,
the reply to Talleyrand resembles Cushing's correspondence with Adams in several important respects. Marshall's reasoning was menda-
cious rather than unclear unless he was rejecting any simple equation
of the meaning of freedom of the press in the United States with Blackstone's discussion in the *Commentaries*. Like Cushing, Marshall
thought that the compatibility of "regulations" of expression with a
constitutionally free press had to be determined by examining the impact of the regulation on the freedom actually enjoyed by the press and,
through the press, "any individual [who] may chuse to offer to the public eye" his views. And Marshall's description, earlier in the reply, of the
state of free expression in the United States is on its face as incompatible

with subsequent governmental punishment as it is with prior censorship: "[n]o individual fears to utter what his judgment or his passions may dictate [and] an unrestrained press conveys alike to the public eye the labors of virtue & the efforts of particular interests."[21] When, a few months later, debate over the Sedition Act squarely presented the question whether the speech and press clauses apply to subsequent liability, it was the Act's critics, not its defenders, who invoked "that sublime and just construction of the Constitution itself, as to the liberty of the press, to be found in the negotiations of the late envoys to France."[22] Contemporaneous readers of the reply to Talleyrand, it would seem, did not see in it an endorsement of Blackstone.

* * *

WE ARE NOW IN A POSITION to summarize what can be garnered from the earliest history of the First Amendment that is relevant to the argument we are presenting.

As an initial matter, Madison introduced and defended what became the First Amendment (along with the other provisions of the federal Bill of Rights), on the express understanding that it would enjoy the same status in federal constitutional law that Cushing and Adams simply assumed Article 16 possessed in the fundamental law of Massachusetts: the First Amendment was to be law—supreme law— and the courts were to act "in a peculiar manner [as] the guardians of these rights." The subsequent debate over the Sedition Act showed that Madison's understanding was universally shared.[23] These points may seem trite, since both are unquestioned commonplaces in contemporary American law, but their combined force bears on one of the central themes to emerge out of Part Two of this book. As we have seen, the history of federal-court adjudication with respect to copyrights and patents is largely one of judicial acquiescence in statutory developments that have radically affected the actual line between expression that is free and expression that is subject to government control. And yet the very existence of the First Amendment originally implied that the judiciary would be "an impenetrable bulwark against every assumption of power" by the federal government that abridges freedom of speech and press. The Supreme Court's virtual abdication of judicial review in cases like *Eldred* sits uneasily with this Madisonian presupposition.

More importantly, chapter seven shows that the argument that the First Amendment had a clear, determinate original meaning, understood or assumed to be embedded in the words "the freedom of speech, [and] of the press," is historically indefensible. Neither the interpretive conventions of founding-era lawyers, nor evidence about the actual views of free expression of founders important not just for their personal stature but also because they seem to reflect more broadly shared understandings, supports the claim that the First Amendment's original meaning was identical to Blackstone's no-prior-restraint definition of a free press (or any other preexisting) definition. Some of the forms of argument accepted in the legal culture of the day (invocations of settled legal meanings and existing practice) invited recourse to possible meanings fixed, at least relatively, outside and before the process of interpretation. Other orthodox arguments (reasoning from the goals of a legal provision, validating the role of experience and of post-"enactment" controversy in clarifying the meaning of a text) clearly demanded that the interpreter himself make creative decisions about what specific legal rule or rules would best implement the authoritative text. And there was no fixed hierarchy of arguments, which meant that ultimately any interpreter, even one who relied on the backward-looking, "fixed-meaning" arguments, was obliged to make a decision about which arguments were the most plausible and faithful to the text. The views expressed (or endorsed) by such representative and major figures as Cushing, Adams, and Marshall show that these are not merely abstract, logical deductions: even before the Sedition Act crisis, sophisticated American lawyers felt, apparently sincerely, no obligation to read free press constitutional provisions as encoding a determinate meaning. The original setting of the First Amendment licenses, or rather demands, the exercise of discretion and judgment in the interpretation of freedom of speech, and of the press.

At the same time, as we have already observed, there is no indication that any founder thought the interpretation of the First Amendment was a matter of labeling whatever views one preferred on personal or political grounds the "meaning" of the First Amendment. Everyone—Hamilton in *Federalist* 84 an exception, perhaps—assumed that it was sensible to think of the words of Article 16 or the First Amendment as meaningful, as a text that could be construed rather than an empty vessel into which meaning had to be poured. And there are interesting signs of agreement, known or otherwise, on how one might build a convincing argument. Blackstone and Cushing and Marshall all share a basically teleological view of free expression: a free press exists to serve certain goals, and its legal meaning ought to accomplish that end. Even Hamilton's skeptical argument rested on the same view: Hamilton's criticism of written guarantees of press freedom assumed the existence of a reasonably clear understanding of the purpose of such a liberty, and denied the value of a written provision on the ground that none could be drafted that would achieve that purpose in the teeth of clever attempts to circumvent the provision's intent. There were signs, additionally, of a certain general level of agreement on what the goal of a free press really is. Blackstone's exaltation of free will, Cushing's concern for the illumination of the mind and his equation of prior restraints with subsequent punishments, Marshall's portrayal of a United States in which no one fears to say whatever he thinks or feels—each suggested that the affirmative purpose of a free press concerns the individual's autonomy of thought and expression as well as the needs of a politically free society. A parallel convergence can be detected in the references to what a free press prevents: the tyranny of prejudice and arbitrary judgment on the part of government censors, of official attempts to distinguish what is truly liberty from what is mere licentiousness.

There was no original meaning to the speech and press clauses of the First Amendment, if by that one means a legal rule or rules behind their words but fixed in significance. The amendment was an unmistakable example of what Madison meant when he asserted that legal provisions are "more or less obscure until their meaning be liquidated and ascertained by a series of particular discussions and adjudications."[24] The First Amendment's operational significance would become clear only after such a series of discussions and adjudications. But in a different sense, there was an original meaning to the amendment. By adopting it, the Republic committed itself to a search for legal rules, enforceable by courts, that would safeguard the existence of free speech and a free press and, consequently, to an ongoing debate over such questions as when a person is really free to say what she means and mean what she says. Such questions may have more than one plausible answer but they are not, by that token, meaningless.

CHAPTER 8

The Sedition Act of 1798 and the First
First Amendment Crisis

THE XYZ AFFAIR that we encountered in the previous chapter was one more episode in the process that, by 1798, led the United States and France from the status of allies bound by the Treaty of 1778 to enemies engaged in hostilities. One product of the American fear and antagonism generated by this process was, as it turned out, a turning point in the history of the First Amendment, or what (with the benefit of hindsight) we might call the original First Amendment. But we must begin the story a little earlier, with the initial cracks in the relationship between America and France.

From its beginning, the French Revolution complicated American relations with France. Around the year 1790, most Americans probably felt gratitude toward the French allies with whom they had won the Revolutionary War, but the abolition of the monarchy and the increasingly militant policies of the republic that replaced it strained many Americans' sense of connection, and pushed others into outright hostility. International issues played into the partisan divisions which had been coalescing gradually into a party system of Federalists and Republicans—very roughly the supporters of a strong federal government and their critics. Differing emotional responses to France and Britain, divergent perspectives on the relative threat each great power posed to the United States, contrary evaluations of the political systems of monarchical Britain and republican France—all contributed to the mixtures of conviction, passion, and expediency that increasingly pushed politically active Americans into accepting for themselves one label or the other. By the beginning of George Washington's second term, the coalition that had fought for the Constitution's adoption had shattered beyond repair: Hamilton and Marshall, for example, had become Federalists, while Madison and Jefferson were leading Republicans. A decision to identify with one group or the other wielded its influence, in turn, on the individual's statements, actions, and, at least much of the time, private opinions as well. Federalists were generally Anglophilic and fearful that France's social turmoil would spill over into the United States; Republicans tended to be Francophiles, and suspicious of anything that seemed likely to draw the country closer to a Britain they saw as arrogant and unrepentantly colonialist.

The outbreak of war between France and Britain in 1793 thus presented the Washington administration with a series of hard choices. American public opinion was, unsurprisingly, deeply divided over what obligations (if any) the country owed France under the 1778 treaty. When President Washington decided to issue a declaration of neutrality on his own authority and to institute and carry out a concerted policy of denying access to American resources to either belligerent, many Republicans were outraged, both at Washington's presumption in acting alone and at what they saw as dramatic proof of the president's Federalist tendencies. While Washington's neutrality policies were in form and intent evenhanded between the belligerent powers, they weighed more heavily on the French, who hoped to use American ports as a dockyard and safe harbor for the privateers with which they sought to contest the seas with the British, the maritime superpower of the age. Diplomatic relations between the United States and France deteriorated, a process that continued after John Adams succeeded Washington in the presidency. The breaking point in American public opinion came with Adams's reluctant decision at the beginning of April 1798 to disclose the XYZ affair. Congressional Republicans, who had been demanding that the President disclose the dispatches from Marshall and the other envoys, were thunderstruck: rather than concealing its own unreasonable dealings with France, the administration had been moving cautiously in response to overweening French arrogance. American public opinion turned swiftly and strongly against France and toward the Federalists, and Congress authorized naval action against the French. What ultimately ensued amounted to a naval war, and despite the absence of a formal declaration of war both the United States attorney general and the Supreme Court interpreted Congress's actions as creating a state of limited public war.[1]

In the view of the Federalist majority in Congress and of some officers in the executive branch, the national security of the United States in 1798 was at risk not only from French attack but also from the possibility of subversive action at home. Although public opinion was at first strongly behind the government's vigorous reaction to French provocations, the Federalists suspected the enthusiasm and even the loyalty of the Republicans, and also of the growing number of foreign immigrants. After extensive debate, in the summer of 1798 Congress passed and President Adams signed into law a battery of four statutes intended to safeguard domestic security. Collectively, these laws have gone down in history as the notorious Alien and Sedition Acts. Three of the statutes dealt with the threats perceived to exist from the immigrant population; our concern is with the fourth, the Sedition Act passed on July 4, 1798.[2]

As enacted, Section 2 of the Sedition Act made it a crime, punishable by a fine of up to $5,000 and a prison term of up to two years, for any person to

write, print, utter or publish, or . . . cause or procure to be written, printed, uttered or published, or . . . knowingly and willingly assist or aid in writing, printing, uttering or publishing any false, scandalous and malicious writing or writings against the government of the United States, or either house of the Congress of the United States, or the President of the United States with intent to defame the said government, or either house of the said Congress, or the said President, or to bring them, or either of them, into contempt or disrepute; or to excite against them, or either or any of them, the hatred of the good people of the United States. . . .

Unlike other parts of the Act, this provision sparked the first great debate in American history over the meaning of the First Amendment.[3]

There was nothing unfamiliar about Section 2 to any founding-era lawyer, or indeed, to any reader of the previous chapter in this book. Section 2 of the Act was unmistakably a statutory version of the crime of seditious libel which Blackstone had described in his *Commentaries*. The crime created by Section 2 was not a novelty, then, but the proposal that Congress enact it into federal law was immediately controversial along predictable partisan lines. The Act's Republican opponents denounced it as a naked attempt by the Federalists to suppress public debate and perpetuate their grip on power. In turn, the Act's Federalist proponents argued that the stability of the federal government and the very independence of the Republic were at risk and that only those who approved of "false, scandalous, and malicious" attacks on the government had any reason to fear the Act. From the beginning, however, debate over the Act was couched largely in constitutional terms. When a Senate version of the bill reached the House of Representatives on July 5,[4] the first recorded response was a pointed call by Republican Carter B. Harrison "for the reading of the amendments to the Constitution," and from that point on, the constitutional battle was joined.[5]

Federalists and Republicans alike described the constitutionality of the proposed Act as involving two distinct, if related, questions. Republican John Nicholas's formulation, while partisan, reflected the analytic approach shared by both sides: he had, he said, "looked in vain amongst the enumerated powers given to Congress in the Constitution, for an authority to pass a law like the present; but he found [instead] what he considered as an express prohibition against passing it." Thus, the first question was whether Congress had the affirmative power to enact such a bill. The Federalists insisted that the Act was a lawful exercise of Congressional authority because "[e]very independent Government has a right to preserve and defend itself" and such a power is therefore implicit in the Constitution's creation of a government. As a textual matter, the bill was constitutional under the Necessary and Proper Clause of Article I, Section 8, which empowers Congress to "make all Laws which shall be necessary and proper for carrying into Execution" the powers of the federal government; a law punishing actions with a direct tendency to lead to interference with the operations of the federal government is a law necessary and proper to the execution of those operations. The Republicans responded by flatly denying that the Constitution delegated any power over the press to Congress, correctly pointing out that the advocates of ratification in 1787–88 had repeatedly issued the same denial. If this left the federal government weaker than it needed to be—a claim the Republicans rejected—that was a constitutional flaw that could not be remedied by legislation.[6]

With few if any exceptions, the defenders of the Act accepted Madison's 1791 argument that constitutionally protected liberties are not merely that area of freedom lying beyond the outer limits of federal authority but actually may overlap with, and in those circumstances override, the Constitution's grants of power. It was not enough, then, to point to some affirmative authorization for the bill to prove its constitutionality under the First Amendment, for the Federalists conceded that the First Amendment would invalidate a law which violated the amendment's provisions even if the law fell within the scope of one of Congress's grants of power. The second question, therefore, was that of deciding what in fact the speech and press clauses of the First Amendment prohibit, and the Federalists came prepared with a clear answer, one (as we have seen) echoed by some modern scholars: the text of the speech and press clauses had a single determinate meaning, derived from existing legal usages.

The amendment, according to Federalist politician and lawyer Harrison Gray Otis, used "a phraseology perfectly familiar in the jurisprudence of every State, and of a certain and technical meaning. It was a mode of expression which we had borrowed from the only country in which [freedom of speech and of the press] had been tolerated." In other words, the language of the First Amendment had a settled meaning at law, the one accepted by English common law and, many Federalists pointed out, endorsed by Blackstone. So understood, the First Amendment and the Sedition Act were entirely compatible. "This freedom . . . is nothing more than the liberty of writing, publishing, and speaking one's thoughts, under the condition of being answerable to the injured party, whether it be the Government or an individual, for false, malicious, and seditious expressions, whether spoken or written; and the liberty of the press is merely an exemption from all previous restraints."[7] Practice in the states, several of which had free press guarantees in their constitutions, the Federalists continued, corroborated the inference that the First Amendment should be construed to protect the freedom from prior restraints on expression that was recognized by the common law, and only that freedom. The Sedition Act, which made no effort to impose any form of prior censorship on expression, thus left the liberty to which the First Amendment refers entirely unabridged. Indeed, its proponents pointed out correctly, the Act went beyond the common law to incorporate the further protections for free expression demanded by advanced libertarian thinking in Britain, the admission of truth as a defense and the submission of the criminality of the publication to the jury.

The Federalists did not argue the case for the Sedition Act's constitutionality solely on textual grounds, however: they were equally insistent that their interpretation of the speech and press clauses gave the fullest intelligible scope to free expression. A prohibition on any form of censorship or licensing scheme, which the Federalists admitted and insisted that the First Amendment embodied, left every person entirely free to speak, "at liberty to print what he pleases," with (as one put it in a later debate on the Act), "the privilege of expressing unreservedly whatever he thinks." "Every man m[ay] publish what he please[s]."[8] The Federalist reading of the First Amendment denied to the federal government the power to control expression; what it permitted was the imposition of liability for harm done. The constitutional freedom of speech protected by the amendment, Harrison Gray Otis explained, is "the liberty of writing, publishing, and speaking one's thoughts, under the condition of being answerable to [an] injured party."[9] Such a condition left the choice of what to say or write in the absolute discretion of each individual, the governmental power it permitted being the power to vindicate the rights of others (including public officials and the government itself) by imposing liability after the fact for licentious, false, and scandalous expression.[10]

The Republican attack on the Sedition Act joined issue with the Federalists on every point. As a textual matter, the Republicans expressed astonishment that anyone would defend a bill exercising control over the press in the teeth of the First Amendment's words. Republican Nathaniel Macon commented that in the past, "[s]everal laws had been passed which he thought violated the spirit, but none before this which directly violated the letter of the Constitution."[11] The Federalist invocation of the common law as the key to interpreting the amendment was illogical and inconsistent with the text of the amendment:

"unless gentlemen chose to assert that the Constitution had given Congress a power to seal the mouths or to cut the tongues of the citizens of the Union," Albert Gallatin remarked sarcastically, the only way in which freedom of *speech* could be abridged was by subsequent punishment, and "a sound construction [of the parallel speech and press clauses] must be such as to be applicable to both."[12] In any event, citing Blackstone's definition of liberty of the press in interpreting the First Amendment was "a manifest abuse of [his] authority" because it ignored the definition's context and its author's purpose. "He had advanced into the fourth volume of a panegyric on the laws of England, and after stating the law on this subject, makes a theory to justify the actual state of the law."[13]

A central theme in the Republicans' constitutional argument was their answer to the claim that a prohibition on prior restraints, in itself, was sufficient to leave freedom of expression unfettered. (The Republicans agreed with the Federalists that the First Amendment forbade such restraints.)[14] As a factual matter, taking into account what no one would deny about the incentives and deterrents to human behavior, imposing subsequent liability for expression would inevitably abridge expression through the most effective means of all—self-censorship.

Under such circumstances, it must be seen that the printers of papers would be deterred from printing anything which should be in the least offensive to a power which might so greatly harass them. They would not only refrain from publishing anything of the least questionable nature, but they would be afraid of publishing the truth, as, though true, it might not always be in their power to establish the truth to the satisfaction of a court of justice. This bill would, therefore, go to the suppression of every printing press in the country, which is not obsequious to the will of Government.[15]

Blackstone's no-prior-restraint view of press freedom, James Madison wrote in a state legislative report published in early 1800, "can never be admitted to be the American idea of it; since a law inflicting penalties on printed publications would have a similar effect with a law authorizing a previous restraint on them."[16]

As John Nicholas summarized the Republican position a few months later, the Federalist interpretation of the speech and press clauses did little to avoid the possibility of governmental control over or limitation of expression: their "definition, if true, so reduces the effect of the amendment, that the power of Congress is left unlimited over the productions of the press, and they are merely deprived of one mode of restraint."[17] If the amendment were to achieve the goal of unreserved speech and thought which even the Federalists purported to acknowledge as its aim, it had to be construed literally to leave Congress "under an obligation . . . of passing no law, either directly or indirectly, affecting that liberty."[18] Madison's 1800 report, perhaps the most sustained presentation of the Republican arguments, was emphatic in stating this conclusion: "the amendment is a denial to Congress of all power over the press," "a positive denial to Congress of any power whatever on this subject," so that "the press [is] wholly exempt from the power of Congress." The First Amendment, in short, is to be read not simply or even primarily as creating an individual privilege or immunity (although it no doubt does that) but as a structural provision that addresses Congress's affirmative powers. After the ratification of the First Amendment, the Republicans insisted, the federal government could lay claim to no authority to abridge the freedom of speech and press: that freedom simply lay altogether beyond the outer limits of federal authority. The First Amendment had laid to rest the claim (which the Republicans also denied) that as originally adopted the Constitution granted powers to Congress that could be used, directly or tangentially, to infringe the exercise of speech and press freedoms.

The Republicans of 1798 to 1800 spent little time developing the significance of this last argument, that the First Amendment (unlike state constitutional provisions concerning liberty of the press) addresses the affirmative scope of (federal) governmental power. They sometimes rebutted the Federalist argument that they were stripping individuals of any legal protection for their reputations with the observation that nothing in the Republican interpretation of the First Amendment had any effect on state law protections for personal interests. Subsequent nineteenth-century discussions often ignored the twofold nature of the Republican critique of the Sedition Act, with Justice Story's great treatise on constitutional law being an exception. Story strongly endorsed Blackstone's view as defining the proper scope of the individual liberty to speak and publish, but he distinguished that issue from what he labeled "a question of a very different nature," the existence of any power in "the national government . . . to pass any law . . . punishing the licentiousness of the press." On this latter issue, Story "abstain[ed] from expressing any opinion."[19] As we shall see, the mainstream of modern judicial thought about the amendment has simply ignored the power-denial aspect of the Republican argument against the Sedition Act.

* * *

DESPITE THE REPUBLICANS' BEST EFFORTS, Congress passed and President Adams signed the Sedition Act. Foreseeing that outcome, several Republican speakers in the House expressed the "hop[e] that the Judges would exercise the power placed in them of declaring the law as unconstitutional,"[20] but the hope was disappointed. While the Act never came before the Supreme Court, several justices presided on circuit over prosecutions under the Act and rejected any suggestion that it was invalid, which led Congressional Federalists to assert later on that the Republicans should abandon their constitutional quibbles now that the Act enjoyed "the solemn decision and concurrence of the judiciary." (The Republicans, needless to say, did no such thing, muttering instead about "hasty adjudications" that did not deserve the usual respect to be accorded decisions made "with all [the] moderation and solemnity that usually attend judicial decisions.")[21] The Federalists' success, however, was short-lived: as the House Republicans had predicted, the Act proved as controversial "out of doors" as in Congress, and provided the Republicans with an issue over which to excoriate Federalist tyranny and high-handedness during the presidential and House elections of 1800. Although most leading Federalists continued to defend the Act, and the Congressional leadership even attempted to extend it as its mandated expiration on March 3, 1801 drew near, others found it a distinctly awkward law with which to be associated. (John Marshall, seeking election to the House in the 1798 fall elections, carefully avoided endorsing the Act or pronouncing on its constitutionality.) After the fact, the Republicans invariably attributed their electoral victory in 1800, which gave them control of both political branches of the federal government, in part to the people's anger over the Federalists' violation of the First Amendment.

We shall return in the next chapter to the significance of this Republican interpretation of the events surrounding the Sedition Act; the immediate task is to avoid the benefits and liabilities of hindsight and examine what the contemporaneous debate over the Act may say about the First Amendment and its interpretation. In 1801, toward the end of the most active period of discussion of the Act,[22] an anonymous pamphleteer in Boston ("An Impartial Citizen") published *A Dissertation Upon the Constitutional Freedom of the Press*.[23] Impartial Citizen insisted that he was not writing "under the influence of any party," and that "[s]ome of each party will be displeased with" the pamphlet, and in truth he took a set of positions on the First Amendment that corresponded to the mainstream position of neither the Federalists nor the Republicans. Impartial Citizen believed it was possible to construe the First Amendment faithfully, not simply impose the "interpreter's" preferences on it, and indeed that doing so was an obligation: "whatever he may wish the constitution," every "candid, sober man . . . must be content to take it as it is." But in Impartial Citizen's opinion, doing so was no simple matter of reconstructing a clear original meaning or understanding. The debate over freedom of speech and press, and more generally the previous decade's arguments over the meaning of many provisions of the Constitution, proved that at least in many instances, the First Amendment paramount among them, the faithful interpreter could not assume that historical inquiry into the intentions of the Framers and ratifiers would resolve his questions. "Our constitution of national government is in our own hands . . . we know the men who formed it. . . . They remain among us, as men of like passions, subjected to the same errors, follies and weakness, as other men. So far are they from boasting of an inspiration in this work, that neither two of them can agree to understand the instrument in the same sense." Impartial Citizen, to be sure, spoke with hyperbole, but the debate over the Sedition Act, read without anachronism, demonstrated clearly the solid truth in his rhetoric: confronted with a serious disagreement over how to understand the First Amendment's guarantee of freedom of speech and press, Americans sharply divided over how to interpret the amendment's command.

The arguments on both sides were self-serving, but that does not mean that we should not take them seriously; indeed the central arguments of both Federalists and Republicans were intellectually and professionally plausible. And yet those arguments led to opposed conclusions. As Impartial Citizen concluded with an air of disgust, the Sedition Act debates showed that in the partisan setting of that discussion it was impossible for interpreters to come to agreement over which legal rules would be appropriate to carry out the purposes of the First Amendment. But severe as the divide between Federalists and Republicans was, it is possible to overstate their disagreement. All agreed that prior restraints on expression are forbidden by the First Amendment: as a 1799 Federalist committee report put it, a law "to impose previous restraint upon the press . . . would be a law to abridge the liberty of the press, and, as such, unconstitutional."[24] Put in positive terms, the First Amendment protects not just expression in the abstract but the individual's choice about what to write (or say). As the same Federalist document asserted, "the liberty of the press consists . . . in a permission to publish, without previous restraint, whatever he may think proper."[25] Republicans disagreed with at least the tone of the word "permission" as well as, of course, with the report's endorsement of the constitutionality of subsequent punishment of "wicked and malicious publications."[26] But no one seems to have thought that the First Amendment was compatible with a federal power literally to prevent expression or to shape beforehand how an individual is to say "whatever he may think proper."

The constitutional arguments over the Sedition Act also share a negative common denominator: no one at the time viewed constitutional interpretation generally, or the construction of the First Amendment in particular, in the mode so common to twenty-first century constitutional lawyers, as a balancing of interests (in the case of the First Amendment the individual's free expression interests against the interests of government). This may seem a truism, but even if so it is one the importance of which should not be overlooked. The Federalists and Republicans of 1798–1801 thought in terms that by today's standards seem too sharp edged, too lacking in nuance and sophistication to serve in the articulation of a system of free expression adequate to contemporary social needs. There are too many situations in which it would simply be unthinkable (would it not?) to limit the First Amendment to a ban on prior restraints, or expand it to deny Congress any power whatever that affects free expression. At this point we do not ask the reader to question this assumption, but only to notice that it is an assumption, not an inherent element of the First Amendment. A balancing approach to issues of free expression enables the interpreter to take into account opposing considerations in a fashion that neither the Federalist nor the Republican approaches could achieve, but the reverse may be true as well.

Beyond the existence of a degree of substantive accord underlying sharp disagreement, from the perspective of two centuries later the debates over the Sedition Act bring out into the open the implications of our discussion, in the previous chapter, of the First Amendment and original meaning. The fact that in a context of severe, partisan debate the warring parties were able to articulate and defend contradictory interpretations of the amendment was not the result of either party ignoring a preexisting determinate meaning, although both strove to make that appear to be so, and some modern scholars have (mistakenly, in our view) accepted the invitation to think so. The truth is that on the first occasion when the American Republic had to consider in a serious and sustained fashion the fundamental meaning of freedom of expression under the Constitution, it became clear that any basic approach to the First Amendment will involve, inevitably, the exercise of a sort of judgment that cannot be reduced to an algorithm or applied without the involvement of the interpreter's sense of the overall structure, purpose, and meaning of the American constitutional experiment. The modern history of the First Amendment's interpretation proceeds along that unstated premise, to be sure, but this is not (as is sometimes claimed) an innovation or a deviation from constitutional orthodoxy: the necessity for this sort of judgment and, indeed, creativity, has been present from the beginning.

It follows as a matter of necessity that arguments over the meaning of the First Amendment, or at least those arguments that address fundamental issues of interpretation, are persuasive (or not) because of their overall appeal as a means of making sense of the words of the amendment in the light of a portrayal of the broader constitutional setting of those words that will itself be contestable. First Amendment reasoning, when the issue is not the application of an agreed-upon framework but rather a proposal about what such a framework should be, is a matter not of syllogism but of rhetoric, although not in the degraded modern sense of the merely plausible or even specious—it is rhetorical, instead, in that it invites assent rather than demanding compliance. The leading Federalists and Republicans in 1798–1801 were all competent constitutionalists, some were brilliant, and the choice, then and now, between their basic views (or anyone else's) is closer to making a commitment than to solving an equation. This suggests, if it does not prove, that in a situation of similar interpretive crisis it is both legitimate and—dare we say—necessary to engage in the same sort of creative reasoning they employed.

CHAPTER 9

Justice Holmes and the Arrival of Balancing

IT IS A COMMONPLACE in legal circles—and a reasonably accurate one—that modern First Amendment law has its origins in the response to the Espionage Act of 1917. The story is a familiar one in constitutional scholarship, its interest lying not just in the importance of the topic but in the great personalities out of whose clash of thought, temperament, and will the highly speech-protective First Amendment of the present day was created—Judge Learned Hand, Herbert Croly (editor of the leading progressive magazine *The New Republic*), political scientist Harold Laski, legal scholars Zechariah Chafee, Jr. and Ernst Freund, and—most importantly—Justice Oliver Wendell Holmes, Jr. It is, in particular, two of Holmes's opinions, filed in the series of Espionage Act cases which the Supreme Court decided in 1919—his opinion for the Court in *Schenck v. United States* and his dissent in *Abrams v. United States*[1]—that seem from a contemporary perspective to have raised the curtain on serious consideration of the First Amendment, so much so that earlier discussions are regularly ignored or treated as mere foils for Holmes and what came after Holmes. In *Schenck* (decided in March 1919), Justice Holmes rejected the claim that the Espionage Act was flatly—what a contemporary lawyer would call facially—unconstitutional, but in passing he stated, rather cryptically, that the "question in every case is whether the words used are used in such circumstances and are of such a nature as to create a clear and present danger that they will bring about the substantive evils that Congress has a right to prevent."[2] By November, Holmes was treating the language of "clear and present danger" as a constitutional definition of the only circumstance under which the federal government may impose liability for speech without violating the First Amendment: "Only the emergency that makes it immediately dangerous to leave the correction of evil counsels to time warrants making any exception to the sweeping command, 'Congress shall make no law abridging the freedom of speech.'"[3]

Despite Holmes's insistence that his dissent in *Abrams* was consistent with *Schenck*,[4] most readers then and since have seen *Abrams* as a novel departure, both from Holmes's position of the previous March and from existing First Amendment thought. With the *Abrams* dissent, the modern law of the First Amendment is off and running. The story of how this came to be is an oft-told tale, not only with its familiar cast of characters but with familiar difficulties of interpretation, including the crucial issues of when and why Holmes changed his mind, and precisely what he changed his mind to.[5] We do not intend to contribute to the rich literature on these questions: our interest lies elsewhere, but not because we do not respect Holmes's importance. His opinions are central to the modern constitutional tradition of protecting free speech—Justice John Marshall Harlan II once referred to *Schenck* and *Abrams* as "fountainhead opinions."[6] Those opinions, furthermore, remain paradigmatic examples of the sort of reasoning presupposed in modern First Amendment law. But our concern is with what the foundations of that law ignore, and with what is simply presupposed away, without attention or concern, in that tradition of legal argument.

The first presupposition of importance is the basic irrelevance of the constitutional debates over the Sedition Act of 1798. Or perhaps we should say the content of those debates, for the memory of the Sedition Act hovered over the Espionage Act in a complex fashion. The Espionage Act was the product of the Wilson administration's anxiety, in the context of the Great War, over the federal government's legal authority to respond to "warfare by propaganda" on the part of hostile foreign powers or domestic political radicals.[7] The administration first proposed legislation addressing the issue in 1916, prior to America's entrance into World War I, but it was only after the declaration of war on Germany on April 6, 1917, that Congress passed and the president signed the Espionage Act. The legislation as originally drafted by the Department of Justice would have authorized executive censorship of the press by making it unlawful to publish any information which the president determined was "of such character that it is or might be useful to the enemy"; another provision in the Justice Department draft would have criminalized any attempt "to cause or attempt to cause disaffection in the military or naval forces of the United States."[8]

Both proposals, as well as a related one permitting the postmaster general to exclude from the mails any writing "of a treasonable or anarchistic character," provoked strong reactions in Congress and, particularly with respect to the press censorship provision, in the press. Critics of the legislation attacked these provisions as an effort to reprise the 1798 Sedition Act, and their invocation of that statute's lingering bad odor as an act of unconstitutional oppression proved effective enough to force the administration and its allies to settle for a less far-reaching statute than they preferred. In the end, the House of Representatives defeated the censorship provision, and Congress modified the language of the other speech-restrictive sections in an apparent effort to confine the bill's intrusion into free expression. Nevertheless, as finally approved the Act created three new federal offenses which bore directly on freedom of expression: Section 3 of Title I of the Act made it a crime, during wartime, for anyone "to make or convey false reports or false statements with intent to interfere" with military operations, to "cause or attempt to cause insubordination, disloyalty, mutiny, or refusal of duty, in the military or naval forces of the United States," or to "obstruct" the recruitment or enlistment of military personnel.[9]

The 1917 Congressional deliberations over the Espionage Act were reminiscent of the 1798 House debates over the Sedition Act, but only up to a point. The Republican opposition of 1917[10] provided most of the criticism and most of the votes to defeat the press censorship provision, but most Republicans wished only to soften, not to defeat the proposed legislation, and President Wilson's fellow Democrats in turn were not monolithic in support of the administration's preferences. The 1917 Act did not play the polarizing role in political-party ways which the 1798 Act had done. Nevertheless, the Espionage Act—the first federal seditious libel legislation since 1798—clearly raised, for many people, issues akin to those presented by the Sedition Act. "Never in the history of our country, since the Alien and Sedition Laws of 1798, has the meaning of free speech been the subject of such sharp controversy as to-day," civil libertarian Zechariah Chafee, Jr. wrote in the middle of the discussion.[11] As Chafee's observation suggests, the Sedition Act and its impact on constitutional law were important to the discussion of the Espionage Act. But what, in fact, was that impact? The answer, it seems, was rather ironic.

As a political matter, within a few years after the Sedition Act's expiration in March 1801, many Americans looked back on the period between 1798 and 1801 as a temporary aberration. The Sedition Act was gone, not only because by its own terms it had expired, but more importantly because the country had repudiated it as an unconscionable violation of the First Amendment.[12] The election of 1800 swept Jefferson into the presidency and the Republicans into a commanding position in both houses of Congress, and the Republicans' dominance of national politics after that ensured that in the nation's memory, the Sedition Act was generally viewed as a discreditable and unconstitutional attack on freedom of speech and press.[13] In the country's political culture, the First Amendment and the Act became isomorphic opposites: the absence of a federal statute criminalizing seditious libel became the proof that the government was obedient to the First Amendment, and between 1798 and 1917 Congress enacted no statute of that sort.

At the same time, the Republican view of the First Amendment's political triumph was a Pyrrhic victory for legal reflection on the First Amendment. No bill that could be categorized by its critics as a new sedition act had any political legs in a nineteenth-century Congress, but that fact served to embalm, not enthrone, orthodox legal thought about the First Amendment. Modern scholars such as David Rabban and Michael Kent Curtis have painstakingly reconstructed the rich history of struggle over free speech during the First Amendment's "forgotten years," a history that generated an "alternative free speech jurisprudence" by "commentators of sharply divergent ideological perspectives,"[14] but their efforts serve only to underline the fact that in court, and especially in federal court, the First Amendment entered the twentieth century in a state of intellectual undress, with the judiciary addressing free speech issues, to the extent that the courts addressed them at all, at a level far below that achieved by the Federalists and Republicans of 1798 to 1801.

The primitive nature of judicial thought on free expression on the eve of the Espionage Act is well illustrated by a 1908 decision of the United States Supreme Court, *Patterson v. Colorado*.[15] The defendant in the case, Thomas M. Patterson, was the editor of two newspapers which had attacked a decision of the Colorado Supreme Court and implied that the decision was dictated by partisan political motives. After he was convicted of criminal contempt by the Colorado court, Patterson sought review by the federal Supreme Court claiming, among other arguments, that what his papers had reported was true and that as a consequence his conviction was a violation of the freedom of speech and press guaranteed by the Constitution of the United States. Over two dissents (one on technical grounds), the Supreme Court rejected his argument and refused to interfere with his conviction.

Patterson's argument on the constitutional meaning of free expression, the reader will note, went no further than the interpretation of liberty of the press which William Cushing had proposed to John Adams in 1789, and was fully consistent with the 1798 Sedition Act itself.[16] The Supreme Court's response, in an opinion written by none other than Justice Holmes, basically adopted Blackstone as defining the constitutional meaning of freedom of speech. "[T]he main purpose of such constitutional provisions is 'to prevent all such *previous restraints* upon publications as had been practiced by other governments,'"[17] Holmes asserted, quoting from an 1825 criminal libel decision by the Supreme Judicial Court of Massachusetts, on which Holmes had served for many years before his appointment to the federal high court. In support of this view, which implicitly endorsed the Federalist claim that the Sedition Act had been more protective of free speech than the First Amendment requires, Holmes cited in addition a 1788 state case and Blackstone. His only substantive comment was to confirm what his quotation implied, that the constitutional liberty in question sheltered individual choice about what to say even if it did not prohibit subsequent punishment for the exercise of that liberty.[18] Holmes's opinion simply ignored the debate over the Sedition Act and made no effort to give any rationale for his construction of the amendment. Instead, he treated the First Amendment's language about freedom of speech and press in a woodenly positivist fashion, as a codification of Blackstone. The only hint of any movement beyond Blackstone was Holmes's reference to a ban on prior restraints being the *main* purpose of constitutional guarantees of those freedoms.

As *Patterson* illustrates, the consequence of the Sedition Act's political burial was a century of First Amendment neglect on the part of the mainstream legal tradition. The enactment of the Espionage Act put the question of the First Amendment's meaning back before the legal profession and the courts, but without leading to any serious reconsideration of the arguments of either the Federalists or the Republicans of 1798 to 1800. Some of the briefs filed with the Supreme Court in Espionage Act cases invoked the Republicans' stance, and in particular the name of Jefferson, but the justices seem to have paid little attention. In *Schenck*, indeed, Holmes in speaking for the Court scarcely moved beyond *Patterson*, only reluctantly conceding that "[i]t well may be that the prohibition of laws abridging the freedom of speech is not confined to previous restraints," while insisting that "to prevent them may have been the main purpose, as intimated in *Patterson v. Colorado*."[19] The concession was one the government had already made, without Holmes's evident hesitation, in its brief: the executive's position in all the Espionage Act cases was that the First Amendment, while protecting fair criticism of government officials and measures against subsequent punishment, did not shield incitements to illegal action.[20] In *Abrams*, to be sure, Holmes announced that he "wholly disagree[d] with the argument of the Government that the First Amendment left the common law as to seditious libel in force,"[21] but his statement showed no actual engagement with the history of the 1798 legislation, or for that matter with the government's actual argument, which was more complex than Holmes admitted but which, like Holmes, ignored rather than addressed the 1798 Republican interpretation of the First Amendment.[22]

In its inception, then, modern First Amendment law owed virtually nothing to the founding era's extensive consideration of the meaning of the First Amendment, not because Holmes and his contemporaries weighed the founding-era arguments and found them wanting, but rather because they simply took no interest in those arguments. They were, to be sure, evenhanded in their willed ignorance: the Federalists' sophisticated defense of a Blackstonian interpretation of the amendment received no more attention from the Court or the academic commentators than did the Republican arguments. The result, inevitably, was that the modern First Amendment was built out of purely modern elements, responsive to modern legal concerns. In some sense, of course, this is always true of law: the questions and the assumptions of the day work together to channel even the most creative intellectual response to the problems of the day. In the case of the First Amendment, the consequences are both clear and present.

Ignorant by choice of their founding-era predecessors' thinking, Holmes and his contemporaries thus built a First Amendment in their own image. One consequence was their acceptance of the presupposition that the speech and press clauses of the First Amendment address an issue of individual rights or interests, that the amendment has to do with protecting individuals against certain exercises of governmental power rather than with disabling government from employing a certain power. Holmes's language in *Schenck* makes this clear. In his opinion for the Court in that case, he wrote of the defendants' "constitutional rights" and suggested that the First Amendment inquiry was to ascertain the outer limits of the "protection of free speech"; in *Abrams* he expressly assumed the constitutionality of the Espionage Act and treated the First Amendment issue as one of an individual immunity against liability under the Act. In this respect, Holmes's opinions reflect the same jurisprudential world view Roscoe Pound invoked in an article published a year before the passage of the Espionage Act. In April 1916, Pound (already one of the nation's premier legal scholars) published an article on "Equitable Relief Against Defamation and Injuries to Personality"[23] in which he reviewed the state of the constitutional law of free expression. As the article's title suggests, Pound dealt with the issue in a similar context to that of Blackstone's definition of liberty of the press a century and a half earlier, but Pound's conclusions, although tentative, were critical of Blackstone as an authority on the constitutional issue. Without much discussion, Pound asserted as common ground that "[h]istorically, [the federal and state constitutional] provisions are connected with censorship of publications in England," and that "our bills of rights guarantee freedom of speech and of publication as an individual natural right." He made no mention of the 1798–1800 Republican argument that the First Amendment was different in that it was a denial of power to the federal government as well as a guarantee of an individual liberty.[24]

Pound classed existing thought about "the scope" of the individual right of speech and publication into three "doctrines" which he identified with three famous legal scholars: Blackstone (the constitutional freedom is defined by the absence of prior restraints), Story (such provisions protect the liberty of publishing the truth with good motives and for a proper end) and Thomas Cooley (the freedom involves "complete immunity from legal censure and punishment" unless the expression is harmful in its character). Pound believed that existing case law was "most nearly in accord with [Cooley's] view,"[25] and he argued that Blackstone's position was both too narrow (the usual criticism, as he noted) and too broad. Limiting a guarantee of free speech and press to a ban on prior restraints "proceeds on a formal interpretation of the guarantee that deprives it of substantial efficacy when applied to legislation imposing prohibitive penalties" and thus "restricts the scope of the guarantee too narrowly." At the same time, taking the Blackstone position seriously as a rule of constitutional law would define the personal liberty too widely, at the expense of other important social interests. "Equally it goes too far in denying to the law all power of restraint before publication. . . . [S]o interpreted, [for example,] the constitution would forbid administrative prevention of false labels under a pure food law."[26] Despite his criticism of the Blackstone/*Patterson* view, however, Pound refrained from coming to a settled conclusion, and only suggested that in the absence of language imperatively demanding a Blackstonian reading, either of the other two approaches "might well be" a preferable interpretation of a constitutional guarantee of free expression.[27]

Pound's article interpreted American constitutional provisions guaranteeing freedom of speech and press to protect an individual right—he did not consider the possibility that the First Amendment might be unique in some respect—and he thought it wrong to limit the scope of that individual right to what he believed was its historical, original meaning (the absence of prior restraints). Pound took it for granted that there had to be limitations to the individual rights of speech and press imposed by the existence of other social interests which the legal system ought to recognize and foster, and he assumed that in reasoning about the proper construction of such provisions it was legitimate to consider the consequences of a proposed interpretation. On a fundamental level, he understood the very notion of a constitutional right to be the instantiation of a particular social interest, rightly shaped by legal judgments about its weight, proper scope, and cost. In such a world view, a provision such as the First Amendment makes no sense except and to the extent that it is harmonized with the other concerns of the legal system. Pound's own focus in his article was on the legal system's legitimate interest in protecting personal and intangible interests such as reputation, but the point was a general one, as his reference to labeling under a pure food law showed.

In his 1916 article, Pound was not concerned of course with the 1917 Espionage Act, although the article was periodically invoked during the Congressional and legal arguments over the Act. In 1919, during the interim between the Supreme Court's decisions in *Schenck* and *Abrams*, Pound's colleague Zechariah Chafee, Jr., published an article on "Freedom of Speech in War Time"[28] that expressly dealt with the Espionage Act and focused on the proper interpretation of the speech and press clauses of the First Amendment. There is good reason to think that Justice Holmes read the article and that his opinion in *Abrams* was influenced by Chafee's argument, but for present purposes we need not reach any conclusion on those historical questions.[29] What is important now about Chafee's article is the fact that it expressed the same perspective on First Amendment thought which Holmes held, or came to hold.

Chafee was not neutral or indifferent about the issues he was addressing: he was a dedicated civil libertarian and his goal in the article was to present as powerful an intellectual case as could be made for as speech-protective an interpretation of the First Amendment as he thought plausible. The Espionage Act, in Chafee's opinion, had provoked a crisis in constitutional understanding and constitutional government as profound as that of 1798 (although, like Pound and Holmes, Chafee puzzlingly showed almost no interest in the constitutional arguments of that earlier era). Given his ideological commitments, and his alarm over what he saw as a darkening climate of repression, Chafee had every incentive to interpret the First Amendment as broadly as he could. It is telling, therefore, that he shared much of Pound's fundamental approach, if not all of Pound's terminology or Pound's relatively subdued appreciation for the importance of free expression.

Chafee began his substantive legal argument by "reject[ing] two extreme views in the controversy," the argument that the First Amendment is suspended during wartime, and "the belief of many agitators that the First Amendment renders unconstitutional any Act of Congress without exception 'abridging the freedom of speech, or of the press.'" The government itself, Chafee noted, had repudiated the former view, but the absolutism of the "agitators" was "equally untenable." "The provisions of the Bill of Rights cannot be applied with absolute literalness but are subject to exceptions. . . . The difficulty, of course, is to define the principle on which the implied exceptions are based."[30] It was inconceivable to Chafee that one could resolve the apparent conflict between the command of the First Amendment and the demands of national security by according to either an absolute status: "let us recognize the issue as a conflict between two vital principles, and endeavor to find the basis of reconciliation between order and freedom."[31]

The First Amendment issue was thus, for Chafee, a question of "determin[ing] where the line runs between utterance which is protected by the Constitution from governmental control and that which is not."[32] The text of the amendment does not, of course, provide much assistance in performing this task, and Chafee dismissed any argument that the amendment's original meaning might be controlling. "[T]he meaning of the First Amendment did not crystallize in 1791. The framers would probably have been horrified at the thought of protecting books by Darwin or Bernard Shaw, but 'liberty of speech' is no more confined to the speech they thought permissible than 'commerce' in another clause is limited to the sailing vessels and horse-drawn vehicles of 1787." The task of interpreting the First Amendment was, rather, a matter of understanding what the real issues at stake were, and then devising judicial doctrine or doctrines that would address those issues properly.

Chafee acknowledged that existing case law both before and under the Espionage Act reflected "two mutually inconsistent theories" about the line between protected and unprotected speech, but found them both inadequate. Like Pound, he criticized the Blackstonian no-prior-restraint interpretation as simultaneously too narrow and too broad: "In some respects this theory goes altogether too far in restricting state action," while "it is hardly necessary to argue that the Blackstonian definition gives very inadequate protection" to legitimate speech interests.[33] The argument that the First Amendment protects free speech but not its abuse, which Chafee found to be frequently invoked in the Espionage Act cases, was useless as a practical guide to decision making by a judge confronted with conflicting claims on the part of an individual and the government. "What is abuse? What is license? . . . Saying that the line lies between [use and abuse] gets us nowhere."[34]

Indeed, Chafee thought the very language of "rights," with its overtones of absoluteness, was misleading.

[T]o put the matter another way, it is useless to define free speech by talk about rights. The agitator expresses his constitutional right to speak, the government asserts its constitutional right to wage war. The result is a deadlock . . . To find the boundary line of any right, we must get behind rules of law to human facts. In our problem, we must regard the desires and needs of the individual human being who wants to speak and those of the great group of human beings among whom he speaks. That is, in technical language, there are individual interests and social interests, which must be balanced against each other, if they conflict, in order to determine which interest shall be sacrificed under the circumstances and which shall be protected and become the foundation of a legal right.[35]

It is because of "this necessity of balancing such interests [that] the clauses" of the Constitution protecting individual liberty "cannot be construed with absolute literalness."[36] The proper resolution of free speech claims under the Espionage Act was, therefore, a matter of correctly determining the weight and incidence both of the individual interest in expressing one's opinion and "the social interest in the attainment of truth."[37] The problem with the Espionage Act cases was, ironically, that the judges had so focused their attention on the individual interests of the defendants (which they then concluded "must readily give way like

other personal desires the moment [they] interfere[ ] with the social interest in national security") that they had neglected the social interest in
public discussion, a social interest "especially important in war time."[38]
Applying the correct approach, Chafee argued, the Court was right in
Schenck to uphold the constitutionality of the Espionage Act on its face,
but in individual cases the Act "may have been construed so extremely
as to violate the Amendment" by failing to fix "the boundary line of free
speech . . . close to the point where words will give rise to unlawful
acts."[39] Whether or not Justice Holmes was actually swayed by Chafee's
article, his dissent in *Abrams* echoes many of Chafee's themes and rests
on essentially the same perspective about the relationship between individual rights and governmental powers, a perspective that, to be sure,
Holmes had held as a general jurisprudential matter for many years.
Like Chafee, Holmes was suspicious of the language of rights because of
its potential to mislead. And Holmes too rejected as absurd the notion
that an individual interest or right can be absolute; he regarded it as the
product of a failure to understand that all legal distinctions are matters
of degree. Holmes made the point expressly with reference to a different
constitutional right a few years later: "The great ordinances of the Constitution do not establish and divide fields of black and white. Even the
more specific of them are found to terminate in a penumbra shading
gradually from one extreme to the other. Property must not be taken
without compensation, but . . . some property may be taken or destroyed
for public use without paying for it, if you do not take too much."[40] The
adjudication of claims of constitutional rights was simply a specialized
example of the general judicial role of "weighing considerations of social advantage," which Holmes had long been arguing to be an inevitable duty of the judicial office.[41]

Holmes's *Abrams* dissent discussed the First Amendment in terms
fully consistent with this perspective. He flatly rejected the defendants'
argument that the Espionage Act was itself unconstitutional:[42]

I never have seen any reason to doubt that the questions of law that alone were before this
Court in the Cases of Schenck, Frohwerk, and Debs, were rightly decided. I do not doubt
for a moment that by the same reasoning that would justify punishing persuasion to mur-

der, the United States constitutionally may punish speech that produces or is intended to produce a clear and imminent danger that it will bring about forthwith certain substantive evils that the United States constitutionally may seek to prevent.[43]

In other words, assuming the existence of federal legislative jurisdiction over a given field, Holmes had no doubt of the existence of federal legislative power to punish speech. The actual effect of the First Amendment, as Holmes described it in *Abrams*, was simply to narrow the circumstances in which Congress could use its power over speech. The judicial task in a case in which someone invokes the right of free speech thus becomes one of weighing the urgency of the social need to restrict that speech. Holmes described the urgency required by the First Amendment in strong terms—"Only the emergency that makes it immediately dangerous to leave the correction of evil counsels to time warrants making any exception to the sweeping command, 'Congress shall make no law abridging the freedom of speech.' "[44] But one should not allow Holmes's sweeping rhetoric to obscure the fact that like Pound and Chafee he assumed that the First Amendment protects an individual right, but only up to the point that some other social interest is weighty enough to justify restricting the exercise of the right.

* * *

JUDGE RICHARD A. POSNER, one of the best known legal scholars and judges in recent American history, has written of Justice Holmes that his opinions "laid the foundations . . . for the expansive modern American view of free speech."[45] Posner is right. Early twenty-first century First Amendment doctrine rests on largely unexamined presuppositions that stem directly from the assumptions Holmes consciously employed in developing his view of free speech law. The story of precisely how Holmes's views achieved this dominance will be touched on in the next chapter; for present purposes it is sufficient to restate what presuppositions he bequeathed to subsequent constitutional law. In a Holmesian world, the First Amendment cannot be seen as an absolute prohibition on Congress, but only as a direction to Congress to effect a reconciliation between conflicting interests—the societal (or other) interests expressed through the legislative process and the cross-cutting interests (or "rights") of individuals brought to light through litigation. Despite the amendment's apparently absolute language ("Congress shall make no law"), it is to be enforced by balancing the government's asserted interests against those of the individual invoking the amendment. "The most stringent protection of free speech would not protect a man in falsely shouting fire in a theater, and causing a panic," Justice Holmes wrote, and went on to describe the permissibility of restrictions on speech as requiring judgments about issues of dangerousness—"clear and present danger," "proximity and degree." From this beginning the Court has elaborated a number of tests or patterns of analysis, tailored to different sorts of expression and different forms of restriction. Many of these tests are highly protective of expression; all invite and require a court to attend to the interests of the government in imposing the restriction. However important First Amendment liberties may be, they sensibly can be compared with, weighed against, the values the government is seeking to advance. There is nothing conceptually unique about the First Amendment, and its claims must invariably be measured against the claims of other constitutional provisions and concerns, including (of course) the powers delegated and property rights created by the copyright and patent clause.[46]

CHAPTER 10

Justice Black and the Absolute First Amendment

THE IMPLICATIONS OF THE APPROACH to First Amendment free speech issues adumbrated in Justice Holmes's dissent in *Abrams* remained unclear for some time. In part this was because of Holmes's own uncertainty concerning precisely what it was he was saying about the First Amendment's meaning and application, in part because from *Abrams* until near the very end of Holmes's tenure on the Court, he and Justice Brandeis never found themselves in a majority on the interpretation of freedom of speech. Holmes and Brandeis forged a speech-protective construction of the Constitution not only to protect dissenters but *as* dissenters, and they had neither need nor opportunity to explore the systematic implications of taking the First Amendment seriously as a limitation on governmental power. Their immediate task, and it doubtless seemed enough, was to maintain their claim about the Constitution's solicitude for expression by political dissidents in the teeth of state and federal governments seemingly bent on eliminating "radical" speech.

After 1930, under the new chief justice, Charles Evans Hughes a majority on the Court emerged which was prepared to accept the free-speech views of Holmes and Brandeis. The decade of the 1930s was, of course, a tumultuous and critical period in American constitutional history. Both on the federal and the state levels, legislators and executive officers reacted to the Great Depression in a fury of governmental initiatives, and the Supreme Court in its turn lurched uncertainly from an initial willingness to find accommodations between traditional constitutional norms and novel exercises of power, through a brief but intense negative reaction, to what proved to be a settled acquiescence, after 1937, in a degree of governmental regulation, particularly by the federal government, that was unprecedented. Beneath the surface swings in the Court's decisions, however, there were deeper intellectual trends, trends that clearly contributed to the ultimate resolution of the constitutional controversies without being themselves inextricably linked to substantive constitutional conclusions. One of the most important of these trends was the Court's gradual acceptance of the Holmesian axiom that all legal distinctions are matters of degree and his corollary presupposition that the adjudication of "rights" is necessarily the reconciliation of the countervailing interests and policies at stake in a given controversy.

The intellectual climate in which the Court began building the modern law of the First Amendment is well illustrated by one of the most important constitutional-law decisions of the 1930s, *Home Building & Loan Association v. Blaisdell.*[1] *Blaisdell* upheld the constitutionality of a state statute, enacted in response to the Great Depression, authorizing a court to delay enforcing the terms of a mortgage contract on a showing of hardship. The statute on its face looked like a flagrant violation of the provision of Article I, Section 10 of the Constitution that prohibits the states from enacting "any . . . Law impairing the Obligation of Contracts," and the dissenting justices argued (probably correctly) that the clause was "framed and adopted with the specific and studied purpose of preventing legislation designed to relieve debtors especially in time of financial distress."[2] The Court, however, in an opinion by Chief Justice Hughes, reasoned that the contracts clause must be applied in the light of what Hughes called "a growing appreciation of public needs and of the necessity of finding ground for a rational compromise between individual rights and public welfare."[3] In the majority's view, since the state law worked a reasonable accommodation between the contractual claims of mortgagees and the public interest in mitigating the effects of the Depression, it was constitutional. The apparent absoluteness of the contract clause's language and the arguable clarity of its historical purpose, were not determinative: for the majority it was "beyond question that the prohibition is not an absolute and is not to be read with literal exactness like a mathematical formula."[4]

The 1930s majority on the Court which took up the Holmes and Brandeis stance toward freedom of expression thus was ready to accept the presuppositions undergirding that stance which we discussed in the previous chapter. To be sure, the first cases upholding free speech and press claims did not always use the language of "clear and present danger," but were just as likely to adopt some other brief and formulaic description of the legal rule which follows from the First Amendment's command. One of the most famous of the early decisions, *West Virginia State Board of Education v. Barnette*,[5] appeared to state as an absolute First Amendment rule the principle that "no official, high or petty, can prescribe what shall be orthodox in politics, nationalism, religion, or other matters of opinion or force citizens to confess by word or act their faith therein."[6] But even in *Barnette*, three members of the six-justice majority joined in concurring opinions that put a balancing gloss on the decision,[7] and the other free-expression cases in the 1930s and 1940s followed Holmes (and Pound and Chafee) in stating or implying that the Constitution's protection of free expression is not absolute and that in determining its scope and application courts must take into account other pressing social interests. As an opinion of the Court in 1939 put it, "[a]s cases arise, the delicate and difficult task falls upon the courts to weigh the circumstances and to appraise the substantiality of the reasons advanced in support of the regulation of the free enjoyment of the rights."[8] The fact that the opinion was written by Justice Owen Roberts, one of the Court's intellectual conservatives, is an indicator of the extent to which the Court as a whole was building its nascent law of the First Amendment on Holmesian foundations. The modern First Amendment was off and running along its path to the dead end of *Eldred*.

But not without opposition. Even as a majority of the justices were embedding Holmes's antiabsolutism into the constitutional law of free speech, one justice, Hugo L. Black, was developing an opposing, absolutist understanding of the First Amendment. In later years, Justice Black and his critics sparred over the extent to which Black's mature views were or were not consistent with those he evidenced in his first years on the Court (he was appointed in 1937), but that historical or biographical debate is of little relevance to our discussion. In any event, from an early point Black showed signs of uneasiness with the Holmesian foundations of the Court's developing First Amendment jurisprudence. Writing for the Court in *Bridges v. California*, in 1941 Black described the clear and present danger test as "a working principle." The cases invoking it, according to Black,

do not purport to mark the furthermost constitutional boundaries of protected expression, nor do we here. They do no more than recognize a minimum compulsion of the Bill of Rights. For the First Amendment does not speak equivocally. It prohibits any law "abridging the freedom of speech, or of the press." It must be taken as a command of the broadest scope that explicit language, read in the context of a liberty-loving society, will allow.[9]

Black's language in *Bridges* does not, of course, show any clear break with Holmes, and indeed the last sentence in the passage quoted seems to imply a role for judicial discretion of a Holmesian sort in determining just what the amendment's language requires in the light of society's needs, even if those needs are themselves described in terms ("liberty-loving") favorable to free expression. At the same time, it is clear that Black was already questioning the compatibility of Holmes's presuppositions with the language and mandatory nature of the First Amendment. Within about a decade, his questions were to become certainties, and Black had embarked on a twenty-year career as the advocate on the high court of an "absolute" interpretation of the First Amendment that emphatically rejected Holmes's (and *Blaisdell*'s) sneering attitude toward reading a constitutional prohibition with "literal exactness."[10] Indeed, it was Black's claim that with respect to the First Amendment, literal exactness is exactly what the Constitution requires.

In order to understand fully the origins and significance of Black's First Amendment views, we must first take a short detour into a related but quite distinct constitutional issue, the so-called incorporation debate. As we noted in earlier chapters, when James Madison introduced a set of proposed amendments in the First Congress in 1789, he included one that would have expressly protected liberty of the press against state infringement. That proposal never made its way out of Congress, and as adopted the federal Bill of Rights probably was generally understood to restrain only federal authority, an assumption which the Supreme Court endorsed in 1833.[11] In 1866, however, the nation adopted the Fourteenth Amendment, the first section of which reads in part: "No State shall make or enforce any law which shall abridge the privileges or immunities of citizens of the United States; nor shall any State deprive any person of life, liberty, or property, without due process of law; nor deny to any person within its jurisdiction the equal protection of the laws." There is an argument that the amendment's reference to "privileges and immunities of citizens of the United States" was intended to include the liberties protected by the Bill of Rights, and although the Supreme Court has never endorsed that interpretation, from the end of the nineteenth century onward the justices have wrestled with arguments that one or the other provision of the Bill of Rights is "incorporated" into the liberty protected by the Fourteenth Amendment's due process clause.

In 1897, the Supreme Court held that the Fourteenth Amendment's due process clause protected property from state appropriation without just compensation, a requirement the Fifth Amendment expressly imposes on the federal government, but the early twentieth-century Court's most prominent use of the clause was to protect "freedom of contract," a liberty not mentioned in the Bill of Rights, against what a majority of the Court deemed unreasonable regulation. Justices Holmes and Brandeis were hostile on principle to this use of the clause, since they viewed the freedom of contract cases as wholesale importations into constitutional law of the majority's personal policy preferences, but in the 1920s they reluctantly invoked the same interpretive move as a means of imposing their speech-protective view of the First Amendment on the states.

Brandeis puts it succinctly.

Despite arguments to the contrary which had seemed to me persuasive, it is settled that the due process clause of the Fourteenth Amendment applies to matters of substantive law as well as to matters of procedure. Thus all fundamental rights comprised within the term liberty are protected by the federal Constitution from invasion by the states. The right of free speech, the right to teach and the right of assembly are, of course, fundamental rights.[12]

Even as it resisted the substantive interpretation of constitutional free speech Holmes and Brandeis proposed, the Court majority of the 1920s accepted, with surprising alacrity, their argument that freedom of speech is an aspect of Fourteenth Amendment liberty, and the speech-protective majority of the following decade naturally followed suit, even after the Court's repudiation, in 1937, of the practice of protecting freedom of contract through the Fourteenth Amendment.[13]

Black did not at first question the Court's continued use of Fourteenth Amendment liberty to protect free expression and certain other personal rights, although as a fervent New Dealer he had been a harsh critic of the Court's freedom of contract jurisprudence. During the 1940s, however, Black came to reject the Court's approach to interpreting the Fourteenth Amendment, regarding it as an illegitimate perpetuation, even if for other policy goals, of the pre-1937 majority's error. The new majority endorsed at once the "old" Court's rejection of the argument that the Fourteenth Amendment incorporated all of the Bill of Rights; only those provisions of the first eight amendments that are truly fundamental are incorporated. "If the Fourteenth Amendment has absorbed them, the process of absorption has had its source in the belief that neither liberty nor justice would exist if they were sacrificed."[14] This rationale, furthermore, allowed the possibility that the Fourteenth Amendment would protect only the core of the liberty guaranteed by the corresponding Bill of Rights provision rather than the entirety of the federal right, a possibility which Holmes had expressly noted with respect to free speech.[15] And finally, as became clear during the 1940s, the Court's approach allowed for the further possibility that the Fourteenth Amendment could be employed to protect liberties with no textual root in the Bill of Rights at all, in exactly the same fashion as the "old" Court had protected freedom of contract.

From Black's perspective, each step in this progression appeared (or had come to appear) to be an error, and in the end the same error: it was the *Court*, not the Constitution, which would decide what rights were so fundamental that "neither liberty nor justice would exist" in their absence. The Court was claiming the duty—but a duty that is in practice a power—to choose among liberties written down in the Bill of Rights, to distinguish "within" those written provisions what was truly fundamental and what was secondary, and even to promote to equality with Bill of Rights liberties rights with no footing in the language of the Constitution at all. Of necessity, then, it was not the constitutional text that would control the Court's decisions, but the discretion—or rather the policy preferences—of the justices themselves:

> To hold that the Fourteenth Amendment was intended to and did provide protection from state invasions of the right of free speech and other clearly defined protections contained in the Bill of Rights, is quite different from holding that "due process," an historical expression relating to procedure, confers a broad judicial power to invalidate all legislation which seems "unreasonable" to courts. In the one instance, courts proceeding within clearly marked constitutional boundaries seek to execute policies written into the Constitution; in the other they roam at will in the limitless area of their own beliefs as to reasonableness and actually select policies, a responsibility which the Constitution entrusts to the legislative representatives of the people.[16]

For Black, the fundamental error in the Court's arrogation to itself of such a power, whether employed to frustrate economic regulations or to protect personal liberty, lay in its unfaithfulness to the Court's sole legitimate function, that of upholding the commands of the Constitution. "To hold that this Court can determine what, if any, provisions of the Bill of Rights will be enforced, and if so to what degree, is to frustrate the great design of a written Constitution."[17] The Court's use of what Black mocked as an extratextual "natural law," consisting of what a majority of justices thought liberty and justice might entail, subverted the truly fundamental constitutional proposition that the Constitution is supreme law for the judiciary as much as for the rest of government and, as such, was "itself a violation of our Constitution."[18] Furthermore, Black concluded, the practical effect of substituting judicial discretion for constitutional text was likely in the long run to be a judicially sanctioned contraction of the liberties the Constitution was meant to safeguard.[19]

Black did not conclude from this analysis of the majority's understanding of the relationship between the Fourteenth Amendment and provisions of the Bill of Rights such as the First Amendment that the Court ought to renounce its earlier decisions holding that freedom of speech and press are protected against state abridgment. Instead, as he announced in *Adamson v. California* in 1947, Black believed that the Court should treat the Fourteenth Amendment as incorporating all of the Bill of Rights, and making every provision of the Bill fully enforceable against state interference just as the original amendments did against federal, while according the judiciary no power to enforce non-textual notions of liberty or justice. Black justified this position with the historical assertion that "the original purpose of the Fourteenth Amendment [was] to extend to all the people of the nation the complete protection of the Bill of Rights,"[20] but his *Adamson* opinion also made it clear that he believed his total incorporation approach was superior to the Court's because it avoided the vice of judicial choice in favor of the judicial virtue of adherence to the text of the Constitution. It was just as important, from a jurisprudential perspective, that total incorporation limited the Court to enforcing the Bill of Rights as that it required the Court to do so.[21]

Only one other justice fully agreed with Black's argument in *Adamson*,[22] and thereafter Black was never able to persuade the Court to adopt the total incorporation solution to the problem of how to relate the Bill of Rights to the Fourteenth Amendment. But Black remained committed to this view, and in the 1960s, the Court bit by bit held virtually all of the Bill of Rights guarantees applicable to the states through the Fourteenth Amendment in the same manner they apply to the federal government, thus accomplishing (most of) Black's goal through the use of the means he rejected.[23] Despite his ostensible failure to win the incorporation debate, by his continued and consistent advocacy of total incorporation Black shaped in far-reaching ways the conclusions the Court as a whole was willing to accept.

We are now in a position to return to our consideration of Justice Black's absolutist interpretation of the First Amendment, for that interpretation was driven by the same concerns and shaped by the same considerations as his approach to the incorporation issue. Black himself occasionally alluded to the relationship in his thinking between the two issues. Not all of the provisions of the Bill of Rights are framed in parallel terms, and Black acknowledged that fidelity to interpreting the

Constitution's text involves, among other obligations, a need to recognize the distinctive attributes of the particular provision under scrutiny. In *Rochin v. California* (an early incorporation opinion), Black therefore drew a distinction between two different sorts of constitutional text.

Some constitutional provisions are stated in absolute and unqualified language such, for illustration, as the First Amendment stating that no law shall be passed prohibiting the free exercise of religion or abridging the freedom of speech or press. Other constitutional provisions do require courts to choose between competing policies, such as the Fourth Amendment which, by its terms, necessitates a judicial decision as to what is an "unreasonable" search or seizure.[24]

In both cases a court acting appropriately would be guided by standards expressed by the text, and so even in applying the latter category, Black insisted, the justices are not free "to invalidate every state law of every kind deemed 'unreasonable' or contrary to the Court's notion of civilized decencies":[25] the text of the Fourth Amendment defines the circumstances as to which the amendment requires, and thus empowers, the judiciary to determine reasonability. But with respect to a text such as the First Amendment stated in absolute terms, fidelity to the text demands an even more circumscribed exercise of judgment. Unlike the Fourth Amendment, the First Amendment's text asks courts not to resolve a conflict between "competing policies" but to enforce the precise resolution embedded in the language of the amendment, neither curtailing nor (less likely, Black thought) overextending the amendment's scope as defined by its words.

One of the first cases in which Black clearly articulated his absolutist reading of the First Amendment was the Court's 1952 decision in *Beauharnais v. Illinois*.[26] The defendant in *Beauharnais* had been convicted of violating a state statute that in essence made it a crime to libel any racial or religious group, by distributing a circular petitioning the Chicago municipal government to prevent further "encroachment" by black people on white people. Beauharnais challenged his conviction on the ground that the statute violated constitutionally protected freedom of expression. Justice Felix Frankfurter's opinion for the majority rejected this claim on two distinct grounds. First, Frankfurter insisted that libelous utterances are not "within the area of constitutionally protected speech"; the explanation for this definitional limitation on the scope of the constitutional right was that "such utterances are no essential part of any exposition of ideas, and are of such slight social value as a step to truth that any benefit that may be derived from them is clearly outweighed by the social interest in order and morality."[27] In any event, Frankfurter further reasoned, "[t]here are limits to the exercise of these liberties (of speech and of the press)," and it "would deny experience to say that the Illinois legislature was without reason in seeking ways to curb false or malicious defamation of racial and religious groups, made in public places and by means calculated to have a powerful emotional impact on those to whom it was presented."[28] Even viewed as a restriction on constitutionally significant expression, the state's group libel law was justified by the importance of the social concerns the legislature was addressing. In reaching this conclusion, Frankfurter assured the reader that legitimate expression was in no way at risk. " 'While this Court sits' it retains and exercises authority to nullify action which encroaches on freedom of utterance under the guise of punishing libel. Of course discussion cannot be denied and the right, as well as the duty, of criticism must not be stifled."[29]

For Black in dissent, Frankfurter's opinion was a perfect illustration of the consequences of attempting to decide a free speech or press claim other than by applying the language of the First Amendment.[30] The circular in question, Black pointed out, undeniably incorporated a call on the (municipal) government to respond to the complaints of Beauharnais and his associates: in short, it was quite literally within the language of the First Amendment about "the right of the people . . . to petition the Government for a redress of grievances:"[31] As he continued, "[w]ithout distortion, this First Amendment could not possibly be read so as to hold that Congress has power to punish Beauharnais and others for petitioning Congress as they have here sought to petition the Chicago authorities."[32] But instead of a straightforward application of the First Amendment's "unequivocal command," the Court had imposed its own interests-balancing judgment, both to define the scope of what speech deserves any protection at all and to evaluate—and uphold—a statute abridging expression. The Court's approach, Black argued, patently converted freedom of speech and press from a right enjoyed by constitutional command into a privilege subject to any restrictions that a majority of the justices found appropriate. For Black, Frankfurter's smug invocation of the Court as the ultimate safeguard of free expression merely confirmed Black's claim that the majority's approach exalted the justices' own discretion over the Constitution they were supposed to serve.

We are told that freedom of petition and discussion are in no danger "while this Court sits." This case raises considerable doubt. Since those who peacefully petition for changes in the law are not to be protected "while this Court sits," who is? I do not agree that the Constitution leaves freedom of petition, assembly, speech, press or worship at the mercy of a case-by-case, day-by-day majority of this Court. I had supposed that our people could rely for their freedom on the Constitution's commands, rather than on the grace of this Court on an individual case basis. To say that a legislative body can, with this Court's approval, make it a crime to petition for and publicly discuss proposed legislation seems as farfetched to me as it would be to say that a valid law could be enacted to punish a candidate for President for telling the people his views. I think the First Amendment, with the Fourteenth, "absolutely" forbids such laws without any "ifs" or "buts" or "whereases." Whatever the danger, if any, in such public discussions, it is a danger the Founders deemed outweighed by the danger incident to the stifling of thought and speech. The Court does not act on this view of the Founders. It calculates what it deems to be the danger of public discussion, holds the scales are tipped on the side of state suppression, and upholds state censorship. This method of decision offers little protection to First Amendment liberties "while this Court sits."[33]

Although reflection and later cases led Black to work out various details, the core of his absolutist interpretation of the First Amendment can already be seen in *Beauharnais*. At the heart of that interpretation was a particular view of the importance of the text of the Constitution, and as a result Black's absolutism was (and is) sometimes misunderstood as a simplistic literalism—a misconstruction that Black himself encouraged by puckish references to "being a rather backward country fellow [who] understand[s] it to mean what the words say."[34] In fact, however, as the relationship between his views on incorporation and his First Amendment absolutism suggests, Black's insistence on the primacy of the constitutional text stemmed from a sophisticated concern about the function of a written Constitution, the role of the judiciary in our constitutional system, and the consequences of judicial review based not on the Constitution's language but on extratextual abstractions.[35] The very point of having a written Constitution was to subject government to the rule of a fundamental law beyond the legitimate authority of government to flout: "since government . . . is a powerful institution, its officials—*all of them*—must be compelled to exercise their powers within strictly defined boundaries."[36] While Black fully accepted the importance of judicial review to the enforcement of the Constitution (and was a harsh critic of the view that the Court should avoid reaching constitutional questions whenever possible), he was insistent that the Constitution's constraining force applied no less to judges than to any other governmental officials. "[T]he Founders wrote into our Constitution their unending fear of granting too much power to judges,"[37] primarily by creating a system in which the only judicial power to overturn legislative or executive action stems from the judicial duty to interpret and obey the (written) law of the Constitution. "The courts are given power to interpret the Constitution and laws, which means to explain and expound, not to alter, amend, or remake."[38]

The fundamental objective of restraining *all* of government by a written Constitution, Black repeatedly pointed out, necessarily assumes that words have meaning, that it is in fact possible to write constitutional provisions that can be understood and applied through legitimate acts of interpretation, and that there is a difference between construing constitutional language to decide a controversy and using it as an excuse for announcing whatever resolution commends itself most to the "interpreter." If text-bound constitutional interpretation is inevitably an illusion or a sham, then the whole project of the American founders rests on a basic error, a conclusion that Black believed implicit in the criticisms of his absolutism on and off the Court, although one that for obvious reasons the critics were unwilling to acknowledge or perhaps even to recognize. But Black was untroubled by the charge that the absolutist approach is simplistic.[39] In addition to leaving the critic without a clear explanation of the difference between constitutional law based on a written instrument and the British sort of customary constitutionalism,[40] nihilism about text-bound interpretation undermines the only legitimate basis for judicial review, the judiciary's capacity to assert that it is invalidating legislative or executive action on the basis not of the judges' contrary preferences (or views about justice, liberty, and so on) but on the strength of the written and supreme law. And on the most fundamental of levels, in Black's view, the self-proclaimed sophistication of his critics was contrary to the assumptions underlying all verbal communication.[41] The real force driving the criticisms of absolutism, Black believed, was the critics' dislike of the consequences of following it.

It is clear that Black did not think that an insistence on the primacy of the text in constitutional interpretation made that task easy in every circumstance. As we earlier saw in his *Rochin* opinion, precisely because Black was a textualist, he was not an absolutist on the interpretation of every provision of the Constitution: the individual provision's text indicates whether it requires the interpreter to make a judgment about the weight of conflicting interests (think again of the Fourth Amendment's ban on "unreasonable" searches and seizures) or issues an unequivocal command. Even when (as with the First Amendment) a provision is absolute in its terms, Black conceded that there can be difficulty and honest disagreement over what matters properly fall within the sphere of the provision's words. Invoking the disagreement on the Court over whether "obscene" expression is constitutionally protected, for example, Black referred to the "complex problem of the marginal scope of each individual amendment as applied to the particular facts of particular cases."[42] But that question, Black insisted, is "wholly different" from the issue of how a court should apply an absolute Bill of Rights provision to a liberty admitted to be within the provision's scope. In the latter situation, Black insisted, there can be no room for disagreement:

If the Constitution withdraws from Government all power over subject matter in an area, such as religion, speech, press, assembly, and petition, there is nothing over which authority may be exerted. . . . [T]here is, at least in those areas, no justification whatever for "balancing" a particular right against some expressly granted power of Congress. . . .

[P]rotecting speech and press may involve dangers to a particular government. [The founders] appreciated the risks involved and they decided that certain rights should be guaranteed regardless of these risks. Courts have neither the right nor the power to review this original decision of the Framers and to attempt to make a different evaluation of the importance of the rights granted in the Constitution.[43]

The "First Amendment's unequivocal command that there shall be no abridgment of the rights of free speech and assembly shows that the men who drafted our Bill of Rights did all the 'balancing' that was to be done in this field."[44] Any judicial intervention beyond enforcing the resolution of conflicting interests struck in the provision itself is an exercise of illegitimate and unconstitutional power.

On the other side of the coin, Black often insisted that judicial deviation from the courts' proper function of interpreting and applying the text of the First Amendment puts both political democracy and individual freedom at risk: both require protection from the penchant of temporary majorities, acting out of self-aggrandizement or fear, to use governmental power to suppress opponents and prevent (or punish) political "error." The transmogrification of the First Amendment from an absolute into a judicial weighing of the interests misreads "the First Amendment to say 'Congress shall make no law abridging freedom of speech, press, assembly and petition, unless Congress and the Supreme Court reach the joint conclusion that on balance the interest of the Government in stifling these freedoms is greater than the interest of the people in having them exercised.' " But beyond that, the result is likely to be a failure to take into account "the real interest" in the individual's First Amendment freedoms, "the interest of the people as a whole in being able to join organizations, advocate causes, and make political 'mistakes' without later being subjected to governmental penalties for having dared to think for themselves."[45] Judicial interference, in the name of free expression, with legislative or executive action not in fact within the scope of the First Amendment's text threatens democracy from the other direction, by substituting rule by judges for government by electorally responsible officials.

As with his advocacy of the total incorporation thesis, Justice Black did not succeed at any point in persuading the Court to adopt his absolutist interpretation of the First Amendment. Even colleagues as committed to broad protection for free expression such as Chief Justice Earl Warren and Justice William Brennan were unwilling to adopt the absolutist interpretation, in part perhaps because they were unwilling to accept the limitations on constitutional protection of expressive conduct which Black insisted were part of the logic of the position.[46] Justices more inclined to accept governmental arguments about the need for some restriction or the other on expression were even more hostile to absolutism, with Frankfurter as Black's most sustained judicial critic until the former's retirement in 1962. The weight of academic commentary, much of it written by disciples or former students of Frankfurter, was against what Dean Erwin Griswold derided as Black's "'Fundamentalist' approach" to judging.[47] And yet in 1967, the distinguished constitutional scholar Paul A. Freund (a professor at Frankfurter's and Griswold's Harvard), wrote, with Black's approach to the First Amendment largely although not exclusively in view, that Black "is without doubt the most influential of the many strong figures who have sat during the thirty years that have passed in his Justiceship."[48] Although Freund himself was a critic, albeit a moderate one, of Black's absolutism, his evaluation rested on his recognition of the "cumulative moral force" that Black's consistency had exerted on the Court's decisions.

As with the incorporation controversy, where Black's ostensible failure to persuade his colleagues had eventually been paralleled by the Court's substantive adoption of most of the specific implications of his argument, so with respect to the First Amendment. The constant presence of Black's absolutism on the Court from *Beauharnais* on ensured that the majority's compromises with governmental regulation or suppression of radical speech in the 1950s never escaped identification and critique, and that during the more receptive 1960s the Court moved very far toward Black's substantive positions on important issues, including the proper First Amendment treatment of defamation and of seditious speech. At least with respect to allegedly libelous speech involving public officials or affairs, Black's consistent view was that such speech was plainly within the scope of the First Amendment, and thus that laws imposing criminal or civil liability for it were unconstitutional. In 1964, the Supreme Court decided in *New York Times v. Sullivan* that the First Amendment, as fully incorporated into the Fourteenth, severely circumscribed the states' power to award damages to public officials, effecting a far-reaching and dramatic reworking of the tort laws of all fifty states in the name of the Constitution. There were no dissents.[49] And in *Brandenburg v. Ohio*, in 1969, the Court quietly repudiated the language of clear and present danger, hallowed in First Amendment tradition because of its early use by Holmes and Brandeis but long rejected by Black, as the First Amendment standard for dealing with speech advocating unlawful action. Once again, no justice dissented.[50]

Perhaps the most striking example of Black's influence on the substance of the law of the First Amendment can be found in the last opinion he ever wrote. In *New York Times v. United States*, the famous Pentagon Papers case decided in June 1971, the executive branch sought an injunction against the publication of documents which, it submitted, would compromise American security interests and intelligence operations. The reader will recognize that the case presented once again the question whether the government ever may curtail expression plainly within the scope of the First Amendment, but on this occasion with a plausible argument that the government's position was supported by the extraordinarily weighty public interest in national security. Arguing for the executive, the solicitor general—who was none other than Black's prominent critic Erwin Griswold—portrayed the case not as one in which he was asking the Court to place the executive's policy preference above free speech, but rather as involving the issue of how to construe the Constitution as a whole. Griswold insisted that as a result the Court could not properly decide the case by looking narrowly at the First Amendment alone. "There are other parts of the Constitution that grant powers and responsibilities to the Executive, and . . . the First

Amendment was not intended to make it impossible for the Executive to function or to protect the security of the United States."[51] However, by a six-to-three margin, the Court rejected Griswold's arguments and held that the First Amendment forbade the judiciary from granting the executive the prior restraints it sought.

The judgment of the Court was announced in a brief per curiam (unsigned) opinion that cited earlier cases stating that "[t]he Government thus carries a heavy burden of showing justification for the imposition of such a restraint" and then simply asserted, without explanation, that "the Government had not met that burden."[52] This formulation was plainly a compromise, and each of the six justices in the majority filed a separate concurrence. It is clear from Justice Black's that, as one would expect, he did not in fact agree with the per curiam's invocation of a less than absolute view of the First Amendment's meaning. Instead, at the very end of his career, Black had the opportunity to restate his absolutist position with respect to the one substantive question about which there was no known disagreement in the founding generation: the validity under the First Amendment of prior restraints on the press. As we saw in an earlier chapter, Federalists and Republicans alike agreed in 1798 and after that the amendment denied any power to the federal government to impose such restraints. In 1971, Black made it clear that he believed that this historical core to the First Amendment remained valid and mandatory.

I adhere to the view that the Government's case against the *Washington Post* should have been dismissed and that the injunction against the *New York Times* should have been vacated without oral argument when the cases were first presented to this Court. I believe that every moment's continuance of the injunctions against these newspapers amounts to a flagrant, indefensible, and continuing violation of the First Amendment.

In seeking injunctions against these newspapers and in its presentation to the Court, the Executive Branch seems to have forgotten the essential purpose and history of the First Amendment. . . . The [first ten] amendments were offered to curtail and restrict the general powers granted to the Executive, Legislative, and Judicial Branches two years before in the original Constitution. The Bill of Rights changed the original Constitution into a new charter under which no branch of government could abridge the people's freedoms of press, speech, religion, and assembly. Yet the Solicitor General argues and some members of the Court appear to agree that the general powers of the Government adopted in the original Constitution should be interpreted to limit and restrict the specific and emphatic guarantees of the Bill of Rights adopted later. I can imagine no greater perversion of history. Madison and the other Framers of the First Amendment, able men that they were, wrote in language they earnestly believed could never be misunderstood: "Congress shall make no law . . . abridging the freedom . . . of the press . . . ." Both the history and language of the First Amendment support the view that the press must be left free to publish news, whatever the source, without censorship, injunctions, or prior restraints.[53]

Solicitor General Griswold's argument, in other words, turned the original history of the First Amendment upside down: instead of treating the amendment, as its language and its origins require, as a restraint on the powers granted by the original text of the Constitution, Griswold wanted the Court to use the powers granted in 1787–88 to adjust, by judicial fiat but in what the executive deemed a socially valuable fashion, the denial of power adopted in 1789–91. In a quietly sardonic footnote, Black invited his reader to "[c]ompare the views of the Solicitor General with those of James Madison," who had assured Congress that the courts would be "an impenetrable bulwark against every assumption of power in the Legislative or Executive."[54] For Black, the Pentagon Papers case was one last opportunity to make the point that there is a difference between the judiciary acting as a bulwark against the assumption of power, and the courts "tak[ing] it upon themselves to 'make' a law abridging freedom of the press" by creating exceptions in power's favor to the First Amendment's command.[55] He could measure his success and his failure in teaching this lesson by the fact that by his lights the Court came to the right conclusion through the votes of justices who themselves rejected his reasoning.[56]

* * *

WITH THE RETIREMENTS OF JUSTICE BLACK in 1971 and Justice Douglas in 1975, the Supreme Court's membership has consisted entirely of justices who give the First Amendment a nonabsolute interpretation. In the opinion of most constitutional scholars this is as it should and indeed as it must be, for the majority view is that Black's absolutism is both undesirable and, in the final analysis, unworkable. On the level of results, as the critics (correctly) observe, Black's approach leaves unprotected much expressive behavior, despite the negative impact on civil-libertarian values, while disabling government from constraining expression certain to cause catastrophic harm. To be workable, furthermore, Black's absolutism involves line drawing that is complicated and may not even make a great deal of sense. For example, Black sharply distinguished (protected) "speech" and (unprotected) "conduct," a dichotomy that is difficult to apply in many circumstances: is burning a United States flag in order to express a political view "speech" protected by the First Amendment or "conduct" subject to regulation? (Black thought it conduct and subject to prohibition; in 1989 the Supreme Court held it to be expression protected by the free speech clause.)[57] Black himself further complicated his approach by according First Amendment protection to some "conduct"[58] while refusing to protect speech when "it is so closely brigaded with illegal action as to be an inseparable part of it."[59] The apparent simplicity of Black's absolutism, in the words of the distinguished civil libertarian Henry J. Abraham, is in fact "[d]eceptive" and any workable and coherent interpretation of the First Amendment "necessarily" requires "balancing between individual and societal prerogatives and responsibilities."[60]

In this book we do not intend to resolve the question whether Justice Black's critics are right in attacking his First Amendment absolutism as unmanageable and internally inconsistent.[61] We are, rather, immediately interested in certain aspects of his First Amendment jurisprudence that are usually not in focus, and (as the reader will see in later chapters) in the possibility that Black's absolutism can be appropriately and consistently restated, in terms he himself only hinted at, in the contemporary interpretation and application of the First Amendment. Our first observation is that Black's colleagues never squarely responded to the claim at the heart of his insistence on fidelity to the text of the First Amendment—that only by absolute textual fidelity could the Court enforce the First Amendment as a prohibition on government without implicitly treating it as a delegation of power to one branch of government (the judiciary) to make what are inevitably policy judgments about the relative value of expression and other (claimed) social interests. The Pentagon Papers case nicely illustrates the point. If we take them at their word, the Federalists and the Republicans of the Sedition Act crisis would have had little trouble in concluding, as did Justice Black, that the First Amendment simply forbade the imposition of a prior restraint on a publication of the sort at issue. While they disagreed vehemently over the amendment's relevance to postpublication penalties, such as those ordained by the Sedition Act itself, they shared the view that the amendment banned attempts by the government to decide before publication whether the public good would be served if the papers should print something. With the exception of Justices Black and Douglas, however, every justice on the *New York Times* Court believed that the First Amendment permits precisely such an exercise of discretion, ultimately by the Supreme Court itself in its exercise of the power of judicial review.[62]

To be sure, the nonabsolutist justices' assumption of the power to determine when the social calculus permits a prior restraint is the inevitable corollary to their adherence to the Holmesian presuppositions that govern the modern law of constitutional free speech. Here too, however, Justice Black's absolutism poses a question to the majority position on the First Amendment that we do not believe has been answered so much as it has been assumed away. Modern thought about constitutional issues, as we discussed in an earlier chapter, is generally allergic to anything resembling an absolute rule. But there is nothing self-evidently correct, and in fact something rather peculiar as an historical matter, in the assumption that because Justice Holmes brought his early-twentieth-century interest-balancing understanding of "rights" to the First Amendment, modern interpretation of that eighteenth-century amendment must "necessarily" proceed along Holmesian lines. At this point in the Court's elaboration of what is now a vast body of free-expression case law, there is clearly a significant argument to be made that it would be too disruptive simply to toss out this case law in its entirety and start over on some other basis. But Black's formulation of a twentieth-century alternative to Holmes raises the issue of whether there should be limits to the dominance granted to the Holmesian paradigm.

A third aspect of Black's absolutism is related to but in a sense the reverse of that just mentioned. In one respect, Black generally followed Holmes: for the most part Black conceptualized the First Amendment as a guarantee of certain individual liberties or rights—in other words, as parallel (in this respect) to, say, the Sixth Amendment, which begins with the words "In all criminal prosecutions, the accused shall enjoy the right. . . ." As a syntactical matter, of course, the First Amendment begins quite differently, with a command to Congress about what powers it shall not exercise ("Congress shall make no law"); and in an earlier chapter we pointed out that founding-era constitutionalists sometimes treated the amendment as a provision respecting governmental power rather than as a guarantee of individual liberty. Black himself not infrequently referred to the First Amendment in this fashion as well,[63] and he believed that there was "a crucially important distinction" between "those areas where government [is] not to act at all and those areas where it [is] to act only in a particular manner."[64] But Black never systematically explored the possibility that more could be at stake in the distinction between a denial of power and the guarantee of a right than a simple choice of phraseology.

Finally, Black's approach to the First Amendment suggests intriguing issues about how to deploy fundamental constitutional modalities of interpretation in applying the First Amendment.[65] As we have seen, Black's absolutism, far from being a simplistic idolization of the amendment's words, was grounded in a sophisticated linking of normative views about the role of the judiciary with reflections on the assumptions implicit in the creation of constitutional texts as well as with a (quite underdeveloped) historical claim about the First Amendment's origins. Modern First Amendment law, in contrast, is focused almost entirely on doctrinal concerns about the Supreme Court's case law and on prudential arguments about the consequences of particular decisions. While Black was by no means oblivious to doctrine, and frequently invoked prudential worries about threats to freedom of expression in defense of his positions, the influence his absolutist views exercised even without being accepted by the Court indicates the possible value of examining once again the role of text, structure, and history for the light they might shed on how to avoid the conundrum of *Eldred*: a powerful First Amendment that is essentially helpless in the face of intellectual property's massive invasion of the realm of free expression.

PART IV

The Absolute First Amendment Revisited:
The Amendment as a Prohibition on Power

CHAPTER II

Constitutional Absolutes in
a Holmesian World

JUSTICE BLACK FAILED. Despite the force of his repeated admonition that the First Amendment says "Congress shall make *no* law," not that it shall refrain from making some laws; despite the verbal congruence between his absolutism and that of founding-era constitutionalists including James Madison; despite the fact that Black's colleagues increasingly came to adopt his speech-protective outcomes as their own and even, arguably, at times to go beyond the master himself; despite all of this, Hugo Black failed, both as a formal matter and in terms of the working presuppositions of First Amendment doctrine. Black pushed the Court toward an increasingly sensitive appreciation of the constitutional value of free expression; but that is, in a sense, precisely what he did not want to do—to encourage the justices to see the First Amendment as an invitation, or even a command, for the Court to assign an appropriate value to expression. For Black, the First Amendment was a denial of power to all parts of government, including the Court, to engage in any such evaluation. But the Court and the legal profession generally, wedded as they were and are to the assumptions Holmes built into free speech law at its modern inception, have been able to make sense of this only as a hyperbolic way of insisting that the value of expression generally ought to be assigned a high value in the constitutional calculus.

This has been true, for the most part, even of sympathetic readers of Justice Black's absolutism. In a 1961 article discussing Justice Black's contribution to First Amendment law, Professor Charles L. Black, Jr., a leading academic lawyer and a strong proponent of vigorous First Amendment protection for speech, wrote that

taken literally, Mr. Justice Black is wrong. No right, however defined, ever turns out to be really "absolute," if you think about it long enough. Take torture.

General immunity from being tortured is something all of us would regard as an essential of civilized life. We might carelessly refer to it as an "absolute." But what if an atom bomb were ticking somewhere in the city, and the roads were closed and trains were not running, and the man who knew where the bomb was hidden sat grinning and silent in a chair at the country police station twenty miles away? Could the "absolute right" not to be tortured really prevail? . . . There are no absolutes, not even in the construction of the word "absolute" when it is used by a sensible man.[1]

The constitutional protection of individual liberties, in other words, is invariably circumscribed both by the definitions we give to a given liberty and by the possibility that exigent social need will make respecting the liberty too costly to endure in a particular situation. While we suspect that Professor Black's own absolute assertion that there are no absolutes was a slight exaggeration (are there any circumstances imaginable in which Congress could prescribe a theological creed?), his article was an unusually candid statement of the Holmesian presupposition about the nature of individual rights (a presupposition the influence of which runs throughout modern constitutional-rights decisions), that "rights" are in practice that area of freedom remaining after judges have determined the relative weights of the interests of the individual and society. Even if the text and early understanding of the First Amendment indicate an absolutist reading of the speech and press clauses, such a reading contradicts a fundamental assumption of the modern Court's deeply *non*-absolutist view of individual rights. It will repay us to spend a little time considering the shape of that understanding of constitutional liberty.

A court exercising the power of judicial review under the United States Constitution always has one or more provisions of the constitutional text before it.[2] This emphatically does not mean that the only legitimate form of constitutional argument consists of narrowly textual observations about the Constitution's wording, but it does suggest that it is fruitful to think about constitutional argument in terms of its relationship to the different types of provisions found in the document. Broadly speaking and as we now understand the matter, the Constitution's clauses can be grouped into three distinct categories: structural provisions, delegations of power, and guarantees of individual liberty.[3] Structural provisions address issues of the denial to a governmental institution of some power, of the separation of powers within government, of the processes by which the institutions and offices of the federal government are created and operate, and other matters involving interaction between governmental entities, including the pervasive distinction between the federal and state governments. Delegations of power convey the substantive grants of power the Constitution vests in the three branches of the federal government. Guarantees of individual liberty create personal privileges and immunities against the exercise of otherwise valid federal or state power. Any action by any part of the federal government must accord with all relevant provisions in each category: it must satisfy the requirements of the Constitution's structural provisions; it must stem, immediately or derivatively, from a grant of power found in the Constitution; and it must not violate any of the guarantees of individual liberty.[4] The First Amendment, as it is currently understood and applied by the courts, is a guarantee (or rather set of guarantees) of individual liberty.

In the founding era, it was sometimes reasoned that the power-granting and liberty-protecting provisions give rise to mutually exclusive conceptual domains—if an action is authorized by a provision granting power it is by definition not a violation of a provision protecting liberty, whereas an unconstitutional invasion of a protected liberty is by definition unauthorized by any provision delegating power. This understanding was contested from the beginning, however, and modern constitutional law emphatically rejects it. Under the current (and long-standing) view, individual liberties protected by the Constitution exist, as it were, on a different plane or level from the Constitution's grants of power to the federal government.[5] The rights safeguarded by the Bill of Rights and other liberty-protecting provisions address possible actions by government that are *within* the scope of the government's affirmative authority. (A federal action that is not affirmatively authorized, or which violates a structural provision, is unconstitutional regardless of whether it invades a protected liberty.) Conflict between constitutional rights and constitutional powers, rather than being a conceptual impossibility, is on the modern view a logical corollary of what rights-protecting provisions exist to do.

To say this, however, is not to answer the question of how to resolve such a conflict. Being part of the Constitution, provisions protecting individual rights share of course in the Constitution's status as "the supreme Law of the Land," and as such American courts treat them as requiring judicial enforcement even in the teeth of a statutory command to the contrary.[6] Automatically giving effect to a constitutional grant of power in the event of conflict with a constitutionally protected liberty would seem to undermine the liberty provision's status as law, and no modern court would seriously entertain such an argument. But modern constitutional law has also almost universally rejected the diametrically opposite approach—automatically giving effect to the provision protecting liberty—as well. As many beginning constitutional-law students learn each year to their surprise and dismay, there are very few absolute rights in United States constitutional law.[7] Neither constitutional liberties nor constitutional powers are, generally speaking, unlimited, and as a result modern constitutional-law doctrines almost invariably involve some sort of balancing between the governmental power(s) involved in a given conflict and the individual right or rights at issue. The implications of this general mindset for working out the relationship between the First Amendment and intellectual property are enormous.

Most contemporary constitutional lawyers probably see the notion of absolute rights, generally speaking, as naive and unworkable. From Holmes on it has been increasingly a commonplace that legal distinctions are all matters of degree, that legal controversies all involve questions of competing interests, that any intelligent resolution of a genuinely contestable issue requires a careful examination of the relative scope and importance of the claims on each side of the dispute. The black-and-white conceptualism attributed (sometimes inaccurately) to nineteenth-century lawyers is derided as a kind of mechanical jurisprudence remote from the practical concerns the law exists to address. In 1963, the distinguished dean of the Harvard Law School, Erwin Griswold (the solicitor general of the Pentagon Papers case), repudiated the notion that some legal distinctions and categories are absolute as a kind of legal fundamentalism:

[A]bsolutes are likely to be phantoms, eluding our grasp. Even if we think we have embraced them, they are likely to be misleading. If we start from absolute premises, we may find that we only oversimplify our problems and thus reach unsound results. It may well be that absolutes are the greatest hindrance to sound and useful thought—in law, as in other fields of human knowledge. . . . [Absolutism] provides its own anodyne for the pains of reasoning. It states the result with delusive finality. But it is, I think, a thoroughly unsatisfactory form of judging.[8]

In its extreme form, this attitude culminates in the self-described "pragmatism" of a Richard Posner,[9] but in a less radical (or perhaps only less overt) manner, this understanding of the judicial process is, we believe, an orthodoxy among American judges and the elite bar. The consequence, applied to constitutional law, is that courts treat a vast range of claims that government is infringing constitutionally protected liberty as requiring the judiciary to balance or weigh the competing governmental and private interests seen to be at stake in the litigation.

The reader is already acquainted with Holmes's application of this line of thought to the First Amendment, and also with the Supreme Court's endorsement of this view, with respect to the First Amendment and to constitutional liberties generally, in the 1930s. A few examples will serve to remind the reader of the balancing-of-interests model with which the modern judiciary approaches almost all issues involving individual rights. Section 2 of Article IV of the Constitution provides that "[t]he Citizens of each State shall be entitled to all Privileges and Immunities of Citizens in the several States," but this, the Supreme Court has announced, "is not an absolute."[10] In evaluating a claim that a state has violated the privileges and immunities clause, the Court will uphold an instance of discrimination against nonresidents if the discriminating state has "a substantial reason for the difference in treatment" and the discrimination "bears a substantial relationship to the State's objective."[11] Governmental discrimination on the basis of race is "suspect" under the principle of equal protection guaranteed by the Fifth and Fourteenth Amendments, but a racial classification is constitutional if its goal rests on a "compelling governmental interest" and the classification is "narrowly tailored" to achieve that end.[12] Since 1992, the controlling test for whether to restrict a woman's freedom to terminate a pregnancy before the fetus is viable has been whether the restriction would place an "undue burden" on the woman's choice, and the Supreme Court has explained that whether a restriction amounts to an undue burden depends on whether it has "the purpose or effect of placing a substantial obstacle in the path of a woman seeking an abortion of a nonviable fetus."[13] The list could be extended indefinitely, particularly in the area of free expression, where the Supreme Court has articulated a variety of tests or doctrines through which it applies the First Amendment to exercises of governmental power.

Two features of these variously worded doctrines are important for our purposes. First, all of them treat the constitutionally protected liberty as in some sense commensurable with the purposes government might have for infringing the liberty: the value judgments implicit in terms such as "substantial," "compelling," and "undue" make sense only if it is appropriate to measure the government's interests on a metaphorical scale that also weighs the individual constitutional right. This assumption of commensurability becomes express when the Supreme Court refers to individual rights as "liberty interests" or calibrates its standard of review according to whether the individual's right or interest is "fundamental" or of lesser status.[14] There is nothing conceptually unique, then, about the liberty-protecting provisions of the Constitution, and even when they are stated in absolute terms their scope and application must invariably be measured against the claims of other constitutional provisions and concerns.[15]

Second, the balancing-of-interests model upholds the judiciary's special responsibility for safeguarding constitutionally protected liberty, but it does so by licensing the courts to engage in their own evaluation of the respective claims of government and the individual. North Carolina's disfavoring treatment of South Carolina's citizens is constitutional or not, depending on whether in the judiciary's view North Carolina has a good enough reason for the discrimination and, again in the judiciary's view, the discrimination is a good enough means of pursuing

North Carolina's goals.[16] Governmental intrusion on someone's "liberty interest" is subject to serious review if in the court's opinion the interest is important ("fundamental") enough to warrant such review. Such judgments are, we think, unmistakably interlaced with the sort of considerations of policy and politics—in the broad rather than the narrow or partisan sense—that characterize legislative debate. Once the courts invite themselves to make such judgments, the judicial enforcement of constitutional rights becomes in itself an exercise of discretionary governmental power, not, to be sure, in the sense of arbitrary power, but in the sense of making choices driven at least in part by policy (or policy-like) arguments and assumptions.

We believe that in this chapter we so far have said nothing that should be controversial in substance, although the way in which we have made our point is heterodox to the point of heresy in a world in which Oliver Wendell Holmes, Jr.'s, assumptions are taken as givens. Our proposal is, at its base, that those assumptions should be rejected, that the First Amendment should be uncoupled from the early-twentieth-century mindset that conditions its current interpretation, and that constitutional law should return to the founding era's predominant understanding of the amendment as a ban on the exercise of a certain power rather than as a guarantee of individual liberty. We suggested, at the end of Part Two, that the First Amendment would make more sense in relation to intellectual property law if this were done. Here we assert that the First Amendment would make more sense *in relation to constitutional law* if the amendment were thought of as a structural provision defining the scope of federal power and not, or not primarily, as a provision protecting individual liberty.

Our starting point for this rethinking is similar to Justice Black's for his version of First Amendment absolutism: the text of the amendment is best read in that way, and the earliest interpreters of the amendment, above all James Madison, construed the amendment in this manner. The text of the amendment, after all, is a command to Congress not to exercise a certain power ("Congress shall make no law"), and the founders took the text at its word: as we have seen, when the issue of the First Amendment's meaning was first squarely and fully addressed during the

Sedition Act crisis, it was generally agreed that its "no law" wording was to be taken seriously and indeed literally. Federalists and Republicans *agreed* that the federal government is powerless to abridge "the freedom of speech, or of the press." Their disagreement lay in the variant definitions they gave to that freedom. In other words, to the extent that early views on constitutional interpretation matter—and the Supreme Court has often stressed that early views are important—amidst the clamor of early disagreement over the meaning of the speech and press clauses we can discern a consensus that those clauses put an absolute limitation on federal power, wherever precisely that limitation should be located.

Where we differ from Justice Black, it should now be clear, lies in the one respect in which he did not escape the dead hand of Justice Holmes: Black accepted Holmes's assumption that the First Amendment's central function is to protect individual rights. In doing so, Black placed his absolutist interpretation of the First Amendment in the conceptual domain controlled by the modern Supreme Court's almost unvarying refusal to treat liberty as an absolute. In addition, by doing so Black opened himself to the charge of inconsistency when he rejected First Amendment arguments, that where he himself wished to place a limit on the scope of expressive freedom he simply did so by manipulating the definition of the liberty.[17] We propose to avoid both difficulties. The First Amendment is, at its core, not a liberty-protecting provision but a structural clause limiting the scope of Congress's power. The Holmesian weighing of government's interests against those of the individual simply does not apply, because within the absolute First Amendment's limits, the government is powerless to act. The boundaries of the absolute First Amendment, furthermore, are set not arbitrarily but by the logic of the power that the First Amendment forbids government to employ.

We propose, then, to read the free speech and free press clauses as denials of power to Congress, and to give that denial its full textual force. Whatever the power "to abridge the freedom of speech, or of the press" is, it is a power that the federal government simply may not exercise. This entails, a little shockingly in light of modern assumptions, that the speech and press clauses are not primarily about the rights of the individual, although, as we argue below, one need not reject the claim that the clauses do, as a secondary function, create individual rights. But in their primary role, the clauses are constitutional definitions of the outer scope of the federal government's jurisdiction. They define a boundary beyond which no exercise of federal power—legislative, executive, or judicial—may go. The whole interest-balancing mindset Holmes applied to constitutional free expression in *Schenck* and *Abrams* and after, which the Court as an institution endorsed in the 1930s and 1940s and reaffirmed by its formal rejection of Black's absolutism in the 1950s and 1960s, is simply irrelevant to the application of the speech and press clauses in their core meanings. Put aside the Holmesian interest-balancing presupposition applied to liberty-protecting provisions, and treat the First Amendment's limitation on federal power as structural, and absolutism becomes a conceivable approach to a constitutional provision.

Or does it? Recall Professor Black and Dean Griswold dismissing the very nature of absolutism as foolish or even conceptually impossible. Could modern constitutional law accommodate the idea of an absolute First Amendment? As it happens, contemporary constitutional doctrine *does* embrace, in one area, an absolutist position, and on a question of constitutional structure and federal authority. In a series of decisions in the past decade, a majority of the justices have insisted emphatically that the powers delegated to Congress by Article I are absolutely limited by the Constitution's denial of any power to subject a state to lawsuits brought by individuals without the state's consent. To understand the Court's reasoning, and the relevance of that reasoning to the First Amendment, the reader must go on a short excursus into what is often called (a bit inaccurately) the law of the Eleventh Amendment.

During the debates over adopting the Constitution in 1787 and 1788, one of the many charges brought against it was the claim that the federal judiciary created or authorized under Article III would have compulsory jurisdiction over cases brought against states by individuals, and in particular by citizens of other states or foreign countries. If so, this raised not only theoretical qualms about the states' loss of sovereignty but more practically the specter of the new federal courts forcing the states to pay the large debts that many of them owed to out-of-state creditors. In response a number of prominent supporters of ratification, including Madison, Hamilton, and Marshall, denied that Article III would have that effect, but in 1793, in *Chisholm v. Georgia* (its first significant case) the Supreme Court held that the critics had been right and that Article III did strip the states of sovereign immunity from suit.[18] The political reaction to the *Chisholm* decision was overwhelmingly negative. The Georgia legislature considered making it a capital offense for a federal marshal to attempt to enforce the judgment in *Chisholm*, and in September 1794 Congress proposed what is now the Eleventh Amendment as a means of overturning the decision: "The judicial power of the United States shall not be construed to extend to any suit in law, or equity, commenced or prosecuted against one of the United States by Citizens of another State, or by Citizens or Subjects of any Foreign State." By the following February the requisite number of state legislatures had approved the amendment, although several failed at first to inform the federal government of that fact, so that it was not until January 1798 that the amendment's adoption was officially proclaimed.[19]

The subsequent history of the interpretation of the Eleventh Amendment is lengthy and complex and much of it is remote from our concerns. But in a recent series of cases involving the Eleventh Amendment, the Supreme Court has had occasion to consider the question of how to relate an amendment restricting federal authority to the powers delegated to Congress in Article I of the Constitution, an issue directly relevant to our concern with the relationship between the copyright and patent clauses and the First Amendment. The roots of the decisions in which we are interested lie in a much older case, *Hans v. Louisiana*, decided in 1890.[20] The plaintiff in *Hans* sued the state of Louisiana in federal court to recover interest allegedly due on some state bond instruments. The state raised the defense that it could not be sued without its consent under the old notion of sovereign immunity, and the plaintiff responded that he, "being a citizen of Louisiana, [was] not embarrassed by the obstacle of the Eleventh Amendment, inasmuch as that amendment only prohibits suits against a state which are brought by the citizens of another state, or by citizens or subjects of a foreign state."[21] The

Supreme Court, however, concluded that the state sovereign immunity safeguarded by the Eleventh Amendment was not limited to the terms of the amendment; it was, rather, a general constitutional principle which the *Chisholm* Court had mistakenly ignored. Since the Eleventh Amendment's immediate purpose was to reverse *Chisholm*, it was drafted in terms specifically designed to correct *Chisholm*'s specific interpretive error,[22] but its broader goal was to restore what the *Hans* Court believed to be the original understanding of Article III.[23]

The immediate and direct significance of *Hans* lay in the significant limitation it placed (or recognized) on the authority of the federal courts, and for almost a century the Eleventh Amendment cases following it were concerned with the scope of this limitation, and its relationship to the Court's somewhat later decision in *Ex parte Young* that state sovereign immunity does not protect a state officer from being enjoined in his or her own person from seeking to enforce an unconstitutional state statute.[24] In *Fitzpatrick v. Bitzer*,[25] however, the Supreme Court was directly confronted with the impact of the Eleventh Amendment (addressed as it is to "the judicial power") on the powers of Congress. The state law at issue in *Fitzpatrick* discriminated against female state employees in the administration of the state's retirement plan, which violated the federal Civil Rights Act of 1964, as amended in 1972 to cover the states as employers.[26] In form the defendants in *Fitzpatrick* were the state officials who administered the retirement plan, but the plaintiffs were seeking not only an injunction against future discrimination but also retroactive money damages for past violations, which would in fact be paid by the state, not its officials. Since the Court had held in an earlier case that the award of retroactive damages to be paid by the state in an *Ex parte Young* action is within the scope of the Eleventh Amendment (on the reasoning that the effect of such an award is identical to a judgment formally entered against the state itself), the defendants argued that the federal courts could not entertain the *Fitzpatrick* plaintiffs' claim for damages. The Supreme Court disagreed. Noting that Congress had enacted the 1972 amendments to the Civil Rights Act pursuant to its power to enforce the *Fourteenth* Amendment, the Court held that the *Eleventh* Amendment was no bar.

[H]ere . . . the Eleventh Amendment defense is asserted in the context of legislation passed pursuant to Congress' authority under [Section] 5 of the Fourteenth Amendment. As ratified by the States after the Civil War, that Amendment quite clearly contemplates limitations on their authority [and] we think that the Eleventh Amendment, and the principle of state sovereignty which it embodies are necessarily limited by the enforcement provisions of [Section] 5 of the Fourteenth Amendment.[27]

The Court's explanation of its decision in *Fitzpatrick* was consistent both with the view that *Chisholm v. Georgia* was wrongly decided and the Eleventh Amendment was a restoration of the Constitution's original meaning, and with the view that the amendment contracted the original scope of national authority. Either way, the Eleventh Amendment could not circumscribe the Fourteenth Amendment's subsequent grant of power to Congress. Thirteen years after *Fitzpatrick*, however, in *Pennsylvania v. Union Gas Co.*,[28] a four-justice plurality went further, and concluded that the Eleventh Amendment did not circumscribe Article I, Section 8's antecedent grant of power to Congress to regulate interstate commerce. The plurality reasoned that the Court had often described Congress's commerce power as "plenary" and that "it makes no sense to conceive of [Section] 5 [of the Fourteenth Amendment] as somehow being an 'ultra-plenary' grant of authority"[29]—plenary is plenary, and if one plenary Congressional power enables Congress to impose liability on the states (as *Fitzpatrick* held) so will another. The four justices who dissented from the constitutional holding in *Union Gas* responded that this was to ignore the importance of chronology to *Fitzpatrick*'s reasoning: "Nothing in this reasoning justifies limitation of the principle embodied in the Eleventh Amendment through appeal to antecedent provisions of the Constitution."[30]

In *Seminole Tribe v. Florida*,[31] decided in 1995, a five-justice majority resolved the analytical disagreement revealed in *Union Gas* by overruling that decision and squarely rejecting any argument that Congress can abrogate state sovereign immunity "through appeal to antecedent provisions of the Constitution." In equating Congress's power under Article I with its power under the Fourteenth Amendment for the purposes of deciding an Eleventh Amendment claim, the *Union Gas* plurality had fundamentally misunderstood *Fitzpatrick*, and even more fundamentally the logic of constitutional amendments affecting the scope of Congressional power. "*Fitzpatrick* was based upon a rationale wholly inapplicable to the Interstate Commerce Clause, viz., that the Fourteenth Amendment, adopted well after the adoption of the Eleventh Amendment and the ratification of the Constitution, operated to alter the preexisting balance between state and federal power achieved by Article III and the Eleventh Amendment."[32] The very purpose of the Fourteenth Amendment's grant of power to Congress was to increase the scope of national authority under the original Constitution-plus-the -Eleventh-Amendment. Antecedent constitutional provisions cannot limit such a subsequent grant of authority. But what of the Eleventh Amendment vis-à-vis the original Constitution? It would be an error to limit the Fourteenth Amendment's grant of power to Congress by reference to antecedent provisions of the Constitution (such as the Eleventh Amendment), an error which *Fitzpatrick v. Bitzer* avoided. But the *Union Gas* plurality had committed precisely the same error in constitutional logic when it concluded that the scope of the Eleventh Amendment restriction on national authority was limited—or more precisely was to be interpreted as limited—by the antecedent grant of authority over commerce to Congress in Article I, Section 8. In both cases, the correct line of reasoning is to recognize that amendments that address the sweep of federal power are enacted precisely in order to alter the preexisting distribution of constitutional authority; that later-adopted provisions take precedence over earlier ones in determining the current scope of national power. The correct view, the *Seminole Tribe* Court concluded, is that the Eleventh Amendment limits the legitimate interpretation of *all* the grants of power to *any* of the branches of the federal government in the original Constitution. Since the amendment comes later in time, "[e]ven when [Article I] vests in Congress complete lawmaking authority over an area, the Eleventh Amendment prevents congressional authorization of suits by private parties against unconsenting States."[33] Furthermore, since the Eleventh Amendment is a blanket prohibition against the use of Article I powers to abrogate state immunity, the weight of importance of the federal interest in doing so is irrelevant: the prohibition is absolute.[34]

To be sure, as the cases following *Seminole Tribe* have made clear, the justices who made up the majority there believe that the Eleventh Amendment was a correction of an error the Court made in *Chisholm v. Georgia*, and that properly construed the original Constitution itself did not extend federal court jurisdiction to suits over unconsenting states or authorize Congress itself to do so. But this does not affect the meaning or significance of *Seminole Tribe*'s repudiation of *Union Gas* (where the plurality made no claim that *Chisholm* was correctly decided). Whether rightly or wrongly, *Chisholm* read the original Constitution as granting power to the national government, a state of affairs which the Eleventh Amendment then "operated to alter." "The Eleventh Amendment restricts the judicial power under Article III, and Article I cannot be used to circumvent the constitutional limitations placed upon federal jurisdiction."[35]

Seminole Tribe was decided by a deeply divided Court, and at the time of this writing the four justices who dissented in that case continue to reject its authority. In our view, however, this does not affect the value of the case for our purposes, for two reasons. (And thus we need not and do not take a position on whether *Seminole Tribe* was correctly decided *on its facts*.) First, the continuing objections of the dissenting justices appear in our reading of the cases to rest chiefly on their fundamental rejection of the substantive interpretation of the Eleventh Amendment first advanced in *Hans v. Louisiana* and fully articulated in recent cases by the *Seminole Tribe* majority.[36] In other words, their primary disagreement with *Seminole Tribe* is that in their view the majority has misconstrued what the nation did in adopting the Eleventh Amendment, not with the majority's insistence that whatever legal effects the Eleventh Amendment has take precedence over contradictory provisions in the original Constitution. (The dissenting justices, who appear to think *Chisholm* correctly decided, do not question that the amendment overrode *Chisholm*'s application of Article III.)[37] Second, in our judgment, regardless of who has the better of the argument about the original meaning of the Eleventh Amendment, *Seminole Tribe* is completely persuasive about its methodological point, that absent special circumstances an amendment varying the preexisting scope of Congressional power ought to be given its full force and not trimmed in its application to powers exercised under antecedent provisions of the Constitution, no matter how plenary or important those powers may otherwise be. Even if a majority of the justices were someday to reject *Seminole Tribe*'s interpretation of the Eleventh Amendment, we believe that the Court should and would adhere to *Seminole Tribe*'s understanding of what we have called the logic of constitutional amendments.

* * *

THE *SEMINOLE TRIBE* LINE OF CASES shows that the modern Supreme Court can entertain and apply an absolute rule, at least where the rule concerns a denial of power to Congress as opposed to an individual right to be asserted against otherwise valid exercises of Congressional power. Under *Seminole Tribe*, in exercising its powers under Article I, Section 8, Congress may never abrogate the sovereign immunity of an unwilling state. The Eleventh Amendment (or as the Court prefers to put it, the principle exemplified by or embodied in that amendment) is an absolute denial to Congress of that power. There is no balancing of the federal interests Congress may wish to advance against the contrary interests of the state: the rule is that Congress shall make no law. The only exceptions the Court has recognized are the bankruptcy clause (for reasons unique to that clause) and situations where an amendment adopted after the Eleventh Amendment affirmatively confers the power of abrogation.

It is worth pausing for a moment to ask why the Court would be willing to treat a rule denying power to Congress as absolute while in enforcing even the most potent individual liberty the Court (almost) always recognizes the possibility that the government may assert an interest so weighty that the individual claim must give way. Is there any difference in the end between saying in one instance that "Congress has no power to do X," and in the other that "the individual has a right that Congress may not violate by doing X?" Perhaps not, from some jurisprudential perspectives, but as a matter of constitutional law we think the *Seminole Tribe* cases indicate why the Court might sensibly wish to draw such a line. As the Court has interpreted the Eleventh Amendment, in its application to Congress the amendment denies a specific power to Congress—it may not use its Article I powers to strip the states of their immunity from suit brought by an individual plaintiff. That prohibition is absolute, but it is also limited in its impact on Congress's ability to pursue those national interests Congress deems important. The Eleventh Amendment denial of power neither prevents Congress from imposing substantive obligations on the states, nor does it even prohibit Congress from subjecting the states to suit when the plaintiff is the United States, or when Congress is acting validly under the Fourteenth Amendment. In contrast, when the Constitution protects an individual right, while the scope of the right is of course limited, within its scope it applies to all exercises of governmental power, regardless of the source of the power being exercised. The impact of an absolute individual right is potentially broader and less predictable, cross-cutting as it does all Congressional powers and all national interests. The Holmesian presupposition that at some point any individual interest needs to be defeasible is, in this light, understandable, and thus for a Holmesian Court it makes sense to recognize some denials of power, but few if any individual rights as absolute within their scope.

At this point, we hope that the relevance of the recent Eleventh Amendment cases is clear. On its face the First Amendment instructs Congress that it shall not exercise a certain legislative authority: the power to make laws that effect certain results. Many early interpreters of the amendment, and Madison in particular, read the First Amendment in precisely this way, as a structural provision prohibiting to Congress the power to wield certain powers, not as a limitation on the manner in which Congress can exercise power. The contemporary Supreme Court is not flatly opposed to the argument that a given denial to Congress of a power is absolute. As in the Eleventh Amendment context, it makes no difference for our purposes whether one agrees with Madison that no such power was delegated in the first place, or (as Madison also acknowledged could be argued) that the amendment deprived Congress of any implied power to abridge speech and press that might be incidental to its exercise of its enumerated powers. On either view, after the First Amendment is adopted, Congress is entirely without such a power—as the text on its face appears to state. Viewing an amendment as a denial of power, *Seminole Tribe* shows that there is no reason not to give the language of the First Amendment a literal reading, that is to say an absolute one: Congress shall make no law.

An absolute structural interpretation of the First Amendment thus cannot be dismissed on the ground that the contemporary Supreme Court does not accept constitutional absolutes—the Court is willing to do so in precisely the area of structural restraints on legislative power where the justices' Holmesian conception of individual rights does not hold sway. But another objection to the plausibility of a structural reading of the First Amendment remains. For nearly a century the Supreme Court and American society generally has seen the amendment not in structural terms but as a source of individual rights. Whatever the Court's willingness to entertain absolute readings of structural features of the Constitution is simply not how the justices or anyone else sees *this* provision. To argue against the modern understanding of the First Amendment as a liberty-protecting provision might seem quixotic, rather like arguing that the commerce clause should have the scope in the twenty-first century that a nineteenth-century lawyer would have acknowledged.[38]

The answer to this objection is implicit in the history of debate over the First Amendment which we recounted in Part III. As we showed there, the modern law of constitutional free expression is in no sense the simple working out of a fixed and determinate meaning embedded in the First Amendment when it was adopted, or implicit in the concepts of freedom of speech and press. Contemporary constitutional lawyers frequently elide or ignore this fact because they simply begin their thinking about the First Amendment with the Holmes opinions of 1919.[39] Starting the story not with 1919 but instead with the adoption of the First Amendment in 1789 makes it possible to see the importance of creativity and innovation in the interpretation of the First Amendment.

In the world of 1789, as the reader has seen, there was no consensus view of exactly what a constitutional provision protecting freedom of speech and press meant: both in theory and practice the interpretive conventions of that era allowed for a number of divergent answers to the question of what the amendment forbade and what it protected. It was only with the proposal in Congress in 1798 to enact a federal law prohibiting seditious libel that the issue of the First Amendment's meaning became a central and important issue. The response, both Federalist and Republican, was to propose an interpretation of the amendment that was plausible from a professional perspective and harmonious with the interpreter's more general sense of the Constitution *and* with his particular political goals. There is no reason to dismiss either Federalist or Republican arguments because the motivations at play were in part political: constitutional arguments that break new ground often, perhaps usually, stem from mixed motives. (It is entirely possible, for example, that Holmes's move in 1919 from *Schenck* to *Abrams* was driven in part by his desire not to lose the adulation of politically liberal commentators whose praise he had come to relish but who were critical of the decisions upholding convictions under the Espionage Act.) Constitutional interpretation does not take place in a hermetically sealed box, immune from all earthly influences. The question of the Sedition Act's constitutionality could not be answered through a purely neutral legal analysis, because the amendment did not embody a settled meaning adequate to resolving the issue. What is important, for present purposes, is that the interpretive crisis of 1798—how are we to understand the First Amendment in its application to the Sedition Act?—provoked responses that were intellectually creative even as they strove to make good sense of the text and previous thinking about press freedom.

The political aftermath of the Sedition Act debate turned out to be so dramatic and one-sided that the issue of how to understand the First Amendment escaped serious attention from the legal mainstream for over a century. But the proposal in Congress in 1917 to enact another federal law banning seditious speech once again made the amendment's interpretation a question recognized as crucial by many. And once again, the response was to propose interpretations of the amendment that were at the same time professionally plausible and ideologically (and politically) palatable. The answers of 1798 played only a subordinate role in Holmes's thinking because they did not fit well with his presuppositions about legal rights and legal analysis; they virtually disappeared from view when the Court as an institution moved to Holmes's position on free speech because by then a majority of the justices shared Holmes's assumptions. Confronted with the interpretive crisis of 1919 and later, the Court responded not by invoking some preexisting legal schema but through arguments that were intellectually novel even if they were also attempts to make faithful sense out of the amendment.

Even as the Court was settling on a view of the First Amendment that depended on Holmesian premises, one of its members, Hugo Black, was coming to believe that there was another interpretive crisis forming. As a chronological matter, the first problem to which Black proposed a different view of the amendment as a solution was the Court's lapse, as he saw it, into the same sort of extratextual and illegitimate judicial legislation the old Court of the *Lochner* era had practiced. His total incorporation approach to construing the due process clause of the Fourteenth Amendment was not limited to issues involving freedom of expression but proposed a general solution with respect to a broad range of possible issues. By the early 1950s, however, Black thought he had been sadly prescient in his earlier warnings that judicial interest balancing poses a threat to free speech: in Black's view the Court majority's acquiescence in the government's repression of radical speech was a crisis parallel to those of 1798 and 1919. Just as Holmes had attempted to be a faithful interpreter of the First Amendment through a creative approach to a problem that preexisting materials did not seem to answer satisfactorily, so Black constructed his mature First Amendment absolutism by proposing an innovative solution to the problems he perceived, although not, to be sure, without some debt both to Holmes and to the Republicans of 1798. Unlike Holmes, as a formal matter, Black failed: the Court refused to adopt his approach even as it came to concur in many of his conclusions.

It should be clear by now that what links all three of these episodes in the history of the First Amendment is an historical pattern. The federal government takes some action—the enactment of the Sedition and Espionage Acts, McCarthy-era governmental repression—that implicates freedom of expression. Controversy over that action leads to a deep division over its compatibility with the speech and press clauses of the First Amendment. Proposals about a fundamental and significantly novel approach to interpreting the amendment are made in an effort to overcome the division. Eventually a broad orthodoxy about the meaning of constitutional free expression emerges, one that owes many of its features to those originally novel notions.

The modern constitutional law of free expression was shaped in a fundamental fashion by the second and third instances of this historical pattern. It rests on the early twentieth-century presuppositions that Justice Holmes embedded in his innovative opinions from *Abrams* on, whereas much of its substantive reach stems from the pressure that Justice Black's absolutism put on the Holmesian paradigm. The resulting web of First Amendment principles, doctrines, and cases is so dominant intellectually and institutionally that it easily assumes an air of inevitability, as if our present-day understandings were somehow implicit in the First Amendment from the beginning or, perhaps, are normative in some almost Platonic sense as the embodiment of what protecting free speech must entail. It is, however, a mistake to succumb to this misperception, for in doing so we almost certainly will miss the most important lessons of First Amendment history—that novel problems have generated novel solutions and that the current state of First Amendment law owes its existence to the willingness of the American legal system to consider and ultimately incorporate innovative approaches to First Amendment problems. If then one accepts the legitimacy, as a general matter, of the Supreme Court's contemporary First Amendment jurisprudence, it is also necessary as a matter of consistency and logic to accept the possibility that the existence of yet another crisis over the interpretation of the First Amendment may provoke still other novel approaches that may in their turn eventually become accepted into mainstream legal thought. As the reader knows, our view is that the contradiction between the orthodox account of free expression in America and the increasingly restrictive impact of intellectual property on free expression is in fact a crisis of meaning and of freedom. The lesson of the First Amendment's history is that the floor is, or ought to be, open to creative responses to this crisis.

The idea of reconceptualizing the First Amendment in structural terms as an absolute limitation on the exercise of federal power cannot be rejected on the ground that modern free speech doctrine views the amendment differently—to reject out of hand the legitimacy of innovation in First Amendment thinking is to cut the grounds of legitimacy from under modern free speech doctrine itself. As we have seen, nothing in contemporary constitutional law makes it beyond professional or intellectual plausibility to interpret the First Amendment in this fashion. Of course, the bare possibility of innovation in free speech law says nothing in itself about what innovation might be persuasive. That depends on the details of the proposed innovation. So, at this point we must now answer the question: What is the power to abridge the freedom of speech or of the press to which the First Amendment refers, and which it absolutely forbids Congress from exercising?

CHAPTER 12

Forward to the Eighteenth Century

RECALL ALEXANDER HAMILTON'S CLAIM in the *Federalist* that it would have been a useless mistake to incorporate into the Constitution a provision protecting liberty of the press.[1] Hamilton based this assertion on the observation that, in essence, reasonable people can differ over the proper scope of such liberty, and that since that is the case such a provision would be too ambiguous in meaning to be effective. The First Amendment, viewed from this perspective, would be (as Judge Robert Bork said famously of the Ninth Amendment) "an inkblot," a constitutional text without discernible operational significance, and certainly incapable of providing a satisfactory basis for the courts to disregard an act of the national legislature.[2] It is striking that this argument, which from the standpoint of expediency would have been valuable to the Federalists of 1798, was made by none of them. Without known exception, the defenders of the Sedition Act justified the Act not by denying that the First Amendment was an appropriate basis for invalidating an act of Congress but instead by insisting that the Act was consistent with the meaning properly to be ascribed to the amendment. The First Amendment does have operational significance, they readily admitted, and to determine that significance the Federalists introduced the first doctrinal innovation in the amendment's history: they invoked Blackstone's definition of liberty of the press as the key to interpreting the amendment's prohibition on federal laws abridging the freedom of speech or of the press. The power to enact such abridgments, in other words, is the power to "lay . . . *previous* restraints upon publications," that prevent anyone from "laying what sentiments he pleases before the public." It is thus the power "to subject all freedom of sentiment to the prejudices" of someone acting with governmental authority, and "make him the arbitrary and infallible judge of all controverted points in learning, religion, and government."[3]

As the reader knows, the Republicans of the late 1790s refused to acquiesce in the Federalist reading of the First Amendment, but the Republican dissent was not a rejection in its entirety of the Federalists' innovative resort to Blackstone. Instead, they argued that precisely because the Federalists were right to invoke Blackstone to define the power of authorizing prior restraints as the power to abridge freedom of speech and press, it would be illogical to limit the amendment's operative significance to a ban on prior restraints. "[T]his idea of the freedom of the press can never be admitted to be the American idea of it; since a law inflicting penalties on printed publications would have a similar effect with a law authorizing a previous restraint on them."[4] If a law authorizing a governmental official to censor, according to the official's criteria, whatever sentiments a person wishes to lay before the public is beyond Congress's authority, then a law authorizing an official to penalize expression after the fact, according to the official's criteria, must equally be beyond the scope of the national government. The controversy over the First Amendment's meaning which the Sedition Act sparked was a debate over the logical scope of the Federalists' innovative use of Blackstone.

In the course of their attacks on the Federalists, various Republicans found themselves blasting Blackstone as well, a logically peculiar but rhetorically unsurprising position.[5] The Republicans' rhetorical equation of Blackstone with a narrow view of the First Amendment has left its traces in modern First Amendment literature. While Blackstone is sometimes more or less favorably acknowledged as an important source of the First Amendment doctrine of prior restraint, his primary role in the literature is to serve as the First Amendment's bugbear: the frightening exemplar of how the amendment could be, or could have been, read in a crabbed and minimal fashion. The Republican legacy of disapproval, furthermore, has been reinforced by the disjuncture between Holmes's mature view of freedom of speech and the Republican-originated portrayal of Blackstone as the father of suppression. Holmes, in modern constitutional law lore, initiated the legal tradition of giving a broad reading to First Amendment freedoms—and came to that view only by implicitly rejecting his prior, Blackstonian view of what freedom of expression meant. From a Holmesian perspective, the First Amendment is a command to weigh the value of free expression against the importance of governmental control of that expression. On this view, the effect of Blackstone's defining liberty of the press in terms of prior restraints can only be to limit the range of situations in which a court should undertake whatever weighing of the interests the First Amendment might require. Under Holmes's (mis)reading of Blackstone, in other words, prior restraints are not banned but balanced, whereas after-the-fact interferences with speech are simply free from judicial scrutiny altogether. The dispute between Blackstone and Holmes thus is purely a disagreement over whether to give freedom of expression a narrower or a broader range of protection. The path of greater protection, for Holmesians after 1919 just as for Jeffersonian Republicans after 1798, lay in dismissing Blackstone except as a footnote or an object lesson.[6]

Object lessons are seldom given dispassionate consideration, and legal citations often take on a life of their own uncoupled from close examination of exactly what the cited author says. Modern First Amendment thought rests not on a rejection of Blackstone, but on a refusal to consider what it might mean to take him seriously. Modern First Amendment thought has also failed to generate a model of the First Amendment that leaves the amendment with any significant role to play in constraining the deleterious effects of intellectual property on the range of free expression American law actually, as a matter of fact, tolerates. We have already argued that this situation demands a reevaluation of the relationship between intellectual property and the First Amendment. Now we suggest that such a reevaluation can be aided by a reconsideration of Blackstone himself.

Blackstone did define liberty of the press quite clearly in terms of what modern American lawyers call prior restraints. "The liberty of the press is indeed essential to the nature of a free state: but this consists in laying no *previous* restraints upon publications, and not in freedom from censure for criminal matter when published."[7] But Blackstone did not simply lay down an unexplained *ipse dixit*: there was in his mind a clear reason and course of logic to this definition of liberty of the press.

Consider again his explanation for *why* press freedom is "essential to the nature of a free state":

Every freeman has an undoubted right to lay what sentiments he pleases before the public: to forbid this, is to destroy the freedom of the press: but if he publishes what is improper, mischievous, or illegal, he must take the consequences of his temerity. To subject the press to the restrictive power of a licenser . . . is to subject all freedom of sentiment to the prejudices of one man, and make him the arbitrary and infallible judge of all controverted points in learning, religion, and government . . . Thus the will of individuals is still left free; the abuse only of that free will is the object of legal punishment. Neither is any restraint hereby laid upon freedom of thought or enquiry: liberty of private sentiment is still left; the disseminating, or making public, of bad sentiments . . . is the crime which society corrects.[8]

It is, in other words, in the nature of a free state that "the will of individuals" on matters of expression should be left free, and this freedom is absolute: "Every freeman has an undoubted right to lay *what sentiments he pleases* before the public."

The concept of "sentiment" was in Blackstone's English a capacious one. Dr. Johnson gave as the word's primary definition "Thought; notion; opinion"[9]; Blackstone's point was not limited to matters of public interest—a misreading of Blackstone's meaning perhaps tempting to those who associate free expression closely with democratic politics—or statements of fact, or original ideas, but perfectly general. A genuinely free state is one in which the individual is perfectly free to express whatever is in his mind, even if his ideas seem whimsical, pointless, obnoxious, or valueless to others. As Blackstone immediately went on to note, in this manner the exterior liberty of the "freeman" to publicize "what sentiments he pleases" accords with his interior freedoms of thought and enquiry, an echo, almost certainly deliberate of the Roman historian Tacitus's description of the reign of Trajan: "times having the rare good fortune that you may think what you like and say what you think."[10]

But what exactly is wrong with "previous restraints upon publications" which distinguishes them from subsequent punishment? Blackstone had no objection to such punishment, or any problem with the notion that there are "bad sentiments," dissemination of which ought to lead to legal consequences even though the law would not prevent their publication ahead of time. (This is a point to which we shall return.) He was perfectly aware of the fact that the threat of liability has, or is likely to have, a deterrent effect on what individuals choose to do in the exercise of their free wills: indeed, in the next-to-last sentence of his discussion of liberty of the press he commended "a reasonable exertion of the laws"—in context, the laws of criminal libel—precisely because such an exertion would produce a deterrent effect on those harboring harmful ideas. What is uniquely injurious about prior restraints, to Blackstone, is the power their use necessarily vests in those entrusted with their issuance. English law, he explained, had initially viewed printing not as a means of exercising personal freedom but as a privilege subject to distribution by royal prerogative or, after the break between Charles I and Parliament, pursuant to legislation:

The art of printing, soon after its introduction, was looked upon (as well in England as in other countries) as merely a matter of state, and subject to the coercion of the crown. It was therefore regulated with us by the king's proclamations, prohibitions, charters of privilege and of license, and finally by the decrees of the court of starchamber; which limited the number of printers, and of presses which each should employ, and prohibited new publications unless previously approved by proper licensers. On the demolition of this odious jurisdiction in 1641, the long parliament of Charles I . . . assumed the same powers as the starchamber exercised with respect to the licensing of books.[11]

The exercise of governmentally authorized discretion by a licenser to determine what may be published was necessarily, in Blackstone's view, "to subject all freedom of sentiment to the prejudices of one man, and make him the arbitrary and infallible judge of all controverted points in learning, religion, and government,"[12] to transfer to that decision maker the choices about expression which in a free state rest with each individual. It was therefore only upon the expiration of the last licensing statute, in 1694, that Blackstone thought that "the press became properly free."[13]

There are three themes in Blackstone's discussion of liberty of the press which we wish to highlight. The first is that the liberty, as he understood it, is absolute: the presence of any prior restraint, even one sanctioned by legislation, renders the press unfree, and the scope of the liberty extends to all "sentiments" an individual may entertain and wish to express. The second is that what is ultimately wrong with the exercise of authority to interfere ex ante with the individual's right to publish as he wishes is that doing so empowers whoever has that authority to substitute his own (perhaps prejudiced or erroneous) judgment and will for that of the individual about what the latter shall say or publish. But third, Blackstone did not define this power simply in formal, temporal terms as the imposition of ex ante as opposed to ex post control over expression; instead, he clearly identified this "odious" power with the historical governmental practice in England of "laying previous restraints upon publications" for the purpose of enforcing "prohibitions and charters of privilege and of license" established by royal or, later, parliamentary authority. Unlike the modern constitutional law of free expression, which defines prior restraints chiefly in terms of the timing of governmental interference with expression,[14] Blackstone understood the idea in a more complex manner. A "previous" or prior restraint of the sort inconsistent with liberty of the press is, for him, an ex ante prohibition on individual choices about what to publish *in the enforcement of some governmental exercise of, or grant to another of, monopoly over expression.* Prior restraints enforce such a monopoly in the most direct and literal manner, but the rationale for objecting to them is not inextricably linked to their temporal relationship to the expression as a logical matter, although Blackstone himself did not perceive this. From Blackstone's perspective, liberty of the press is the absence of governmentally created and enforced monopolies in the realm of the expression of "sentiments."[15] Blackstone, in other words, thought of liberty of the press as defined by what authority the government exercises, and not in the first instance by the scope of an individual's legal rights. The object, certainly, was to safeguard the individual's freedom, but it was to be achieved by a limitation—voluntarily undertaken by

Parliament, Blackstone would have acknowledged—on the government's powers.

Blackstone's approach was not intellectually novel, nor was it a product of his sometimes overstated conformism. In broad outline, Blackstone's discussion in his *Commentaries* tracks closely the reasoning of that fountainhead of English libertarian thought on expression, John Milton's *Areopagitica*, published in 1644 to protest Parliament's 1643 order that no book be published without license from a governmental board of licensers. Blackstone was a devotee of Milton's poetry,[16] and his understanding of the relationship between liberty and authority parallels Milton's views. The *Areopagitica* attacked Parliament's assumption of the censorial powers practiced earlier by the monarch as a cowardly surrender to the vices of civic passivity and conformity; Milton argued that the robustly confident, divinely blessed commonwealth of England should reject it. Licensing of the sort Milton rejected demands capacities that the licensers could not be expected to display. In part, this is the product of the "economic self-interest of monopoly privilege"[17] that the parliamentary licensing system employed and that contemporary American intellectual property law reproduces: those who invoke parliamentary authority to suppress expression do so on self-interested grounds.[18]

Even more fundamentally, however, Milton objected to licensing because the licenser necessarily makes judgments about the future effects of present expression. Such judgments are likely to be overly conservative in dealing with what the licenser sees as "new and dangerous opinions," but regardless of the individual decision maker's character or courage, in any case he is being asked to "forejudge" the expression of others "ere we understand them" or the consequences of their speech. The very capacity of choice which Milton thought central to human freedom—"Give me the liberty to know, to utter, and to argue freely according to conscience, above all liberties"[19]—is subverted by an official's fears about the future effects of present expression.

The licensing of other men's expression thus asserts a privilege which Milton, and also Blackstone (a devout Protestant Christian), thought disavowed by God himself. In Book Three of *Paradise Lost*,

God the Father comments to his Son on the spiritual and moral state of the first human couple in their original innocence. Will humanity lose this innocence, he ponders, "easily transgress[ing] the sole Command" placed on Adam and Eve as a "pledge" of their obedience? If so, Milton portrays the Father asserting, it will be Man's choice: "I made him just and right, / Sufficient to have stood, though free to fall."[20] The relationship between freedom and authority, in this tradition of thought, does not entail freedom from responsibility, but it does demand freedom from the prevenient intervention of authority. Whatever else may be said of this view, it is not one of subservience to authority, but of a determined commitment to allow individual choice in the face of authority.

* * *

WHAT DOES THIS DISCUSSION of the views of an eighteenth-century lawyer suggest about the relationship between the First Amendment and intellectual property? Blackstone, to be sure, held a view of liberty of the press narrower in many ways than modern American free speech doctrine understands the First Amendment. He did not see after-the-fact punishment for "improper, mischievous, or illegal" publications as a violation of press freedom although, as we have argued, this was not out of a simple hidebound conservatism but because his conception of that freedom treated it as a function of the scope of governmental power rather than the extent of a personal right. After-the-fact punishment does not directly maintain a governmental monopoly over expression; in such circumstances neither the grantee of special privileges nor governmental officials enforcing such privileges usurp or override the choices of the individual about what to express, or the availability of the individual's expressive choices to the public. But where government creates a monopoly on certain expression, and then prevents anyone else from violating the monopoly, this is in Blackstone's terms a denial of liberty of the press. And thus, the modern American law of intellectual property, insofar as it relies on the use of prior restraints—which is to a great and indeed increasing degree—is a clear and ongoing abridgment of freedom of speech and of the press as Blackstone understood that freedom. Copyrights and patents in American law are "charters of privilege" or monopoly created by legislative authority. Indeed, the very language of the copyright and patent clause, which speaks of Congress "securing for limited Times to Authors and Inventors the exclusive Right to their respective Writings and Discoveries," is a blatant reminder that intellectual property rights, unlike most other forms of property,[21] are founded not on some normative source beyond the purview of the Constitution but are instead a grant of monopoly privilege by Congress acting pursuant to the Constitution.

To be sure, Blackstone himself did not understand copyright to be a violation of press freedom, even though the English law of his day knew of injunctions against the violation of copyright. This observation is not, however, inconsistent with the tentative conclusion we have just stated: that a major practical component of modern intellectual property law cannot be squared with the Blackstonian logic of press freedom. As we shall explain shortly, we are not arguing that Blackstone's views should simply determine the meaning to be ascribed to the First Amendment. But even within Blackstone's own discussion of copyright we think one can detect the seeds of a justification for the application of Blackstone's logic to a case where Blackstone himself did not go.

Blackstone addressed copyright in the second volume of the *Commentaries*, which concerns "the rights of Things," or in other words property law understood broadly.[22] He locates his discussion in a series of chapters on "the *title* to things personal, or the various means of *acquiring*, and of *losing*, such property as may be had therein," and more specifically in a chapter devoted to title by occupancy.[23] The result is that the analysis of copyright sits close to Blackstone's treatment of the acquisition of property rights to wild animals and to "corn growing on the ground, or other *emblements*, by any *possessor* of the land"[24] even where the underlying title to the real property lies in someone else. (Emblements are the profits from crops.) In both cases, Blackstone understood the property right to stem from the right holder's investment of energy and labor: wild animals become the subject of private property when someone seizes them, crops belong to the person who has had "the labour and expense of tilling, manuring, and sowing, the lands." So with copyright, which "being grounded on labour and invention, is more properly reducible to the head of occupancy than any other; since the right of occupancy itself is supposed by Mr. Locke, and many others, to be founded on the personal labour of the occupant."[25]

For Blackstone, in other words, copyright gives rise to a certain kind of property right out of considerations of natural justice, or perhaps even natural law: his invocation of Locke (like an earlier reference to the will of "the creator") and his statement that although "in England" there has been "direct determination upon the right of authors at the common law . . . much may be gathered from the frequent injunctions of the court of chancery, prohibiting the invasion of this property,"[26] both support the conclusion that for Blackstone the quality of property he saw in copyright rested on moral grounds. Recognizing liberty of the press as a reason for declining to protect such a "natural" moral claim would have seemed strange or even distasteful to Blackstone, who regularly insisted on the moral stature and beauty of English law. In contrast, it is long settled in the United States that the rights enforceable under the federal Copyright Act are the creatures of the Act, and mediately of the copyright clause.[27] To the extent that moral or natural-law reasoning lies at the base of Blackstone's failure to relate copyright to press freedom, his failure to do so simply is not relevant in the American context.

A second basis within Blackstone's own reasoning for expanding his views on press freedom to copyright rests in his understanding of the positive-law rules found in the Statute of Anne governing copyright. Those rules, he asserted, were themselves borrowed from the exception for patents recognized in the Statute of Monopolies of James I. Blackstone, in short, did in fact understand copyright as the sort of governmental privilege which—in another context and when combined with the use of prior restraints—he identified as the evil to which liberty of the press is the opposite. It is nevertheless unsurprising that he did not conclude or apparently even consider the possibility that copyright protection was a violation of press freedom: Parliament having passed the Statute of Anne, it would have been inconsistent with Blackstone's premise of parliamentary omnipotence to question the enforceability of copyright, and inconsistent with his generally laudatory account of English law to conceive of copyright enforceability as an evil.

Like Blackstone, founding-era constitutionalists did not investigate the relationship between the areas of law we call free expression and intellectual property, not (it must be stressed) because they had considered and rejected the possibility that the First Amendment put limits on Congress's authority under the copyright and patent clause, but—as was the case with Blackstone—because the possibility of a conflict did not occur to them. But once again, unless we are to denounce as illegitimate virtually the whole of modern First Amendment law, this cannot be dispositive. The founders equally failed to consider the possibility that tort law might violate the First Amendment through imposing civil liability for defamation, but the Supreme Court held in *New York Times v. Sullivan* that such is the case, despite the fact that this involved the upending of tort law as it had existed from the dawn of the Republic without regard to the fact that nothing in founding-era thinking directed the Court to do so.[28]

With Blackstone, and we think also with the founders themselves, the proper question is not to ask what they thought specifically on a topic about which they did not think at all, but what we can learn about the First Amendment and our issues from what they said.[29] Blackstone has troubled those committed to a broad First Amendment ever since the Court embraced such an interpretation on the foundation of Justice Holmes's 1919 opinions. The argument that it is sensible to understand Blackstone's views on liberty of the press as the most likely original meaning of the speech and press clauses has a simplicity and cogency that by that very token has been troubling. That great First Amendment absolutist, Justice Black, lamented Leonard Levy's historical conclusion that Blackstone's views were the amendment's original meaning as "probably one of the most devastating blows . . . delivered against civil liberty in America for a long time,"[30] and those less committed than Black to original meaning as the lode-star of constitutional interpretation have nonetheless generally agreed with him that Blackstone's understanding of liberty of the press is unacceptable.

As we have seen, however, Blackstone's views were considerably more complex than most modern lawyers have recognized. Justice Black's fear of Blackstone was based on his acceptance of the wooden reading that Levy and others gave Blackstone. Ironically, as the reader can now see, there are important themes shared by Blackstone's explanation of liberty of the press and Black's absolutist reasoning. Blackstone identified press freedom with prior restraints because he believed that English historical experience had shown the threat to a free state, to the liberty to think and speak as one thinks, lies in the creation of governmental monopolies over publication, and that there can be no true individual freedom of thought or expression wherever governmental power enforces such monopolies by denying choice to the individual. Like Black, Blackstone perceived the exercise by governmental officials of discretion over what is to be published as a central evil. Furthermore, Blackstone, like Black but unlike some modern First Amendment theorists, did not distinguish between political speech and expression on other matters, nor distinguish "high" from "low value" speech, unlike some modern First Amendment case law: the content, quality, and perceived social utility of expression were irrelevant to resolving what an individual may print without prior interference ("what sentiments he pleases"). With respect to liberty of the press, Blackstone placed all potential speakers on an even plane ("every freeman"), and he insisted that a free state necessarily leaves the choice of how and what to publish up to each individual. In all of these respects, Blackstone's vision of liberty of the press equals or exceeds the contemporary orthodox view of the First Amendment.

We do not disagree that freedom of speech and press may, and indeed should, require more than Blackstone allowed. But it is intolerable that the First Amendment should be construed to permit the government to exercise powers that Blackstone's own logic and the constitutional reasoning shared by all participants in the 1798 Sedition Act debates condemn.

* * *

THE FEASIBILITY AND DESIRABILITY of the absolute reading of the First Amendment that we are proposing can best be shown by a detailed examination of how intellectual property would be reconfigured by that reading: Part V will provide that examination. We turn now to some more general and in some respects technical points that need brief attention if our basic thesis is to be clear.

THE RELATIONSHIP BETWEEN THE PROPOSAL AND THE EXISTING FIRST AMENDMENT DOCTRINE OF PRIOR RESTRAINTS

Our proposal is not the equivalent of redefining the First Amendment as nothing more than the existing "prohibition" on prior restraints. As the reader has seen, contemporary case law treats the doctrine of prior restraints as triggered by the prospective timing of a governmental interference with expression, and as permitting such interference upon a sufficiently strong showing.[31] To be sure, even with respect to prior restraints, an absolute First Amendment would work a major change in the remedies available to holders of copyrights and patents. The paradigm expression of the power to abridge the freedom of speech and of the press is the imposition of censorship, licensing, or prior restraint on expression. Because under our proposal the First Amendment imposes an absolute structural limitation on federal power, any such prior restraint is simply beyond the authority of Congress to authorize or the courts to employ. The Pentagon Papers case was correctly decided, as Justice Black maintained, because the executive branch was asking the judiciary to exercise a power no branch of the federal government possesses, not (as the laconic per curiam opinion implied) because the government had failed to meet some stringent burden imposed on a party seeking an injunction. No matter how demanding the test, such an approach ultimately involves an instrumentality of government (a federal court) balancing private and public interests, and thus reintroduces the central vice at which the absolute First Amendment is directed, governmental choice about who is to say what. The absolute First Amendment rules out any such balancing, regardless of the justification government advances to defend its attempt to maintain or create a monopoly over expression. A constitutional amendment subsequent to the First Amendment could, of course, authorize Congressional legislation contravening the speech and press clauses, but there is no plausible argument that any subsequent amendment does so, and thus the absolute First Amendment would apply to Congressional legislation regardless of which Article I power Congress purported to employ.

The hoary counterexample to any absolute ban on prior restraints, *Near v. Minnesota*'s[32] injunction to prevent publication of troopship sailing times during a war is, we suspect, better seen as an example of how the use of extreme hypotheticals distorts constitutional thinking than as a serious objection to our proposal. Nothing in the absolute First Amendment would prevent the federal government from creating national security classifications for sensitive information and legislating criminal penalties for their enforcement. Nor are such ex post sanctions self-evidently less effective a means of protecting appropriate governmental secrecy than a prior restraint; injunctions, after all, are enforced by after-the-fact punishment for their violation.

DISCERNING THE EXISTENCE AND SCOPE
OF A MONOPOLY OVER EXPRESSION

The absolute First Amendment is the not the omnipresent First Amendment: all sorts of governmental interference with expression or expressive activity (a distinction of no relevance under our absolute interpretation) would be beyond its scope, not because the government won the metaphorical weighing of interests but because by definition the governmental power in play is not the power to maintain a monopoly over expression, which is *the* power the absolute First Amendment denies to government. (See the next heading for a consideration of whether other, nonabsolute First Amendment principles might still apply.) The unauthorized disclosure of national security secrets could be made a criminal offense under the absolute First Amendment because Congress would not be deciding, or authorizing the executive or the courts to decide, that only certain speakers could utter the secrets, and thus the criminal statute in itself would not be part of a system of monopoly over expression in the relevant sense. (Recall that a prior restraint automatically sets up a system of monopoly over expression and thus is invalid even when it is not part of a larger system of monopoly.) While there undoubtedly would be controversies on the outer margin, we will show in Part V that the concept of a monopoly over expression is susceptible to clear enough definition to make it possible to reach principled decisions about what governmental actions fall within the absolute First Amendment's ban.

THE RELATIONSHIP BETWEEN THE PROPOSAL AND OTHER INTERPRETATIONS OF THE SPEECH AND PRESS CLAUSES AS PROTECTING INDIVIDUAL RIGHTS

As the reader knows, the courts have developed a rich web of case law and doctrine premised on the Holmesian understanding of the First Amendment as concerned with individual rights. Would these individual-rights doctrines continue to exist or would they be entirely displaced if the First Amendment were reconceptualized as a structural provision prohibiting the exercise of federal power? There is, we think, no reason why an absolute, structural reading of the amendment is inconsistent with the continued employment, as a general matter, of individual-rights interpretations of the amendment. Constitutional lawyers are familiar with provisions that play more than one role in the law. Since *Strauder v. West Virginia*, for example, the Supreme Court has recognized that the equal protection clause of the Fourteenth Amendment is both a command to the states and, by implication, a creator of affirmative individual rights,[33] while the Court's enforcement of the commerce clause—primarily a delegation of power to Congress and secondarily a restraint on state legislation—is even older. To be sure, adopting our proposal would require modification of existing doctrine where that doctrine permits violations of the absolute structural ban, as we have seen with the existing doctrine of prior restraints, but this need not involve a wholesale revision of First Amendment law: most First Amendment doctrines do not address governmentally created monopolies on expression and as a consequence would be unaffected by our proposal.

THE RELATIONSHIP BETWEEN THE PROPOSAL AND THE OTHER CLAUSES OF THE FIRST AMENDMENT

Our approach takes seriously the underlying unity in the First Amendment's provisions, all of which have to do with monopolies in some fashion. In particular, it indicates the mutually reinforcing connections between the religion clauses and the speech and press clauses: all should be read to deny to government the power, as the Court long ago wrote, to dictate what people say or think, or to pursue this goal by making laws upholding monopolies over expression: "If there is any fixed star in our constitutional constellation, it is that no official, high or petty, can prescribe what shall be orthodox in politics, nationalism, religion, or other matters of opinion or force citizens to confess by word or act their faith therein. If there are any circumstances which permit an exception, they do not now occur to us."[34] Giving an absolute, structural reading to the speech and press clauses might well lead to a similar reconsideration of the establishment clause in particular, but that is a question beyond the scope of this book.

THE RELATIONSHIP BETWEEN THE PROPOSAL AND FEDERALISM

On its face and as originally understood, the First Amendment addressed only Congress (and by necessary implication the other two branches of the federal government).[35] Modern constitutional doctrine treats the clauses of the First Amendment as applicable to the laws and actions of the states by their incorporation into the Fourteenth Amendment. (The reader will recall our discussion of the incorporation controversy in chapter ten.) It would be theoretically possible, and indeed would accord with statements by some founding-era constitutionalists including Madison, to treat the structural First Amendment as, in essence, a federalism provision that shifts to the states responsibility for the matters in issue by denying competence over them to the federal government.[36] It is difficult to see what the modern rationale would be for so limiting the First Amendment's prohibition on the enforcement of monopolies over expression, and so we think the most natural conclusion is that the absolute First Amendment would be fully applicable to state law.

* * *

CONSIDER THE FOLLOWING PROPOSITIONS, which we believe we have established:

(1) Construing the First Amendment as, at its core, a prohibition on the exercise of a certain power makes better sense of the text of the First Amendment than the current interest-balancing understanding.

(2) A structural reading of the First Amendment is the interpretive framework that Madison initially advanced in proposing the amendment, and it was common ground in the first great First Amendment debate, the struggle over the Sedition Act of 1798.

(3) It is an artifact of the intellectual history of free speech thinking in this country, not a notion inherent in the concept, that modern First Amendment doctrine construes the amendment as, at its core, a safeguard of individual liberty which requires a balancing of the value of the liberty against the societal interests advanced by government.

(4) There is a structural, historically plausible reading of the First Amendment: Blackstone's understanding of liberty of the press, read with more emphasis than is customary on the evil Blackstone was inveighing against (monopoly over expression).

(5) Interpreting the First Amendment as, in its primary function at any rate, an absolute ban on the exercise of the power to maintain a monopoly over expression addresses the problem of governmental discretion to permit or prohibit speech; this is the problem that Justice Black highlighted and that contemporary doctrine exacerbates by invariably resorting to some form of judicial balancing.

(6) There is nothing in the history of First Amendment thought (characterized as it is by radical change at crisis points) or in the logic of

constitutional law (think of the Eleventh Amendment) that makes it unthinkable to view a prohibition on the exercise of a specific power as absolute.

Now think the supposedly unthinkable: the First Amendment to the Constitution of the United States forbids American government, in any of its parts including the courts, to undertake in any fashion to create or maintain a monopoly over expression.

PART V

Summing Up

CHAPTER 13

Intellectual Property in the Image
of an Absolute First Amendment

In prior chapters we have acknowledged the merit in intellectual property while questioning the understanding, common to all the doctrines in which expression plays an important part, that exclusive interests in expression can be recognized and protected without substantial concern for the obvious conflict between such interests and the First Amendment. We have suggested that this conflict has always existed, but that it has grown more evident, more insistent, and more destructive in our time. We have suggested that our present understanding of the First Amendment is not only inadequate to the need, but is additionally flawed in itself, and have argued accordingly that the amendment would be better understood were it to be interpreted at large as a straightforward constraint against the exercise of Congressional (or state) power abridging speech and press. Nothing in what we suggest presupposes that all of the amendment's affirmative or penumbral benefits, defined in the course of a century's contemplation, would necessarily be relinquished. On the other hand, we have no necessary quarrel with carrying the limitations implicit in our arguments beyond the immediate role they play in our endeavor.[1] Paying heed to a plenary reinterpretation of the amendment at large is not essential to our undertaking. The Court's easy dismissal of the underlying conflict of concern to us here has never resulted in a considered judgment on any ground; at most, it has been a device for deferring such a judgment. We propose accordingly that the First Amendment be read absolutely, in keeping with its first and most obvious meaning: *that Congress shall make no law abridging freedom of speech or of the press by conferring monopolies in expression that otherwise would belong to the universe of discourses in which all are free to share and share alike.* In at least this sense, "no law" should mean *no law.*

RESHAPING THE DOCTRINES

We approach what is new in this concluding portion of our book, then, by reiterating briefly the shape that intellectual property doctrines assume when reassessed against the constraints imposed by an absolute First Amendment. The first thing to be said is that they retain (or can retain) their present shape to a remarkable degree. The subject matter of the doctrines, the reasons for recognizing them, the disposition of the underlying interests, the incentives and rewards, the acknowledgment of creativity itself—all of these and more remain essentially the same. Even exclusivity is not entirely forbidden. Protection can still be provided for works that have not yet been made available to the public, or which, having been made available in limited formats or settings, are thus to be secured effectively against appropriation. The public gains no right to enter Emily Dickinson's bedroom or similarly private domains; or to suborn breaches of fiduciary obligations (between author and agent, producer or publisher, for example); or to storm gated venues or record the events presented there (admission into the precincts of the concert hall or venue can still require a ticket; whether the event can be recorded is still a matter of contract); or (in settings substantially equivalent to gated venues) to breach the security measures that may be taken to prevent works in a particular embodiment from being mechanically recorded—measures in settings such as those that are contemplated and provided for by the Digital Millennium Copyright Act, to offer but one example.

What will change most dramatically is the single thing that makes intellectual property obviously objectionable under the Constitution at present. Congress will simply have no power to create or recognize monopolies in expression that otherwise would press itself upon the public consciousness at large, and this is so whether the monopolies are justified under the patent and copyright clause, the commerce clause, the treaty power, or otherwise. When exclusive interests in expression are conferred for no better reason than that exclusivity will encourage the production of such interests, or make them valuable in the hands of a favored few, the First Amendment will then intervene. Congress may not thus forbid our common participation in the universe of discourses. This will be so, of course, when appropriation is essentially for noncommercial purposes, whether personal, private, or otherwise. But it will be no less so even when the purpose of the appropriation is to engage in competition with the creators of the interests, or otherwise to pursue financial gain. Interests in expression will no longer be consigned exclusively to proprietors recognized by the state. Justifications grounded in our understanding of property will prove likewise unavailing. Proprietorship and property are irrelevant in the setting of an absolute First Amendment. The issue is freedom, not property.[2] The central purpose of the First Amendment's constraint upon state power is, we think, as Brandeis suggested in *Whitney v. California*, to confer upon each individual citizen the freedom to think as he pleases or to speak as she thinks.[3] This the First Amendment will now do by withdrawing from Congress all power to abridge this freedom. The standard against which intellectual property must be fashioned will be accordingly absolute.

What Will Intellectual Property Look Like When Constrained as We Have Proposed?

In expressive works, interests will no longer much resemble "property," assuming that they do so now. We think it may be closer to the mark to envision a regulatory regime of the sort that Professors Patterson and Joyce (and others) have argued was the Framers' original expectation with respect to copyright and patents.[4] In any event, as we have just said, what will most assuredly change first is the exclusivity that is characteristic of intellectual property today. Constraints against appropriation of expressive works that are protected for no other reason than to confer proprietary rights in speech itself will be swept away by the force of a First Amendment that will no longer permit the creation or protection of such rights. The customary justifications will no longer answer. The intellectual property clause cannot continue to give to Congress powers that the First Amendment withdraws. "Progress" cannot suffice: expression may not be abridged merely in order to encourage more or better expression. This is so for the same reason that it may not be abridged in order to limit or discourage unwelcome expression. The

First Amendment must withdraw from Congress the power to judge expression in these terms altogether. "Property" cannot suffice either, and for the same fundamental reason: estates in expression built upon monopolies that abridge expression for the purpose of improving, increasing, or limiting it simply do not lie within the gift of Congress.[5]

This does not mean that all works now recognized as intellectual property will be affected. Copyright will change fundamentally, of course, for its central emphasis upon exclusivity in expression generally depends upon the exercise of a power to be forbidden by the First Amendment. In the language of copyright, protection subsists in expression. In the parlance of the First Amendment, speech and expression are used interchangeably. Is expression equivalent to expression in these two settings? It would certainly seem so. The subject matter of copyright includes, in the language of the Copyright Act itself, "literary works; musical works, including any accompanying words; dramatic works, including any accompanying music; pantomimes and choreographic works; pictorial, graphic, and sculptural works; motion pictures and other audiovisual works; sound recordings; and architectural works."[6] The First Amendment also embraces each category of these works. The equivalence in subject matter is essentially complete. Expression appears to be expression (or speech), for the purposes of both copyright and the First Amendment. But Congress is forbidden by the First Amendment to enact legislation abridging free expression in these and all other similar works, while copyright presupposes that Congress may confer monopolies in them upon favored proprietors. Were copyrighted expression not entitled to some form of categorical exception or prior claim (as Professor Nimmer believed to be the case), then (as he also conceded) a conflict between copyright and the First Amendment could scarcely be doubted.[7]

Interests in other realms will change or not, according to the corresponding realities of their individual existences. Utility patent rights that do not amount to a confinement of expression can retain their exclusivity: drug and medical patents, for example, are unlikely candidates for change; but patentable rights in designs will almost surely be altered. Rights touching equivalently upon expression in still other ways, as may be the case with patents covering business methods or genetic improvements, also will be affected by our changed understanding of the amendment.[8]

In trademark law, interests recognized primarily for the sake of avoiding confusion, deception, misrepresentation, or mistakes in the marketplace are unlikely to be altered. To be sure, we recognize these interests in some sense as though they were exclusive properties, but that is so for reasons that have nothing to do primarily with judging the merits in expression as such or establishing monopolies in the universe of discourses. Indeed, in classic doctrine, we limit trademark interests when the fact of proprietorship is at odds with freedom of discourse, as is the case when a mark becomes generic or functional or is used fairly to describe rather than to signify goods or services in the marketplace. Even at that we must remember that it is still the First Amendment and not the devices internal to the system of protection that count: we are not to repeat Professor Nimmer's error in supposing that the idea/expression dichotomy (or something like it) offers a sufficient response to the new constraints imposed by the amendment.[9] Trademark rights that are recognized primarily for the sake of conferring monopoly interests in their proprietors as a device for controlling discourses will be affected, even when they masquerade as something else. Courts that see in the mere fact of appropriation itself an indication of likelihood of confusion will err, for no such connection can fairly be made. Whether rights against dilution can survive intact will depend on whether they are seen as a logical extension of classic trademark interests or, instead, as a device for conferring copyright-like monopolies.[10]

Meanwhile, trade secrets do not seem to us likely candidates for change. The interests at the heart of this regime are ordinarily utilitarian in nature, and thus are not conferred primarily in order to establish monopolies in discourses otherwise available to all. Only those secrets that are in fact not generally available, but are rather closely held and strictly controlled, qualify as trade secrets under present law.[11] And even then, the law does not object when someone not privy to the secret nevertheless manages to discover it by the process known as "reverse engineering": in that instance the secret is "loosed upon the world," where it is thereafter "free as the air for all to use."[12] Finally, the interests protected by trade secrets classically have had far more to do with constraints against objectionable conduct—such as physical trespass, breaches of fiduciary obligations, and unseemly actions in the too-aggressive pursuit of competition—than they have had with the subject matter of the secrets themselves.[13] Though the concept of misappropriation may play a role in how trade secrets are protected, still we think the essential underpinnings of trade secrets doctrines are to be seen in the sort of transient wrongs customarily recognized in the field of torts, rather than in theories of protection grounded in property.[14]

Other doctrines identified by the *Restatement (Third) of Unfair Competition* as having descended from a theory of misappropriation reminiscent of the majority's reasoning in *International News Service v. Associated Press* will require closer examination; these include common law copyright and the right of publicity.[15] Here we think the *Restatement* may be an incomplete guide for our purposes. As we have seen, common law copyright may have had its origins in unpublished works; these works are protected for reasons that lie beyond a mere concern for property or productivity.[16] An unpublished work may remain protected in the hands of its creator for reasons grounded in concerns for privacy; this we expect will be so whether the work is otherwise eligible for federal protection or not. Virtually by definition, however, the right of publicity arises only when the subject of its protection—for the sake of convenience let us think of it as a celebrity's fame—is well known. Its primary raison d'etre is in the desire to establish exclusivity in expression where otherwise there would be none. On the face of it, then, one must expect that interests in publicity will be limited in the way that most copyright interests in published works will be. Appropriation is to be expected in either instance, offset by acknowledgments that are meant to respond to a creator's moral sensibilities, and offset as well by limitations intended to avoid confusion, deception, and the like. In commercial settings (most actionable appropriations of publicity rights today take place in exactly such settings), apportionment of net revenues can follow on terms equivalent to those governing copyright. Of course a fuller analysis will be required, one that may well take decades before a conclusion is achieved.

We have summarized these results with a seeming confidence that belies our own doubts, uncertainties, and reservations. In truth these will not be easy decisions, but then drawing lines in law is rarely easy, whether in theory or in practice. The question in all cases will be whether the interest at issue corresponds substantially to the interests in expression that the First Amendment guards against abridgment at the hands of Congress or the state. Such correspondence seems evident enough in copyright, where only the existence of the monopoly itself prevents us now from asserting our right to think and speak exactly as we please. Congress may still act in pursuit of any number of laudable or permissible goals, including the goals envisioned by the intellectual property clause. It is not wrong to encourage expressive productivity; but it is impermissible to do so by creating monopolies in the very expression we mean to encourage. This was always a doubtful undertaking and arguably one that did not receive the close attention it deserved when the copyright and patent clause was adopted, much less when that clause was followed by the First Amendment. Perhaps the Framers nodded; or perhaps they envisioned regimes quite different from the ones we know today. When the patent and copyright clause refers to an "exclusive right" for authors and inventors[17] it may have meant no more than something like "the exclusive right to the emblements or emoluments accruing therefrom." That would be consistent with Congress's later adoption of compulsory licenses;[18] modified as we (and others) have suggested, to provide for sharing in net revenues from commercial undertakings, it would be consistent with an absolute First Amendment as well. We could also come to understand that the clause may reflect some concern for the provenance of works. We have suggested that a desire for recognition is probably closer to the heart of what is "natural" to authors and inventors than is money. And we have argued that responding to an interest of this sort need not abridge expression.

In the end we cannot say with certainty what was in the Framers' minds, for such records of debate as they left behind them do not tell us. But we can say now, with the benefit of two hundred years of accumulated wisdom, that exclusive intellectual property regimes in expression qua expression cannot be squared with the vision of the First Amendment we have presented here. A grant of monopoly in expression can be justified only when the object of the grant (its purpose) is essentially other than the subject of the grant (the expression). A trademark may thus qualify to the extent that its recognition is for the purpose of avoiding confusion in the marketplace. A grant of copyright cannot qualify even if its purpose is to promote expression, for even in that case both the object and the subject of the grant are identical. To grant a monopoly in speech to one person is to abridge that speech as to all others. That is precisely what Congress may not (and cannot) do. That power the First Amendment withdraws on the face of the text. Read absolutely, the text does not admit of any defense or justification in the case of abridgement. No law simply means no law.

SOME CONCLUDING QUESTIONS
AND OUR RESPONSES

How Will We Approach the Decisions that Lie Ahead?

To begin, we will learn to distinguish more carefully and deliberately than we now do between works of expression as such, and their particular embodiment, format, or reduction to practice, as well as the particular setting in which we encounter them. What this means in practical terms can be sketched in quickly, in accordance with our own expectations. What it may mean in detail must await analysis, argument, definitions, and decisions still to come in years ahead.

The primary consequence of an absolute First Amendment will be to constrain the state against abridging expression that otherwise has been "divulged." We suppose that the practical standard against which to measure the availability of a work will often correspond to the well-established distinction in copyright between published and unpublished works. But the metastandard will always be measured more appropriately by the telling insight Jefferson offered in his letter to McPherson: the moment a work is divulged, "it forces itself into the possession of every one" so that we cannot dispossess ourselves of it.[19] At that point, whether we (or others) like it or not, it is necessarily ours. And at that point, accordingly, the First Amendment must withdraw from the state the power to confer monopolies in expression that otherwise would belong to all of us.

As we have also said, however, the impact of a First Amendment so read will be absolute but not unlimited. No plausible interpretation of the amendment will confer the right to invade privacy, or break down the doors of the Metropolitan Opera, Madison Square Garden, or the Southpoint Cinema 16. Nor will it confer the right to set aside obligations grounded in fiduciary duty, or interfere with contractual relations entered into willingly and in fact, in the course of a deliberate and affirmative manifestation of an assent to be bound. Contract law in its more odious contemporary aspects—including quasi-contracts, shrink-wrap licensing, prepackaged conventions approved by Uniform Commissioners, and other forms of unconscionable "bargains"—will necessarily give way when ersatz efforts in the name of agreement plainly amount to nothing more than an attempt to reintroduce the very sort of exclusivity that the First Amendment will now oppose.[20] Doubtful cases will be resolved appropriately against an extension of such protection, rather than the other way around.[21]

Physical copies of works may of course be protected against theft, as any article of personal property may be. Beyond that, we may be forbidden to record a play or motion picture or concert in a theater or other venue; we may be similarly forbidden to copy a painting or photograph in a museum, whether with cameras or brush and canvas; and so on. In each instance the proprietor of the traditional venue presumably can continue to limit the immediate conduct of patrons on grounds that stand apart from the mere wish to avoid appropriation of the work itself. Of course no such limits could be imposed so as to carry their effect beyond the precincts of the venue, at least not unless a contractual undertaking as deliberate as the ones we have just described could be shown. This, it seems to us, will be a rare circumstance, and will require a deliberate agreement to be bound going well beyond anything merely implicit in fact or circumstance, much less implied in law.

In our judgment, similar limitations on conduct can extend to a setting in which a party engages in deliberate efforts to control access and concomitant conduct with respect to a digitally formatted work;

such limitations may be necessary to enable the party to exploit the work effectively in that setting. Of course copy-protected embodiments of works in digital formats—including movies, music, art, literary works, and the like, as well as computer programs—can be protected against appropriation to the extent that the copy protection is effective. That much is merely existential. But efforts to control the work in a particular setting may go further: with the assistance of Congress or the state, a would-be exploiter of a work may protect it in substantially the manner (for example) that the present-day Digital Millennium Copyright Act now provides. A central hallmark of the DMCA is to be seen in its provisions forbidding circumvention of access technology. It is the circumvention that is forbidden in this context, however, rather than copying the underlying work as such.[22] The chief concern is with particular efforts to exploit the work in a digitally enclosed setting.[23] Nothing in this part of the DMCA ultimately forbids appropriating the work itself, not even for directly competitive purposes, as one may still do once the work becomes part of the universe of discourses in which all are free to share. Nor will anything in an absolute First Amendment necessarily prevent the DMCA (or preferably, some more aptly-crafted successor to it) from achieving the end that we have described.

The DMCA may not be a wise policy choice with respect to copyrighted interests protected under the present copyright regime. Its provisions forbidding publication of information enabling circumvention seem plainly impermissible, even when considered against our present understanding of the First Amendment.[24] Its notorious lacunae with respect to fair use may offend against the present First Amendment as well, given the opposing roles exclusivity and fair use play within the current copyright regime; arguments to this effect are legion. But we must remember, again, that a work of the intellect and its embodiment are not the same thing. It is the expression in the work itself that is to be free in consequence of an absolute First Amendment. A particular embodiment of the work can continue to be protected against appropriation by the digital fences and virtual arenas the DMCA (or legislation like it) authorizes, without objection under an absolute First Amendment—just as has been the case with fences and arenas in the previrtual world.

The digital technologies justify us in seeking to define and establish new venues. As we have said, the analogies we think compelling are to the drawing room, the concert hall, the museum, the theater, the sports palace, the convention center—or to Fillmore West, Woodstock, and their older cousins and latter-day successors (such as the Grand Ole Opry, Branson, and Bonnaroo). The interest to be protected in each instance is the effective exploitation of a work in a particular setting, rather than the work itself. Nothing in the First Amendment, or in any of its essential history, suggests that the state may not offer its assistance in an endeavor of this sort. Nothing in an absolute First Amendment as we envision it appears at odds with such an effort either. Carefully circumscribed so as to avoid direct or intentional impediments to a separate appropriation of the work itself, legislation fashioned to establish the equivalent of a virtual venue can bring the digital technologies into alignment with the world of expositions we have known for millenniums.[25]

To students of the intellectual property field who now decry the ability of the established doctrines to impede the advancing technologies, the indifference of the First Amendment to these issues as such will seem frustrating and perhaps indefensible. We can offer three responses.

We have said that our book began with just such concerns. But in pursuing them we have in fact taken on a very different quest. We have attempted to refashion both the First Amendment and intellectual property directly, and then to understand them in a more satisfactory way—first individually, and then in their relationship one to another. Our mission thus is to inquire into the shape of the field when measured against a First Amendment whose essential function is to limit Congress in its ability to grant monopolies in discourses that otherwise would be free. Congress may very well respond to the rising chorus of protests against constraints upon technology. In our judgment, those constraints do matter and should be constantly revisited and revised. But the First Amendment cannot be counted on to extend as far as one might like. Congressional judgment and wisdom will still be necessary when sound policy choices carry us beyond its reach.[26]

Moreover, we think the prevailing concerns today are often fundamentally misassessed. The conflict between exclusivity in expression and freedom of expression is ancient; it did not begin with the advent of the new technologies, and it is not to be understood chiefly as an outgrowth of that advent either. Long before there was an Internet there was an issue of freedom deserving of acknowledgment. Professor Nimmer recognized as much, and as to that he was entirely right. Copyright as we have come to know it has always posed a threat to freedom of expression. It may have taken the digital technologies and the Internet to bring that conflict to widespread attention, but the conflict itself is in no sense new. We can be grateful for the attention without mistaking it for novelty.

Ultimately, the value of the new technologies does not lie primarily in copying for the sake of copying, but rather in the extraordinary degree to which they enable additional expression. What has changed most dramatically since their arrival is the ease with which works can be expressed. Copying is part of that, of course, but only part, and only sometimes the most important part. It is what the new technologies enable us to do with works newly liberated that matters most.

Will Fair Use Continue to Play a Role?

Presumably so. In any instance in which the availability of a work is still less than "fairness" requires in the circumstances, there is every reason to suppose that the fair use doctrine will continue to be responsive. This we would expect to be as fully the case under the regime of an absolute First Amendment as it is now.

But is it possible that its role may be even greater than at present?

As our colleague Jed Purdy has observed, there are times when what we must have in order to express ourselves fully is not merely the underlying work but rather its particular embodiment as well. Professor Nimmer himself acknowledged that some works are impressed with a public interest that requires recognition even under a First Amendment flawed (we would say) by the principle of definitional balancing.[27] Zapruder's film of the assassination of JFK, and the "I Have a Dream" speech delivered by Martin Luther King, are two examples of works that must be approached directly (or at least through the medium of direct copies) in order to yield the authenticity that is vital to their fullest expression.[28] Nimmer believed these to be fit subjects for First Amendment

protection, as against the exclusivity that copyright otherwise would afford; in his opinion, this would be true even though fair use itself might
well be inapposite in such settings. We can readily concur in this view,
given the First Amendment as Nimmer understood it at the time he
wrote, and no less so as it is currently construed.[29]

Will a similar outcome follow under an absolute First Amendment?
We think it will. But does this mean that we will be at the mercy of definitional balancing (or something like it) after all? In our opinion it does
not. What it means is nothing more nor less than what we have already
conceded: lines will continue to require drawing even when the First
Amendment is read absolutely. Perhaps, in the strictest understanding of
an absolute First Amendment, the effect would be to withdraw power
from Congress to abridge expression, without any offsetting affirmative
obligations arising under the amendment at all. In that view, fair use
might well take on added meaning as it assumed the burden of coping
with exigencies no longer within the reach of the amendment. We think
such a construction unlikely, however, given the history of the amendment in the past century. Indeed, it is equally an exercise in definition to
hypothesize that some forms of expression may reflect penumbral meaning, as is the case at present.[30] Examples of expression like the ones that
commanded the attention of Nimmer are no less likely, in our judgment,
to command corresponding additional attention from future courts.[31]
As we have said, we have no quarrel with such a prospect. Exercises in
definition cannot be avoided. It will be enough that, at the center of the
First Amendment inquiry, hierarchical balances like the ones that are
struck at present will have no place.

Won't Piracy Flourish in the Shadow of an Absolute First Amendment?

On the contrary, "piracy" is more likely to decline. It is difficult to be a
pirate (or wish or need to be one) when one is entitled to share freely and
without penalty in the treasures of the world. Works will be available
for commercial and noncommercial uses alike, as indeed they often were
prior to the passage of the 1976 Copyright Revision. This will not be a
simple matter of returning to a better legislative scheme, however, but

rather the consequence that follows when the treasure to be shared is expression protected against abridgement by the First Amendment.

But Won't Millions of Unlicensed Appropriations of Works Now Protected by Copyright Exclusivity Undermine the Goal of Progress in Expressive Works?

No. For the first time we will see instead that First Amendment constraints against monopolies in the universe of discourses will "drive the engine" of such progress, rather than the other way around.

How Will Copyright Proprietors Know When They Are Entitled to Compensation for Commercial Appropriations of Their Works?

One way, of course, will be to continue a limited version of the system that we now have, which presupposes an obligation to pay for substantial commercial exploitation of a copyrighted work in defined settings. Suitably limited, a new regime can establish an obligation to share net revenues, along lines we have previously discussed. (In fact, of course, parties to such transactions will likely bargain around an obligation of this character, exactly as is the case now.) Another possibility will be to adapt our experience with clearinghouses to the new need in the marketplace. Still another will be to adopt proposals for subsidies like the ones we have also discussed previously. In short, Congress will be free to deal with this in any way that does not abridge expression.

What About the Question of Acknowledgment to Creators of Works?

In making provision for an acknowledgment of the provenance of a work, Congress presumably will address concerns grounded primarily in such considerations as authenticity and confusion, but will be obliged to avoid requirements effectively amounting to an abridgment of expression. Against that standard, and also as a practical matter, such requirements probably will prove unsuited to appropriations and uses of works in noncommercial settings. We suppose meanwhile that acknowledgment in commercial settings can be required most obviously when an obligation to share in net revenues begins. Again, however, this will be a matter for Congress to decide. No direct entitlement of this sort arises under existing copyright law. The First Amendment itself will not require its recognition in future law.

How Are We to Think About the Economics of Intellectual Property in the Image of an Absolute First Amendment?

The First Amendment reflects a commitment to freedom that we think wholly compatible with sound economics. Should that not seem so to others, however, we must nevertheless treat the role of the First Amendment as paramount, and the role of economics as subordinate. In effect we will reverse the approach we now take to questions of this sort: we will give place to the First Amendment first; and only then will we begin to assess what remains against the precepts of sound economics.

Will It Still Be Possible for Congress to Provide Continuing Economic Incentives to the Production of Creative Works?

The answer is yes, of course. To begin with, Congress will be free to adopt altogether new and different systems of incentives. Systems such as those proposed by Professor Fisher, for example—in which direct, tax-supported patronage of intellectual productivity would augment, supplant, or displace the present intellectual property regimes—probably would not in themselves contravene an absolute First Amendment, so long as patronage is not conditioned upon the content of the expression itself.[32] But interventions substantially less sweeping than these will also be possible. The incentives in a regime of fair competition, with apportionment of net profits measured by the value of one work in the commercial success of another, will prove powerful enough to encourage productivity at least equal to the productivity we now know or have known under past regimes. In reality, present-day regimes flourish through contracting, rather than through penalties or sanctions; compulsory licenses exist mainly in order to encourage parties to contract around the actual terms imposed by these regimes. Penalties and sanctions will now vanish; licenses will be modified accordingly. Market failure will be less frequent, for the reason that the emerging regimes will rely more directly on market incentives, and less on the influence of such irrational forces as the endowment effect that economically dubious monopolies produce. It may even be likely that the new regimes will play an increasingly slender role in the marketplace. As we have suggested in an earlier chapter, Justice Stephen Breyer's classic inquiry into the "uneasy case" for copyright may finally come into its own, as competitors learn to rely on markets rather than monopolies.[33]

Will the Nature of Creative Works Change?

We have suggested that industrial property is likely to change only in limited ways. But what about intellectual productivity? Will there still be music, art, books, television, theater, movies, and the like as we have known them? To each of these questions, the answer is again yes. Let us all understand this, once more, quickly: only three things really change immediately and of necessity under the regime we propose. One is that notions of propertied exclusivity will no longer prevent appropriation of expressive works. The second is that private appropriation for personal (noncommercial) uses will be permissible without license or payment. The third is that commercial uses of appropriated works will result (or can result if Congress chooses) in an equitable apportionment of net revenues according to the value of the appropriated work in the commercial setting. As against each of these changes let us also understand that no one will be obliged to make creative works available in a format that is readily amenable to direct copying. And as to each of these, let us understand still further that contracting around these changes will become commonplace, as is the case with virtually all other transactions in a free market economy. This will be the new metareality, as it were. It is not the end of policy choices in the doctrinal fields we now know as intellectual property, however, but rather the occasion for a new beginning—a beginning grounded in a new appreciation for a First Amendment reality denied for far too long.

Music will adapt to this new reality, as it has adapted through the entire history of its existence. It is worth remembering, again, that the recording industry in America had no copyright protection at all until the adoption of the Sound Recording Amendment of 1971;[34] performing artists have gained a measure of copyright protection only recently;[35] composers and publishers have been subject to compulsory licensing since 1909.[36] And yet in fact the music business in America has always proven remarkably adaptable to changing conditions. We do not dispute the startling presence of digital copying in the last two decades; nor do we doubt that the recording industry has struggled to keep pace with the changes that confront it. The industry will struggle harder, as it ought to, and in the end it will survive and flourish or not, according to its wits. This is as it should be. And music? (For remember that music and the music business are not the same thing.) Music will make its way into our lives no less surely than before. It is a telling datum in this context: music in all its forms has never been more at the center of our lives than it is in our time. No other generation has ever had the access to music that the high school and college-age generation of our time now has. Music is undergoing a moment of reinvention.[37] The digital technologies and file sharing are at the center of this metamorphosis. Already we can see the shape of the recording industry's response to the new reality of file sharing.

Lower prices for CDs, new formats, and new methods of distribution, augmented by new efforts at marketing and service, have begun to give the industry new viability. Meanwhile, a new and startling reality has begun to suggest itself. Far from dampening the appetite for music at large, file sharing appears to increase it. As the roles now played out separately by musicians and audiences begin to merge, and the distance between them erodes, the importance of music in individual lives increases. Music is the dominant medium of our time. The demographic trends are positive and powerful. Money and music can still go hand in hand.[38] If the graybeards in the music business cannot find a market in these circumstances, then let them step aside and make room for a younger generation that can.

And movies? Again, we need not fear their loss. Smaller independent features should flourish in an environment that frees them from the weight of clearances and rights. At present the motion picture industry is dominated by producers and distributors whose market power is considerably derived from their control over content and its exploitation. Intellectual property monopolies impose barriers to entry that often operate as capriciously as they do powerfully. Copyright in the motion picture industry means, as a practical matter, that good people do not often work—and often do not work at all. Modified as we propose, rights and clearances of the sort that make these insights valid will no longer operate with the force that they now bring to the field. The general effect will be to level the field, with beneficial results for the production and distribution of independent features, by newcomers and established players alike.

But will the changes we propose doom the studios or the big budget feature? Can *Saving Private Ryan, Titanic,* and *Casino Royale* (or *Ishtar* and *Heaven's Gate*) still thrive in the legal environment we envision? Presupposing copy-guarded embodiments of film and other recorded works as we ourselves do, the answer is yes—though still subject to the same ultimate aesthetic challenges and resultant uncertainties at the box office. What the industry will lose in its present-day reliance on intellectual property exclusivity it will more than make up for in access to works that are now unavailable, or are now available on terms that make them doubtful or unattractive. Consider *Gone With the Wind.* Neither sequel nor remake is feasible now in the absence of a license. Either will become immediately feasible when exclusivity is no longer a central feature of copyright protection. But can a studio afford to invest heavily in a project if the story cannot be protected? Of course. Anyone is free to tell the story of D-Day or the *Titanic.* Even the extended term of protection upheld by the Court's decision in *Eldred* does not afford exclusive protection for those scenarios in any significant sense. The events are in the public domain; anyone can produce a picture based on them. Even if expression itself is no longer to be protected in quite the same way, the reality is that few competitors will choose to develop projects willingly without concern for what others may already have underway, and this is so for at least two reasons: one is to be seen in Justice Breyer's larger economic analysis of lead time advantage, and the other is reflected in the related but more immediate fact that market demand will not ordinarily justify the closely sequential release of a closely similar (much less identical) picture. *Wyatt Earp* may or may not have been as good a picture as the earlier and financially more successful *Tombstone,* but it wasn't their relative merits at storytelling that made the difference between them. It was the race to the box office. *Wyatt Earp*, the second of the two pictures, was foredoomed by its later release date. The public had been reminded of all it had need of in the earlier work.[39] Calculations of this kind count for far more than copyright in the studio's decision to green-light a film or not. Some changes in know-how are bound to follow from what we propose. Changes in the essential profitability of motion pictures at large will not.

We can offer essentially the same responses to questions about the other principal entertainment industries. Books will still be published, theatrical productions mounted, television shows produced. As we have suggested, some changes in the way those industries now do business will follow, but to no significant disadvantage, whether as to expression or profitability. We can expect that markets will perform better in the service of these endeavors than they now do, for we think (in concert with many others) that markets generally function better unimpeded by monopolies and subsidies, intellectual or otherwise.

All of this said, let us be clear about our priorities. We have meant to acknowledge the costs to freedom of expression inherent in the regimes we now have, and to suggest how they can be transformed in the image of a First Amendment whose central function is to withdraw power from Congress to grant or withhold monopolies in the universe of discourses. We have recognized the utility in continuing incentives to intellectual productivity; nothing in our understanding of an absolute First Amendment requires us to forego them. Whether in the model of fair competition and apportionment of profits, or otherwise, it is clear that adequate incentives can continue to be offered. It will be up to Congress to choose among them, taking into account the myriad considerations that will affect the choice. Perhaps the best choice will resemble a clearinghouse, fashioned roughly after the performing rights societies that have served copyright for decades,[40] but modified of course so as to remove all state-sanctioned and content-determined disparities among those who are parties to the transactions to be arbitrated from time to time. We imagine that parties will contract around this formal structure, however, finding in freedom of contract the least transaction costs and the greatest mutual satisfaction.[41] Meanwhile, outrage and despair, leavened by hopeful condescension and contempt, will undoubtedly be voiced by those to whom any change in the accustomed way of doing business will seem a form of sacrilege. (It has occurred to us that perhaps another chapter, this one on the Establishment Clause, may be needed before our work is finished.) But the influence of reactionaries will have a limited half-life. The advantage will shift quickly to the nimble and swift-witted. Eventually, we are confident that the traditional creative products of the entertainment industries will appear to most observers, whether inside or out, to have remained essentially unchanged—except in the degree to which they will have been augmented by an even greater array of expressive works.

Ultimately, however, it is still the First Amendment that will matter most. In this result, we think, the Constitution, as well as public and private interests in intellectual productivity and freedom of expression alike, will be well served.*

---

* What about the impact on global commerce as a result of the suggestions made in this book? What about the question of our obligations under treaties with other nations? (And why are questions as important as these relegated to a place in a final note?)

Taking freedom seriously will not mean abandoning global commerce, nor will it mean abandoning effective competition. In much of the world, frankly, the change will scarcely be noticed, inasmuch as present-day regimes have yet to achieve a full measure of enforcement. The more important aspects of our treaty obligations will survive, though some modifications will be required in the language and practices of the Universal Copyright Convention, the Berne Convention, certain bi- or multilateral treaties, and of course in the more recent TRIPS Accords that were ratified in 1994 in the aftermath of the Uruguay Round of the General Agreement on Tariffs and Trade. The United States will find it necessary to lead the way in further negotiations leading toward necessary modifications. This will no doubt seem daunting at the outset, but is likely to prove more embarrassing than formidable: elsewhere in the world (even in countries of the European Union which treat intellectual property as a matter of "human rights"), resistance to the idea of exclusivity in expression as a fundamental "right" is mounting. The United States' recognition of a philosophy of intellectual property that places the primary emphasis on freedom of expression ultimately will be of a piece with these global undercurrents.

Meanwhile, the First Amendment applies as fully to the treaty power as to any other provision in the original articles of the Constitution. The government can enter into only those treaties that do not violate the amendment. If it appears that we have undertaken to ratify a treaty improvidently, then it is the treaty that must be reconsidered.

But these are matters ultimately beyond the scope of our book. We do not doubt that they will deserve additional attention in subsequent works. In this book, they are matters for a footnote. This footnote takes us as far as we are prepared to go.

Reference Matter

Notes

CHAPTER 1

1. We think we remember encountering a similar analogy elsewhere, but cannot locate the source. Kindly consider this footnote an acknowledgment in absentia.

2. See, e.g., Madhavi Sunder, "IP³," *Stanford Law Review* 59 (2006): 257.

3. Note here a conventional distinction between "industrial property" (unfair competition, trade secrets, trademarks, patents, and utility models) and "intellectual property" (copyright and neighboring rights, such as *droit moral*), a distinction widely observed elsewhere in the world but largely ignored in the United States, where the latter term is taken to embrace all of the doctrines. We begin our discussion of the subject in plenary terms according to the fashion in the United States. But our interest ultimately is in expression. Thus, in the end, our usage of the term will often accord with the more limited understanding it is given elsewhere. Meanwhile, our colleague Jerome Reichman has observed in a personal conversation that a more elaborate understanding of the conceptual origins of intellectual property is possible than we have offered in the text. We do not understand him to disagree with us, however, when we describe our narrative as "conventional." For our purposes, we think it will suffice to begin our discussion as we have done, leaving the more detailed account of origins for others to whom that account may have greater significance than it does for our project.

4. Laura Underkuffler, *The Idea of Property: Its Meaning and Power* (New York: Oxford University Press, 2003).

5. Wendy Gordon, "An Inquiry into the Merits of Copyright: The Challenges of Consistency, Consent, and Encouragement Theory," *Stanford Law Review* 41 (1989): 1343; see also Mark Lemley, "Ex Ante Versus Ex Post Justifications for Intellectual Property," *University of Chicago Law Review* 71 (2004): 129.

6. Readers who are already familiar sssith the doctrines may choose to skip ahead, presumably without loss—though in our narrative here we may assume or propose an understanding that is in fact foreign to their own.

7. Our discussion of the subject begins, as is conventional, with the semiobligatory paean to competition. See generally *Restatement (Third) of Unfair Competition*, § 1 cmt. a (1995). The reader will eventually see, however, that intellectual property and competition are fundamentally antithetical. For further discussion on Wal-Mart and its effect on the modern economy, see generally Charles Fishman, *The Wal-Mart Effect: How the World's Most Powerful Company Really Works—and How It's Transforming the American Economy* (New York: Penguin Books, 2007).

8. See Richard Posner, *The Economics of Justice* (Cambridge, MA: Harvard University Press, 1981): 94–95.

9. *Tuttle v. Buck*, 107 Minn. 145 (1909).

10. See generally J. Thomas McCarthy, *McCarthy on Trademarks and Unfair Competition*, §§ 1:1, 1:18, 2:2, 5:2 (Eagan, MN: West, 2005) (noting that actions for unfair competition arose from the tort of fraud and deceit). McCarthy observes that competitive standards within a given enterprise or property regime determine what is moral and fair and, thus, what constitutes unfair competition as well.

11. Justice Holmes addressed this form of passing off (or "palming off," as he called it) in *International News Service v. Associated Press*, 248 U.S. 215, 247 (1918), which we discuss at greater length in Part Two of our book.

12. See *McCarthy on Trademarks*, §§ 1:18–19.

13. The cause of action that arises from passing off is not ordinarily conceptualized as "property," for much the same reason that we do not think of actions for personal injury as "property." In law these actions are not recognized apart from the interests of those who are entitled to bring them, and are not amenable to sale as property interests are. Instead, they are commonly viewed as transient interests governed by liability rules of general applicability, and are thus the province of tort law. Yet the action for passing off is quite commonly treated as an aspect of intellectual property, and we have included it here for that reason.

14. *INS*, 248 U.S. 215 (1918).

15. Dennis Karjala has been the leading proponent of a wider recognition of misappropriation as a force in intellectual property law. See Dennis Karjala, "Misappropriation as a Third Intellectual Property Paradigm," *Columbia Law Review* 94 (1994): 2594; Karjala, "Copyright and Misappropriation," *University of Dayton Law Review* 17 (1992): 885, 904–9. But contemporary opinion has generally run to the contrary. See *Restatement (Third) of Unfair Competition*, § 38 cmt. b-c; see also *McCarthy on Trademark*, §§ 1:12, 1:18, 10:48, 10:51, 10:60; Douglas Baird, "The Story of INS v. AP: Property, Natural Monopoly, and the Uneasy Legacy of a Concocted Controversy," in *Intellectual Property Stories*, ed. Jane Ginsburg & Rochelle Dreyfuss (New York: Foundation Press, 2006): 9–35; Richard Posner, "Misappropriation: A Dirge," *Houston Law Review* 40 (2003): 621.

16. See Gordon, "An Inquiry into the Merits of Copyright," 1446 n. 445, discussing John Locke's theory of property and its relevance to copyright.

17. *Mazer v. Stein*, 347 U.S. 201, 219 (1954). ("The economic philosophy behind the clause empowering Congress to grant patents and copyrights is the conviction that encouragement of individual effort by personal gain is the best way to advance public welfare through the talents of authors and inventors in 'Science and useful Arts.'")

18. Mark Lemley, "Ex Ante Versus Ex Post Justifications for Intellectual Property," *University of Chicago Law Review* 71 (2004): 129.

19. *Restatement (Third) of Unfair Competition*, § 38 cmt. b-c; Gary Myers, "The Restatement's Rejection of the Misappropriation Tort: A Victory for the Public Domain," *South Carolina Law Review* 47 (1996): 673, 688.

20. The account that follows in the text is drawn primarily from authorities cited in David Lange, "The Speech & Press Clauses," *UCLA Law Review* 23 (1975): 77. But the subject has been treated in numerous works, with occasional variances among them. Compare, for example, Mark Rose, "Nine-Tenths of the

Law: The English Copyright Debates and the Rhetoric of the Public Domain," *Law & Contemporary Problems* 66 (2003): 75 with L. Ray Patterson, *Copyright in Historical Perspective* (Nashville, TN: Vanderbilt University Press, 1968). See also Howard Abrams, "The Historic Foundation of American Copyright Law: Exploding the Myth of Common Law Copyright," *Wayne Law Review* 29 (1983): 1119. Siva Vaidhyanathan offers a still more recent treatment in *Copyrights and Copywrongs: The Rise of Intellectual Property and How It Threatens Creativity* (New York: New York University Press, 2001).

21. See Patterson, *Copyright in Historical Perspective*, 130–42.
22. We assume More's story needs no citation. For the rest, compare Michel Foucault, "What Is an Author?" in *Textual Strategies: Perspectives in Post-Structuralist Criticism*, ed. Josué Harari (Ithaca, NY: Cornell University Press, 1979) with William M. Landes and Richard A. Posner, "An Economic Analysis of Copyright Law," *Journal of Legal Studies* 18 (1989): 325.
23. See Abrams, "The Historic Foundation of American Copyright Law." For alternative arguments about the existence of common-law copyright before 1709, as well as its importance, see generally R. C. DeWolf, *Outline of Copyright Law* (Boston: John W. Luce, 1925) and Philip Wittenberg, *The Law of Literary Property* (New York: World Publishing Co., 1957): 25–31. See also Craig Joyce, "A Curious Chapter in the History of Judicature: *Wheaton v. Peters* and the Rest of the Story (of Copyright in the New Republic)," *Houston Law Review* 42 (2005): 325.
24. Melville Nimmer, *Nimmer on Copyright* § 4.03 (Newark, NJ: Matthew Bender, 2005).
25. See generally *Wheaton v. Peters*, 33 U.S. 591 (1834). See also Joyce, "A Curious Chapter in the History of Judicature."
26. *Nimmer on Copyright* § 2.02; see also 17 U.S.C. § 301(a).
27. Samuel D. Warren & Louis D. Brandeis, "The Right to Privacy," *Harvard Law Review* 4 (1890): 193.
28. *Restatement (Third) of Unfair Competition* § 38 cmt. b-d.
29. *Restatement (Third) of Unfair Competition* § 39.
30. *E. I. duPont de Nemours v. Christopher*, 431 F.2d 41 (5th Cir. 1970).
31. See, e.g., *ILG Industries, Inc. v. Scott*, 49 Ill.2d 88, 97 (1971). (Noting that "in many cases the question of whether a specific matter is a trade secret is an extremely close one, often not readily predictable until a court has announced its ruling.")
32. *Restatement (Third) of Unfair Competition*, §§ 38, 39 et seq.
33. Warren & Brandeis, "The Right to Privacy," 193.
34. William Prosser, "Privacy," *California Law Review* 48 (1960): 383.
35. Harry Kalven, Jr., "Privacy in Tort Law—Were Warren and Brandeis Wrong?" *Law & Contemporary Problems* 31 (1966): 326, 334.
36. See, e.g., *Jacqueline Kennedy Onassis v. Christian Dior, Inc.*, 472 N.Y.S.2d 254 (N.Y. Sup. Ct., Special Term 1984).
37. Roberta Kwall, "Fame," *Indiana Law Journal* 73 (1997): 1; Samantha Barbas, *Movie Crazy: Fans, Stars, and the Cult of the Celebrity* (New York: Palgrave MacMillan, 2001).

38. Melville Nimmer, "The Right of Publicity," *Law & Contemporary Problems* 19 (1954): 203.

39. *Restatement (Second) of Contracts*, § 547(1)(d): "An assignment of a claim against a third person or a bargain to assign such a claim is illegal and ineffective if the claim is for . . . (d) damages for an injury the gist of which is to the person rather than to property"; see also *Dodd v. Middlesex Mut. Assurance Co.*, 698 A.2d 859 (Conn. 1999) ("Under common law a cause of action for personal injuries cannot be assigned."); *Horton v. New South Ins. Co.*, 122 N.C. App. 265 (1996) (assignments of personal tort claims are void as against public policy because they promote champerty).

40. Harriet Pilpel, an eminent member of the New York bar and noted practitioner in the field of literary law, believed that the provenance of the publicity right was fundamentally unrelated to privacy, and thus substantially different from the more conventional narrative we are relating here. See generally Harriet Pilpel, "The Right of Publicity," *Bulletin of the Copyright Society (USA)* 27 (1980): 249. In another context we might pursue her views at greater length, but time and space forbid our doing more than noting the divergence here.

41. *Haelan v. Topps Chewing Gum*, 202 F.2d 866 (2d Cir. 1953.)

42. The *Haelan* court held:

in addition to and independent of that right of privacy (which in New York derives from statute), a man has a right in the publicity value of his photograph, i.e., the right to grant the exclusive privilege of publishing his picture, and that such a grant may validly be made "in gross," i.e., without an accompanying transfer of a business or of anything else. Whether it be labeled a "property" right is immaterial; for here, as often elsewhere, the tag "property" simply symbolizes the fact that courts enforce a claim which has pecuniary worth.

202 F.2d at 868.

43. *Metropolitan Opera Ass'n v. Wagner-Nichols Recorder Corp.*, 101 N.Y.S.2d 483, 492 (1950).

44. Nimmer, "The Right of Publicity," 214.

45. See generally J. Thomas McCarthy, *The Rights of Publicity and Privacy* § 1:29 (Eagan, MN: West, 2005) (discussing the development of the right of publicity and noting that judges "were understandably reluctant to buy what they perceived as a 'pig in a poke.' Sometimes plaintiffs' attorneys referred to a 'right of publicity' in their complaint, but when pressed by the court to define exactly what it meant, were unable to set a judge's mind at ease. Few trial judges were willing to risk reversal by resting liability entirely upon this new and untested concept.")

46. *Lugosi v. Universal Pictures*, 25 Cal. 3d 813 (1979).

47. *Guglielmi v. Spelling-Goldberg Prods.*, 25 Cal. 3d 860 (1979). Though filed in 1971, this case (and *Lugosi*) lingered during most of the decade before arriving in the California Supreme Court.

48. *Restatement (Second) of Torts* § 652C.

49. *Lugosi*, 25 Cal. 3d at 819 ("'a right of value' to create a business, product or service of value is embraced in the law of privacy and is protectable during one's lifetime but it does not survive the death of Lugosi"); *Guglielmi*, 25 Cal. 3d at 862 (noting that *Lugosi* controlled and, therefore, the privacy or publicity rights of

Rudolph Valentino, the plaintiff, were not descendible). In 1984, the California legislature enacted legislation in favor of a descendible right of publicity. Cal. Civ. Code § 990 (1984).

50. The Second Circuit originally applied New York law to affirm a preliminary injunction against the sale of Elvis Presley posters. See *Factors Etc., Inc. v. Pro Arts, Inc.*, 579 F.2d 215 (2d Cir. 1978), *cert. denied*, 440 U.S. 215 (1979) ("*Factors I*"). But then the Second Circuit reversed itself after the Sixth Circuit applied Tennessee common law to the same facts and, consequently, concluded that Tennessee did not have any cognizable "right of publicity." See *Memphis Dev. Foundation v. Factors Etc., Inc.*, 616 F.2d 956, 959–60 (6th Cir.), *cert. denied*, 449 U.S. 953 (1980) ("*Factors II*"). The Tennessee legislature, intending to reverse the outcome in *Factors II*, subsequently enacted a right-of-publicity statute. Tenn. Code Ann. § 47-25-1104 (after a ten-year period, the exclusive right is terminable by proof of nonuse of decedent's name, likeness or image "for a period of two (2) years"). But the Tennessee Court of Appeals then decided that the Tennessee Legislature's judgment fell short, declaring that publicity rights were descendible under common law with respect to rights of publicity that were in existence *prior to* the effective date of the statute. See *ex rel. Elvis Presley Int'l Memorial Foundation v. Crowell*, 733 S.W.2d 89, 99 (Tenn. Ct. App. 1987).

51. McCarthy identifies the following states: California, Connecticut, Florida, Georgia, Hawaii, Illinois, Indiana, Kentucky, Massachusetts, Michigan, Minnesota, Missouri, Nevada, Nebraska, New Jersey, New York, Ohio, Oklahoma, Pennsylvania, Rhode Island, Tennessee, Texas, Utah, Virginia, and Wisconsin. See generally McCarthy, *The Rights of Publicity and Privacy* § 6:6.

52. California, Florida, Illinois, Indiana, Kentucky, Nevada, New York, Oklahoma, Tennessee, Texas, and Virginia. See McCarthy, *The Rights of Publicity and Privacy*, § 6:6.

53. *Restatement (Third) of Unfair Competition* § 38 cmt. b.

54. *Restatement (Third) of Unfair Competition* § 46. ("One who appropriates the commercial value of a person's identity by using without consent the person's name, likeness, or other indicia of identity for purposes of trade is subject to liability for the relief appropriate under the rules stated in §§ 48 and 49.")

55. *Restatement (Third) of Unfair Competition* § 38 cmt. B. ("In many cases [*INS*] has been invoked when narrower rules of unfair competition would have achieved the same result. In most of the areas in which it has been expansively applied, its application has now been supplanted by legislation.")

56. We are obliged to note that Professor Lange was among the advisors to the reporter.

57. *Restatement (Third) of Unfair Competition* § 9. The principal source of federal protection is in the Lanham Act of 1946, which the Supreme Court has construed broadly. See, e.g., *Qualitex Co. v. Jacobson Prods. Co.*, 514 U.S. 159, 162 (1995) (a trademark can be "anything at all that is capable of carrying meaning").

58. *Two Pesos, Inc., v. Taco Cabana, Inc.*, 505 U.S. 763, 765 n. 1 (1992).

59. *Wal-Mart Stores v. Samara Bros.* 529 U.S. 205 (2000).

60. McCarthy, *McCarthy on Trademarks* § 2:8. ("Today, the keystone of that portion of unfair competition law which relates to trademarks is the avoidance of a

likelihood of confusion in the minds of the buying public. Whatever route one travels, whether by trademark infringement or unfair competition, the signs give direction to the same enquiry—whether defendant's acts are likely to cause confusion.")

61. Cf. Monica Wallace, "Using the Past to Predict the Future: Refocusing the Analysis of a Federal Dilution Claim," *University of Cincinnati Law Review* 73 (2005): 945, 946 (noting that "if a consumer intends to purchase the 'Cheerios' brand cereal but instead purchases 'Cheeri-ohes' cereal, the sale clearly belongs to the owner of the Cheerios mark and an infringement claim protects the senior trademark holder").

62. *Restatement (Third) of Unfair Competition* § 13–17. These and other similarly useful examples appear recurrently and interchangeably in discussions of trademark law. Cf. Mary LaFrance, *Understanding Trademark Law* §§ 2.05–7 (Newark, NJ: Matthew Bender, 2005). Additional distinctions between state and federal protection are important but need not detain us here. While continued use is the key to continuing priority and protection as a general matter, some statutory protection may require formal steps amounting to renewal to be taken periodically.

63. See generally Daniel McClure, "Trademarks and Unfair Competition: A Critical History of Legal Thought," *Trademark Reporter* 69 (1979): 305.

64. See generally *Restatement (Third) of Unfair Competition* § 30; see also *United Drug Co. v. Theodore Rectanus Co.*, 248 U.S. 90, 97 (1918) (holding that "[t]here is no such thing as property in a trade-mark except as a right appurtenant to an established business or trade in connection with which the mark is employed"); *Major League Baseball Properties, Inc. v. Sed Non Olet Denarius, Ltd.*, 817 F. Supp. 1103 (S.D.N.Y. 1993), *vacated*, 859 F. Supp. 80 (S.D.N.Y. 1994) (famed "Brooklyn Dodgers" mark deemed abandoned after the Dodgers team moved to Los Angeles and changed its name to the "Los Angeles Dodgers"; court found that the Los Angeles Dodgers' use of "Brooklyn Dodgers" was merely historical use and insufficient to demonstrate a presently identifiable, antecedent source).

65. See generally *Restatement (Third) of Unfair Competition* § 34; see also *Fisk v. Fisk*, 3 F.2d 7 (8th Cir. 1924); *Sands, Taylor & Wood Co. v. Quaker Oats Co.*, 978 F.2d 947 (7th Cir. 1992), *cert. denied*, 507 U.S. 1042 (1993).

66. This is consistent with the view generally taken by any court which deals with the species of unfair competition known as "passing off." See generally *Clothier Case*, 1656 Poph. 144 (1619) (arguably the first trademark case; passing off found when one clothier deceptively used the mark of another clothier in making his cloth); *Crowell Pub. Co. v. Italian Monthly Co.*, 28 F.2d 613 (2d Cir. 1928) (claim for unfair competition based on passing off of another's mark; court found that the use of the phrase "The New American" [magazine title] did not infringe on alleged proprietary interest in a similar phrase, "The American Magazine"); *Dixi-Cola Laboratories v. Coca-Cola Co.*, 117 F.2d 352 (4th Cir. 1941); *Avon Periodicals v. Ziff-Davis Pub. Co.*, 113 N.Y.S.2d 737 (N.Y. Sup. 1952); see also McClure, "Trademarks and Unfair Competition."

67. In re *Trade-Mark Cases*, 100 U.S. 82 (1879) (holding the federal trademark statute of 1870 unconstitutional as it exceeded the scope of congressional authority,

evidenced by the lack of any intent on Congress' part to regulate interstate or foreign use of trademarks); see also William Landes & Richard Posner, "The Economics of Trademark Law," *Trademark Reporter* 78 (1988): 267, 267–70 (observing, before arguing in favor of a rivalrous-property system for trademarks, that a "property right is a legally enforceable power to exclude others from using a resource, without need to contract with them"); *McCarthy on Trademarks and Unfair Competition* § 5:2.

68. *Restatement (Third) of Unfair Competition* § 19.

69. See generally Wendy Gordon, "On Owning Information: Intellectual Property and the Restitutionary Impulse," *Virginia Law Review* 78 (1992): 149, 277. As Gordon puts it, the

> recent trend in intellectual property rights finds that all appropriations are in danger of being treated as misappropriations and that the interdependence upon which our cultural life rests is on the verge of becoming a cash-and-carry operation. I speculate that judges may feel no need to examine the trend because the restitutionary notion that one deserves to keep the 'fruits of his labor' seems so evidently correct, so evidently in accord with traditional notions of corrective justice and traditional conceptions of the judicial role, that giving legal protection to intellectual products appears to require no special justification.

> Graeme Austin, in "Trademarks and the Burdened Imagination," *Brooklyn Law Review* 69 (2004): 827, 846 makes much the same point and notes that "[d]espite the instrumentalist emphasis on 'search costs,' courts also rationalize imposing liability for trademark infringement on general principles of commercial morality, basing their analyses on broad unfair competition concepts. A related development is that trademarks are often, and increasingly, conceptualized as property in their own right, allowing trademark proprietors to borrow from the rhetoric associated with the enforcement of property rights in other intellectual property contexts."

70. Frank Schechter, "The Rational Basis of Trademark Protection," *Harvard Law Review* 40 (1927): 813.

71. As Schechter elaborates:

> The true functions of the trademark are . . . to identify a product as satisfactory and thereby stimulate further purchase by the consuming public. . . . To describe a trademark merely as a symbol of good will, without recognizing it as an agency for the actual creation and perpetuation of good will, ignores the most potent aspect of the nature of a trademark and that phase most in need of protection. . . . [T]oday the trademark is not merely the symbol of good will but [also] the most effective agent for the creation of good will.

"The Rational Basis of Trademark Protection," 818.

72. The essential point for Schechter was that the mark not derive its primary meaning from common language, usage, or understanding. See Schechter, "The Rational Basis of Trademark Protection," 825–31.

73. Lanham Act § 43(c). The law came into effect early in 1996.

74. In the first case to reach it involving § 43(c), the Supreme Court held that the section was to be construed with some strictness. *Moseley v. V Secret Catalogue, Inc.*, 537 U.S. 418 (2003). Thus it was not enough, as some had supposed, that a

plaintiff be able to show a likelihood of dilution, or even a gradual "whittling away" of the mark's distinctiveness; instead, actual dilution in fact, resulting in a present diminution in distinctiveness, must be pleaded and must be plausibly susceptible to proof. Congress responded to this holding in 2006 with an amendment to § 43(c) that changed the standard to "likelihood of dilution."

CHAPTER 2

1. Section 102(a) of the Copyright Act of 1976 lists eight categories of copyrightable works: (1) literary works; (2) musical works, including any accompanying words; (3) dramatic works, including any accompanying music; (4) pantomimes and choreographic works; (5) pictorial, graphic, and sculptural works; (6) motion pictures and other audiovisual works; (7) sound recordings; and (8) architectural works. This classification scheme quickly becomes far more complex than it might appear. Computer programs, for example, are considered to be literary works. Until 1991 data collections could hope for some protection from copyright on what was termed the "sweat of the brow" theory, a substitute for the originality that both the copyright clause and the 1976 General Revision each required. In *Feist Publications, Inc. v. Rural Telephone Service Co.*, 499 U.S. 340 (1991), the Supreme Court held that "sweat of the brow" could not sustain copyright. Since then, data have had an uneasy existence as the disinherited children of the intellectual property regime. Congressional action to restore them to the table has not yet earned passage, though at some point a general system of protection for data seems likely.

2. Patent Act § 101. In addition to utility patents, the Act provides protection for certain works of industrial design as well as asexually reproduced plants.

3. One exception to this generalization may lie in the computer program field, where practitioners must be aware of the availability and differing utility in both copyright and patent law. In this area of practice, the common subjects of the rights, rather than the rights themselves, provide coherence.

4. U.S. Const. art. I, § 8, cl. 8.

5. For further discussion on the semantics of Art. I, § 8, cl. 8, see Karl Fenning, "The Origin of the Patent and Copyright Clause of the Constitution," *Journal of the Patent Office Society* 11 (1929): 438, 445 (noting that the framers avoided doctrinal terms, "possibly lest the power be limited to the particular forms . . . at that time known as copyrights and patents"); Tom Arnold, "A Philosophy on the Protections Afforded by Patent, Trademark, Copyright and Unfair Competition Law: The Sources and Nature of Product Simulation Law," *Trademark Reporter* 54 (1964): 413, 418 (noting that the framers likely intended to omit the words "patent" and "copyright"; also discussing, along with the nomenclature of the clause, how the colonies frequently mandated inventions to have a "public use" value to secure patentlike protection; books, on the other hand, had two requirements for copyrightlike protection: (1) availability (enough copies printed to avoid scarcity or hoarding of information) and (2) price; but cf. Benjamin Kaplan, "Performer's Right and Copyright: The Capitol Records Case," *Harvard Law Review* 69 (1956): 409, 423. ("Yet even in 1787 lawyers were familiar with the importance of publication in copyright law, and the failure to use the term [publication] in the copyright clause may indicate that no distinction was intended for constitutional purposes between published and unpublished works.")

6. See generally Frank Schechter, *The Historical Foundations of the Law Relating to Trademarks* (New York: Columbia University Press, 1925); Bruce Bugbee, *Genesis of American Patent and Copyright Law* (Washington, DC: Public Affairs Press, 1967); Irah Donner, "The Copyright Clause of the U.S. Constitution: Why Did the Framers Include It with Unanimous Approval?" *American Journal of Legal History* 36 (1992): 361; Milton Handler & Charles Pickett, "Trade-marks and Trade Names—An Analysis and Synthesis," *Columbia Law Review* 30 (1930): 168; Frank Prager, "Historic Background and Foundation of American Patent Law," *American Journal of Legal History* 5 (1961): 309.

7. Lawrence Lessig, *Free Culture* (New York: Penguin Press, 2004), 131.

8. *Graham v. John Deere Co.*, 38 U.S. 1, 5 (1966).

9. Colonial patent laws, which were the result of intense lobbying and only enabled brief protection for "new inventions," were rough versions of the Statute of Monopolies. Edward Walterscheid, "The Early Evolution of the United States Patent Law: Antecedents (5 Part I)," *Journal of the Patent & Trademark Office Society* 78 (1996): 615, 626. Colonial copyright laws were likewise based on the laws of the mother country, specifically the Statute of Anne. As the late Professor L. Ray Patterson has pointed out, the Statute of Anne, discussed in Chapter 1, gave *publishers* a monopoly right to copy. That was the essence of the statute; it was narrowly drawn for the publisher's (or bookseller's) benefit. Likewise, Massachusetts, the first colony to enact a copyright statute, protected only publishers, not authors, and issued an order in 1662 forbidding any printer from publishing without a license; this regime was the mirror image of the Statute of Anne. See generally L. Ray Patterson, *Copyright in Historical Perspective* (Nashville, TN: Vanderbilt University Press, 1968), 143–49, 183–84; see also Siva Vaidhyanathan, *Copyrights and Copywrongs: The Rise of Intellectual Property and How It Threatens Creativity* (New York: New York University Press, 2001), 38.

10. James Madison and Charles Pinckney are largely credited with providing the foundation for the progress clause. Dotan Oliar notes that it was from the elements of Madison and Pinckney's proposals—both of which clearly included contemporary language and understandings of copyright and patent—that the clause derived its substance. And that substance was, specifically, to "confer upon Congress two means (patents and copyrights) . . . in order to achieve one end (promotion of progress of science and useful arts) but not another (mere encouragement of industry)." Dotan Oliar, "Making Sense of the Intellectual Property Clause: Promotion of Progress as a Limitation on Congress's Intellectual Property Power," *Georgetown Law Journal* 94 (2006): 1771, 1796.

11. Paul Goldstein, *Copyright's Highway: From Gutenberg to the Celestial Jukebox* (Stanford, CA: Stanford University Press, 2003), 28.

12. U.S. Const. art. I, § 8, cl. 8; see also *Feist*, 499 U.S. 340; *Graham v. John Deere Co.*, 383 U.S. 1 (1966).

13. See *Wheaton v. Peters*, 33 U.S. 591, 592 (1834) (rejecting the appellant's argument that statutory copyright supplemented common-law rights—which would have prolonged proprietary interests in intangible goods—and holding instead that all intellectual property must eventually enter the public domain). For subsequent patent cases that followed *Wheaton*, see *U.S. v. American Bell Tel. Co.*,

167 U.S. 224, 243 (1897) (holding that Alexander Graham Bell's patent had "expired and all the monopoly which attaches to it alone has ceased, and the right to use that invention has become public property"); *McCormick v. Talcott*, 61 U.S. 402, 406 (1857) (declaring that the plaintiff's patent "is now public property"); *Atty. Gen. v. Rumford Chem. Works*, 32 F. 608, 617 (C.C.D.R.I. 1876) (an invention "becomes public property at the expiration of the term of the patent"); *Page v. Ferry*, 18 F. Cas. 979, 983 (C.C.E.D. Mich. 1857) (holding that patentable subject matter becomes public property after expiration); *Wintermute v. Redington*, 30 F. Cas. 367, 369 (C.C.N.D. Ohio 1856). ("[T]he consideration for which the patent issues to him, is the benefit he confers on the community, by his discovery eventually becoming public property.") As for later copyright cases, see *Merriam v. Famous Shoe & Clothing Co.*, 47 F. 411, 413 (C.C.E.D. Mo. 1891) ("[A]s the copyright on that edition has expired, it has now become public property. Any one may reprint that edition of the work . . ."); *Merriam v. Holloway Pub. Co.*, 43 F. 450, 451 (C.C.E.D. Mo. 1890). ("When a man takes out a copyright, for any of his writings or works, he impliedly agrees that, at the expiration of that copyright, such writings or works shall go to the public and become public property . . . . The copyright law gives an author or proprietor a monopoly of the sale of his writings for a definite period, but the grant of a monopoly implies that, after the monopoly has expired, the public shall be entitled ever afterwards to the unrestricted use of the book.")

14. See generally Patent Act of 1836 § 6 (expanding upon the 1793 Patent Act by requiring patent applicants to prove novelty [no "prior art"] by "particularly specifying and pointing out the part, improvement or combination, which he claims as his own invention or discovery"); today, the novelty requirement is specifically spelled out in 35 U.S.C. § 102(a).

15. Constructive knowledge of the prior art may be imputed by public use or knowledge prior to invention, as well as prior publications or patents, 35 U.S.C. § 102.

16. Ibid., § 103. See *Graham v. John Deere Co.*, 383 U.S. 1, 3–10 (1966).

17. *Hotchkiss v. Greenwood*, 52 U.S. 248 (1850) (holding that a ceramic doorknob needed more "ingenuity and skill" to be patentable).

18. *Alfred Bell & Co. v. Catalda Fine Arts*, 191 F.2d 99 (2d Cir. 1951) (reasoning that the "Constitution, as so interpreted, recognizes that the standards for patents and copyrights are basically different"); see also Melville Nimmer & David Nimmer, *Nimmer on Copyright* (Newark: Matthew Bender & Co., 2006, § 2.01[A]).

19. *Sheldon v. Metro-Goldwyn Pictures Corporation*, 81 F.2d 49, 54 (1936), *cert. denied*, 298 U.S. 669 (1936).

20. Nimmer & Nimmer, *Nimmer on Copyright*.

21. David Nimmer, "Copyright in the Dead Sea Scrolls: Authorship and Originality," *Houston Law Review* 38 (2001): 1, 39 n. 152.

22. *Matthew Bender & Co. v. West Publ'g Co.*, 158 F.3d 674, 681 (2d Cir. 1998) (holding that the " 'originality' standard requires that the work result from 'independent creation' and that the author demonstrate that such creation entails a 'modicum of creativity' ").

23. *Eldred v. Ashcroft*, 537 U.S. 186 (2003).

24. 17 U.S.C. § 102(b).

25. But cf. Kristen Knudsen, "Tomorrow Never Dies: The Protection of James Bond

and Other Fictional Characters Under the Federal Trademark Dilution Act," *Vanderbilt Journal of Entertainment Law & Practice* 2 (2000): 13, 19.

26. For an historical account of the Bond genre, see Lars Sauerberg, *Secret Agents in Fiction: Ian Fleming, John Le Carré, and Len Deighton* (New York: St. Martin's Press, 1984); see also Ronald Grover, "Is James Bond Worth $1 Billion?" *Business Week*, September 20, 2004.

27. "The paramount purpose of the idea-expression dichotomy, whether statutory or judicial, is to prevent copyright protection from becoming overbroad . . . and, specifically, to distinguish copyright protection from patent protection." Howard Abrams, *The Law of Copyright*, § 3:2 (Eagan, MN: West, 2004).

28. See *Hotchkiss v. Greenwood*, 52 U.S. 248 (1850).

29. See Donald Chisum, *Chisum on Patents*, § 3.05 (Albany, NY: Matthew Bender & Co., 2006); see also *Paulik v. Rizkalla*, 760 F.2d 1270, 1273 (Fed Cir. 1985). ("There is no impediment in the law to holding that a long period of inactivity need not be a fatal forfeiture, if the first inventor resumes work on the invention before the second inventor enters the field."); *Brenner v. Manson*, 383 U.S. 519, 534–35 (1966). (holding that utility is not met "[u]nless and until a process is refined and developed to this point—where specific benefit exists in currently available form—there is insufficient justification for permitting an applicant to engross what may prove to be a broad field. . . . [Otherwise,] [s]uch a patent may confer power to block off whole areas of scientific development, without compensating benefit to the public.")

30. 17 U.S.C. § 102(a).

31. *Nimmer on Copyright*, § 2.03[G].

32. Ibid.

33. 17 U.S.C. §§ 408, 411–12.

34. "The Copyright Office has substantial discretion to deny registration if the subject matter is not copyrightable. Nonetheless, it uses its power to deny registration of copyright claims very sparingly, under a policy known as the 'rule of doubt.' This means that all doubts are resolved in favor of the applicant and any resulting problems are left for the courts to resolve." Bruce Keller & Jeffrey Cunard, *Copyright Law: A Practitioner's Guide*, § 5:3[C] (New York: PLI Press, 2005).

35. 17 U.S.C. § 410(c).

36. 35 U.S.C. §§ 102, 103.

37. 35 U.S.C. § 103(c); see *Hazeltine Research, Inc. v. Brenner*, 382 U.S. 252, 254–55 (1965); *Chisum on Patents*, §§ 11.02, 11.04.

38. *Chisum on Patents*, § 11.03.

39. These are the principal rights provided by § 106(1)–(5) of the 1976 Act; they were part of the Act when it first took effect on January 1, 1978. We omit discussion here of an additional public performance right made available in 1996 to proprietors of sound recordings that are transmitted digitally to subscribers (as in the case of an FM broadcast in digital format) (17 U.S.C. § 106[6]), as well as rights accruing to the creators of visual fine arts in limited copies (17 U.S.C. § 106A).

40. 17 U.S.C. § 501(a).

41. *Wihtol v. Crow*, 309 F.2d 777 (8th Cir. 1962).

42. *Metro-Goldwyn-Mayer Studios Inc. v. Grokster, Ltd.*, 125 S. Ct. 2764, 2780 (2005); see also David Lange, "Students, Music and the Net: A Comment on Peer-To-Peer File Sharing," *Duke Law & Technology Review*, 2003, no. 0021.

43. Section 154 of the Patent Act of 1952. The provisions quoted in the text apply to utility and design patents. See § 171. Plant patents confer the right to exclude others from asexually reproducing the plant and from selling the plant or its parts. Like copyright, patent law is territorial, in that in the absence of a treaty it is effective primarily throughout the United States. It also permits the patentee to preclude the importation of discoveries, designs, or plants that would infringe were they to be made here.

44. 35 U.S.C. § 271(a) ("whoever without authority makes, uses, offers to sell, or sells any patented invention, within the United States or imports into the United States any patented invention during the term of the patent therefor, infringes the patent").

45. *Bio-Techn. Gen. Corp. v. Genentech, Inc.*, 80 F.3d 1553, 1559 (Fed. Cir. 1996). ("It is elementary that a patent grants only the right to exclude others and confers no right on its holder to make, use, or sell."); *Animal Legal Defense Fund v. Quigg*, 932 F.2d 920, 935 n.15 (Fed. Cir. 1991). ("A patent provides only a right to exclude others from practicing the invention for a limited time.")

46. *Bio-Techn. Gen. Corp.*, 80 F.3d 1553. See also Trevor Carter, "Legalizing Patent Infringement: Application of the Patent Exhaustion Doctrine to Foundry Agreements," *Indiana Law Review* 28 (1995): 689, 691 (explaining that the "right that a patent gives the patent owner is described as a negative right because it permits the patent owner to prevent others from making, using or selling the invention").

47. See *Wihtol v. Crow*, 309 F.2d 777; *Princeton Univ. Press v. Michigan Document Services*, 99 F.3d 1813 (6th Cir. 1996) (en banc) (rejecting fair use and finding infringement because the defendants used substantial portions of copyrighted material in developing student course packs); *American Geophysical Union v. Texaco*, 60 F.3d 913 (2d Cir. 1994) (infringement found and fair use rejected when defendant copied entire work for archival purposes); 17 U.S.C. § 501 et seq.

48. This is often called "literal infringement," and occurs "when every limitation recited in the claim appears in the accused device, i.e., when the properly construed claim reads on the accused device exactly." *Amhil Enters., Ltd. v. Wawa, Inc.*, 81 F.3d 1554, 1562 (Fed. Cir. 1996).

49. *Nichols v. Universal Pictures Corp.*, 45 F.2d 119, 121 (2d Cir. 1930), *cert. denied*, 282 U.S. 902 (1931) (citations omitted).

50. See *Computer Associates Intern., Inc. v. Altai, Inc.*, 982 F.2d 693 (2d Cir. 1992). For further discussion, see John Ogilvie, "Defining Computer Program Parts Under Learned Hand's Abstractions Test in Software Copyright Infringement Cases," *Michigan Law Review* 91 (1992): 526.

51. *Autogiro Company of America v. United States*, 384 F.2d 391, 400 (Ct. Cl. 1967).

52. *Graver Tank & Mfg. Co. v. Linde Air Products Co.*, 339 U.S. 605 (1950).

53. The Federal Circuit is a specialist court that decides most patent disputes on appeal. A court sits *en banc* when all of the members participate in deciding the case, rather than a panel of three judges as is far more common.

54. See *Hilton Davis Chem. Co. v. Warner-Jenkinson Co.*, 62 F.3d 1512, 1522 (Fed. Cir. 1995) (en banc) (per curiam), *rev'd and remanded*, 520 U.S. 17 (1997).

55. *Festo Corp. v. Shoketsu Kinzoku Kogyo Kabushiki Co., Ltd.*, 535 U.S. 722 (2002). In both *Warner-Jenkinson* and *Festo* the Court imposed new requirements as a condition of finding equivalency, but preserved the underlying doctrine. The Federal Circuit subsequently adopted a comprehensive set of standards to accord with the Court's decisions. See *Festo Corp. v. Shoketsu Kinzoku Kogyo Kabushiki Co.*, 304 F.3d 1289, 1698 (Fed. Cir. 2002) (ordering a rehearing of the case remanded by the U.S. Supreme Court). The details of these limitations are well beyond the scope of this book.

56. See Jessica Litman, *Digital Copyright* (Amherst, NY: Prometheus Books, 2001) (discussing "The Art of Making Copyright Laws" and emphasizing the role of lobbyists in the legislative process).

57. To see just how worried these industries are, simply visit their web sites: http://www.riaa.com/issues/piracy/riaa.asp and http://www.mpaa.org/piracy.asp (last visited June 30, 2006).

58. Lessig, *Free Culture*, 302.

59. For further discussion on this point, see David Lange, "Reimagining the Public Domain," *Law & Contemporary Problems* 66 (2003): 463, 471; David Lange, "Students, Music and the Net," *Duke Law & Technology Review*, 2003, no. 0021.

60. See generally *Harper & Row Publishers, Inc. v. Nation Enterprises*, 471 U.S. 539, 560 (1985) (recognizing fair use as one of two First Amendment safeguards—the other being the idea/expression dichotomy—as being already embodied in copyright law); see also *Eldred v. Ashcroft*, 221(2003) (noting that "copyright's built-in free speech safeguards are generally adequate to address [First Amendment concerns]").

61. See *Nimmer on Copyright*, § 8B.01[D][2]; see also M. B. W. Sinclair, "Fair Use Old and New: The *Betamax* Case and its Forebears," *Buffalo Law Review* 33 (1984): 269, citing S. Rep. No. 473, 94th Cong., 1st Sess. 61 (1975). ("Prior to the 1976 Copyright Act, the doctrine had developed entirely at the hands of judges, as an 'equitable rule of reason.'")

62. E.g., *Sony Corp. v. Universal City Studios, Inc.*, 464 U.S. 417, 481–82 (1984) (Blackmun, J., dissenting). ("Photocopying an old newspaper clipping to send to a friend may be an example; pinning a quotation on one's bulletin board may be another. In each of these cases, the effect on the author is truly *de minimis*.")

63. *Fred Fisher, Inc. v. Dillingham*, 298 F. 145, 152 (S.D.N.Y. 1924).

64. Abrams, *The Law of Copyright*, § 15:2.

65. *Lawrence v. Dana*, 15 F. Cas. 26, 59 (C.C.D. Mass. 1869) (holding that users were free to create abridgements); *Stowe v. Thomas*, 23 F. Cas. 201, 208 (C.C.E.D. Pa. 1853) (translation of a prior work not infringement); but cf. *Folsom v. Marsh*, 9 F. Cas. 342 (C.C.D. Mass. 1841) (defendant held liable for infringement because of the amount of copying—i.e., substantial copying—made the junior work a copy and not an abridgement).

66. 17 U.S.C. § 106(2).

67. See generally Alan Latman, "Fair Use of Copyrighted Works," reprinted in *Studies on Copyright*, ed. Copyright Society of the USA (South Hackensack, NJ: F. B. Rothman, 1963); L. Ray Patterson & Christopher Thomas, "Personal Use in Copyright Law: An Unrecognized Constitutional Right," *Journal of the Copyright Society of the U.S.A.* 50 (2003): 475, 501.

68. See Pierre Leval, "Toward a Fair Use Standard," *Harvard Law Review* 103 (1990): 1105, 1127 n. 94 (reporting the following decisions as evidence of judicial attitudes in early fair use decisions: *Cary v. Kearsley*, 170 Eng.Rep. 679, 4 Esp. 168 [1802]); *Jarrold v. Houlston*, 69 Eng.Rep. 1294, 1298, 3 K. & J. 708, 716–17 (1857); see also *Marcus v. Rowley*, 695 F.2d 1171, 1175 (9th Cir. 1983). ("[F]air use presupposes that the defendant has acted fairly and in good faith. . . ."); *Iowa State Univ. Research Found., Inc. v. American Broadcasting Co.*, 621 F.2d 57, 62 (2d Cir. 1980) (noting the relevance of conduct to fair use). See also *Time, Inc. v. Bernard Geis Associates*, 293 F. Supp. 130 (S.D.N.Y. 1968) (an oft-cited case holding that it was fair use to reproduce frames of Abraham Zapruder's "home movie pictures").

69. Wendy Gordon, "Fair Use as Market Failure: A Structural and Economic Analysis of the *Betamax* Case and Its Predecessors," *Columbia Law Review* 82 (1982): 1600.

70. Michael Madison suggests that

> the case for fair use is strongest when the defendant can persuasively argue that the value of her activity to society clearly outweighs even stipulated loss to the copyright owner. That balance tips most sharply in favor of fair use when the defendant is doing the sort of thing that society wants done regardless of, and even in spite of, the claim of some rights holder to authorize the activity. Second, the phrasing addresses the concern that fair use decision-making is at least unpredictable and at worst arbitrary. Judicial treatment of fair use as a case-by-case "safety valve" for a variety of policy, fairness, and/or personal autonomy concerns has tended, over time, substantially to reduce its usefulness in dealing with substantive policy concerns, as well as its usefulness in day-to-day planning in intellectual property economies.

> Madison, "Rewriting Fair Use and the Future of Copyright Reform," *Cardozo Arts & Entertainment Law Journal* 23 (2005): 391, 406; see also Polk Wagner, "The Perfect Storm: Intellectual Property and Public Values," *Fordham Law Review* 74 (2005): 423 (arguing that "reform of fair use itself must, in my view, address the root causes of the current controversy: uncertainty").

71. *Wihtol v. Crow*, 309 F.2d 777 (8th Cir. 1962).

72. *Nimmer on Copyright*, § 13.05[A]; see also David Nimmer, "'Fairest of Them All' and Other Fairy Tales of Fair Use," *Law & Contemporary Problems* 66 (2003): 263, 287, quoting *Harper & Row Publishers, Inc. v. Nation Enterprises*, 471 U.S. 539, 550 n. 3 (1985).

73. Economists sometimes appear to think that fair use requires a "transaction costs" analysis—that is, recognizing the doctrine only when the cost of acquiring rights outweighs the benefit of appropriating a senior work. E.g., Mary Barry, "Multiple Photocopying by Educators and the Fair Use Doctrine: The Court's Role in Reducing Transaction Costs," *University of Illinois Law Review* 1994: 387; William Landes & Richard Posner, "An Economic Analysis of Copyright Law," *Journal of Legal Studies* 18 (1989): 325. Professor Lessig suggests that "fair use" seemingly means, at least in America, the right to hire a lawyer to defend one's right to create. See Lessig, *Free Culture*, 187.

74. In this category, courts generally find infringement as opposed to fair use, almost without exception. Courts appear to find this kind of appropriation—

displacing the market value of a given work—particularly objectionable because it defeats the incentive rationale of copyright law. E.g., *Sony Corp. v. Universal City Studios, Inc.*, 464 U.S. 417, 432 (1984). ("The immediate effect of our copyright law is to secure a fair return for an 'author's' creative labor. But the ultimate aim is, by this incentive, to stimulate artistic creativity for the general public good.")

75. Section 107 specifically contemplates "the purpose and character of the use, including whether such use is of a commercial nature or is for nonprofit educational purposes." 17 U.S.C. § 107(1).

76. Copyright protection does not extend to ideas. See 17 U.S.C. § 102(b) ("In no case does copyright protection for an original work of authorship extend to any idea . . ."). This is a central tenet of copyright law, though it is notoriously difficult to apply in practice. See, e.g., *Hoehling v. Universal City Studios*, 618 F.2d 972 (2d Cir. 1980) (historical facts of the Hindenburg disaster were not capable of being copyrighted); *Educational Testing Services v. Katzman*, 793 F.2d 533 (3d Cir. 1986) (famous SAT examination and SAT test-prep service case).

77. This goes to the "nature of the copyrighted work." 17 U.S.C. § 107(2). The Court has stated that "some works are closer to the core of intended copyright protection than others." *Campbell v. Acuff-Rose Music, Inc.*, 510 U.S. 569, 586 (1994). And these works are, precisely, "more creative in nature." *A&M Records, Inc. v. Napster, Inc.*, 239 F.3d 1004, 1016 (9th Cir. 2001), citing *Campbell* at 586.

78. *Harper & Row Publishers, Inc. v. Nation Enteprises*, 471 U.S. 539, 564 (1985); see also *Nimmer on Copyright*, § 13.05[A].

79. See Leval, "Toward a Fair Use Standard," 1111.

80. Ibid. Transformative use can justify appropriation of an antecedent work by adding new expression or meaning. See *Campbell*, 510 U.S. at 579 (noting that the "enquiry focuses on whether the new work merely supersedes the objects of the original creation, or whether and to what extent it is transformative, altering the original with new expression, meaning, or message"). The Second Circuit has given the role to be played by transformative use additional prominence in *Bill Graham Archives v. Dorling Kindersley Ltd.*, 448 F.3d 605 (2d Cir. 2006).

81. *Campbell*, 510 U.S. at 570. See also *Warner Bros., Inc. v. American Broadcasting Companies, Inc.*, 720 F.2d 231, 242 (2d Cir. 1983) (TV show parodying Superman); *Elsmere Music, Inc. v. National Broadcasting Co.*, 623 F.2d 252, 253 n. 1 (2d Cir. 1980) (*Saturday Night Live* episode that parodied song "I Love New York"); *Berlin v. E.C. Publications, Inc.*, 329 F.2d 541, 544–45 (2d Cir.) (parodies of Irving Berlin songs in *Mad Magazine*), cert. denied, 379 U.S. 822 (1964).

82. E.g., *Mattel, Inc. v. Walking Mountain Prods.*, 353 F.3d 792, 806 (9th Cir. 2003) ("[T]he public benefit in allowing artistic creativity and social criticism to flourish is great"), cited in *Nimmer on Copyright*, §13.05[C][2] (discussing *Campbell*).

83. See generally *Loew's Inc. v. Columbia Broadcasting Sys., Inc.*, 131 F. Supp. 165 (S.D. Cal. 1955), aff'd sub nom. *Benny v. Loew's, Inc.*, 239 F.2d 532 (9th Cir. 1956), aff'd by an equally divided court, 356 U.S. 43 (1958); see also *Nimmer on Copyright*, § 13.05[C][1].

84. Leval, "Toward a Fair Use Standard," 1106. ("Curiously, judges generally have neither complained of the absence of guidance, nor made substantial efforts to fill the void.")

85. *Williams & Wilkins Co. v. United States*, 487 F.2d 1345 (Ct. Cl. 1973), *aff'd by an equally divided Court*, 420 U.S. 376 (1975).

86. *Williams & Wilkins Co.*, 487 F.2d 1345, 1362 ("we find that these practices have up to now been 'fair'").

87. Goldstein, *Copyright's Highway*, 132–44 (reviewing photocopying aspects of the 1976 Copyright Act).

88. See, e.g., 17 U.S.C. § 108. While technically known to practitioners as a "limitation on exclusive rights," this section really is a more prescriptive form of fair use. It is directed at libraries and archives, and it is the result of "an agreement reached by an Ad Hoc Committee of Educational Institutions and Organizations on Copyright Law Revision in negotiation with the Authors League of America and the Association of American Publishers which was incorporated in the discussion of the fair use doctrine in the House Committee Report on the 1976 Copyright Revision Act. H.R. Rep. No. 1476, 94th Cong., 2d Sess. 66–70 (1976)." Abrams, *The Law of Copyright*, § 1:32 at n. 7. We should note that this section is undergoing reexamination by a study group appointed by the Register of Copyrights.

89. 17 U.S.C. § 107.

90. *Nimmer on Copyright*, § 13.05[A][4].

91. See generally Julie Cohen et al., *Copyright in a Global Information Economy* (New York: Aspen Law & Business, 2002), 31–32; Rebecca Tushnet, "Copy This Essay," *Yale Law Journal* 114 (2004): 535, 590; Wagner, "The Perfect Storm," 439; Jeremy Kudon, "Form over Function: Expanding the Transformative Use Test for Fair Use," *Boston University Law Review* 80 (2000): 579.

92. Lange, "Reimagining the Public Domain," 482; see also Brett Kaplicer, "Rap Music and De Minimis Copying: Applying the Ringgold and Sandoval Approach to Digital Samples," *Cardozo Arts & Entertainment Law Journal* 18 (2000): 227, 254 (noting that "evaluating the four factors is a tedious and intricate process").

93. Nimmer, "'Fairest of Them All,'" 284.

94. See generally *Metro-Goldwyn-Mayer Studios Inc. v. Grokster, Ltd.*, 125 S. Ct. 2764, 2780 (2005); *UMG Recordings, Inc. v. MP3.Com, Inc.*, 92 F. Supp. 2d 349, 350 (S.D.N.Y. 2000); *In re Aimster Copyright Litigation*, 334 F.3d 643 (7th Cir. 2003) (applying *Sony* to technologies capable of both noninfringing uses and "mass infringement"); *A&M Records, Inc. v. Napster, Inc.*, 239 F.3d 1004 (2001); *Sony Corp. v. Universal City Studios, Inc.*, 464 U.S. 417 (1984).

95. 17 U.S.C. § 107.

96. H.R. Rep. No. 94-1476, reprinted in 1976 U.S.C.C.A.N. 5659 at 5679 (because fair use "is an equitable rule of reason, no generally applicable definition is possible, and each case raising the question must be decided on its own facts").

97. Ibid.

98. See generally *Grokster, Napster, Aimster, MP3.Com*, cited in note 94 above.

99. See generally, Kristina Groennings, "Costs and Benefits of the Recording Industry's Litigation Against Individuals," *Berkeley Technology Law Journal* 20 (2005): 571; Valerie Alter, "Building Rome in a Day: What Should We Expect from the RIAA?" *Hastings Communications & Entertainment Law Journal* 26 (2003): 155; see also Tom Zeller, "The Imps of File Sharing May Lose in Court, But They Are Winning in the Marketplace," *New York Times*, July 4, 2005; Bruce

Orwall, "Movie Industry to Begin Filing Lawsuits Against Online Pirates," *Wall Street Journal*, November 4, 2004.

100. *Sony Corp. v. Universal City Studios, Inc.*, 464 U.S. 417 (1984).

101. *Sony*, 433, quoting Peter Rosenberg, *Patent Law Fundamentals* (St. Paul, MN: West Group, 1982), § 17.02[2]. ("[A] sale of an article which though adapted to an infringing use is also adapted to other and lawful uses, is not enough to make the seller a contributory infringer. Such a rule would block the wheels of commerce.")

102. *Grokster*, 125 S. Ct. at 2772. ("The record is replete with evidence that from the moment Grokster and StreamCast began to distribute their free software, each one clearly voiced the objective that recipients use it to download copyrighted works, and each took active steps to encourage infringement.")

103. *Grokster*, 125 S. Ct. at 2782 (stating that *Grokster* was "significantly different from Sony" and noting that "Sony dealt with a claim of liability based solely on distributing a product with alternative lawful and unlawful uses, with knowledge that some users would follow the unlawful course. The case struck a balance between the interests of protection and innovation by holding that the product's capability of substantial lawful employment should bar the imputation of fault and consequent secondary liability for the unlawful acts of others. MGM's evidence in this case most obviously addresses a different basis of liability for distributing a product open to alternative uses.")

104. Compulsory licenses are scattered throughout Title 17. A sampling includes: (1) mechanical reproductions (17 U.S.C. § 115); (2) digital audio home recording (17 U.S.C. § 114); (3) cable television (17 U.S.C. § 111); (4) public broadcasting (17 U.S.C. § 118); (5) satellite retransmission (17 U.S.C. § 119); and (6) local market retransmission (17 U.S.C. § 122).

105. See *Nimmer on Copyright*, § 8.04; see also Timothy Brennan, "Copyright, Property, and the Right to Deny," *Chicago-Kent Law Review* 68 (1993): 675, 708 ("Fair use is nothing more than a zero-price compulsory license of copyrighted works"); Trotter Hardy, "Property (and Copyright) in Cyberspace," *University of Chicago Legal Forum*, 1996, 217, 233 ("Fair use . . . can be seen as a kind of compulsory license, albeit one for which the payment required is exactly zero dollars."); Ralph Oman, "The Compulsory License Redux: Will It Survive in a Changing Marketplace?" *Cardozo Arts & Entertainment Law Journal* 5 (1986): 37.

106. *White-Smith Music Pub. Co. v. Apollo Co.*, 209 U.S. 1, 17 (1908).

107. At the time, Italy was the only country to protect mechanical reproductions. Congress observed that "Fonotipia, of Milan, Italy, is perhaps the largest music-publishing company in the world, and has a practical monopoly of the business of producing music by mechanical means in Italy." Fonotipia was "taking steps to form an international trust" to "establish [a] monopoly [throughout] the Berne Union." Sensing that an Italian monopoly would limit "the market for what the composer has to sell to one customer," Congress enacted subsection (e) to "give to the composer the exclusive right to prohibit the reproduction of his music by mechanical means on the part of anybody if he desired, to secure to him adequate compensation from all reproducers if he did not desire to exercise this exclusive right to prohibit and to prevent the establishment of a great trade monopoly." See The House Report 1 on the

Copyright Act of 1909; see also Michael Landau, " 'Publication,' Musical Compositions, and the Copyright Act of 1909: Still Crazy after All These Years," *Vanderbilt
Journal of Entertainment Law & Practice* 2 (2000): 29.

108. Copyright Act of 1909 § 1(e).

109. Today, the compulsory license applicable to musical composition is contained in
Section 115 of the 1976 Act. For additional discussion, see M. William Krasi-
lovsky & Sidney Shemel, *This Business of Music,* 7th ed. (New York: Billboard
Books, 1995), 237–38; Lydia Loren, "Untangling the Web of Music Copyrights,"
Case Western Reserve Law Review 53 (2003): 673, 682 ("While the creators of
most sound recordings do not utilize the statutory provisions for the compulsory
mechanical license, the availability of such a license does affect the rate paid . . .");
Ralph Oman, "The Compulsory License Redux: Will It Survive in a Changing
Marketplace?" *Cardozo Arts & Entertainment Law Journal* 5 (1986): 37; Robert
P. Merges, "Contracting into Liability Rules: Intellectual Property Rights and
Collective Rights Organizations," *California Law Review* 84 (1996): 1293, 1311
("mechanical royalty transactions are largely handled by private entities").

110. See provisions cited in note 104 above; see also *Nimmer on Copyright,* § 8.18;
Joseph Liu, "Regulatory Copyright," *North Carolina Law Review* 83 (2004): 87,
91 (arguing that copyright law has become "increasingly more detailed and
industry-specific, relying more on compulsory licenses and, in some cases, mandating adoption of certain technologies and banning others").

111. Robert Cassler, "Copyright Compulsory Licenses—Are They Coming or Going?"
Journal of the Copyright Society of the USA 37 (1990): 231, 242–43.

112. Jon Garon, "Normative Copyright: A Conceptual Framework for Copyright
Philosophy and Ethics," *Cornell Law Review* 88 (2003): 1278, 1322. ("These provisions of the law limit the scope of the copyright holder's interest. In real property
language, these 110 provisions create an easement over the copyright owner's interest. In tort terms, these provisions provide limited immunity from suit.")

113. U.S. Const. art. I, § 8, cl. 8.

114. See, e.g, *Fogerty v. Fantasy, Inc.,* 510 U.S. 517, 524 (1994) ("The primary objective of the Copyright Act is to encourage the production of original literary, artistic, and musical expression for the good of the public."); *Feist Publications, Inc. v.
Rural Telephone Service Co.,* 499 U.S. 340, 349 (1991) ("The primary objective of
copyright is not to reward the labor of authors, but '[t]o promote the Progress of
Science and useful Arts.' "); *Bonito Boats, Inc. v. Thunder Craft Boats, Inc.,* 489
U.S. 141, 167 (1989) (highlighting the "patent statute's careful balance between
public right and private monopoly to promote certain creative activity"); *Graham
v. John Deere Co.,* 383 U.S. 1, 9 (1966) ("The patent monopoly was not designed
to secure to the inventor his natural right in his discoveries," but rather "was a
reward, an inducement, to bring forth new knowledge."); *Mazer v. Stein,* 347 U.S.
201, 219 (1954) ("The economic philosophy behind the clause empowering Congress to grant patents and copyrights is the conviction that encouragement of individual effort by personal gain is the best way to advance public welfare. . . ."); see
also Adam Mossoff, "What Is Property? Putting the Pieces Back Together,"
Arizona Law Review 45 (2003): 371.

115. *Feist Publications. Inc. v. Rural Telephone Service Co.,* 499 U.S. 340 (1991); *Sony
Corp. v. Universal City Studios, Inc.,* 464 U.S. 417, 429 (1984) (noting that the

"task of defining the scope of the limited monopoly . . . involves a difficult balance between the interests of authors and inventors in the control and exploitation of their writings and discoveries on the one hand, and society's competing interest in the free flow of ideas, information, and commerce on the other hand"); *Graham v. John Deere Co.*, 383 U.S. 1 (1966); see also David Lange, "Recognizing the Public Domain," *Law and Contemporary Problems* 44 (1981): 147; Robert Kastenmeier, "The 1989 Horace S. Manges Lecture—'Copyright in an Era of Technological Change: A Political Perspective,'" *Columbia–VLA Journal of Law & the Arts* 14 (1990): 1, 6 (noting that, when determining copyright legislation, "Congress will attempt to recognize and balance the legitimate rights of producers, creators or copyright holders and the interests of the public").

116. U.S. Const. art. I, § 8, cl. 8.

117. See *McCarthy on Trademarks*, §§ 6:2, 6:3. ("A fundamental distinction between patents and copyrights on the one hand and trademarks on the other, is the fact that Congress has passed laws providing for patent and copyright protection under a specific grant of power in the Constitution.")

118. Here we note the broad distinction between moral rights and the intellectual economy—the latter being the formal basis upon which U.S. copyright and patent law is founded. Note also that this is in contrast to these systems elsewhere (notably in France and other European countries) where moral rights are more prominent in the formal jurisprudence.

119. For further discussion on the moral right, its ascension and history, see Russell DaSilva, "Droit Moral and the Amoral Copyright: A Comparison of Artists' Rights in France and the United States," *Bulletin of the Copyright Society of the USA* 28 (1980): 1; Roberta Kwall, "Copyright and the Moral Right: Is an American Marriage Possible?" *Vanderbilt Law Review* 38 (1985): 1; *Nimmer on Copyright*, § 8D.01[A].

120. *Nimmer on Copyright*, § 8D.01[B]; Rebecca Martin, "The WIPO Performances and Phonograms Treaty: Will the U.S. Whistle a New Tune?" *Journal of the Copyright Society of the USA* 44 (1997): 157, 167–72 (offering an analysis of the interplay between Rome Convention, moral rights, and the enactment of the Digital Performance Right in Sound Recording Act of 1995).

121. See Kwall "Copyright and the Moral Right" (comparing the U.S. "tradition of safeguarding only the pecuniary rights of a copyright owner" with the more European approach of protecting the "product of the creator's mind, heart, and soul").

122. Berne Convention for the Protection of Literary and Artistic Works, Art. 6 *bis*.

123. See Kathryn Kelly, "Moral Rights and the First Amendment: Putting Honor Before Free Speech?" *University of Miami Entertainment & Sports Law Review* 11 (1994): 211; Molly Torsen, "'Anonymous, Untitled, Mixed Media': Mixing Intellectual Property Law with Other Legal Philosophies to Protect Traditional Cultural Expressions," *Journal of the Copyright Society of the USA* 53 (2006): 287, 300.

124. Catherine Fisk, "Credit Where It's Due: The Law and Norms of Attribution," *Georgetown Law Journal* 95 (2006): 49. See also Roberta Kwall, "Fame," *Indiana Law Journal* 73 (1997): 1; Roberta Kwall, "Copyright and the Moral Right: Is an American Marriage Possible?" *Vanderbilt Law Review* 38 (1985): 1.

125. *Nichols v. Universal Pictures Corp*, 45 F.2d 119, *cert. denied*, 282 U.S. 902 (1931).

126. See, e.g., *Dastar Corp. v. Twentieth Century Fox Film Corp.*, 539 U.S. 23 (2003).

127. See David Lange, "Recognizing the Public Domain," 147, n. 20; L. Ray Patterson & Stanley Lindberg, *The Nature of Copyright: A Law of User's Rights* (Athens: University of Georgia Press, 1991) (noting that the "public domain is whatever is left over when copyright expires, is lost, or never existed"); see also Ralph Brown, "Unification: A Cheerful Requiem for Common Law Copyright," *UCLA Law Review* 24 (1977): 1070.

128. Edward Samuels, "The Public Domain in Copyright Law," *Journal of the Copyright Society of the USA* 41 (1993): 137 (expressing an almost hostile view of the public domain and perceiving its legal existence as that which is left over after exclusivity runs its natural course).

129. See Lange, "Recognizing the Public Domain"; see also James Boyle, "The Second Enclosure Movement of the Public Domain," *Law & Contemporary Problems* 66 (2003): 33; Keith Aoki, "Authors, Inventors and Trademark Owners: Private Intellectual Property and the Public Domain (Part I)," *Columbia-VLA Journal of Law and the Arts* 18 (1994): 1.

130. See generally David Lange, "Reimagining the Public Domain," 474; see also Jed Rubenfeld, "Freedom of Imagination: Copyright's Constitutionality," *Yale Law Journal* 112 (2002): 1, 54.

131. Maintaining a commons in physical things may prove problematic, thanks to the likelihood of "overgrazing," just as Garrett Hardin famously suggested in "The Tragedy of the Commons," *Science,* 1968, 1243. But as many IP scholars have noted, an intellectual property commons is a generally sustainable concept, since the subject matter is nonrivalrous.

132. See Boyle, "The Second Enclosure Movement"; Benjamin Kaplan, *An Unhurried View of Copyright* (New York: Columbia University Press, 1967), 55.

133. See Lange, "Reimagining the Public Domain," 474. See also Pamela Samuelson, "Enriching Discourse on Public Domain," *Duke Law Journal* 55 (2006): 783.

134. See Lange, "Reimagining the Public Domain," 469.

CHAPTER 3

1. See Edwin Mansfield et al., *Technology Transfer, Productivity, and Economic Policy* (New York: W. W. Norton, 1982) (concluding that ninety percent of "pharmaceutical innovations" would never have happened but for patent protection); see also Edwin Mansfield, "Patents and Innovation: An Empirical Study," *Management Science* 32 (1986): 173, 180 (concluding that while patent protection in most industries has little effect, there are "a few industries, particularly pharmaceuticals and chemicals, [in which] the effects of the patent systems [are] very substantial"); Arti Rai, "Fostering Cumulative Innovation in the Biopharmaceutical Industry: The Role of Patents and Antitrust," *Berkeley Technology Law Journal* 16 (2001): 813, 828 (discussing, inter alia, how "[i]n the specific context of the biopharmaceutical industry, the claim that broad, monopoly-conferring rights on nascent inventions can provide a necessary spur to further innovation may well have merit").

2. Stephen Breyer, "The Uneasy Case for Copyright: A Study of Copyright in Books, Photocopies, and Computer Programs," *Harvard Law Review* 84 (1970): 281.

Though in form Breyer's essay was a modest work of scholarship, its implications were enormous and have proved long-lasting (and by no means merely because its author ascended to the Supreme Court bench). Breyer himself has claimed no more for his thesis than that extensions of intellectual property protection should be assessed with some reservations grounded in economic analysis, a "youthful skepticism" duly noted by more enthusiastic proponents of IP protection. See, Edmund W. Kitch, "Elementary and Persistent Errors in the Economic Analysis of Intellectual Property," *Vanderbilt Law Review* 53 (2000): 1727. We ourselves are no longer quite youthful nor are we economists; our own present skepticism may well be considerably greater than Justice Breyer's, whether measured then or now. In our view, Breyer's long-ago study continues to offer the basis for important countervailing arguments against the easy assumptions some economists have made (then and now) in favor of wider protection. We may thus be willing to carry the implications in his essay considerably farther than he himself would do were he free (or inclined) to express himself fully.

3. Breyer, "The Uneasy Case for Copyright," 299.

4. Not all architects wanted the Architectural Works Copyright Protection Act of 1990 (codified in the Copyright Act at various sections). Many saw it as superfluous because, prior to 1990, architectural plans and drawings were "clearly protected." See William Patry, *Copyright Law & Practice* (Washington, DC: Bureau of National Affairs, 1994), 302–4. Further, critics (including architects) responded with skepticism and concern about how the legislation would affect a building owner's rights. See Antoinette Vacca, "The Architectural Works Copyright Protection Act: Much Ado About Something?" *Marquette Intellectual Property Law Review* 9 (2005): 111, 118. Yet, since the U.S. did not protect "built designs of structures," Congress found that the U.S. was not in compliance with the Berne Convention, specifically Article 2(1), and thus moved to enact the AWCPA. Patry, *Copyright Law & Practice*, 302–4.

5. "Copyright law," for instance, "presupposes that . . . authors and publishers will invest sufficient resources in producing and publishing works only if they are promised property rights that will enable them to control and profit from their works' dissemination in the marketplace." Paul Goldstein, *Copyright*, § 1.14 (New York: Aspen, 2004). See also William Landes & Richard Posner, "An Economic Analysis of Copyright Law," *Journal of Legal Studies* 18 (1989): 325.

6. Edgardo Buscaglia & William Ratliff, *Law & Economics in Developing Countries* (Stanford, CA: Hoover Institution Press, 2000), 1–29 (discussing, inter alia, how "inadequate intellectual property protection influence[s] the willingness of firms to transfer technology to developing countries"); Keith Maskus & Jerome Reichman, "The Globalization of Private Knowledge Goods and the Privatization of Global Public Goods," in *International Public Goods & Transfer of Technology Under a Globalized Intellectual Property Regime*, ed. Keith Masksus & Jerome Reichman (New York: Cambridge University Press, 2005), 3–45. But a careful reading of these materials reveals reservations on the part of the authors about the ultimate relationship to be seen between intellectual property regimes and foreign direct investment.

7. See, e.g., David Opderbeck, "The Penguin's Genome, or Coase and Open Source Biotechnology," *Harvard Journal of Law & Technology* 18 (2004): 167, 197 (discussing

how venture capitalists "depend on intellectual property protections" and declaring that "[w]ithout intellectual property protection at crucial developmental milestones, this funding would evaporate, depleting the biotechnology commons").

8. "The problem," says Mark Lemley, "is that we don't have a clue how innovation works." Mark Lemley, "Reconceiving Patents in the Age of Venture Capital," *Journal of Small & Emerging Business Law* 4 (2000): 137, 139. Further, if intellectual property regimes do encourage intellectual productivity, it appears that such a benefit is entirely industry specific. For further discussion on this topic, see Wesley Cohen & Stephen Merrill, ed., *Patents In The Knowledge-Based Economy* (Washington, DC: National Academies Press, 2003), and Wesley Cohen et al., "Protecting Their Intellectual Assets: Appropriability Conditions and Why U.S. Manufacturing Firms Patent (or Not)," (Nat'l Bureau of Econ. Research, Working Paper No. 7552, 2002).

9. Some authors conclude that intellectual property protection is only useful in the context of a "patent portfolio." See, e.g., Gideon Parchomovsky & R. Polk Wagner, "Patent Portfolios," *University of Pennsylvania Law Review* 154 (2005): 1, 10 (noting that while a firm's pursuit of a patent portfolio might lead to more patents or "progress," on balance "the net effects are almost certainly negative from a social perspective"). Other authors entirely reject the idea that intellectual property protection is necessary. See, e.g., George Priest, "What Economists Can Tell Lawyers About Intellectual Property: Comment on Cheung," *Research in Law & Economics* 8 (1986): 19; Richard Levin et al., "Appropriating the Returns from Industrial Research & Development," in *Brookings Papers on Economic Activity*, ed. William Brainard & George Perry (Washington, DC: The Brookings Institution, 1987), 783. Others argue that protection is only useful for particular industries. See Cohen & Merrill, *Patents In the Knowledge-Based Economy*. In the words of the respected economist Fritz Machlup, "No economist, on the basis of present knowledge, could possibly state with certainty that the patent system, as it now operates, confers a net benefit or a net loss upon society." Fritz Machlup, "An Economic Review of the Patent System," Subcommittee on Patents, Trademarks, and Copyrights of the Senate Comm. on the Judiciary, 85th Cong., Study No. 15, 1958, 79–80. Nothing in the years since Machlup offered this comment has seriously undermined his insight.

10. Mark Lemley convincingly argues that intellectual property laws are increasingly enacted and interpreted to help creators manage, rather than create, intellectual property. See Mark Lemley, "Ex Ante versus Ex Post Justification for Intellectual Property," *University of Chicago Law Review* 71 (2004): 129.

11. Breyer, "The Uneasy Case for Copyright," 344. ("One should become suspicious of the need for protection at present upon learning that the software industry is currently burgeoning without the use of copyright.")

12. Software makers now frequently concede that competition, rather than copyright or patent protection, drives innovation. See Federal Trade Commission, *To Promote Innovation: The Proper Balance of Competition and Patent Law and Policy*, October 2003, p. 46, available at http://ftc.gov/os/2003/10/innovationrpt.pdf.

13. For example, Microsoft doesn't sell Windows XP or Microsoft Word; Microsoft grants a purported license to use these products. This manipulation of contract

(and, some might say, copyright) law enables Microsoft to maintain some control over its product by keeping the right of distribution under 17 U.S.C. § 106(3) and extinguishing the consumer's first-sale interests under 17 U.S.C. § 109(d). And if one were to crack the code of, say, Windows XP, and tinker with it, making it safer against viruses, worms, and the like, then that use might well be a violation of Microsoft's right of adaptation under 17 U.S.C. § 106(2). Cf. *U.S. v. Microsoft Corp.*, 87 F. Supp. 2d 30, 40 (2000) (in which Microsoft sought a Sherman Act exemption because "as a general proposition, Microsoft argues that the federal Copyright Act, 17 U.S.C. § 101 et seq., endows the holder of a valid copyright in software with an absolute right to prevent licensees, in this case the OEMs, from shipping modified versions of its product without its express permission").

14. This is especially true in the open-source software movement in which programmers—frequently volunteers—create products that are often superior to products from established vendors. The success of the Firefox web browser is a prime example: many critics believe it is actually superior to Microsoft's Internet Explorer.

15. Michael Dryja, "Looking to the Changing Nature of Software for Clues to its Protection," *University of Baltimore Intellectual Property Law Journal* 3 (1995): 109, 120 (noting that "a computer programmer views her work as an intangible, abstract creation similar to a literary work. . . . A programmer composes a program through careful construction of computer language commands. The programmer thoughtfully chooses each command in order to achieve just the effect she wishes to convey. It is no accident, then, that copyright law was the first choice for protecting computer software. The persons receiving these freshly given copyrights seem no different than any other artisan.")

16. Breyer, "The Uneasy Case for Copyright," 299–300 ("By the time a copier chooses a book, prints it, and distributes it to retailers, he may be six to eight weeks behind, by which time the initial publisher will have provided retailers with substantial inventories."); see also *Eldred v. Ashcroft*, 537 U.S. 186, 242–69 (2003) (Breyer, S., dissenting).

17. See *Nimmer on Copyright*, § 1.01 (noting that "Congress had explicitly refused to extend copyright laws so as to cover the field of industrial designs") and § 2.08[D] for general discussion.

18. See Jay Dratler, "Trademark Protection for Industrial Designs," *University of Illinois Law Review* 1998: 887.

19. *Chisum on Patents*, § 1.02[5] (noting that design patents are "difficult to obtain" because of "the requirement of novelty and nonobviousness").

20. See, e.g., U.S. Trademark No. 1,063,799 (registered Apr. 19, 1977) (Rolls Royce grilles) and U.S. Trademark Nos. 1,606,324 (registered July 17, 1990) and 1,415,749 (registered Nov. 4, 1986) (BMW grilles); see also Lars Smith, "Trade Distinctiveness: Solving Scalia's Tertium Quid Trade Dress Conundrum," *Michigan State Law Review* 2005: 243, 277–81.

21. See Christine Cox & Jennifer Jenkins, "Between the Cracks, a Fertile Commons: An Overview of the Relationship Between Fashion and Intellectual Property," in *Ready to Share: Fashion & the Ownership of Creativity*, ed. David Bollier & Laurie Racine (Annenberg School for Communication, 2006) (analyzing the fashion industry's custom of sampling and appropriating antecedent designs). See

generally Kal Raustiala & Christopher Sprigman, "The Piracy Paradox: Innovation and Intellectual Property in Fashion Design," *University of Virginia Law Review* 92 (2006): 1687. See also Ben Winograd & Cheryl Lu-lien Tan, "Can Fashion Be Copyrighted? Designers Want to Halt Knockoffs, But Some Say They Spur Sales; 'Few People Can Spend $4,000,'" *Wall Street Journal,* eastern edition, p. B1, September 11, 2006.

22. Microsoft employed this strategy with its release of the Xbox 360. The first Xbox was superior to Sony's Playstation 2, but Sony still won eighty percent of the market share because Sony built "an insurmountable lead mainly because it went on sale nearly two years ahead of the Xbox. But this time, Microsoft expects to sell 3 million 360s in the first 90 days, long before the next version of PlayStation makes its debut." Hiawatha Bray, "A High-Stakes Xbox," *Boston Globe,* November 18, 2005.

23. See, e.g., *Peter Pan Fabrics, Inc. v. Martin Weiner Corp.,* 274 F.2d 487 (2d Cir. 1960).

24. See, e.g., *Tufenkian Import/Export Ventures, Inc. v. Einstein Moomjy, Inc.,* 338 F.3d 127 (2d Cir. 2003) (infringement found on the basis of "substantial similarity"); *Odegard, Inc. v. Costikyan Classic Carpets, Inc.,* 963 F. Supp. 1328 (S.D.N.Y. 1997) (willful infringement of a carpet design).

25. For a different view as to designs, however, see Jerome Reichman, "Design Protection and the Legislative Agenda," *Law and Contemporary Problems* 55 (1992): 281 (and works cited therein).

26. *Feist Publications, Inc. v. Rural Telephone Service Co.,* 499 U.S. 340 (1991). For a thorough discussion on this topic, see Jerome Reichman & Pamda Samuelson, "Intellectual Property Rights in Data?" *Vanderbilt Law Review* 50 (1997): 51.

27. The most common example has been the telephone white pages, where the alphabetized arrangement of names, addresses, and phone numbers was thought to be proprietary; but also in collections far more extensive, such as the numerous demographic compilations gathered by such data proprietors as Dun & Bradstreet. See *Financial Info., Inc. v. Moody's Investors Serv., Inc.,* 808 F.2d 204 (2d Cir. 1986).

28. See *Southern Bell Tel. & Tel. v. Associated Telephone Directory Publishers,* 756 F.2d 801, 809 (11th Cir. 1985) and *West Publishing Co. v. Mead Data Central, Inc.,* 799 F.2d 1219 (8th Cir. 1986) (both recognizing copyright in compilations and affirming the long-standing "sweat of the brow" theory). Cf. *Lane v. First Nat. Bank of Boston,* 687 F. Supp. 11, 17 (D. Mass. 1988), *aff'd,* 871 F.2d 166 (1st Cir. 1989) (dismissing the "'sweat of the brow' theory [as] irrelevant" and finding copyrightability based on the arrangement of the plaintiff's compilation). The opinions in these cases include citations to older cases.

29. *Feist,* 499 U.S. at 359–60. ("[T]he Copyright Act leave[s] no doubt that originality, not 'sweat of the brow,' is the touchstone of copyright protection in directories and other fact-based works.")

30. See, e.g., Laura Tyson & Edward Sherry, "Statutory Protection for Databases: Economic & Public Policy Issues," Information Industry Association, October 23, 1997, http://judiciary.house.gov/legacy/41118.htm (last visited July 5, 2006).

31. See, e.g., Database and Collections of Information Misappropriation Act, H.R. 3261, 108th Cong. (2004); Consumer and Investors Access to Information Act of 1999, H.R. 1858, 106th Cong. (1999); Collections of Information Antipiracy Act, H.R. 354, 106th Cong. (1999) (originally H.R. 2652, 105th Cong. [1997]).

32. See Reichman & Samuelson, "Intellectual Property Rights in Data?"
33. For instance, Westlaw and LexisNexis presumably make profits despite the fact that much of their content—cases, statutes, etc.—is either in the public domain or, alternatively, offered over the web for free (in law journals, for instance). In short, Westlaw and Lexis are "competing with free." This naturally leads one to conclude that their success is grounded in the convenience or quality of their services. For further discussion, see Jonathan Barnett, "Private Protection of Patentable Goods," *Cardozo Law Review* 25 (2004): 1251, 1309 (noting that "calls on U.S. lawmakers to imitate the European Union's generous intellectual property protections for electronic databases may be misguided given that the U.S. database industry apparently flourishes even though formal intellectual property protection of database products is highly uncertain"); Raymond Nimmer, *Nimmer on Information Law,* § 1:4 (Eagan, MN: West, 2005) (noting that *Feist* and its brethren are ultimately the result of a "digital transformation of society," creating a conundrum on how to deal with the "marketplace of information").
34. Breyer, "The Uneasy Case for Copyright," 299–300.
35. *Harper & Row Publishers, Inc. v. Nation Enters.,* 471 U.S. 539, 558 (1985); *Eldred,* 534 U.S. 1126, 219 (quoting *Harper & Row* and then going on to discuss how "copyright law contains built-in First Amendment accommodations").
36. Circulation and advertising historically have been print media's bread and butter. Some have described this as a "history of easy money," giving the industry little incentive to change its business model. See Philip Meyer, *The Vanishing Newspaper: Saving Journalism in the Information Age* (Columbia, MO: University of Missouri Press, 2004), 46 (noting that print media's "inherent conservatism, a consequence of their easy-money history, places them at a disadvantage in attempts at innovation").
37. Harry Fox, for example, has long empowered the music industry by issuing mechanical licenses, collecting fees, employing accounting agencies, and instituting litigation on behalf of copyright holders and music publishers. See William Krasilovsky et al., *This Business of Music: The Definitive Guide to the Music Industry,* 9th ed. (New York: Watson-Guptill, 2003), 154–61.
38. Trotter Hardy nicely describes the nature of copyright in the early twentieth century in "Copyright and 'New-Use' Technologies," *Nova Law Review* 23 (1999): 659.
39. David Lange, "Recognizing the Public Domain," *Law & Contemporary Problems* 44 (1981): 147, 158–59.
40. See Leroy Ashby, *With Amusement for All: A History of American Popular Culture Since 1830* (Lexington, KY: University Press of Kentucky, 2006) (retelling, in detail, the ascension and demise of burlesque and vaudeville).
41. Blue laws silenced perfectly innocent films, as well. Consider *Mutual Film Corp. v. Industrial Commission of Ohio,* 236 U.S. 230 (1915). In that case, Ohio enacted a statute creating a "censor board" whose charge was to screen and then allow the showing of those "films [that] in the judgment and discretion of the board of censors [are] of a moral, educational or amusing and harmless character." Mutual Film, a distributor of movies, objected not to the content of the statute but rather the burden it placed on them; in effect, Mutual Film had to incur the cost of having

the "censor board" inspect its many movies and then approve them for showings in Ohio. But the Supreme Court didn't consider the First Amendment implications of the law, and summarily signed off on the Ohio censorship law. See Ira Carmen, *Movies, Censorship, and the Law* (Ann Arbor, MI: University of Michigan Press, 1966), 10–16.

42. Cf. Ashby, *With Amusement for All*, 55, 249–50 (discussing the impact of copyright laws on the music industry).

43. For a synopsis of how the Dead used this kind of "free riding" to their financial advantage, see Seth Schiesel, "Jerry Garcia: The Man, The Myth, the Area Rug," *New York Times*, August 9, 2005; see also Michael Parish, "More Bands are 'Bootlegging' Own Concerts," *Chicago Tribune*, May 18, 2003. (We expect the reader will soon sense, correctly, that we are describing the Dead largely from within the matrix of our own memories and experiences. We think we remember having read a similar account of the Dead's financial success in a European edition of an American newspaper—perhaps the *International Herald-Tribune*—some twenty years earlier, but we have been unable to recall the exact date or place where we read it, or locate the account itself. In any event, this is by no means a new story. As we also seem to remember, the earlier newspaper account compared the Dead's success with that of Bob Dylan who insisted on strict copyright protection—a contrast we will acknowledge presently in our own text.) John Tehranian discusses how the Dead's success was driven by "familiarity rather than scarcity" in "All Rights Reserved? Reassessing Copyright and Patent Enforcement in the Digital Age," *University of Cincinnati Law Review* 72 (2003): 45, 71. ("[T]he Grateful Dead utilized a different model for profit that recognized the uses and limits of intellectual property.") For a recent discussion about the Dead and digital technologies, see Jesse Mayshark, "Downloads of the Dead Are Not Dead Yet," *New York Times*, December 1, 2005 (telling the curious story of how the Dead objected to archive.org's initiative to make recordings available for free over the Internet—something that was in direct competition to the Dead's own pay site, gdstore.com; after a worldwide Deadhead uproar, the Dead relented and allowed the project to go forward. Phil Lesh, the Dead's bassist, reasoned that it is the "Grateful Dead's legacy [to make their content free] and I hope that one way or another all of it is available for those who want it."); see also Jon Pareles, "The Dead's Gamble: Free Music for Sale," *New York Times*, December 3, 2005 (offering an outstanding exegesis of the Dead's business model and then juxtaposing it with popular copyright protection regimes).

44. Michal Senft, "Fan-recorded Concerts Are Far from Dead," *Arizona Republic*, August 30, 2005 (quoting David Lemieux, the Dead's official archivist, as saying "[Jerry] believed that once they had played the music, it belonged to the audience, and they could do with it what they wanted").

45. Rose Jones, "Jerry's Kids: Young Deadheads Aren't In It for the Nostalgia," *Los Angeles Times*, January 13, 1995. ("The band lets the taping happen; in fact, fan taping sections using the latest [digital audio taping] equipment are set aside at the concerts. As one of the largest moneymaking enterprises in rock 'n' roll, the Grateful Dead view the exchange as an integral part of the culture that has flourished around it since making the Haight-Ashbury scene in 1966.")

46. In the year before Garcia died, for example, the Dead's "business enterprise earned more than $70 million, $52 million from touring alone. [Additionally, its] mail-order catalog, featuring everything from albums to snow skis and software, draws an estimated $20 million in annual orders." Micah Morrison, "Icons or Knockoffs? A True Original," *Wall Street Journal*, August 17, 1995.

47. For a more detailed account, see Steve Parish et al, *Home Before Daylight: My Life on the Road with the Grateful Dead* (New York: St. Martin's Press, 2003).

48. For more on "Dead Culture," see Phil Lesh, *Searching for the Sound* (New York: Little, Brown and Co., 2005); Dennis McNally, *A Long Strange Trip: The Inside History of the Grateful Dead* (New York: Broadway Books, 2002); Ed Ward et al., *Rock of Ages: History of Rock and Roll* (New York: Rolling Stone Press, 1986).

49. Harvey Hartman, *Reflections on a Cultural Brand: Connecting with Lifestyles* (Bellevue, WA: Hartman Group, 2003), 69 (analyzing how the Dead employed experience and community to create "substantial profits, long-term financial stability, and an almost unrivaled degree of brand loyalty").

50. See William Fisher, *Promises to Keep* (Stanford, CA: Stanford University Press, 2004); Tom Graves, "Picking Up the Pieces of Grokster: A New Approach To File Sharing," *Hastings Communications & Entertainment Law Journal* 27 (2005): 137 (offering a scathing critique of the recording industry's "antiquated business model" and arguing that *Grokster* has, for the time being, given the industry no incentive to change its "traditional distribution format for the benefit of artists and consumers alike"); see also Jason Riley, "Copyfight," *Wall Street Journal*, November 26, 2005 (criticizing the general Recording Industry Association of America ["RIAA"] business attitude and asking "How viable is a business model based on suing your customers, especially [when the litigation has] no deterrent effect?").

51. 17 U.S.C. § 115.

52. For an analysis of the difference between property and liability/regulatory regimes, see Guido Calabresi & Douglas Melamed, "Property Rules, Liability Rules, and Inalienability: One View of the Cathedral," *Harvard Law Review* 85 (1972): 1089; see also Jerome H. Reichman & Pamela Samuelson, "Intellectual Property Rights in Data?" *Vanderbilt Law Review* 50 (1997): 51; Robert Merges, "Contracting Into Liability Rules: Intellectual Property Rights and Collective Rights Organizations," *California Law Review* 84 (1996): 1293. Jerome H. Reichman, "Legal Hybrids Between the Patent and Copyright Paradigms," *Columbia Law Review* 94 (1994): 2432.

53. William Fisher, *Promises to Keep* (Stanford, CA: Stanford University Press, 2004).

54. Graham Henderson, president of the Canadian Recording Industry Association (CRIA), who criticized Fisher's suggestions (even calling him "Comrade Fisher"), insisted that copyright should be value-based—not used cars value but "moral values"—and left to the free market. See Michael Geist, "Music Industry Doesn't Need More Government Protection," *Toronto Star*, February 21, 2005.

55. See Barak Orbach, "Antitrust & Pricing in the Motion Picture Industry," *Yale Journal on Regulation* 21 (2004): 317, 329–35; Siva Vaidhyanathan, *Copyrights and Copywrongs* (New York: New York University Press, 2001), 87–93.

56. See the authorities cited in the preceding note. See also Lawrence Lessig, *Free Culture* (New York: Penguin Press, 2004), 54–55.

57. E.g., *Kalem Co. v. Harper Bros.*, 222 U.S. 55 (1911) (finding *Ben Hur* the movie to
infringe on *Ben Hur* the book, even though the 1906 Act did not include "moving
pictures" as a protectable subject matter); *Barry v. Hughes*, 103 F.2d 427 (2d Cir.
1939), *cert. denied*, 308 U.S. 604 (1939) (movie based on another's misappropriated work was infringement); *Nichols v. Universal Pictures Corp.*, 45 F.2d 119 (2d
Cir. 1930), *cert. denied*, 282 U.S. 902 (1931) (play's theme, storyline—i.e., its
copyright—does not extend to ideas); *Sheldon v. Metro-Goldwyn Pictures Corp.*,
81 F.2d 49 (2d Cir. 1936), *cert. denied*, 309 U.S. 390 (1940) (movie infringed playwright despite no evidence of copying of the playwright's dialogue); *Shipman v.
R.K.O. Radio Pictures, Inc.*, 100 F.2d 533 (2d Cir. 1938) (movie did not infringe
because the scene in question was so "lacking in novelty so as to be regarded the
common property of all playwrights") quoting *Serrana v. Jefferson*, 33 F. 347, 348
(1888); *Collins v. Metro-Goldwyn Pictures Corp.*, 106 F.2d 83 (2d Cir. 1939) (no
infringement despite substantial similarity between book and later movie); *Dellar
v. Samuel Goldwyn, Inc.*, 104 F.2d 661 (2d Cir. 1939) (" 'theme,' the 'plot,' the
'ideas' may always be freely borrowed"); *Kustoff v. Chaplin*, 120 F.2d 551 (9th
Cir. 1941) (no infringement because "ordinary observer [would not] believe that
the film has picturized appellant's book"); *O'Neill v. General Film Co.*, 157 N.Y.S
1028 (1916) (scenes in a derivative work based on an unpublished, antecedent
playwright did not infringe because the original author failed to publish his play);
Curwood v. Affiliated Distrib., 283 F. 219 (S.D.N.Y. 1922) (curious case in which
a writer licensed his work to a producer and authorized him to "elaborate" "however needed"; the producer, instead, produced a film that only used the title of the
original work; the court held that the "right to elaborate upon an original story"
required the "appropriate expression to the theme, thought, and main action of
that which was originally written"); *Echevarria v. Warner Bros. Pictures, Inc.*, 12
F. Supp. 632 (S.D. Cal. 1935) (story based on a historical incident was not copyrightable and free for use in later motion picture); *Caruthers v. R.K.O. Radio
Pictures, Inc.*, 20 F. Supp. 906 (S.D.N.Y. 1937) (original content at issue lacked
"distinctive qualities"); *Lynch v. Warner Bros. Pictures, Inc.*, 32 F. Supp. 575
(S.D.N.Y. 1940) (no infringement because the plaintiff's original "theme" or story
line was only "superficially simila[r]" to a later moving picture).

58. The Court probably recognized as much in *United States v. Paramount Pictures,
Inc.*, 334 U.S. 131 (1948) (objecting to the industry's attempts to avoid competition by using "clearances," pooling agreements, formula deals, master agreements, franchises, and block booking); for further discussion, see Michael Meurer,
"Copyright Law and Price Discrimination," *Cardozo Law Review* 23 (2001): 55,
120.

59. See Robert Sklar, *Movie-Made America* (New York: Random House, 1975), 170–
270.

60. Indeed, one source reports that the average cost to produce a movie in 1999 was
$50 million dollars. Thomas Inkel, "Internet-Based Fans: Why The Entertainment
Industries Cannot Depend On Traditional Copyright Protections," *Pepperdine
Law Review* 28 (2001): 879, 900. Another says that recently, "the average cost of
a producing and marketing a studio production [is] now topping $100 [million]."
Christopher Kelley, "Where Will They Shoot J.R?" *Fort Worth Star-Telegram*,
February 8, 2006. But the best assessment of cost and consequences is given by

two authors from the *Wall Street Journal*, explaining that "As movie-production costs have soared, awarding first-dollar gross has become an increasingly risky proposition for studios. The average Hollywood picture costs around $64 million today, not including marketing costs, according to the Motion Picture Association of America. But the big-event movies that major studios rely on to bring in the big bucks—like the $207 million 'Kong' or the recently released 'Harry Potter and the Goblet of Fire,' which cost Warner Bros. about $200 million—can cost three times that much or more.'" So, "'[m]athematically, it starts getting difficult with budgets beyond $100 million to recoup money on a movie with major first-dollar gross participants,' says Bill Mechanic, the former head of Twentieth Century Fox and a former top Disney executive. 'First-dollar gross is fine if a movie is successful, but if it's not, participants will continue earning fees which only pushes the studio into further losses.'" Kate Kelly & Merissa Marr, "Sweetheart Star Deals Go Sour," *Wall Street Journal*, January 13, 2006. See also Alexander Lindey & Michael Landau, *Lindey on Entertainment, Publishing, and the Arts* (St. Paul, MN: West, 2004), § 6:49 (discussing how "[p]roduction costs for major motion pictures have been skyrocketing, and the trend does not seem to be slowing down").

61. Two popular, well-received examples of low-budget films are *Super Size Me*, a comical documentary-like film that tells the story of a man who eats nothing but McDonald's for thirty consecutive days, produced at a cost of $65,000 and grossing $11,529,368, and *The Blair Witch Project*, a horror flick about a camping trip gone bad in western Maryland, with a production budget of $35,000 and a gross of $140,539,099. See http://the-numbers.com/movies/records/budgets.html (last visited July 7, 2006).

62. *Borat: Cultural Learnings of America for Make Benefit Glorious Nation of Kazakhstan* is an example of a more typical "low budget" film: its production costs were $18 million, and in its first two weeks it grossed more than $116 million. See Bruce DeMara, "Reality versus Borat," *Toronto Star*, November 16, 2006.

63. *Lindey on Entertainment, Publishing, and the Arts*, § 6:49–50. ("While several years ago it was almost unbelievable for a motion picture to cost $100 million, in 2004 many of the major films topped that benchmark.")

64. Ibid.

65. In 2001, studios took home only fifty to fifty-five percent of *box-office* revenues with remainder going to the theaters, accounting for twenty-six percent overall revenues for the industries. "The Monster That Ate Hollywood," *Frontline* (Boston: WGBH, 2001). In 2004, box-office revenues totaled $7.4 billion, representing a meager sixteen percent of the industry's net. Carrie Rickey, "'Simultaneous Release' of Movies to Large and Small Screens begins Friday. Entertainment Industry Divided," *Philadelphia Inquirer*, January 25, 2006.

66. Pay-per-view (or "video-on-demand") accounted for $530 million in revenues for 2005. See Christopher Shulgan, "Mr. Skoll Goes to Hollywood," *Toronto Globe & Mail*, February 24, 2006.

67. Ibid. (accounting for $21 billion in income and forty-seven percent of the industry's net).

68. "Depending on the company doing the tracking, the video rental business last year ranged from $8 billion to $8.9 billion." Lorne Manly, "Extinction Long Seen, Video Stores Hang On," *New York Times*, August 23, 2005.

69. See *Lindey on Entertainment, Publishing, and the Arts*, § 6:8–6:9.
70. The curious can visit HBO.com to see the studios' penchant for peddling trinkets (toys, games, clothing, etc). A *Sopranos* fan, for example, can buy cookbooks, t-shirts, games, posters, and the like. See http://store.hbo.com (last visited July 7, 2006).
71. See, e.g., Braden Cox, "One Bundle, Many Antitrust Laws: The Dilemma for Digital Products," *Intellectual Property & Technology Law Journal* 4 (2005): 14; Steve Calandrillo, "An Economic Analysis of Property Rights in Information: Justifications and Problems of Exclusive Rights, Incentives to Generate Information, and the Alternative of a Government-Run Reward System," *Fordham Intellectual Property, Media & Entertainment Law Journal* 9 (1998): 301, 325.
72. Production costs of $175,000,000 (1995), $44,000,000 (1980), and $40,000,000 (1987), respectively. See http://the-numbers.com/movies (last visited July 7, 2006).
73. *Star Wars: Revelations*, an online movie, available at http://panicstruckpro.com/revelations (last visited July 7, 2006).
74. This is true as well for earlier derivative adaptations of the Star Wars genre. See Henry Jenkins, *Textual Poachers: Television Fans and Participatory Culture* (New York: Routledge, 1992), 30–31.
75. See, e.g., Jacqueline Ewenstein, "*Seminole Tribe*: Are States Free to Pirate Copyrights with Impunity?" *Columbia-VLA Journal of Law & the Arts* 22 (1997): 91, 118–19. ("With the rise of the welfare state, the rigid distinction between 'inherent rights' and 'privileges' granted by the government has been called into question as both courts and commentators have doubted whether individuals should be subjected to the unfettered discretion of government to withhold such 'privileges.' As with other government benefits such as social security, farm subsidies, or food stamps, the Constitution permits, but does not require, Congress to grant copyrights. Such government 'largess' has been held to be Due Process property when a person has a 'claim of entitlement' that rises above a 'mere expectancy.'")
76. See Act of Aug. 24, 1912, ch. 356, 37 Stat. 488 (1909 Act amended to include "[m]otion-picture photoplays" [movies or motion pictures] and "[m]otion pictures other than photoplays" [documentaries]); see also *Nimmer on Copyright*, § 2.09[D][2].
77. Primarily because the studios controlled or owned the movie theaters and equipment used to screen movies. The whole industry was "vertically integrated." See John Izod, *Hollywood and the Box Office, 1895–1986* (New York: Columbia University Press, 1989), 49, and Ethan Mordden, *The Hollywood Studios: House Style in the Golden Age of the Movies* (New York: Knopf, 1988).
78. Or, as Jack Valenti put it years ago, "[T]he VCR is to the American film producer and the American public as the Boston strangler is to the woman home alone." See *Home Recording of Copyrighted Works: Hearing on H.R. 4783, H.R. 4794, H.R. 4808, H.R. 5250, H.R. 5488, and H.R. 5750*, 97th Cong. 8 (1983).
79. 464 U.S. 417 (1984).
80. *Sony*, 464 U.S. at 455 (affirming the district court's ruling that "home time-shifting is fair use").
81. *Sony*, 464 U.S. at 456.
82. In the year following *Sony*, studios and distributors shipped eighty-two percent more prerecorded cassettes to feed the VCRs that were proliferating across the

consumer landscape. See Michael Cieply, "Movie Cassette Prices Could Fall as Hollywood Gluts Video Stores," *Wall Street Journal*, January 3, 1985; cf. the video-on-demand statistics mentioned in note 66.

83. Aaron Perkins, "Encryption Use: Law and Anarchy on the Digital Frontier," *Houston Law Review* 41 (2005): 1625, 1643–44. ("Although [*Sony* gave] the movie industry [a] legal defeat, an entire industry—the home entertainment industry—was born that created new ways for movie studios to get Americans to part with their money. Piracy never became the economic drain that Universal had feared. One reason this failed to occur was because of the inherent copying limitations of the analog format of beta and VHS tapes. A more significant reason was the adaptation of marketing and pricing models that encouraged consumers to buy legitimate home copies of movies.") (citations omitted)

84. Bandwidth is a problem: movies are generally large files and moving these files—legally or illegally—over the current Internet infrastructure is a time-consuming experience. See David Lazarus, "Bill Would Profoundly Change the Internet," *San Francisco Chronicle*, April 5, 2006; Rob Pegoraro, "Movie Downloads Remain a Production Worth Skipping," *Washington Post*, September 17, 2006. But even if the experience were faster, there is little indication the studios would move to cash in and offer movies for sale via the Internet. "For several years now, the refrain in the movie industry has been: 'We don't want to make the same mistake as the music industry.' Hollywood studios, having ventured billions of dollars on their titles, say they can't afford to let customers get used to finding movies via black-market file-sharing . . . [And today,] [t]he studios continue to show an amazing proficiency for finding reasons not to sell or rent digital downloads in ways that customers might value, all for the sake of protecting their existing retail channels." Rob Pegoraro, "A 'Mistake' Hollywood Had Better Start Making," *Washington Post*, September 13, 2006. For more on the quality of digital content, see http://en.wikipedia.org/wiki/Digital_video (last visited December 8, 2005); for a detailed explanation of peer-to-peer, see http://en.wikipedia.org/wiki/Peer-to -peer (last visited July 7, 2006).

85. Nora Achrati, "Valenti Warns of Piracy," *Milwaukee Journal Sentinel*, February 28, 2003.

86. *Metro-Goldwyn-Mayer Studios, Inc. v. Grokster, Ltd.*, 545 U.S. 913 (2005).

87. William Fisher III, *Promises to Keep* (Stanford, CA: Stanford University Press, 2004).

88. See Jerome H. Reichman, "Legal Hybrids Between the Patent and Copyright Paradigms," *Columbia Law Review* 94 (1994): 2432; Jerome H. Reichman & Pamela Samuelson, "Intellectual Property Rights in Data?" *Vanderbilt Law Review* 50 (1997): 51.

89. 274 U.S. 357, 375 (1927) (Brandeis, J., concurring).

90. 188 U.S. 239, 249–50 (1903).

91. 81 F.2d 49, 54 (2d Cir. 1936), aff'd, 309 U.S. 390 (1940).

92. *Folsom v. Marsh*, 9 F. Cas. 342, 344 (C.C.D. Mass. 1841) (noting that copyright and patent cases are "nearer than any other class of cases belonging to forensic discussions, to what may be called the metaphysics of the law where the distinctions are, or at least may be, very subtle and refined, and, sometimes, almost evanescent").

93. 191 F.2d 99, 104 (2d Cir. 1951) (citations omitted).
94. *Bleistein*, 188 U.S. at 251.
95. 537 U.S. 186, 219–20 (2003).
96. See generally Jed Rubenfeld, "Freedom of Imagination," *Yale Law Journal* 112 (2002): 1.
97. This is implicit in the reservation from the reach of copyright of ideas (and the like). See 17 U.S.C. § 102(b). ("In no case does copyright protection . . . extend to any idea. . . regardless of the form in which it is described, explained, illustrated or embodied.")
98. The Court accepted this rationale in *Harper & Row*, 471 U.S. at 556, and later affirmed it in *Feist*, 499 U.S. at 349–50. In truth the proposition in the text is a commonplace, reflected in numerous opinions.
99. Again, the point in the text is common ground among copyright skeptics at large. It has also gained a wider purchase among those skeptics who are students of the first amendment as well. See, e.g., Rubenfeld, "Freedom of Imagination," 14 (discussing how courts and commentators rely "on the idea/expression distinction to explain why copyright poses no serious free speech problems" and then demonstrating how "distinguishing ideas from expression is notoriously tricky"); Neil Netanel, "Locating Copyright Within the First Amendment Skein," *Stanford Law Review* 54 (2001): 1, 14 (criticizing the "idea/expression dichotomy on First Amendment grounds).
100. *Peter Pan Fabrics, Inc. v. Martin Weiner Corp.*, 274 F.2d 487, 489 (2d Cir. 1960).
101. Netanel, "Locating Copyright," 19 ("First Amendment protection afforded by copyright's idea/expression dichotomy is no less uncertain, unstable, and illusory than the dichotomy itself . . . given the indeterminate character of the idea/expression dichotomy, speakers who seek to do so often risk finding themselves on the receiving end of a copyright infringement action."); Diane Zimmerman, "Information as Speech, Information as Goods: Some Thoughts on Marketplaces and the Bill of Rights," *William & Mary Law Review* 33 (1992): 665, 709. ("Faced with the fuzzed line between idea and expression, would-be speakers, unsure of their rights, might conclude that they are better off bargaining with the copyright owner for permission than risking the costs of litigation, a possible injunction, and an assessment of damages.")
102. Cf. Jerome Frank, *Law and the Modern Mind* (New York: Tudor, 1935), 32–40; see also *Nimmer on Copyright*, § 13.03[A][1].
103. See Rubenfeld, "Freedom of Imagination" and Netanel, "Locating Copyright"; cf. Melville Nimmer, "Does Copyright Abridge the First Amendment Guaranties of Free Speech and Press?" *UCLA Law Review* 17 (1970): 1180, 1186–204.
104. See Netanel, "Locating Copyright," 15 (citing several cases demonstrating that "effective speech sometimes requires the verbatim copying of substantial portions of existing literary expression"); see also *San Francisco Arts & Athletics, Inc. v. U.S. Olympic Committee*, 483 U.S. 522 (1987) (defendants infringed by using the word "Olympic" to describe the "Gay Olympic Games"); *Zacchini v. Scripps-Howard Broadcasting Co.*, 433 U.S. 562 (1977) (news broadcast of a performer's entire "human cannonball" act was infringement and the First Amendment did not apply); *Roth Greeting Cards v. United Card Co.*, 429 F.2d 1106, 1110 (9th Cir. 1970) (greeting card infringed because the "total concept and feel" was sufficiently

similar to an antecedent work "as a whole," even though the defendant copied neither the text nor artistic design of the antecedent work); *Sid & Marty Krofft Television Prods., Inc. v. McDonald's Corp.*, 562 F.2d 1157 (9th Cir. 1977) (total concept and feel).

105. *Nimmer on Copyright*, § 1.10[C][2]; Melville Nimmer, "Does Copyright Abridge First Amendment Guaranties?"; see, e.g., *Ets-Hokin v. Skyy Spirits, Inc.*, 323 F.3d 763 (9th Cir. 2003) (*scenes à faire* and merger precluded an infringement of a vodka bottle picture); *Morrissey v. Procter & Gamble Co.*, 379 F.2d 675 (1st Cir. 1967) (applying doctrine to dispute involving contest rules); *Matthew Bender & Co., Inc. v. Kluwer Law Book Publishers, Inc.*, 672 F. Supp. 107, 110 (S.D.N.Y. 1987) (broader decision allowing a merger defense because "While in theory there are numerous ways to place the information . . . from a practical point of view the number of ways [to do so] in a useful and accessible manner is limited.").

106. See *Matthew Bender*, 672 F. Supp. 107 (S.D.N.Y. 1987); see also Netanel, "Locating Copyright," 14–16 (though we should note that Professor Netanel was advocating a position of First Amendment supremacy, rather than the merger doctrine, when idea and expression cannot be separated sensibly).

107. *Nimmer on Copyright*, § 13.03[B][4].

108. 81 F.2d 49 (2d Cir.), *cert. denied*, 298 U.S. 669 (1936).

109. *Ets-Hokin*, 225 F.3d at 1084 (Nelson, D., dissenting) (district court criticized for not dismissing original claim "because this case could have been dismissed on firmer legal grounds—the originality of the allegedly infringing photographs and the merger doctrine"). See also *Mannion v. Coors Brewing Co.*, 377 F. Supp. 2d 444, 455–61 (S.D.N.Y. 2005), in which Judge Kaplan considers, but in effect dismisses, an argument for merger, on the ground that merger (like the distinction between idea and expression itself) is fundamentally unsuitable in settings involving photographs and other visual arts. The effect of his opinion is to free such works from the burden of merger, while allowing them to search for protection via an even more unsuitable heuristic. See the additional discussion in note 120 of this chapter.

110. See, e.g., *Roth Greeting Cards* and *Krofft*.

111. *Nimmer on Copyright*, § 13.03[A][1][c] (discussing how the phrase "may, conceivably, make sense to refer to . . . a greeting card or game or anthropomorphic fantasy world," but in reality "[t]he phrase is geared towards simplistic works that require only a highly 'intrinsic' (i.e., unanalytic) evaluation. . . . More broadly, the touchstone of 'total concept and feel' threatens to subvert the very essence of copyright, namely the protection of original expression.").

112. We take some satisfaction in Nimmer's repudiation of "concept and feel" as a standard for determining infringement. Ibid. ("'[T]otal concept and feel' should not be viewed as a sine qua non for infringement—similarity that is otherwise actionable cannot be rendered defensible simply because of a different 'concept and feel.' In sum, therefore, the frequent invocations of this standard do little to bring order to the inquiry into what constitutes substantial similarity, and would be better abandoned.") We should emphasize, however, that he does not join us in our more general criticism of the classic idea-expression dichotomy. Indeed, as we will see in due course, the latter doctrine is central to his own understanding of how and why copyright can be defended against charges that it is at odds with freedom of expression.

113. Rubenfeld, "Freedom of Imagination," 14.

114. To express oneself, to speak, "is not to put a word under each thought. . . . Language signifies when instead of copying thought it lets itself be taken apart and put together again by thought. Language bears the meaning of thoughts as a footprint signifies the movement and effort of the body." And, further, "To [speak] is not to possess the objects of thought; it is to use them to mark out a realm to think about that which we therefore are not yet thinking about." Maurice Merleau-Ponty, *Signs* (Evanston, IL: Northwestern University Press, 1964), 44, 160, quoted in Donald Spence, *Narrative Truth and Historical Truth: Meaning and Interpretation in Psychoanalysis* (New York: W. W. Norton, 1982).

115. Donald Spence conveys this point exceptionally well. As a psychoanalyst, he notes that there is "slippage between thoughts and words," and that expression is not "produced by simply lumping the words together, as would be the case if each word carried a piece of the final thought." Instead, "words must be put together in a certain sequence to convey [a] final meaning; once that is accomplished, the words themselves take on somewhat different meanings. In much the same way, the associating patient forms his thoughts into words; he is actively constructing something that will somehow approximate what he has in mind but will never quite contain it all; and once the words are expressed, they take on a particular color from the thought. Rather than being aware of a field of words in his mind's eye, waiting to be named, it is more as if the patient is conscious of bits and pieces of experience, 'written' in a variety of languages (not always in words). He must continually translate from the private language of experience into the common language of speech. Expressed in these terms, free association is hardly free and the patient is hardly passive. The patient is probably not as diligent as the writer and usually not trying to find the exact word (an essentially impossible task and, therefore, a convenient resistance); but viewing speech in this manner puts a different interpretation on the task of the patient. It makes free association much less similar to passively reporting the passing scene and much closer to active composition; and it gives the common expression 'tell me what comes to mind' an ironic twist because, from the patient's point of view, the mind is often empty of words until the patient makes an effort to find them." Spence, *Narrative Truth*, 83–84.

116. See generally Netanel, "Locating Copyright."

117. Granted, there is dispute about what, if anything, King appropriated for his "I Have a Dream" speech, and, if so, whether his doing so was intentional or not. Some assert that he lifted the template for the speech from Archibald Carey's 1952 address to the Republican National Convention. See Theodore Pappas, *Plagiarism and the Culture War: The Writings of Martin Luther King, Jr., and Other Prominent Americans* (Tampa, FL: Hallberg, 1998); Keith Miller, *Voice of Deliverance: The Language of Martin Luther King, Jr., and Its Sources* (New York: Free Press, 1992), 146–49. But we are persuaded by our colleague Rick Lischer of Duke Divinity School, who argues that "there is no such thing as an 'original dream' [speech]." If anything, the speech arose out of the "Bible and the African-American church." And, as far as plagiarism goes, King simply had a "genius for absorbing through his pores the power around him in the church and translating it for wider audiences. He borrowed nothing . . . but he overheard much." Richard Lischer, *The Preacher King* (London: Oxford University Press, 1995), 93–94.

118. Lischer, *The Preacher King*, 93–94.
119. Zapruder's account of his decision is chronicled in *Time, Inc. v. Bernard Geis Associates*, 293 F. Supp. 130 (S.D.N.Y. 1968).
120. But cf. *Mannion v. Coors Brewing Co.*, 377 F. Supp. 2d at 453–55 (analyzing copyright infringement claim by considering the originality requirement in terms of "originality in the rendition," "originality in the creation of the subject," and "originality in the timing"); see also Hugh Laddie et al, *The Modern Law of Copyright and Designs* (London: Butterworths, 2000) (acknowledged and followed in *Mannion*).
121. See Nimmer, "Does Copyright Abridge First Amendment Guaranties?" 1196–203 (discussing *Bernard Geis*); see also *Lindey on Entertainment, Publishing, and the Arts* § 1:60 (comparing merger to conventional understandings of "thin copyright"); Howard Abrams, *The Law of Copyright*, § 14:34 (Eagan, MN: West, 2005) (discussing the similarities and disparities among "thin copyright," merger, and the concept of "inseparable expression.")
122. *Time Inc. v. Bernard Geis Associates*, 293 F. Supp. at 146 (finding fair use because there was "public interest in having the fullest information available on the murder of President Kennedy"). Compare Nimmer, "Does Copyright Abridge First Amendment Guaranties?" 1200 (concurring with *Geis* in its outcome, but remarking how the court "actually relied not on the first amendment but rather on the doctrine of fair use in upholding the defendant's copying of the Zapruder film. I would suggest that a grave danger to copyright may lie in the failure to distinguish between the statutory privilege known as fair use and an emerging constitutional limitation on copyright contained in the first amendment.").
123. Cf. David Fewer, "Constitutionalizing Copyright: Freedom of Expression and the Limits of Copyright in Canada," *University of Toronto Faculty of Law Review* 55 (1997): 175, 229. ("This argument is strong only if one accepts that it is never valid to use another's expression for one's own expressive purposes. Essentially, this argument repeats the claim that appropriated expression is not within the scope of freedom of expression, reading into the right a[n] [originality] requirement. This seems a difficult argument to maintain [because] it is necessary in some instances to use another's speech for socially valuable uses that lie close to the core of values enshrined in freedom of expression, such as educational, critical, and transformative uses.")
124. See Kembrew McCleod, *Freedom of Expression* (New York: Doubleday, 2005) (offering countless examples of how exclusive rights silence a second-in-time artist's expression); Lessig, *Free Culture*, 95–99 (offering an example of how a four-second clip of *The Simpsons*—a clip that was inadvertently included in the background of a documentary about stagehands—foredoomed the entire enterprise, as it became too onerous to obtain a license from the purported copyright holder, Fox). See Fred von Lohmann, "RIAA Says Ripping CDs to Your iPod is NOT Fair Use," *Electronic Frontier Foundation*, available at http://www.eff.org/deeplinks/archives/2006_02.php (last visited July 7, 2006) quoting "Joint Reply Comments" filing of content industry (available at same site).
125. Alice Randall, *The Wind Done Gone* (New York: Houghton Mifflin, 2001). Jed Rubenfeld represented Ms. Randall, his former classmate at Yale, and discusses her case in "Freedom of Imagination."

126. Margaret Mitchell, *Gone With the Wind* (New York: MacMillan, 1936).

127. See Tina Susman, "Brilliant Parody or Blatant Ripoff?" *Newsday*, April 18, 2001; for more on Mitchell, the person, see Patrick Allen, ed., *Margaret Mitchell, Reporter* (Athens, GA: Hill Street Press, 2000).

128. See Plaintiff's Complaint, *SunTrust Bank v. Houghton Mifflin Co.*, Civil Action No. 1:01CV-701, *3 (N.D. Ga. March 15, 2001) (available at http://houghtonmifflinbooks.com/features/randall_url/courtpapers.shtml); Appellee's Brief, *SunTrust Bank v. Houghton Mifflin Co.*, Case No. 01-122-00-HH, *50-52 (11th Cir. May 18, 2001) (available at http://houghtonmifflinbooks.com/features/randall_url/courtpapers.shtml).

129. *SunTrust Bank v. Houghton Mifflin Co.*, 136 F. Supp. 2d 1357 (N.D. Ga.) (using the "substantial similarity" test to find infringement because of the "fragmented literal similarity" and "comprehensive nonliteral similarity" between the two works), *rev'd on first amendment grounds*, 252 F.3d 1165 (11th Cir.), *order vacated and opinion substituted*, 268 F.3d 1257 (11th Cir. 2001).

130. *SunTrust*, 252 F.3d at 1166 (11th Cir. 2001) (per curiam). ("It is manifest that the entry of a preliminary injunction in this copyright case was an abuse of discretion in that it represents an unlawful prior restraint in violation of the First Amendment.")

131. *SunTrust*, 268 F.3d at 1259, 1277.

132. See David Kirkpatrick, "Mitchell Estate Settles 'Gone With the Wind' Suit," *New York Times*, May 10, 2002.

133. Rubenfeld, "Freedom of Imagination," 56–59.

134. MacDonald introduced the world to Travis McGee in 1964 in *The Deep Blue Good-by* (Philadelphia: Lippincott, 1975). (For those who may wonder at what can seem to be a discrepancy in the dates just given, our editor Elisabeth Lewis Corley offers this response: 1975 is the date of the first American hardcover edition. It appears to have been published in 1964 by Fawcett in New York, and in the UK perhaps a year later.) McGee appeared in twenty-one novels, concluding with *The Lonely Silver Rain* (Knopf, 1985).

135. Our description here is of a piece with countless others, all more or less to the same effect (though we ourselves happen also to have read all of the novels, and can thus attest to these qualities in McGee from personal observation and experience). See, e.g., Jonathan Yardley, "John D. MacDonald's Lush Landscape of Crime," *Washington Post*, November 11, 2003. ("McGee is owner of the Busted Flush, 52-foot barge-type houseboat, Slip F-18, Bahia Mar, Lauderdale. He's a World War II veteran, 6 feet 4 inches tall, solidly built. He isn't exactly a clerical type, in the words of one of the many women for whom he does important favors: You are huge and it is obvious you have been whacked upon, and you look as though you damn well enjoyed returning the favor. He's catnip for the ladies, but he is by his own admission an incurable romantic who thinks the man-woman thing shouldn't be a contest, who believes the biggest and most important reason in the world [for lovemaking] is to be together with someone in a way that makes life a little less bleak and solitary and lonesome.")

136. By the time of his death in 1986, MacDonald had already sold over seventy million copies in this series. An untold number have been resold in the used-book market since then. See Kiki Olson, "The Writing Machine," *St. Petersburg Times*, September 17, 2000.

137. See Gerald Fraser, "John D. MacDonald, Novelist, Is Dead," *New York Times*, December 29, 1986.

138. Including one of the coauthors of this book.

139. See 17 U.S.C. § 302(a) (copyright term for a single, identified author is the life of the author plus seventy years).

140. See Lessig, *Free Culture*; McCleod, *Freedom of Expression*.

141. See *Wihtol v. Crow*, 199 F. Supp. 682, 685 (S.D. Iowa 1961), *rev'd*, 309 F.2d 777 (8th Cir. 1962); see also *Nimmer on Copyright*, § 13.05[E][4][b].

142. See, e.g., *Bright Tunes Music Corp. v. Harrisongs Music, Ltd.*, 420 F.Supp. 177, 180–81 (S.D.N.Y. 1976) ("I conclude that the composer in seeking musical materials to clothe his thoughts, was working with various possibilities. As he tried this possibility and that, there came to the surface of his mind a particular combination that pleased him as being one he felt would be appealing to a prospective listener; in other words, that this combination of sounds would work. Why? Because his subconscious knew it already had worked in a song his conscious mind did not remember. Having arrived at this pleasing combination of sounds, the recording was made, the lead sheet prepared for copyright and the song became an enormous success. Did Harrison deliberately use the music of He's So Fine? I do not believe he did so deliberately. Nevertheless, it is clear that My Sweet Lord is the very same song as He's So Fine with different words, and Harrison had access to He's So Fine. This is, under the law, infringement of copyright, and is no less so even though subconsciously accomplished."); see also *Fred Fisher, Inc., v. Dillingham*, 298 F. 145 (S.D.N.Y. 1924) (Hand finding liability because there "must have been" a taking even though doing so was "probably unconscious").

143. See 17 U.S.C. § 107 ("fair use of a copyrighted work [includes] criticism, comment, news reporting, teaching [including multiple copies for classroom use], scholarship, or research"); see also §§ 108–22. Besides fair use, Congress has excepted other uses from the reproduction right, including library photocopying (17 U.S.C. § 108), short recordings for broadcast purposes (17 U.S.C. § 112), reproducing pictorial, graphic, or sculptural works embodied in "useful articles" (17 U.S.C. § 113), sound recordings (17 U.S.C. § 114), mechanical-compulsory licenses for nondramatic musical works (17 U.S.C. § 115), computer programs (17 U.S.C. § 117), compulsory licenses for noncommercial broadcasting (17 U.S.C. § 118), and two-dimensional reproduction of architectural works (17 U.S.C. § 120). Patry, *Copyright Law & Practice*, 717.

144. See 17 U.S.C. § 107(1)–(4) (purpose and character of the use; nature of copyrighted work; amount of the copyrighted work used in relation to its whole; and, effect use has on marketability or market value of the work).

145. See L. Ray Patterson & Stanley Lindberg, *The Nature of Copyright: A Law of User's Rights* (Athens: University of Georgia Press, 1991); cf. Julie Cohen, "The Place of the User in Copyright Law," *Fordham Law Review* 74 (2005): 347 (critiquing differing conceptions of the "user" in copyright and arguing for copyright law to "acknowledge and comprehensively adjust for the situated user's importance"). For a skeptical discussion on the term's origin and modern impact, see Lorin Brennan, "The Public Policy of Information Licensing," *Houston Law Review* 36 (1999): 61, 77. ("A recent trend in discussions of information

has been to advance the idea of 'user's rights.' The concept of user's rights argues that certain exceptions to exclusive rights in the Copyright Act, such as fair use, do not merely create a defense to an infringement action, but also create an affirmative right to use a copyrighted work . . . This concept of user's rights is questionable. Just because an item of information may be used without infringing a copyright does not mean that it may be used without regard to any other law.")

146. L. Ray Patterson & Craig Joyce, "Copyright In 1791: An Essay Concerning The Founders' View of the Copyright Power Granted to Congress in Article I, Section 8, Clause 8 of the U.S. Constitution," *Emory Law Journal* 52 (2003): 909, 950 n. 102.

147. See generally Rebecca Tushnet, "Copy This Essay: How Fair Use Doctrine Harms Free Speech and How Copying Serves It," *Yale Law Journal* 114 (2004): 535, 545 (arguing that even a "successful fair use defense is expensive, and the risk of such a lawsuit deters publishers from investing in potentially infringing works; that kind of self-censorship is traditionally a matter of concern to the First Amendment"); Wendy Gordon, "Excuse and Justification in the Law of Fair Use: Transaction Costs Have Always Been *Part* of the Story," *Journal of the Copyright Society* 50 (2003): 149 (noting that "every plausible litmus test that might simplify the 'fair use' inquiry has proven inadequate"); Jessica Litman, "Reforming Information Law in Copyright's Image," *University of Dayton Law Review* 22 (1997): 587, 612–13. ("Fair use is problematic [to the First Amendment]. . . . It may be that we could design a fair-use-like privilege that provides would-be fair users with reasonable certainty, was indifferent to content, and relied on clear rules, mechanically applied. Once we were done, though, the privilege wouldn't be very fair-use-like.") See also Lloyd Weinreb, "Fair's Fair: A Comment on the Fair Use Doctrine," *Harvard Law Review* 103 (1990): 1137, 1154–56 (describing the Court's approach to fair use in *Sony* as "hopelessly inadequate" and a "procrustean effort to make the correct result fit that analysis rather than stating its real basis directly"); and see JuNelle Harris, "Beyond Fair Use: Expanding Copyright Misuse To Protect Digital Free Speech," *Texas Intellectual Property Law Journal* 13 (2004): 83 (repeatedly stating that "fair use is inadequate" to protect speech interests or to assist in "differentiating between more or less legitimate assertions by copyright owners").

148. See David Nimmer, " 'Fairest of Them All,' and Other Fairy Tales of Fair Use," *Law & Contemporary Problems* 66 (2003): 263, 267–81 (asking "How do the factors work out in practice?" and then demonstrating how the factors work as "convenient pegs on which to hang antecedent conclusions").

149. Nimmer, " 'Fairest of Them All," 287.

150. David Lange, "Copyright and the Constitution in the Age of Intellectual Property," *Journal of Intellectual Property* 1 (1993): 119, 127–28. ("Among jewelers, for example, or potters or glassmakers or metalsmiths or rag doll makers or woodworkers, making the product is also a species of creative play—and this is no less true when what is being made is not original. You don't have to take my word for that. Just take a close look the next time you head for the beach and see for yourself: the child who imitates the next child's sand castle is enjoying herself every bit as much as if she had gotten there first. Sometimes, in fact, the art is in the

appropriation. Shakespeare called it 'The Winter's Tale.' Art historians call it 'making a find.'") See also Tom Bethell & Irvin Matus, "The Case for Oxford," *The Atlantic Monthly*, October 1991, 45–46 (finding "more than a few additional parallels" between Shakespeare's *Hamlet* and an earlier work by Lord Burghley); Ward Elliott & Robert Valenza, "Oxford By The Numbers: What Are the Odds That the Earl of Oxford Could Have Written Shakespeare's Poems and Plays?" *Tennessee Law Review* 72 (2004): 323; but cf. *Encyclopedia Britannica Online*, s.v. "Shakespeare, William," http://search.eb.com/eb/article-232330 (last visited July 10, 2006) (arguing that any "theory [making Shakespeare into a plagiarist] is suspect on a number of counts").

151. "[S]ometimes, far more simply, a pearl is beyond price. Sometimes it is inappropriate, even garish, to think in terms of a market. Sometimes, in short, the market does not fail. Sometimes the market is irrelevant." David Lange & Jennifer Lange Anderson, "Copyright, Fair Use and Transformative Critical Appropriation," paper presented at the Duke Conference on the Public Domain, November 9, 2001, available at http://law.duke.edu/pd/papers/langeand.pdf (last visited May 2006).

152. See generally Julio Cole, "Patents and Copyrights: Do the Benefits Exceed the Costs?" *Journal of Libertarian Studies* 15, no. 4 (2001): 79, 80–89; Mark Lemley, "What's Different about Intellectual Property?" *Texas Law Review* 83 (2005): 1097, 1099–102 (explaining that while "benefits exceed [the] costs" analyses may be helpful in other fields, the "same cannot be said of intellectual property").

153. Roland Barthes, "The Death of the Author," in *Image, Music, Text*, trans. Stephen Heath (New York: Noonday, 1988), 142–48 (arguing that readers, not authors, ultimately assign meaning to an author's work); but cf. Seán Burke, *The Death and Return of the Author*, 2nd ed. (Edinburgh: Edinburgh University Press, 1998) (countering Barthes's theories).

154. See generally Martha Woodmansee, "The Genius and the Copyright: Economic and Legal Conditions of the Emergence of the 'Author,'" *Eighteenth-Century Studies* 17, No. 4 (1984): 425–48; see also James Boyle, "A Theory of Law and Information: Copyright, Spleens, Blackmail, and Insider Trading," *California Law Review* 80 (1992): 1413, 1418–23 (arguing that appeals to "a particular [and particularly romantic] image of information production" and "stereotype[s] of the romantic author" often guide courts in framing and settling copyright disputes).

155. Rubenfeld, "Freedom of Imagination," 37–43.

156. Zechariah Chafee, Jr., "Reflections on the Law of Copyright," *Columbia Law Review* 45 (1945): 503, 511.

157. Rubenfeld, "Freedom of Imagination," 59 (noting that the use of copyright regimes to silence another's expression—whether in the form of imitation, appropriation, or otherwise—"create[s] a private power over public speech that is unacceptable and tantamount to censorship [and] penalize[s] the exercise of the imagination").

158. As Wendell Berry said in the preface to one of his best works, "As I understand it, I am being paid only for my work in arranging the words; my property is that arrangement. The thoughts in this book, on the contrary, are not mine. They came freely to me, and I give them freely away. I have no 'intellectual property,' and I think that all claimants to such property are thieves." *Sex, Economy, Freedom & Community* (New York: Pantheon Books, 1993).

159. PBS has produced an outstanding documentary on Bob Dylan. It extensively discusses Dylan's journey and, of course, his influences—among them Guthrie and Seeger. See *No Direction Home: Bob Dylan*, DVD, directed by Martin Scorsese (Paramount Home Entertainment, 2005); see also "Bob Dylan: Influences Map," http://www.pbs.org/wnet/americanmasters/dylan/influences_flash.html (last visited July 10, 2006); see also the shifting Dylan personae as reinterpreted in *I'm Not There*, written and directed by Todd Haynes (Killer Films/The Weinstein Company, 2007).

160. G. Marx, *Groucho and Me* (New York: Bernard Geis, 1959), 88 quoted in Lange, "Recognizing the Public Domain,"161–62 n. 63.

161. Rubenfeld, "Freedom of Imagination."

162. See Lange, "Recognizing the Public Domain," 161–62 n. 63.

163. Law is simply not a suitable medium for decisions of this sort. In Justice Douglas's words, echoed subsequently by Professor Lessig, "common sense revolts at the idea." See Douglas, J., in *United States v. Causby*, 328 U.S. 256, 261 (1946); Lessig, *Free Culture*, 2–4, 11–13, 183–85 (arguing that "common sense revolts" against extreme intellectual property claims and systems in which IP law serves as a conduit for creativity).

164. *Bleistein*, 188 U.S. at 251.

165. *Peter Pan Fabrics*, 274 F.2d at 489.

166. See, e.g., Richard Posner, *Frontiers of Legal Theory* (Cambridge, MA: Harvard University Press, 2001) 67 (utilizing a cost-benefit analysis to determine whether one's speech is permissible under the law); Landes & Posner, "An Economic Analysis of Copyright Law," 345–55.

167. See Paul Romer, "Endogenous Technological Change," *Journal of Political Economy* 98 (1990): S71, S73–S74 ("A purely rival good has the property that its use by one firm or person precludes its use by another; a purely nonrival good has the property that its use by one firm or person in no way limits its use by another."); Lawrence Lessig, *The Future of Ideas* (New York: Random House, 2001), 21 (noting that the "economists are right" with respect to rivalrous and nonrivalrous categories and noting that a "rivalrous resource" is more problematic). See also *Alabama Power Co. v. F.C.C.*, 311 F.3d 1357, 1369 (11th Cir. 2002) (noting that one party's gain "precisely corresponds to [another's] loss" when goods are rivalrous, whereas the gain of nonrivalrous goods by another party "does not necessarily diminish the use and enjoyment of others").

168. See Wesley Hohfeld, "Fundamental Legal Conceptions as Applied in Judicial Reasoning," *Yale Law Journal* 26 (1917): 710; see also Adam Mossoff, "What is Property? Putting the Pieces Back Together," *Arizona Law Review* 45 (2003): 371, 413–28.

169. See the authorities cited in note 167. See also Lange, "Recognizing the Public Domain," 147.

170. Jefferson to Isaac McPherson, August 13, 1813, in *Life and Selected Writings of Thomas Jefferson*, ed. Adrienne Koch & William Harwood Peden (New York: Random House, 1993), 557.

171. *Chisum on Patents*, § 2.02 (describing the early origins of patents); *Graham v. John Deere Co.*, 383 U.S. 1, 8–9 (1966) (describing Jefferson's philosophical approach to patents); see also Oren Bar-Gill & Gideon Parchomovsky, "A Marketplace for Ideas?" *Texas Law Review* 84 (2005): 395.

172. Edward Walterscheid offers a useful view of Jefferson's perspective on patents and exclusivity in general. See "Patents and the Jeffersonian Mythology," *John Marshall Law Review* 29 (1995): 269, 281–97 (noting that Jefferson sought to make early patent law far less exclusive and describing how he approached the "embarrassment of an exclusive patent").

173. R. Polk Wagner, "Information Wants to Be Free: Intellectual Property and the Mythologies of Control," *Columbia Law Review* 103 (2003): 995; see also John Perry Barlow, "The Economy of Ideas," *Wired*, March 1994.

174. *Whitney v. California*, 274 U.S. 357, 375 (1927) (Brandeis, J., dissenting); see Yochai Benkler, "Free as the Air to Common Use: First Amendment Constraints on Enclosure of the Public Domain," *New York University Law Review* 74 (1999): 354.

175. *Mishawaka Rubber & Woolen Mfg. Co. v. S.S. Kresge Co.*, 316 U.S. 203, 205 (1942).

176. Jefferson to Isaac McPherson, August 13, 1813.

177. Walterscheid, "Patents and the Jeffersonian Mythology," 304–5 (arguing that Jefferson's words to McPherson were a "disavowal of any natural or inherent property right in an invention"); see also Walterscheid, *The Nature of the Intellectual Property Clause: A Study in Historical Perspective* (Buffalo: William S. Hein & Co., 2002), 4–9 ; James Boyle, "The Second Enclosure Movement and the Construction of the Public Domain," *Law & Contemporary Problems* 66 (2003): 33, 53.

178. See Rubenfeld, "Freedom of Imagination," 57–58, making the point in an explicit First Amendment setting. Compare, e.g., the contrary presupposition as to rent-seeking entitlements in 17 U.S.C. § 111 (cable), § 114 (satellite), § 115 (cover songs), or § 116 (coin-operated phonorecord players).

179. The phrase "an insight more important than we can use" originated with the late Professor Harry Kalven in "Broadcasting, Public Policy and the First Amendment," *Journal of Law & Economics* 10 (1967): 15, 30.

180. "In theory" presumes that the song or film is marketable to that specific downloader prior to her mouse click. This is not a black and white issue. And to be sure, not every download or file-sharing instance means that someone is losing as another gains. Professor Lessig offers a smart account of how language of "appropriation" and "piracy" can be illusory in this context. Lessig, *Free Culture*, 68–69.

181. See generally Richard Posner, *Economic Analysis of Law*, 5th ed. (New York: Aspen, 1998), 35–41 (contemporary property system protecting content [copyright] should be expanded until enforcement costs outweigh benefits created by the system [more content]); Goldstein, *Copyright's Highway*, 187–216 (arguing that as digital technologies expand the possible uses of copyrightable content a correlative expansion in copyright protection should likewise take place); Daniel McClure, "Trademarks and Competition: The Recent History," *Law & Contemporary Problems* 59 (1996): 13, 13–14 (linking the "Chicago School" and the 1990s expansion of "law and economics" to the "pendulum [swinging] back in favor of protection"); Neil Netanel, "Copyright and a Democratic Civil Society," *Yale Law Journal* 106 (1996): 283, 367–68; for an international take on this topic, see Joost Pauwelyn, "The Transformation of World Trade," *Michigan Law Review*

104 (2005): 1, 54 (expressing skepticism about "free trade" and demonstrating that economic-centered analysis positions the WTO to be "as much about protectionism as it is about free trade"); Boyle, "Second Enclosure," 40–41 (noting that any opposition to expanding intellectual property regimes is "portrayed as economically illiterate").

182. 17 U.S.C. § 106.

183. Stuart Kaplan, "Let Me Hear Your Web Sights: Visual and Aural Metaphors for the Internet," *Idaho Law Review* 40 (2004): 299, 311–12 (suggesting that, despite the controversy over peer-to-peer technologies, "attention should also be given to the opportunities for advancing a variety of art forms through robust file-sharing capabilities"). See David Lange, "Reimagining the Public Domain," *Law and Contemporary Problems* 66 (2003): 463.

184. Boyle, "Second Enclosure," 46–53.

185. Cf. *Kelly v. Arriba Soft Corp.*, 336 F.3d 811 (9th Cir. 2003) (search engine's display of copyrighted pictures [thumbnails] was noninfringing fair use); and see *Perfect 10 v. Amazon.com, Inc.*, 487 F.3d 701 (9th Cir. 2007) (following *Kelly* in an action brought against Google, and finding "transformative use").

186. 17 U.S.C. § 106A; for further discussion bearing upon these issues, see Jane Ginsburg, "Copyright in the 101st Congress: Commentary on the Visual Artists Rights Act and the Architectural Works Act of 1990," *Columbia Journal of Law & the Arts* 14 (1990): 477.

187. See Bob Thompson, "Search Me? Google Wants to Digitize Every Book," *Washington Post*, August 13, 2006 ("Last fall, the Authors Guild and a group of major publishing houses filed separate suits in U.S. District Court in Manhattan, charging Google with copyright infringement on a massive scale. Google argues that under the 'fair use' provisions of copyright law, it has a perfect right to let its users search the text of copyrighted works—as long as, once the search is complete, it only shows them what it calls 'snippets' of those works. Nonsense, say the authors and publishers: In order to find and display those snippets, Google must first copy whole books without permission."); Kevin Delaney & Andres Cala, "France Mobilizes, Seeks European Allies to Fend Off Google," *Wall Street Journal*, May 12, 2005. In February 2008, as this book was nearing completion, Professor Lange joined other scholars in a declaration in support of a finding of fair use in this matter, to be filed in France in connection with the pending legislation.

188. Lange, "Recognizing the Public Domain," 147.

189. Record Rental Amendment of 1984, Pub. L. 98–450, October 4, 1984, 98 Stat. 1727 (1984), 98th Cong. 2d Sess. (1984); see also Software Rental Amendments of 1990: Hearing Before the Subcomm. on Courts, Intellectual Property and the Admin. of Justice of the House Comm. on the Judiciary, 101st Cong., 2d Sess. 2 (1990) (statement of Rep. Robert Kastenmeier).

190. Pub. L. 105–304, 112 Stat. 2863 (1998) (codified at 17 U.S.C. § 1201 et seq.).

191. By "virtual venue" we mean a digitally generated venue analogous to the Grand Ole Opry, Carnegie Hall, Soldiers' Field, the old Fillmore West, or Woodstock or the new Bonnaroo Festival—or, for that matter, the Southpoint Cinema Sixteen just down the road a piece, or the Royal Albert Hall, or anyplace else in the world where public admission can be controlled so that works can be presented to audiences on terms to be bargained for or otherwise established.

192. No Session of Congress is without such legislation, but no useful purpose would be served by cataloging the bills that are pending as we go to press.

193. See "The Public Domain," *Law & Contemporary Problems* 66 (2003). The Creative Commons, a privately generated consortium of public domain oriented copyright proprietors, offers users a flexible alternative to statutory licensing. *Creative Commons*, http://creativecommons.org.

194. See Lessig, *Free Culture.*

CHAPTER 4

1. David Lange, "The Speech and Press Clauses," *UCLA Law Review* 23 (1975): 77; see *First National Bank of Boston v. Bellotti*, 435 U.S. 765 (1978) (holding that the press clause does not give special status or privilege to any group and that there is no distinction in the First Amendment's freedom to disseminate ideas through one form of media [newspapers] over another).

2. See Jed Rubenfeld, "Freedom of Imagination: Copyright's Constitutionality," *Yale Law Journal* 112 (2002): 1. Rubenfeld envisions the first amendment interests of relevance here as having their origins in the imagination, a view in which we generally concur. His understanding of these interests is more constricted than ours, however, or at least so we understand him to suggest in his essay. Meanwhile, we do not mean to attribute to him our conflation of the speech and press clauses, an issue about which, so far as we know, he has not expressed himself.

3. For more on this topic, see *Texas v. Johnson*, 491 U.S. 397 (1989) (finding that First Amendment protections "do not end at the spoken or written work" and recognizing the expressive nature of burning a flag); see also *Spence v. Washington*, 418 U.S. 405 (1974) (peace symbol affixed to American flag found to be protected expression); *United States v. O'Brien*, 391 U.S. 367 (1968) (declaring that not all conduct "can be labeled as 'speech' whenever [someone] engaging in conduct intends thereby to express an idea").

4. See *New York Times Co. v. United States*, 403 U.S. 713, 717 (1971) (Black, J. concurring); see also Roger Newman, *Hugo Black: A Biography* (New York: Pantheon Books, 1994), 512. It should be acknowledged that Justice Black does not appear to have considered the conflict between the First Amendment and the role that exclusivity plays with respect to expression in copyright or the other intellectual property doctrines. We suppose that his views might have coincided with our own, but our research does not allow us to aver as much, and of course it is not inevitably so. In any event, our views would not change had he aligned himself with the present doctrines.

5. Eugene Volokh addresses this line of demarcation in "Speech as Conduct: Generally Applicable Laws, Illegal Courses of Conduct, 'Situation-Altering Utterances,' and the Uncharted Zones," *Cornell Law Review* 90 (2005): 1277.

6. See 15 U.S.C. § 1125(c).

7. The Court has said the First Amendment represents "a profound national commitment to the principle that debate on public issues should be uninhibited, robust, and wide-open." *New York Times v. Sullivan*, 376 U.S. 254, 270 (1964).

8. See Rubenfeld, "Freedom of Imagination."

9. See John Hart Ely, *Democracy and Distrust: A Theory of Judicial Review* (Cambridge, MA: Harvard University Press, 1980), 109.

10. *West Virginia State Board of Education v. Barnette,* 319 U.S. 624 (1943) (forbidding state law forcing schoolchildren to salute or say a pledge to the flag); *Hurley v. Irish-American Gay, Lesbian and Bisexual Group of Boston,* 515 U.S. 557 (1995) (holding unconstitutional a parade requirement that forced participants to display messages with which they disagreed).

11. *Wooley v. Maynard,* 430 U.S. 705 (1977) (holding that motorists were free to block out the license-plate slogan "Live Free or Die" provided that the plate remained legible enough to identify the automobile).

12. *Grosjean v. American Press Co.,* 297 U.S. 233, 250 (1936) (holding special tax on newspaper invalid because the tax (or the government's motive in implementing it) was "a deliberate and calculated device . . . to limit the circulation of information"); *Minneapolis Star & Tribune Co. v. Minnesota Commissioner of Revenue,* 460 U.S. 575 (1983) (differential taxation on the press suggests an attempt to suppress expression and is therefore presumptively unconstitutional without an adequate, valid, and compelling governmental interest to counterbalance potential harm).

13. *Central Hudson Gas & Elec. Corp. v. Public Service Commission,* 447 U.S. 557 (1980) (holding that commercial speech—mailings—is protectable speech provided that it is neither misleading nor related to an unlawful purpose and satisfies a four-pronged test).

14. See Bipartisan Campaign Finance Reform Act of 2002, Pub. L. No. 107–55, 116 Stat. 81 (2002) (codified at 2 U.S.C. §§ 431–55 [2004]) (commonly termed "McCain-Feingold"); see also *Buckley v. Valeo,* 424 U.S. 1 (1976) (allowing regulation of campaign *donations* but distinguishing and forbidding regulation of campaign *expenditures*); *McConnell v. FEC,* 540 U.S. 93 (2003) (upholding parts of McCain-Feingold).

15. *FCC v. Pacifica Foundation,* 438 U.S. 726 (1978) (famous case involving George Carlin's "seven dirty words" in which the Court upheld a FCC regulation that prohibited the broadcast of "indecent" language during times in which children may be in the audience); but cf. *United States v. Playboy Entertainment Group Inc.,* 529 U.S. 803 (2000) (holding unconstitutional a federal statute that, in its effect, required transmission of sexually oriented content during hours when children would not be in the audience).

16. *Village of Skokie v. National Socialist Party of America,* 69 Ill.2d 605 (1978) (city ordinance barring the display or use of a swastika was unconstitutional; use and display of the swastika was a symbolic form of free speech entitled to First Amendment protections); *R.A.V. v. City of St. Paul,* 505 U.S. 377 (1992) (city ordinance prohibiting the display of a symbol—here, a burning cross—that causes "anger, alarm or resentment in others on the basis of race, color, creed, religion or gender" was unconstitutional).

17. *Watchtower Bible & Tract Society of N.Y., Inc. v. Village of Stratton,* 536 U.S. 150 (2002) (ordinance prohibiting door-to-door solicitations to promote or explain a cause without first registering and obtaining a permit held unconstitutional); *Martin v. City of Struthers,* 319 U.S. 141 (1943) (ordinance banning door-to-door solicitations held unconstitutional); *Hynes v. Mayor of Oradell,* 425 U.S. 610 (1976) (ordinance mandating advance notice of pamphleteering held unconstitutionally vague and overbroad); cf. *Frisby v. Schultz,* 487 U.S. 474 (1988) (upholding a ban on "fo-

cused picketing" because the target was unwilling or "captive" household members and the demonstrators had alternative channels of communications).

18. *Tinker v. Des Moines Independent Community School Dist.*, 393 U.S. 503 (1969) (famous case involving students who were suspended for wearing black armbands to protest the Vietnam war; the Court found the school district's policies and actions unconstitutional and declared that "[s]tudents or teachers [do not lose] their constitutional rights to freedom of speech or expression at the schoolhouse gate"); cf. *Bethel School Dist. No. 403 v. Fraser*, 478 U.S. 675, 683 (1986); *Board of Educ., Island Trees Union Free School Dist. No. 26 v. Pico*, 457 U.S. 853 (1982); see also Todd DeMitchell, "School Uniforms and the Constitution: Common Dress in an Uncommon Time," *Education Law Reporter* 156 (2001): 1.

19. *Fraser*, 478 U.S. 675, 683 (deferring to school administrators and clearly reducing the First Amendment interests of students, reasoning that "it is a highly appropriate function of public school education to prohibit the use of vulgar and offensive terms in public discourse").

20. *Pico*, 457 U.S. 853 (plurality of the Court stressed pupil's right of access to information and ideas—even ideas that are unsavory or offensive—and reversed lower court ruling granting dismissal of a suit challenging a school board's censorship of offensive books from its libraries).

21. See C. Edwin Baker, "Scope of the First Amendment Freedom of Speech," *UCLA Law Review* 25 (1978): 964; David Strauss, "Persuasion, Autonomy, and Freedom of Expression," *Columbia Law Review* 91 (1991): 334, 362–70.

22. Charles Black, Jr., "He Cannot Choose but Hear: The Plight of the Captive Auditor," *Columbia Law Review* 53 (1953): 960; see also Charles Black, Jr., "Mr. Justice Black, the Supreme Court, and the Bill of Rights," in *The Occasions of Justice* (New York: Macmillan, 1963), 89.

23. Mark Twain, *Following the Equator* (Hartford, CT: American Publishing, 1897), 195.

24. See 17 U.S.C. § 506 (setting forth criminal penalties for willful infringement).

25. Rubenfeld, "Freedom of Imagination," 1, n. 1 (noting that "[t]o perform a work publicly means, among other things, 'to recite' it 'at a place open to the public or at any place where a substantial number of persons outside of a normal circle of a family and its social acquaintances is gathered . . . 'Willful' copyright violations can be criminal offenses") (citing 17 U.S.C. § 101, 506); cf. *Nebraska Press Ass'n v. Stuart*, 427 U.S. 539 (1976); *New York Times Co. v. United States*, 403 U.S. 713 (1971) (Pentagon Papers); *Near v. Minnesota*, 283 U.S. 697 (1931); *SunTrust Bank v. Houghton Mifflin Co.*, 136 F. Supp. 2d 1357 (N.D. Ga.), *vacated*, 252 F.3d 1165 (11th Cir.) (per curiam), *order vacated and opinion substituted*, 268 F.3d 1257 (11th Cir. 2001); *Religious Tech. Ctr. v. Netcom On-Line Communications Servs., Inc.*, 923 F. Supp. 1231 (N.D. Cal. 1995).

26. Rubenfeld, "Freedom of Imagination"; Yochai Benkler, "Free as the Air to Common Use: First Amendment Constraints on Enclosure of the Public Domain," *New York University Law Review* 74 (1999): 354; see also Mark Lemley and Eugene Volokh, "Freedom of Speech and Injunctions in Intellectual Property Cases," *Duke Law Journal* 48 (1998): 147; Neil Netanel, "Locating Copyright Within the First Amendment Skein," *Stanford Law Review* 54 (2001): 1, 47–68.

27. *Eldred v. Reno*, 239 F.3d 372 (D.C. Cir. 2001), *aff'd sub nom., Eldred v. Ashcroft*, 534 U.S. 1126 (2002).
28. *Eldred v. Reno*, 239 F.3d at 375.
29. *Eldred v. Reno*, 239 F.3d at 376, quoting *United Video, Inc. v. F.C.C.*, 890 F.2d 1173, 1191 (Fed. Cir. 1989).
30. *Eldred v. Ashcroft*, 537 U.S. 186, 221 (2003).
31. Copyright Term Extension Act of 1998 ("CTEA"), Pub. L. No. 105–298, 112 Stat. 2827 (1998) (codified at scattered sections of 17 U.S.C.) (and frequently cited as the "SBCTEA").
32. 17 U.S.C. § 302(a).
33. Here, we are referring specifically to anonymous or pseudonymous works, as well as "works made for hire." See 17 U.S.C. § 302(c).
34. The reader should be aware that we were counsel on an amicus brief (a brief by a "friend of the court" not a party to the case), which argued that the Act was unconstitutional.
35. *Eldred v. Ashcroft*, 537 U.S. at 218–19.
36. Ibid., 218.
37. Erwin Chemerinsky, *Constitutional Law: Principles and Policies* (New York: Aspen, 1997), 757–58.
38. *R.A.V. v. City of St. Paul*, 505 U.S. at 395–96 (1992) (noting that "[c]ontent-based regulations . . . are presumptively invalid" and invalidating a hate-speech ordinance because of the viability of content-neutral alternatives).
39. *Texas v. Johnson*, 491 U.S. at 412 (1989) (subjecting a state flag-burning statute, as a content-based restriction, to "the most exacting scrutiny" [quoting *Boos v. Barry*, 485 U.S. 312, 321 (1988)]).
40. *Turner Broadcasting System, Inc. v. FCC*, 512 U.S. 622, 662 (1994). We should make it clear again that we believe (as do numerous others who have written on the subject) that copyright (and other similar intellectual property-generated) exclusivity is content-based. Defining content is at the center of this sort of restriction; it is irrelevant that among the reasons for doing so is the wish to achieve the status of property for the preferred version of a particular instance of speech. In our judgment this is quite different from the efficiency in the marketplace that is at the heart of trademark law. Copyright is grounded in threshold judgments about the originality in a work. The threshold may seem absurdly low at times, but its purpose is nevertheless always to advance human knowledge while enriching the public domain, and thus a copyrighted work owes its very entitlement to exclusivity to the existence of content. Property is a subordinate goal, a mere means to an end: thus, a work devoid of content cannot be protected by copyright. *Feist Publications, Inc. v. Rural Tel. Serv. Co., Inc.*, 499 U.S. 340 (1991). Trademark law, on the other hand, is ordinarily content neutral in that it confers or withholds exclusivity essentially without concern one way or another for the originality in content that a particular trademark may encode. The question for the mark is whether it is distinctive, and thus capable of signaling the identity of goods or services in commerce, rather than an inquiry into whether it encodes expressivity in a universe of discourses. *In re Trade-Mark Cases*, 100 U.S. 82 (1879). Were we to be persuaded that trademarks were more or other than this, whether generally or in a particular setting, then they too might well be content based, and would be subject

accordingly to the arguments we advance in this book as to copyright and other doctrines in which expression is protected against appropriation. Copyright, which subsists only in expression, can never be merely content neutral, despite the concession to that effect in the petitioners' briefs in *Eldred*, where even the weaker claim, properly understood by the Court, would have led to the heightened review the petitioners wanted.

41. Rebecca Tushnet suggests that Justice Ginsburg "denigrates" the First Amendment with her "incomplete analysis" in *Eldred* by, inter alia, erecting false distinctions between those who appropriate and those who are "real speakers." In the end, Ginsburg's *Eldred* analysis is "at least impossibly overbroad." See Tushnet, "Copy This Essay: How Fair Use Doctrine Harms Free Speech and How Copying Serves It," *Yale Law Journal* 114 (2004): 535, 548–63.

42. See Graeme Austin, "Keynote Address," *Columbia Journal of Law & the Arts* 28 (2004): 397, 400 (discussing how Justice Ginsburg's analysis in *Eldred* enabled future discussions of copyright and the first amendment to boil down to "a battle of 'traditions'—my tradition [copyright] is better or more venerable than yours [the First Amendment]. If you win the battle of traditions, you've probably got a better chance of also winning the constitutional battle.").

43. 512 U.S. 622, 662 (1994).

44. *Eldred v. Ashcroft*, 537 U.S. at 219.

45. Ibid.

46. On the subject of originalism generally, including its quirks, flaws, and methods, see H. Jefferson Powell, "Original Understanding of Original Intent," *Harvard Law Review* 98 (1985): 885.

47. *Eldred v. Ashcroft*, 537 U.S. at 219.

48. *New York Times Co. v. Sullivan*, 376 U.S. 254 (1964).

49. *Eldred v. Ashcroft*, 537 U.S. at 219 (quoting *Harper & Row*, 471 U.S. 539, 560).

50. Ibid.

51. *Cohen v. California*, 403 U.S. 15, 24 (1971).

52. *Eldred v. Ashcroft*, 537 U.S. at 219–20.

53. Ibid.

54. 512 U.S. 622 (1994).

55. *Eldred v. Ashcroft*, 537 U.S. at 221.

56. Ibid.

57. Ibid., 221 (citations omitted).

58. Ibid., 191.

59. Writing about the Court's treatment of the copyright clause claim in *Eldred*, dissenting Justice John Paul Stevens observed that "[f]airly read, *Eldred* is in effect an announcement that legislation enacted under the copyright and patent clauses is "judicially unreviewable." Stevens's conclusion is equally applicable to the Court's dealings with the first amendment in *Eldred* although unfortunately Stevens did not discuss the free speech issue in his dissent. 537 U.S. at 242 (Stevens, J., dissenting).

60. Justice Stevens's dissent does not directly address the First Amendment. Justice Stephen Breyer's dissent, in contrast, expressly relies on free speech concerns in concluding that the petitioner's claim under the copyright clause is valid. "The statute falls outside the scope of legislative power that the Copyright Clause, read

in light of the First Amendment, grants to Congress." 537 U.S. at 266–67 (Breyer, J., dissenting).

61. In fact, the oral arguments in *Eldred* indicate that a group fog hovered over the justices as the petitioner tried to explain how and why First Amendment interests were at stake. And when it became clear that the petitioner was serious about his First Amendment claim, Chief Justice Rehnquist quipped, "Well, but you want more than that. You want the right to copy verbatim other people's books, don't you?" See Transcript of Oral Argument at 11, *Eldred v. Ashcroft*, 537 U.S. 186, (2003) (No. 01-618), available at http://www.supremecourtus.gov/oral_arguments/argument_transcripts.html (last visited July 12, 2006).

62. See "Pure Fiction: The Attempt to Patent Plot," *Harvard Journal of Law & Technology* 19 (2005): 231.

63. What counts as the appropriate method of interpretation is essentially contested among constitutional theorists and we think it neither necessary nor possible to develop a general theory in the process of presenting a lengthy and complex argument about a specific interpretive issue. Our own view is very similar to that of Philip Bobbitt: all those forms of argument that are generally accepted as cogent by judges and other lawyers are legitimate means of advancing claims about the proper interpretation of the Constitution. We differ from Bobbitt, as we believe the courts and most constitutional lawyers do, in one respect: we recognize that any plausible interpretation of the Constitution must be faithful to the text. We believe, furthermore, that acknowledging the primacy of the text in this sense makes what our colleague Walter Dellinger calls "a moderate originalism" an indispensable starting point for anything that can plausibly claim to be American constitutional law. A refusal to use original meaning to establish the starting point for the words the document uses would render the text infinitely manipulable. The argument we present about the correct interpretation of the First Amendment in this book is grounded in the overt meaning of the amendment's text, as understood by all of its original readers (as far as can be seen); it is buttressed by the subsidiary argument that the Holmesian individual-rights reading of the free speech and press clauses leads to the perverse result that precisely what the amendment's text and original meaning seem to preclude is in fact permissible.

64. See generally, Walterscheid, *The Nature of the Intellectual Property Clause*. For additional discussion, in certain respects essentially at cross-purposes with our own understanding in this passage, see L. Ray Patterson & Craig Joyce, "Copyright in 1791: An Essay Concerning the Founders' View of the Copyright Power Granted to Congress in Article I, Section 8, Clause 8 of the U.S. Constitution," *Emory Law Journal* 52 (2003): 909, 929 passim.

65. See Copyright Act of 1790, ch. 15, § 1.

66. See Benjamin Kaplan, *An Unhurried View of Copyright* (New York: Columbia University Press, 1967), 6–9 (arguing that publishers, not authors, were the targeted beneficiaries of the first copyright statutes); see also Siva Vaidhyanathan, *Copyrights and Copywrongs: The Rise of Intellectual Property and How it Threatens Creativity* (New York: New York University Press, 2001), 37–47; L. Ray Patterson, *Copyright in Historical Perspective* (Nashville: Vanderbilt University Press, 1968).

67. Patent Act of 1793, ch. 11.

68. Patents themselves became especially significant in American life after the passage of the 1836 Patent Act, which established a more rigorous system for inquiring into the issue of novelty. See *Chisum on Patents*, vol. 1, "Overview" §§ 2–3.

69. Lawrence Lessig, "Copyright's First Amendment," *UCLA Law Review* 48 (2001): 1057, 1066.

70. U.S. Const. art. I, sec. 8, cl. 8.

71. But see Patterson & Joyce, "Copyright in 1791."

72. E.g., *Eldred v. Ashcroft*, 190. ("That Amendment and the Copyright Clause were adopted close in time. This proximity indicates the Framers' view that copyright's limited monopolies are compatible with free speech principles.") See also Lemley & Volokh, "Freedom of Speech and Injunctions in Intellectual Property Cases," 147.

73. See Patterson & Joyce, "Copyright in 1791."

74. Zechariah Chafee, Jr., Book Review, *Harvard Law Review* 62 (1949): 891, 898. See David Lange, "The Speech and Press Clauses"; Leonard W. Levy, *Legacy of Suppression: Freedom of Speech and Press in Early American History* (Cambridge, MA: Harvard University Press, 1960). Levy's 1960 volume was followed some twenty years later by a second version of the work, in which he recanted and amended some of his earlier conclusions. See Levy, *Emergence of a Free Press* (New York: Oxford University Press, 1985). The effect of these revisions was meant to suggest a somewhat stronger role for press freedom than Levy had originally propounded. In our view, meanwhile, Chafee's original insight remains apt.

75. See Edward Walterscheid, *The Nature of the Intellectual Property Clause*, 6; see also Walterscheid, "Patents and the Jeffersonian Mythology," *John Marshall Law Review* 29 (1995): 269, 274; Siva Vaidhyanathan, *Copyrights and Copywrongs*, 23; Donald Chisum et al., *Principles of Patent Law* (Albany, NY: Matthew Bender & Co, 2001), 17–18. ("Thomas Jefferson, while no stranger to the inventive process, was skeptical of monopolies and, initially, anything but a devotée of the patent system.")

76. Jefferson to Isaac McPherson, August 13, 1813, in *Life and Selected Writings of Thomas Jefferson*, ed. Adrienne Koch & William Harwood Peden (New York: Random House, 1993); also quoted in *Graham v. John Deere Co.*, 383 U.S. 1, 10 (1966).

77. *Graham v. John Deere Co.*, 383 U.S. at 7–10.

78. *Trade-Mark Cases*, 100 U.S. 82, 93–94 (noting that trademark law "has no necessary relation to invention or discovery"); see also *Prestonettes, Inc. v. Coty*, 264 U.S. 359, 368 (1924).

79. See Thomas Nachbar, "Intellectual Property and Constitutional Norms," *Columbia Law Review* 104 (2004): 272.

80. Walterscheid, "Patents and the Jeffersonian Mythology," 262–65.

81. Rubenfeld, "Freedom of Imagination," 1.

82. See Diane Zimmerman, "Information as Speech, Information as Goods: Some Thoughts on Marketplaces and the Bill of Rights," *William & Mary Law Review* 33 (1992): 665.

83. Christina Bohannan offers a quick account of the development of copyright law (and much more) in "Reclaiming Copyright," *Cardozo Arts and Entertainment Law Journal* 23 (2006): 567; see also *Nimmer on Copyright*, § 8.14.

84. William Landes, "Copyright, Borrowed Images, and Appropriation Art: An Economic Approach," *George Mason Law Review* 9 (2000): 1, 2. (Copyright law's "doctrines are best explained as efforts to create rights in intangible property.")

85. See, e.g., *Mazer v. Stein*, 347 U.S. 201, 219 (1954) ("The economic philosophy behind the clause empowering Congress to grant patents and copyrights is the conviction that encouragement of individual effort by personal gain is the best way to advance public welfare through the talents of authors and inventors in 'Science and useful Arts.'"); *Sony Corp. v. Universal City Studios, Inc.*, 464 U.S. 417, 429 (1984) (noting that the limited monopoly grant "is intended to motivate the creative activity of authors and inventors by the provision of a special reward, and to allow the public access to the products of their genius after the limited period of exclusive control has expired").

86. See L. Ray Patterson, *The Nature of Copyright* (Athens: University of Georgia Press, 1969): 1–15, 50.

87. See *Nimmer on Copyright* § 8D; see also Susan Liemer, "How We Lost Our Moral Rights and the Door Closed on Non-Economic Values in Copyright," *John Marshall Law School Review of Intellectual Property Law* 5 (2005): 1, 35 (noting that prior to around 1990, "the strong economic focus of United States copyright law allowed for little legal recognition of other values"). See Chapter 3 for further analysis of these issues.

88. *Nimmer on Copyright* § 2.01[A] (discussing "Originality Distinguished from Novelty"); *Chisum on Patents* §§ 1.01–05, 3.01, 4.01; Walterscheid, "Divergent Evolution of the Patent Power and the Copyright Power," *Marquette Intellectual Property Law Review* 9 (2005): 307. These issues are discussed further in Chapter 2.

89. A notable exception here is the so-called "business method patent," which our colleague James Boyle criticizes in "Second Enclosure Movement," *Law & Contemporary Problems* 66 (2003): 33, 41–42 (discussing how patents are increasingly employed to cover "ideas" which are otherwise unprotectable); see also Robert Merges et al., *Intellectual Property in the New Technological Age* (New York: Aspen, 2003), 23–27 (noting that "[i]n general copyrights are easier to secure and last substantially longer than patents").

90. As noted earlier, early copyright law was more likely established to protect existing publishers as opposed to incentivizing progress. See L. Ray Patterson, *Copyright in Historical Perspective*.

91. Nimmer, "Copyright vs. The First Amendment," *Bulletin of the Copyright Society (USA)* 16 (1970): 255; Nimmer, "Does Copyright Abridge the First Amendment Guaranties of Free Speech and the Press?" *UCLA Law Review* 17 (1970): 1180.

92. *New York Times Co. v. Sullivan*, 376 U.S. 254, 270 (1964).

93. *Garrison v. Louisiana*, 379 U.S. 64 (1964); *Henry v. Collins*, 380 U.S. 356 (1965); *Linn v. United Plant Guard Workers*, 383 U.S. 53 (1966); *Rosenblatt v. Baer*, 383 U.S. 75 (1966); *Time, Inc. v. Hill*, 385 U.S. 374 (1967); *Curtis Publishing Co. v. Butts*, 388 U.S. 130 (1967); *Beckley Newspapers Corp. v. Hanks*, 389 U.S. 81 (1967); *St. Amant v. Thompson*, 390 U.S. 727 (1968); *Greenbelt Coop. Publishing Ass'n v. Bresler*, 398 U.S. 6 (1970); *Monitor Patriot Co. v. Roy*, 401 U.S. 265 (1971); *Rosenbloom v. Metromedia, Inc.*, 403 U.S. 29 (1971); *Time, Inc. v. Pape*, 401 U.S. 279 (1971).

94. *Smith v. California*, 361 U.S. 147, 157 (1959) (Black, J., concurring) ("I read 'no law . . . abridging' to mean no law abridging."); see also, e.g., Hugo Black, "The Bill of Rights," *New York University Law Review* 35 (1960): 865, 879. ("The phrase 'Congress shall make no law' is composed of plain words, easily understood. The language is absolute.")

95. E.g., *Konigsberg v. State Bar of California*, 366 U.S. 36, 56 (1961) (Black, J., dissenting, joined by Douglas, J.).

96. The majority expressly repudiated Black's view that "freedom of speech and association are absolutes." See *Konigsberg*, 366 U.S. at 49. See also cases cited in note 93.

97. For further discussion about the origins and development of defamation, see Chemerinsky, *Constitutional Law*, 850–66.

98. Melville Nimmer, "The Right to Speak from *Times* to *Time*: First Amendment Theory Applied to Libel and Misapplied to Privacy," *California Law Review* 56 (1968): 935.

99. *Sears, Roebuck & Co. v. Stiffel Co.*, 376 U.S. 225 (1964); *Compco Corp. v. Day-Brite Lighting, Inc.*, 376 U.S. 234 (1964). These cases were decided, with *New York Times*, on March 9, 1964. See Daphne R. Leeds et al., "Product Simulation: A Right or a Wrong?" *Columbia Law Review* 64 (1964): 1178.

100. See *Sears* and *Compco*, cited in the preceding note.

101. But see *Nimmer on Copyright* § 1.01[B][1][f][iii] for a different current analysis.

102. Cf., Paul Goldstein, "The Competitive Mandate: From *Sears* to *Lear*," *California Law Review* 59 (1971): 873.

103. Nimmer, "Does Copyright Abridge First Amendment Guaranties," 1181–83.

104. Ibid., 1189–93. A close reading of Nimmer's discussion of fair use can leave the reader in some doubt as to the relationship he saw between that doctrine and the First Amendment. He was at least concerned, or so it would appear, that fair use not be employed as a substitute for a more direct analysis and recognition of speech interests in circumstances in which appropriation was a paramount concern when viewed from the perspective of public necessity; arguably this could cut somewhat against fair use as an alternative to the First Amendment. All in all, however, we think the better reading of his essay leaves fair use intact as a reason why First Amendment analysis need not ordinarily jeopardize the copyright proprietor's interest in exclusivity. Certainly the Supreme Court itself has subsequently treated both the idea-expression dichotomy and fair use alike as reasons for avoiding a closer examination of the potential conflict Nimmer had addressed. See *Eldred*, 537 U.S. at 219–20. We think Nimmer would have approved.

105. Robert Denicola, "Copyright and Free Speech: Constitutional Limitations on the Protection of Expression," *California Law Review* 67 (1979): 283; Paul Goldstein, "Copyright and the First Amendment," *Columbia Law Review* 70 (1970): 983. Goldstein's work appeared soon after Nimmer's Brace Memorial Lecture, but appears to have been inspired quite independently, by some of the issues we have suggested as inspirations for Nimmer's work.

106. L. Ray Patterson, "Free Speech, Copyright, and Fair Use," *Vanderbilt Law Review* 40 (1987): 1; Patterson & Joyce, "Copyright in 1791." See also Stanley F. Birch, "Copyright Fair Use: A Constitutional Imperative," *Journal of the Copyright Society* 54 (2007): 139 (Brace Memorial Lecture); Lee Ann Lockridge,

"The Myth of Copyright's Fair Use Doctrine as a Protector of Free Speech," *Santa Clara Computer and High Technology Law Journal* 24 (2006): 31.

107. E.g., Keith Aoki, "Authors, Inventors and Trademark Owners: Private Intellectual Property and the Public Domain, Part I," *Columbia-VLA Journal of Law & the Arts* 18 (1993): 1; Yochai Benkler, "Free as the Air to Common Use: First Amendment Constraints on Enclosure of the Public Domain," *New York University Law Review* 74 (1999): 354; Benkler, "Through the Looking Glass: Alice and the Constitutional Foundations of the Public Domain," *Law & Contemporary Problems* 66 (2003): 173; James Boyle, *Shamans, Software, and Spleens: Law and the Construction of the Information Society* (Cambridge, MA: Harvard University Press, 1996); Lawrence Lessig, *Code and Other Laws of Cyberspace* (New York: Basic Books, 1999); Lessig, *Free Culture* (New York: Penguin Press, 2004); Jessica Litman, "Revising Copyright Law for the Information Age," *Oregon Law Review* 75 (1996): 19; Pamela Samuelson, "Some New Kinds of Authorship Made Possible by Computers and Some Intellectual Property Questions They Raise," *University of Pittsburgh Law Review* 53 (1992): 685.

108. E.g., Neil Netanel, "Locating Copyright Within the First Amendment Skein," *Stanford Law Review* 54 (2001): 1; Netanel, "From the Dead Sea Scrolls to the Digital Millennium; Recent Developments in Copyright Law," *Texas Intellectual Property Law Journal* 9 (2000): 19; Netanel, *Copyright's Paradox: Property in Expression/Freedom of Expression* (New York: Oxford University Press, 2008).

109. Alfred Yen, "A First Amendment Perspective on the Idea/Expression Dichotomy and Copyright's 'Total Look and Feel,'" *Emory Law Journal* 38 (1989): 393.

110. Lemley & Volokh, "Freedom of Speech and Injunctions in Intellectual Property Cases," 147.

111. Lemley & Volokh, "Freedom of Speech," 216. See also Eugene Volokh, "Freedom of Speech and the Right of Publicity," *University of Houston Law Review,* 2007, 903; cf. Rebecca Tushnet, "Copyright as a Model for Free Speech Law: What Copyright Has in Common with Anti-Pornography Laws, Campaign Finance Reform, and Telecommunications Regulation," *Boston College Law Review* 42 (2000): 1.

112. C. Edwin Baker, "First Amendment Limits on Copyright," *Vanderbilt Law Review* 55 (2002): 891; Rubenfeld, "Freedom of Imagination"; William Van Alstyne, "Reconciling What the First Amendment Forbids With What the Copyright Clause Permits: A Summary Explanation and Review," *Law & Contemporary Problems* 66 (2003): 225.

113. E.g., James Boyle, *Shamans, Software, and Spleens: Law and the Construction of the Information Society* (Cambridge, MA: Harvard University Press, 1996); Lawrence Lessig, *Free Culture.* See also Lessig, "Copyright's First Amendment," *UCLA Law Review* 48 (2001): 1057.

114. Paul Heald & Suzanna Sherry, "Implied Limits on the Legislative Power: The Intellectual Property Clause as an Absolute Restraint on Congress," *University of Illinois Law Review,* 2000, 1119; Malla Pollack, "Dealing with Old Father William, or Moving from Constitutional Text to Constitutional Doctrine: Progress Clause Review of the Copyright Term Extension Act," *Loyola of Los Angeles Law Review* 36 (2002): 337; Alex Kozinski, "A Market-Oriented Revision of the Patent System," *UCLA Law Review* 21 (1974): 1042. Professor Pollack has been a

regular contributor to the discourse on the intellectual property clause, the First Amendment and the public domain. See, e.g., Malla Pollack, "Unconstitutional Incontestability? The Intersection of the Intellectual Property and Commerce Clauses of the Constitution," *Puget Sound Law Review* 18 (1995): 259; and "The Democratic Public Domain: Resurrecting the Modern First Amendment and the Original Progress Clause (A.K.A. Patent and Copyright Clause)," *Jurimetrics Journal* 45 (2004) 23.

115. Alan Latman, *Fair Use of Copyrighted Works*, Copyright Office Study No. 14, prepared for 87th Cong., 2d. Sess. 40 (Comm. Print 1961).

116. E.g., L. Ray Patterson, "Free Speech, Copyright, and Fair Use," *Vanderbilt Law Review* 40 (1987): 1; L. Ray Patterson & Craig Joyce, "Copyright in 1791: An Essay Concerning the Founders' View of the Copyright Power Granted to Congress in Article I, Section 8, Clause 8 of the U.S. Constitution," *Emory Law Journal* 52 (2003): 909; Wendy Gordon, "Fair Use as Market Failure: A Structural and Economic Analysis of the *Betamax* Case and Its Predecessors," *Columbia Law Review* 82 (1982): 1600; William Fisher, "Reconstructing the Fair Use Doctrine," *Harvard Law Review* 101 (1988): 1659. See also Alex Kozinski & Christopher Newman, "What's So Fair About Fair Use?" *Journal of the Copyright Society* 46 (1999): 573 (Brace Memorial Lecture).

117. Pierre Leval, "Toward a Fair Use Standard," *Harvard Law Review* 103 (1990): 1105, 1111.

118. Lloyd Weinreb, "Fair is Fair: A Comment on the Fair Use Doctrine," *Harvard Law Review* 103 (1990): 1137, 1161.

119. David Nimmer, " 'Fairest of Them All' and Other Fairy Tales of Fair Use," *Law & Contemporary Problems* 66 (2003): 263, 287.

120. Rochelle Dreyfuss, "Information Products: A Challenge to Intellectual Property Theory," *New York University Journal of International Law and Politics* 20 (1988): 897; Peter Jaszi, "Toward a Theory of Copyright: The Metamorphoses of 'Authorship,'" *Duke Law Journal* 40 (1991): 455; Peter Menell, "Envisioning Copyright Law's Digital Future," *New York Law School Law Review* 46 (2002): 63; Robert Merges, "As Many As Six Impossible Patents Before Breakfast: Property Rights for Business Concepts and Patent System Reform," *Berkeley Technology Law Journal* 14 (1999): 577; Maureen O'Rourke, "Toward a Doctrine of Fair Use in Patent Law," *Columbia Law Review* 100 (2000): 1177; Arti Rai & Rebecca Eisenberg, "Bayh-Dole Reform and the Progress of Biomedicine," *Law and Contemporary Problems* 66 (2003): 289; J. H. Reichman & Paul Uhlir, "A Contractually Reconstructed Research Commons for Scientific Data in a Highly Protectionist Intellectual Property Environment," *Law and Contemporary Problems* 66 (2003): 315; Mark Lemley & Douglas Lichtman, "Rethinking Patent Law's Presumption of Validity," *Stanford Law Review* 60 (2007): 45; Anthony Reese, "Copyright and Internet Music Transmissions: Existing Law, Major Controversies, Possible Solutions," *University of Miami Law Review* 55 (2001): 237; Paul Edward Geller, "Beyond the Copyright Crisis: Principles for Change, *Journal of the Copyright Society of the United States of America* 55 (2008): 165.

121. Yochai Benkler, "Through the Looking Glass: Alice and the Constitutional Foundations of the Public Domain," *Law & Contemporary Problems* 66 (2003): 173; James Boyle, "The Second Enclosure Movement and the Construction of

the Public Domain," *Law and Contemporary Problems* 66 (2003): 33; Julie Cohen, "Copyright, Commodification and Culture: Locating the Public Domain," in *The Future of the Public Domain*, ed. Lucie Guibault & P. Bernt Hugenholtz, 121–66 (The Hague: Kluwer Law International, 2006); Peter Jaszi, "Goodbye to All That—A Reluctant (and Perhaps Premature) Adieu to a Constitutionally-Grounded Discourse of Public Interest in Copyright Law," *Vanderbilt Journal of Transnational Law* 29 (1996): 595; Jessica Litman, "The Public Domain," *Emory Law Journal* 39 (1990): 965; Pamela Samuelson, "Enriching Discourse on Public Domain," *Duke Law Journal* 55 (2006): 783; Diane Zimmerman, "Is There a Right to Have Something to Say? One View of the Public Domain," *Fordham Law Review* 73 (2004): 297; Symposium, "The Public Domain," *Law & Contemporary Problems* 66 (2003); Anupam Chander & Mahdavi Sunder, "The Romance of the Public Domain," *California Law Review* 92 (2004): 1332. Professor Boyle's new book (*The Public Domain: An Environmentalism for Information*) will be published by Yale University Press in the fall of 2008.

122. See http://law.duke.edu/cspd (Center for the Study of the Public Domain); http://creativecommons.org (Creative Commons); http://www.law.berkeley.edu/clinics/samuelson/ and http://www.wcl.american.edu/ipclinic/ (Samuelson-Glushko clinics); http://cyber.law.harvard.edu/home/ (Berkman).

123. William Landes & Richard Posner, "An Economic Analysis of Copyright Law," *Journal of Legal Studies* 18 (1989): 325; see also Landes & Posner, "Economics of Trademark Law," *The Trademark Reporter* 78 (1988): 267.

124. Wendy Gordon, "An Inquiry into the Merits of Copyright: The Challenges of Consistency, Consent and Encouragement Theory," *Stanford Law Review* 41 (1989): 1343. See also "Fair Use as Market Failure: A Structural and Economic Analysis of the *Betamax* Case and Its Predecessors," *Columbia Law Review* 82 (1982): 1600.

125. Symposium, "Taking Stock: The Law and Economics of Intellectual Property Rights," *Vanderbilt Law Review* 53 (2000): 1727. Professor Reichman was the convenor of the colloquium, which was also edited by the journal's editors.

126. A sampling of Professor Samuelson's work includes "CONTU Revisited: The Case Against Copyright Protection for Computer Programs in Machine-Readable Form," *Duke Law Journal* 33 (1984): 663; "Creating a New Kind of Intellectual Property: Applying the Lessons of the Chip Law to Computer Programs," *Minnesota Law Review* 70 (1985): 471; "Allocating Ownership Rights in Computer-Generated Works," *University of Pittsburgh Law Review* 47 (1986): 1185; "Some New Kinds of Authorship Made Possible by Computers and Some Intellectual Property Questions They Raise," *University of Pittsburgh Law Review* 53 (1992): 685; "Computer Programs, User Interfaces, and Section 102(b) of the Copyright Act of 1976: A Critique of *Lotus v. Paperback*," *Law & Contemporary Problems* 55 (1992): 311; "Intellectual Property and the Digital Economy: Why the Anti-Circumvention Regulations Need to Be Revised," *Berkeley Technology Law Journal* 14 (1999): 519; "Enriching Discourse on Public Domain," *Duke Law Journal* 55 (2006): 783.

127. Julie Cohen, "*Lochner* in Cyberspace: The New Economic Orthodoxy of 'Rights Management,'" *Michigan Law Review* 97 (1998): 462. Among other scholars of

note who have published in this setting, we have previously acknowledged the work of Professors Aoki, Benkler, Boyle, Lessig, Litman, and Samuelson in note 107. These acknowledgments barely begin to cover the field; we have not attempted to fashion an exhaustive bibliography.

128. See Nimmer, "Does Copyright Abridge First Amendment Guaranties?"

129. Benjamin Kaplan, *An Unhurried View of Copyright* (New York: Columbia University Press, 1967).

130. E.g., Ralph S. Brown, Jr., "Advertising and the Public Interest: Legal Protection of Trade Symbols," *Yale Law Journal* 57 (1948): 1165.

131. Zechariah Chafee, Jr., "Reflections on the Law of Copyright: I," *Columbia Law Review* 45 (1945): 503; Zechariah Chafee, Jr., "Reflections on the Law of Copyright: II," *Columbia Law Review* 45 (1945): 719. Extensive acknowledgments and citations to earlier works appear passim in Lange, "Recognizing the Public Domain."

132. William Fisher, *Promises to Keep* (Stanford, CA: Stanford University Press, 2004). See Rubenfeld, "Freedom of Imagination."

133. *Mazer v. Stein*, 347 U.S. 201, 219 (1954).

CHAPTER 5

1. *International News Service v. Associated Press*, 248 U.S. 215 (1918).

2. See Leonard W. Levy, *Emergence of a Free Press* (New York: Oxford University Press, 1985): 11–16; see also David Lange, "The Speech and Press Clauses," *UCLA Law Review* 23 (1975): 77, 88–98.

3. *Schenck v. United States*, 249 U.S. 47 (1919).

4. See generally Zechariah Chafee, Jr., *Free Speech in the United States* (Cambridge, MA: Harvard University Press, 1941).

5. See Diane Zimmerman, "Information as Speech, Information as Goods," *William & Mary Law Review* 33 (1992): 665, 726–27. ("The fact that the Court decided [*INS*] at a time when its First Amendment jurisprudence was at best nascent may be one reason that it shows little sensitivity to the implications of the dispute for speech lying close to the core of First Amendment values. . . . [The case] seems rather to be a continuation of the prior century's romance with expanding forms of intellectual property protection.")

6. Ray Patterson nicely discusses the growth of copyright and its "dual theoretical basis" in American law. See L. Ray Patterson, "Copyright in the New Millenium: Resolving Conflict Between Property Rights and Political Rights," *Ohio State Law Journal* 62 (2001): 703, 723–32.

7. See Joseph P. Liu, "Regulatory Copyright," *North Carolina Law Review* 83 (2004): 87, 96–98 (discussing lobbyists and the development of the 1909 Act); Dotan Oliar, "Making Sense of the Intellectual Property Clause: Promotion of Progress as a Limitation on Congress's Intellectual Property Power," *Georgetown Law Journal* 94 (2006): 1771, 1774 (noting that "[t]he CTEA was criticized for being tailored to satisfy the interest groups that lobbied for it at the public's expense"); William Patry, "Copyright and the Legislative Process: A Personal Perspective," *Cardozo Arts & Entertainment Law Journal* 14 (1996): 139 (offering a scathing review of the influence of copyright [and more generally IP] development); Jessica Litman, "Copyright, Compromise, and Legislative History," *Cor-*

nell Law Review 72 (1987): 857; Jessica Litman, "Copyright Legislation and Technological Change," *Oregon Law Review* 68 (1989): 275.

8. J. Thomas McCarthy, *McCarthy on Trademarks and Unfair Competition*, 4th ed. (Eagan, MN: West, 2004), § 5:2 (discussing the development of federal trademark law, and in particular the Lanham Act).

9. *Erie Railroad v. Tompkins*, 304 U.S. 64 (1938) (seminal decision requiring federal courts to apply the substantive law of the state where the court sits in cases of diversity jurisdiction).

10. From the beginning of the Republic, federal courts had considered themselves free to establish common law principles in cases in which the federal court's jurisdiction was founded upon diversity of citizenship among the parties under Article III. In 1938, however, the Court held in *Erie Railroad Co. v. Tompkins*, 304 U.S. 64 (1938), that federal courts must rely exclusively on state authority for the precedents to be applied in diversity settings. With this decision, the formal era of federal common law precedent came to an end.

11. See *McCarthy on Trademarks* §§ 5:1–4; see also Daniel McClure, "Trademarks & Unfair Competition: A Critical History of Legal Thought," *Trademark Reporter* 69 (1979): 305.

12. E.g., *Tuttle v. Buck*, 107 Minn. 145 (1909) (claim allowed when the defendant established a competing business—retail barbershop—without any legitimate personal interest and for the purpose of ruining the plaintiff's business by circulating "false and malicious reports and accusations"); *Tooke & Reynolds v. Bastrop Ice & Storage Co.*, 172 La. 781 (1931) (defendant liable under state law for selling below cost in a single area for the purpose of eliminating competition and securing a local monopoly); *Memphis Steam Laundry-Cleaners v. Lindsey*, 192 Miss. 224 (1941) (defendant liable for malicious competition when it sold at below cost to destroy a competing business).

13. See *Restatement (Third) of Unfair Competition* §1 cmt. a (1995).

14. See, e.g, Rudolf Callmann, Note, "He Who Reaps Where He Has Not Sown: Unjust Enrichment in the Law of Unfair Competition," *Harvard Law Review* 55 (1942): 595; Ralph Brown, "Advertising and the Public Interest: Legal Protection of Trade Symbols," *Yale Law Journal* 57 (1948): 1165, 1200; W. Edward Sell, "The Doctrine of Misappropriation in Unfair Competition," *Vanderbilt Law Review* 11 (1958); 483; James A. Rahl, "The Right to 'Appropriate' Trade Values," *Ohio State Law Journal* 23 (1962): 56; Douglas G. Baird, "Common Law Intellectual Property and the Legacy of International News Service v. Associated Press," *University of Chicago Law Review* 50 (1983): 411; Howard B. Abrams, "Copyright, Misappropriation, and Preemption: Constitutional and Statutory Limits of State Law Protection," *Supreme Court Review*, 1983, 509; Leo Raskind, "The Misappropriation Doctrine as a Competitive Norm of Intellectual Property Law," *Minnesota Law Review* 75 (1991): 875; Dennis S. Karjala, "Copyright and Misappropriation," *University of Dayton Law Review* 17 (1992): 885; Wendy J. Gordon, "On Owning Information: Intellectual Property and the Restitutionary Impulse," *Virginia Law Revew* 78 (1992): 149; Dennis S. Karjala, "Misappropriation as a Third Intellectual Property Paradigm," *Columbia Law Review* 94 (1994): 2594; Richard A. Posner, "Misappropriation: A Dirge," *Houston Law Review* 40 (2003): 621; Douglas G. Baird, "The Story of *INS v. AP*: Property, Natural Monopoly, and the Uneasy Legacy of a

Concocted Controversy," in *Intellectual Property Stories*, ed. Jane Ginsburg & Rochelle Dreyfuss (New York: Foundation Press, 2006): 9–35.

15. Some accounts of the dispute suggest that the origins of INS's disadvantage in the field lay in the fact that its owner, William Randolph Hearst, had supported the Central Powers at the outset of the War, thereby leading to recriminatory acts of censorship by Allied authorities. See Richard Posner, "Misappropriation: A Dirge," 627–28.

16. *International News Service v. Associated Press*, 248 U.S. at 229–30 (1918).

17. The Court acknowledged this very point, and Justice Brandeis grounded much of his dissent on it. 248 U.S. at 233, 254–55 (Brandeis, J., dissenting). AP also alleged that INS had suborned AP's employees and affiliated newspapers so as to gain access to materials not yet published or otherwise available. But the opinions in the case consider only the appropriation of news that was published, either in bulletins or in newspapers. Our discussion also presupposes and addresses only this more limited aspect of INS's alleged wrongdoing.

18. "Justice Brandeis dissented, pointing out that the injunction would deprive the readers of hundreds of newspapers of timely access to the latest war news. He did not discuss the possibility that AP would license INS to publish AP's dispatches (though it did not do so even after the injunction was upheld by the Supreme Court), or that if INS could copy AP's dispatches AP would have a diminished incentive to incur the costs of obtaining the news. Justice Holmes also dissented, but on a different ground that I shall discuss shortly." Posner, "Misappropriation: A Dirge," 621. A license? In Posner's world, perhaps. But not likely, we suspect, in the world of the Associated Press and INS, circa 1917–18.

19. *INS*, 248 U.S. at 238.

20. Ibid., 231–32.

21. Commentators often suggest that the tort of misappropriation originated with *INS*. E.g., Dennis S. Karjala, "Misappropriation as a Third Intellectual Property Paradigm," *Columbia Law Review* 94 (1994): 2594, 2598. ("The original misappropriation case [(*INS*)] arose because the new technology of telegraphy permitted fast and inexpensive copying across the continent of hard-won information that was freely copyable under the primary paradigms.") But this is probably oversimplistic. Courts heard misappropriation-like cases (or, more generally, unfair competition cases) before *INS*. See, e.g., *McLean v. Fleming*, 96 U.S. 245 (1877); *Pavesich v. New England Life Insurance* Co., 122 Ga. 190 (1905); *J. I. Case Plow Works v. J. I. Case Threshing Mach.* Co., 162 Wis. 185 (1916).

22. Henry Smith, "The Language of Property: Form, Context, and Audience," *Stanford Law Review* 55 (2003): 1105, 1176 (also noting how "the Supreme Court provided a somewhat novel right against misappropriation of hot news"); Thomas W. Merrill & Henry Smith, "Optimal Standardization in the Law of Property: The Numerus Clausus Principle," *Yale Law Journal* 110 (2000): 1, 19 (decrying the "innovative" approach the Court took in recognizing the misappropriation claim); J. E. Penner, "The 'Bundle of Rights' Picture of Property," *UCLA Law Review* 43 (1996): 711, 715 (critiquing *INS* and *Moore v. Regents of the University of California*—the latter a case raising the question whether intellectual property rights could be claimed in a patient's spleen—as innovative, novel, and successful quests to "treat something as property").

23. *INS*, 248 U.S. at 246.
24. See especially Paul Goldstein, "Copyright and the First Amendment," *Columbia Law Review* 70 (1970): 983. See also Gary Myers, "The Restatement's Rejection of the Misappropriation Tort: A Victory for the Public Domain," *South Carolina Law Review* 47 (1996): 673.
25. See Gordon, "On Owning Information," 149, 281 (noting that *INS* has created a " 'restitutionary impulse,' " which is "the tendency of some courts to assume that 'reaping and sowing' and 'unjust enrichment' automatically give rise to absolute claims, trumping all other considerations").
26. *INS*, 248 U.S. at 232.
27. Ibid., 235.
28. Ibid., 236 (citation omitted).
29. Ibid., 240.
30. See Robert Bone, "Enforcement Costs and Trademark Puzzles," *Virginia Law Review* 90 (2004): 2009–114 (arguing that the phrase "to reap where it has not sown" has greatly influenced the development of intellectual commerce, particularly trademarks, and noting how "the unjust enrichment rhetoric" has become the "moral norm" in intellectual property disputes; Bone finds this to be overreaching at best and ridiculous at worst); see also Gordon "On Owning Information."
31. Wendy Gordon offers a useful analysis of Locke in "A Property Right in Self-Expression: Equality and Individualism in the Natural Law of Intellectual Property," *Yale Law Journal* 102 (1993): 1533.
32. *INS*, 248 U.S. at 240.
33. Richard Epstein, "*International News Service v. Associated Press*: Custom and Law as Sources of Property Rights in News," *Virginia Law Review* 78 (1992): 85, 113–19 (demonstrating how Pitney's reasoning "manage[d] to produce, by diverging at the two critical junctures from the standard conception of common law rights, the very same distribution of outcomes that would have been achieved if he had simply decided that custom within the industry set up the property rights as between industry competitors").
34. Ibid., 121; Douglas Baird, "Common Law Intellectual Property and the Legacy of *International News Service v. Associated Press*," *University of Chicago Law Review* 50 (1983): 411, 427.
35. *INS*, 248 U.S. at 241.
36. Ibid., 245.
37. Compare Goldstein, "Copyright and the First Amendment." Goldstein also saw *INS* as a "paradigm," and pursued his analysis of the case along lines similar to ours in this chapter and the next. Despite these similarities, however, our positions ultimately diverge considerably. He sought to establish "accomodative principles" that would reconcile copyright (and neighboring rights) with the first amendment on terms affording a more satisfactory balance between them. We ourselves are able to imagine a degree of "coexistence" between intellectual productivity and freedom of expression, but only against a clear understanding that the first amendment absolutely forbids any law that would confer a monopoly in expression otherwise falling within the universe of discourses. In the view we ultimately take, the right to appropriate expression is correspondingly absolute.

38. *INS,* 248 U.S. at 246.
39. See Epstein, *"INS v. AP"* and Baird, "The Legacy of *INS v. AP."*
40. Rochelle Dreyfuss expands this topic and deeply criticizes the "if value, then right" theories that guide intellectual property. See Rochelle Dreyfuss, "Expressive Genericity: Trademarks as Language in the Pepsi Generation," *Notre Dame Law Review* 65 (1990): 397, 405–6.
41. Arthur Miller, "Common Law Protection for Products of the Mind: An 'Idea' Whose Time Has Come," *Harvard Law Review* 119 (2006): 703, 765–66.
42. *INS,* 248 U.S. at 246–48.
43. Ibid., 247.
44. Ibid., 246–48.
45. Ibid., 249–50, 263.
46. Ibid., 264.
47. Ibid.
48. Ibid., 267.
49. Ibid., 266 (citations omitted).
50. Copyright Act of 1909 § 1(e).
51. See, e.g., 17 U.S.C. § 111 (cable), § 114 (satellite), or § 115 (cover songs).
52. Jed Rubenfeld, "Freedom of Imagination: Copyright's Constitutionality," *Yale Law Journal* 112 (2002): 1, 57.

CHAPTER 6

1. *International News Service v. Associated Press,* 248 U.S. 215, 250 (1918).
2. Jefferson to Isaac McPherson, August 13, 1813, in Merrill D. Peterson, ed., *The Portable Thomas Jefferson* (New York: Viking Penguin, 1977), 530. See also David L. Lange, "Recognizing the Public Domain," *Law & Contemporary Problems* 44 (1981): 147–50.
3. *Eldred v. Ashcroft,* 537 U.S. 186, 206–7. ("Congress passed the CTEA in light of demographic, economic, and technological changes, and rationally credited projections that longer terms would encourage copyright holders to invest in the restoration and public distribution of their works.")
4. United States courts have overwhelmingly adopted the former view (commonly known as the utilitarian theory). See, e.g., *Fogerty v. Fantasy, Inc.,* 510 U.S. 517, 524 (1994) ("The primary objective of the Copyright Act is to encourage the production of original literary, artistic, and musical expression for the good of the public."); *Feist Publications, Inc. v. Rural Telephone Service Co., Inc.,* 499 U.S. 340, 349 (1991) ("The primary objective of copyright is not to reward the labor of authors, but '[t]o promote the Progress of Science and useful Arts.' "); *Bonito Boats, Inc. v. Thunder Craft Boats, Inc.,* 489 U.S. 141, 167 (1989) (highlighting the "patent statute's careful balance between public right and private monopoly to promote certain creative activity."); *Graham v. John Deere Co.,* 383 U.S. 1, 9 (1966) ("The patent monopoly was not designed to secure to the inventor his natural right in his discoveries," but rather "was a reward, an inducement, to bring forth new knowledge."); *Mazer v. Stein,* 347 U.S. 201, 219 (1954). ("The economic philosophy behind the clause empowering Congress to grant patents and copyrights is the conviction that encouragement of individual effort by personal gain is the best way to advance public welfare.") Moral rights, on the other hand, have

gained relatively little room in U.S. law. Congress has only halfheartedly recognized moral rights—specifically, the rights of attribution and integrity for visual art (17 U.S.C. § 106A)—and only did so as a prerequisite to joining the Berne Convention. See generally *Nimmer on Copyright* § 8D (Dayton, OH: Matthew Bender, 2006).

5. As previously discussed in Chapter 3, Justice Breyer criticized the utilitarian theory of intellectual property in "The Uneasy Case for Copyright: A Study of Copyright in Books, Photocopies, and Computer Programs," *Harvard Law Review* 84 (1970): 281. See also Mark Lemley, "Ex Ante Versus Ex Post Justifications for Intellectual Property," *University of Chicago Law Review* 71 (2004): 129. For a discussion about the dangers of moral rights, see Eric Brooks, Comment, "Tilted Justice: Site-Specific Art and Moral Rights after U.S. Adherence to the Berne Convention," *California Law Review* 77 (1989): 1431.

6. China, for instance, has not traditionally recognized intellectual property in practice. See William P. Alford, *To Steal Is an Elegant Offense: Intellectual Property Law in Chinese Civilization* (Stanford, CA: Stanford University Press, 1995). Meanwhile, "interestingly, the push for stronger copyright protection in the U.S.-Vietnam free trade agreement did not result in more purchases of proprietary software from U.S. manufacturers. Instead, the agreement led the Vietnam government to announce its plan to require all state-owned companies and government ministries to use open source software by 2005." Peter Yu, "Intellectual Property at a Crossroads: The Use of the Past in Intellectual Property Jurisprudence," *Loyola of Los Angeles Law Review* 38 (2004): 323, 352. See also Michael Smith, Note, "Bringing Developing Countries' Intellectual Property Laws to TRIPS Standards: Hurdles and Pitfalls Facing Vietnam's Efforts to Normalize an Intellectual Property Regime," *Case Western Reserve Journal of International Law* 31 (1999): 211.

7. See Lemley, "Ex Ante Versus Ex Post Justifications," 135. ("The argument that a single company is better positioned than the market to make efficient use of an idea should strike us as jarringly counterintuitive in a market economy. Our normal supposition is that the invisible hand of the market will work by permitting different companies to compete with each other. It is competition, not the skill or incentives of any given firm, that drives the market to efficiency. Nothing about the fact that a work was once subject to copyright or patent protection should change our intuition here.")

8. *INS*, 248 U.S. at 239.

9. See Dennis Karjala, "Misappropriation as a Third Intellectual Property Paradigm," *Columbia Law Review* 94 (1994): 2594.

10. See Neal Gabler, *Life the Movie: How Entertainment Conquered Reality* (New York: Knopf, 1998) (a revealing discussion of how the entertainment industries have redefined virtually everything in American culture, including faith, business, academia, and politics).

11. For further discussion, see Margaret Chon, "Intellectual Property and the Development Divide," *Cardozo Law Review* 27 (2006): 2821; see also David Lange & Jerome Reichman, "Bargaining Around the TRIPS Agreement: The Case for Ongoing Public-Private Initiatives to Facilitate Worldwide Intellectual Property Transactions," *Duke Journal of Comparative & International Law* 9 (1998): 11.

12. See generally Andrew Carlson, "The Country Music Television Dispute: An Illustration of the Tensions Between Canadian Cultural Protectionism and Ameri-

can Entertainment Exports," *Minnesota Journal of Global Trade* 6 (1997): 585 (considering Canada's trade relationship with the United States, which "is the dominant producer and exporter of entertainment and popular culture throughout the world"); Jonas Grant, " 'Jurassic' Trade Dispute: The Exclusion of the Audiovisual Sector from the GATT," *Indiana Law Journal* 70 (1995): 1333, 1333–34. ("Trade in services is becoming increasingly important to the United States' economic well-being, and one of the healthiest service sector industries in the U.S. is the entertainment industry. U.S. entertainment exports generate an annual trade surplus of $8 billion—exceeded only by the aerospace industry. In an era of U.S. trade deficits, Hollywood is a self-described trade 'prize.' ")

13. See Keith Maskus, *Intellectual Property Rights in a Global Economy* (Washington, D.C.: Institute for International Economics, 2000); Jerome H. Reichman & Tracy Lewis, "Using Liability Rules to Stimulate Local Innovation in Developing Countries: Application to Traditional Knowledge," in *International Public Goods and Transfer of Technology Under a Globalized Intellectual Property Regime*, ed. Keith E. Maskus & Jerome H. Reichman (New York: Cambridge University Press, 2005): 337–66. As we have previously acknowledged, however, such positive correlation as there may be remains a matter for continuing debate and some skepticism.

14. *Whitney v. California*, 274 U.S. 357 (1927).

15. See generally David Lange, "The Speech & Press Clauses," *UCLA Law Review* 23 (1975): 77, 87, 102; Vincent Blasi, "The First Amendment and the Ideal of Civic Courage: The Brandeis Opinion in Whitney v. California," *William & Mary Law Review* 29 (1988): 653; Douglas Fraleigh & Joseph Tuman, *Freedom of Speech in the Marketplace of Ideas* 100 (New York: St. Martin's Press, 1997). ("Although Brandeis' opinion did little to help Anita Whitney, it developed important ideas about freedom of speech, which would be used by future courts and advocates in defense of that freedom.")

16. *Whitney*, 274 U.S. at 375; see David Lange, "Reimagining the Public Domain," *Law & Contemporary Problems* 66 (2003): 463, 475; Lange, "Speech & Press Clauses," 92–93.

17. See *Eldred v. Ashcroft*, 537 U.S. 186, 219. (Ginsburg, J., quoting *Harper & Row v. Nation Enterprises,* 471 U.S. 539, 558 (1985) and asserting that "copyright's purpose is to *promote* the creation and publication of free expression").

18. See Paul Goldstein, "Copyright and the First Amendment," *Columbia Law Review* 70 (1970): 983; Yochai Benkler, "Free as the Air to Common Use: First Amendment Constraints on Enclosure of the Public Domain," *New York University Law Review* 74 (1999): 354. See also William Van Alstyne, "Reconciling What the First Amendment Forbids With What the Copyright Clause Permits: A Summary Explanation and Review," *Law & Contemporary Problems* 66 (2003): 225; Jed Rubenfeld, "Freedom of Imagination," *Yale Law Journal* 112 (2002): 1, 9.

19. See notes 4–5 of this chapter.

20. Ibid.

21. In our view, Pitney and the majority in *INS* accepted the arguments by AP with respect to incentives as quite real. This was no less true for Holmes, though to different effect; and almost certainly true for Brandeis as well.

22. See Lemley "Ex Ante Versus Ex Post Justifications."

23. See Rubenfeld, "Freedom of Imagination," passim. Meanwhile, the reader should bear in mind that the alternative system of apportionments, proposed by Professor Fisher, is vastly different from the influential Calabresi-Melamed model that would redress purported harms along the lines of conventional liability standards, which enable damages. See William Fisher III, *Promises to Keep* (Stanford, CA: Stanford University Press, 2004); Guido Calabresi & Douglas Melamed, "Property Rules, Liability Rules, and Inalienability: One View of the Cathedral," *Harvard Law Review* 85 (1972): 1089. See also J. H. Reichman & Pamela Samuelson, "Intellectual Property Rights in Data?" *Vanderbilt Law Review* 50 (1997): 51; J. H. Reichman, "Legal Hybrids Between the Patent and Copyright Paradigms," *Columbia Law Review* 94 (1994): 2432, 2531 (arguing that exclusive property rights are better suited for "investment in relatively large-scale innovation than in a small-scale innovation").

24. Jed Rubenfeld characterizes some of them as "Giant-sized First Amendment theories," which "tend to start with one or both of two giant-sized ideas: either democracy or individual autonomy." Rubenfeld, "Freedom of Imagination," 30. We have attempted to acknowledge at least a representative sampling of these works in Chapter 4, as well as works less sweeping in scope.

25. *Whitney v. California*, 274 U.S. at 375.

26. Copyright has proven to enjoy a peculiar "first-amendment immunity." Rubenfeld, "Freedom of Imagination," 5–29. In contrast, trademark and right of publicity claims have sometimes failed on First Amendment grounds. See, e.g., *Mattel, Inc. v. MCA Records, Inc.*, 296 F.3d 894, 901 (9th Cir. 2002) (holding that trademark law does not have the automatic right to trump the First Amendment and that, "[s]imply put, the trademark owner does not have the right to control public discourse whenever the public imbues his mark with a meaning beyond its source-identifying function"); *L.L. Bean v. Drake Publishers, Inc.*, 811 F.2d 26, 34 (1st Cir. 1987) (defeating a tarnishment claim and holding that parodic use of a trademark is "no reason to afford less protection under the first amendment"); *Cardtoons, L.C. v. Major League Baseball Players Ass'n*, 868 F. Supp. 1266 (N.D. Okla. 1994) (parodic use of baseball cards was protected by the First Amendment and not a violation of Oklahoma's right of publicity statute); *CBC Distribution and Marketing Inc. v. Major League Baseball Advanced Media, L.P.*, 443 F. Supp. 2d 1077 (E.D. Mo. 2006). ("CBC's First Amendment right to freedom of expression prevails over the players' claimed right of publicity; none of the justifications for the right of publicity compel a finding that the First Amendment should not trump the right of publicity.")

27. See our discussion on "The Literature, Albeit in Passing," in Chapter 4.

28. Ibid. See Rubenfeld, "Freedom of Imagination," note 30.

29. See Jane Ginsburg, "Authors and Users in Copyright," *Journal of the Copyright Society of the USA* 45 (1997): 1 ("Digital agendas notwithstanding, some of this derogatory discourse is not new; infringers have long found eloquent, if somewhat cynical, ways to justify piracy in the name of progress [not to mention the First Amendment]."); Jane Ginsburg et al., "The Constitutionality of Copyright Term Extension: How Long Is Too Long?" *Cardozo Arts & Entertainment Law Journal* 18 (2000): 651, 701. ("The First Amendment is certainly about the freedom to make your own speech. Whether it is about the freedom to make other people's

speeches again for them, I have some doubt.") See also the comments of Professor Arthur Miller in the same Ginsburg article, supra, at 694 ("As to the First Amendment argument, it is interesting. I will leave that by and large to Professor Ginsburg. The notion that copyright, *ipsi dixit, ipso facto*, suppresses speech, however, boggles my mind. Anyone can take my speech, take my ideas, and make fair use of it. Indeed, that is what the United States Supreme Court said in *Harper & Row v. Nation Enterprises*."); see also Richard Epstein, "Privacy, Publication, and the First Amendment: The Dangers of First Amendment Exceptionalism," *Stanford Law Review* 52 (2000): 1003; Richard Epstein, "Liberty Versus Property? Cracks in the Foundations of Copyright Law," *San Diego Law Review* 42 (2005): 1.

30. Nimmer, "Does Copyright Abridge First Amendment Guaranties?" 1189–93; 1200–4. In Nimmer's view, however, the appropriate role ultimately to be played by fair use was a subject for congressional determination, and probably was narrower than is generally allowed in our time.

31. Ibid., 1196–200.

32. Rubenfeld, "Freedom of Imagination," 13–16; see also Yochai Benkler, "Free as the Air to Common Use: First Amendment Constraints on Enclosure of the Public Domain," *New York University Law Review* 74 (1999): 354.

33. 17 U.S.C. § 102.

34. See, e.g., Lawrence Lessig, *Free Culture* (New York: Penguin Press, 2004): 8, 30, 99, 192–93 (arguing that contemporary copyright regimes force artists and creators to work within a permission culture rather than a free culture).

35. For more on patents of this nature, see *Chisum on Patents* § 1.03[5]; *State St. Bank & Trust Co. v. Signature Fin. Group*, 149 F.3d 1368 (Fed. Cir. 1998); see also *Nimmer on Copyright* § 2.19.

36. In 2006, Congress passed and the president signed the Trademark Dilution Revision Act of 2006 (H.R. 683), which revises the Federal Trademark Dilution Act of 1995. See 15 U.S.C. § 1125(c). This new law modifies the central holding in *Moseley v. V Secret Catalogue, Inc.*, 537 U.S. 418 (2003), discussed in Chapter 1, by replacing the actual dilution standard with a mere "likelihood of dilution."

37. See Jane Ginsburg, "No 'Sweat?' Copyright and Other Protection of Works of Information After *Feist v. Rural Telephone*," *Columbia Law Review* 92 (1992): 338, 375. ("[W]hatever the Supreme Court's prior interpretations of the Patent-Copyright Clause, Congress may nonetheless supply the content of that clause. Even if Congress cannot claim ultimate authority to interpret those portions of the Constitution that bear neither on separation of powers nor on individual rights, Congress should enjoy substantial discretion in implementing its constitutional prerogative to 'promote the Progress of Science.' Congress' determination of what endeavors constitute the 'Writings' of 'Authors' should be viewed as an exercise of fact-finding by the body most competent to evaluate the efficacy of the means chosen to promote the constitutional goal. Supreme Court review of these kinds of congressional findings therefore should be extremely differential.")

38. At one time we believed that the intellectual property clause, preceded and augmented by an affirmative role for the public domain, would offer the better sources of constraint upon the growth of intellectual property. See David Lange, "Recognizing the Public Domain," *Law & Contemporary Problems* 44 (1981):

147; David Lange, "At Play in the Fields of the Word: Copyright and the Construction of Authorship in the Post-Literate Millennium," *Law & Contemporary Problems* 55 (1992): 139; David Lange, "The Intellectual Property Clause in Contemporary Trademark Law: An Appreciation of Two Recent Essays About Why We Ought to Care," *Law & Contemporary Problems* 59 (1996): 213, 240. ("[S]ome indeed have argued that the First Amendment should be more immediately applicable to copyright than has been the case to date. I disagree, and strongly so. The First Amendment presupposes freedom of expression; intellectual property under the Constitution presupposes exclusive rights for limited times. The presumptions in First Amendment jurisprudence run in ways inappropriate to the presumptions in intellectual property. What intellectual property requires, I would argue, is not an expanded First Amendment, but an expanded Intellectual Property Clause, joined with the First Amendment in providing a comprehensive system of protection for individual proprietary rights in authorship and invention that ultimately will serve the public domain and freedom of expression alike.") In still more recent years, however, our thinking on this began to change. See David Lange, "Reimagining the Public Domain," *Law & Contemporary Problems* 66 (2003): 463, 474. This book reflects our judgment today that only an absolute First Amendment can constrain intellectual property in satisfactory measure.

39. *INS*, 248 U.S. at 247–51.
40. E.g., Rubenfeld, "Freedom of Imagination." See also Lange, "Reimagining the Public Domain."
41. *INS*, 248 U.S. at 243–46.
42. Ibid., 262–67.
43. See *Sheldon v. Metro-Goldwyn Pictures Corp.*, 81 F.2d 49, (2d. Cir. 1936) *cert. denied*, 298 U.S. 660 (1936) (a classic opinion by Hand, J., making the point in the context of a film starring Joan Crawford). Compare our text at this point and in the pages immediately following with the closely similar discussion in Rubenfeld, "Freedom of Imagination." We ourselves suggested, many years ago, an increased role for apportionment of profits, as an offset against liability for appropriation. See Lange, "Recognizing the Public Domain," at 174 n. 125, citing the Nimmer treatise and its discussion of *Sheldon*. The general idea has been endorsed by many others, including Goldstein in his earlier work. Its provenance is complex and uncertain. We believe, however, that Rubenfeld was the first to suggest that an apportionment of net profits as a complete alternative to exclusivity in a setting also explicitly advocating a clearly paramount role for the First Amendment. Despite some initial misgivings, we have come to concur in his basic analysis. Our views of the role to be played by appropriation of expression under an absolute First Amendment go well beyond his own position, however, as our book suggests, passim; and meanwhile, our conclusion with respect to the permissible limits of an apportionment of net profits is likely to be considerably narrower.
44. See Calabresi & Melamed, "Property Rules, Liability Rules, and Inalienability."
45. See generally J. H. Reichman, "Legal Hybrids Between the Patent and Copyright Paradigms," *Columbia Law Review* 94 (1994): 2432.
46. See Fisher, *Promises to Keep.*
47. David Lange, "Reimagining the Public Domain," notes 22, 53 and accompanying text; see also Rubenfeld, "Freedom of Imagination."

48. Calabresi & Melamed, "Property Rules, Liability Rules, and Inalienability," 1092. ("Whenever someone may destroy the initial entitlement if he is willing to pay an objectively determined value for it, an entitlement is protected by a liability rule. This value may be what it is thought the original holder of the entitlement would have sold it for. But the holder's complaint that he would have demanded more will not avail him once the objectively determined value is set. Obviously, liability rules involve an additional stage of state intervention: not only are entitlements protected, but their transfer or destruction is allowed on the basis of a value determined by some organ of the state rather than by the parties themselves.")

49. See Catherine Fisk, "Credit Where It's Due: The Law and Norms of Attribution," *Georgetown Law Journal* 95 (2006): 49; Roberta Kwall, "Fame," *Indiana Law Journal* 73 (1997): 1; Roberta Kwall, "Copyright and the Moral Right: Is an American Marriage Possible?" *Vanderbilt Law Review* 38 (1985): 1.

50. For further discussion on the moral right, its ascension and history, see Russell DaSilva, "Droit Moral and the Amoral Copyright: A Comparison of Artists' Rights in France and the United States," *Bulletin of the Copyright Society* 28 (1980): 1; Kwall, "Copyright and the Moral Right;" *Nimmer on Copyright* § 8D.

51. *Nimmer on Copyright* § 8D.

52. For a detailed discussion of French moral rights, see Calvin Peeler, "From the Providence of Kings to Copyrighted Things (and French Moral Rights)," *Indiana International and Comparative Law Review* 9 (1999): 423. It should be noted, also, that California is not far behind the French; it too has enacted a paternal "Preservation of Cultural and Artistic Creations" statute that resembles the efforts of the French. See Cal. Civ. Code § 989.

53. See note 4 of this chapter.

54. 17 U.S.C. § 106A. Here, it is also worth mentioning the *Digital Performance Right in Sound Recordings Act of 1995*, Public Law 104–39, 104th Cong., 1st Sess. (Nov. 1, 1995), which has its roots in moral rights. This law was enacted, in part, because of international influence—namely, the Rome Convention, art. 7(1)(a). See *Nimmer on Copyright* § 8.21; Rebecca Martin, "The WIPO Performances and Phonograms Treaty: Will the U.S. Whistle a New Tune?" *Journal of the Copyright Society* 44 (1997): 157, 167–78.

55. 15 U.S.C. § 1125(a)(1)(B).

56. Moral rights gained a new formal entitlement to recognition after the U.S. accepted Article 6 *bis* of the Berne Convention. But the principal identifiable result of the United States' having joined Berne is the Visual Artists Rights Act (VARA), which was passed in 1990 and codified at 17 U.S.C. § 106A. VARA, standing alone, does not satisfy Berne because it excludes the right to anonymity or pseudonymity; VARA preserves only the rights of integrity and attribution. Further, Congress has provided that Berne is not self-implementing and artists do not have enforceable rights under Berne alone; the reason is that the Berne treaty does not obligate the U.S. to codify and therefore enforce its provisions. Artists have only those rights provided by U.S. law (here VARA). And VARA applies only to paintings, drawings, prints, sculptures, and, in limited circumstances, photographs (produced for an exhibit, each signed by the creator, numbered, and no more than 200). See 17 U.S.C. §§ 106A, 602(2). *Nimmer on Copyright* § 8D.01[B].

57. See *Dastar Corp. v. Twentieth Century Fox Film Corp.*, 539 U.S. 23 (2003) (holding that the phrase "designation of origin" referred to the source of a commercial good and not the idea maker behind the good; the defendant, therefore, did not violate § 43[a] of the Lanham Act "False Designation of Origin," codified at 15 U.S.C. § 1125[a]).

58. We discuss the Digital Millennium Copyright Act and its impact on expression in somewhat greater detail in Chapter 13. But the full scope of the DMCA is ultimately well beyond the reach of this book.

59. See generally *Restatement (Third) of Unfair Competition* § 39 et seq.

60. See *Restatement (Third) of Unfair Competition*, § 43 cmt. (b) (allowing for persons "to exploit any information acquired through such 'reverse engineering' "); see also *Uniform Trade Secret Act* § 1(4) (" 'Trade secret' means information, including a formula, pattern, compilation, program, device, method, technique, or process, that: (i) derives independent economic value, actual or potential, from not being generally known to, and not being readily ascertainable by proper means by, other persons who can obtain economic value from its disclosure or use, and (ii) is the subject of efforts that are reasonable under the circumstances to maintain its secrecy."); N.C. Gen. Stat. § 66–152 ("Derives independent actual or potential commercial value from not being generally known or readily ascertainable through independent development or reverse engineering by persons who can obtain economic value from its disclosure or use."); see also *Computer Care v. Service Sys. Enters., Inc.*, 982 F.2d 1063, 1075 (7th Cir. 1992) (a trade secret must be characterized as "not generally known or easily duplicated by the industry"); *Chicago Lock Co. v. Fanberg*, 676 F.2d 400 (9th Cir. 1982) (discovery of trade secret by collecting information from other locksmiths who had reverse engineered the plaintiff's locks not improper, nor was compiling and publishing the information so obtained).

61. See, e.g., *ILG Industries, Inc. v. Scott*, 273 N.E.2d 393, 398 (Ill. Sup. Ct. 1971). ("In many cases the question of whether a specific matter is a trade secret is an extremely close one, often not readily predictable until a court has announced its ruling.")

62. See *E.I. duPont deNemours & Co., Inc., v. Christopher*, 431 F.2d 1012 (5th Cir. 1970) (maintaining secrecy does not go so far as to include guarding against aerial reconnaissance flights).

63. U.S. Const. art. I, § 8, cl. 8.

64. U.S. Const. art. I, § 8, cl. 3.

65. Erwin Chemerinsky offers a useful summary and analysis of the development of the commerce clause in *Constitutional Law: Principles and Policies* (New York: Aspen, 1997), 174–97.

66. 5 U.S. 137 (1803); see Jed Rubenfeld, *Revolution by Judiciary: The Structure of American Constitutional Law* (Cambridge: Harvard University Press, 2005), 4, passim ("Incredibly, American constitutional case law has almost nothing to say about what judges are supposed to be doing when they go about the business of interpreting the Constitution."); H. Jefferson Powell, "Grand Visions in an Age of Conflict," *Yale Law Journal* 115 (2006): 2067, 2080–89.

67. 537 U.S. 186 (2003).

68. U.S. Const. amend. 1 ("*Congress* shall make no law") (emphasis added).

69. See Rubenfeld, *Revolution by Judiciary*; cf. "Colloquium: Akhil Reed Amar's *America's Constitution* and Jed Rubenfeld's *Revolution by Judiciary*," *Yale Law Journal* 115 (2006): 1843, 1975–2110.

70. The effect wrought by Holmes is now omnipresent. See, e.g., *Smolla & Nimmer on Free Speech* § 2:19 (New York: Matthew Bender, 1994) (discussing how "absolutism is too simplistic" and demonstrating, à la Holmes, why the First Amendment cannot "immunize all use of language").

71. Chapter 9 of this book is dedicated to an examination of Holmes and his influence.

CHAPTER 7

1. Max Farrand, *The Records of the Federal Convention of 1787* (New Haven, CT: Yale University Press, 1966), 2:617–18. Pinckney's later comment, made in the South Carolina House of Representatives the following January, can be found in volume 3 of Farrand, at page 256.

2. Jacob E. Cooke, ed., *The Federalist* (Middletown, CT: Wesleyan University Press, 1961), 84:581, 579. All subsequent citations of the *Federalist Papers* are to this edition.

3. Hamilton mentioned specifically the prohibitions on bills of attainder and ex post facto laws, which §§ 9 and 10 apply to federal and state authority, respectively.

4. *Federalist* 84:575; ibid., 78:524.

5. Ibid., 48:333.

6. Jefferson to Madison, March 15, 1789, in *Papers of Thomas Jefferson*, ed. J. Boyd (Princeton, NJ: Princeton University Press, 1958), 14:659.

7. The quotations from Madison's speech, which he delivered on June 8, 1789, can be found in Philip B. Kurland & Ralph Lerner, ed., *The Founders' Constitution*, vol. 5 (Chicago: University of Chicago Press, 1987), 24–29.

8. The discussion of libel and liberty of the press is found at William Blackstone, *Commentaries*, vol. 4, (London: A. Strahan and W. Woodfall, 1795), 150–53.

9. Blackstone only obliquely glanced at the tension between condemning prior censorship as arbitrary and approving subsequent prosecutions for criminal libel as salutary, by remarking in the last line of his chapter that "to censure the licentiousness, is to maintain the liberty, of the press." Ibid., 153.

10. See, e.g., Hans Baade, " 'Original Intent' in Historical Perspective: Some Critical Glosses," *Texas Law Review* 69 (1991): 1001.

11. For a discussion of both the argument from settled legal meaning and its competitors in founding-era thought, see H. Jefferson Powell, *A Community Built on Words: The Constitution in History and Politics* (Chicago: University of Chicago Press, 2002), 43–66.

12. *Federalist* 83:560.

13. The quoted expressions are from a speech George Mason gave in the Virginia convention which ratified the Constitution. Mason was arguing against the claim by Edmund Randolph that the ex post facto clauses of Article I §§ 9 and 10 would be interpreted in accord with their "technical definitions." In a 1798 case, *Calder v. Bull*, 3 U.S. (3 Dall.) 386, several justices of the United States Supreme Court accepted Randolph's conclusion; our point is not that Randolph was wrong but

that both his and Mason's were reasonable legal arguments at the time of the First Amendment's origins. For further substantiation of this point, see Powell, *A Community Built on Words*, 45–50.

14. The reader will have noted that the First Amendment uses language, "the freedom of speech, and of the press" that actually is not identical to Blackstone's phrase. The point seems overnice—and founding-era lawyers like their modern counterparts were suspicious of arguments based on minute observations about word choice. On the other hand, Article 9 of the English Bill of Rights of 1689 provided that "the freedom of speech, and debates or proceedings in Parliament, ought not to be impeached or questioned in any court or place out of Parliament," a privilege in other words against subsequent legal liability. Technically, one might say, the First Amendment's language suggested that it was this provision, and its lineal descendent in Article I, Section 6 of the Constitution, not Blackstone's definition of "liberty of the press," that should supply the professional meaning relevant to the First Amendment's interpretation.

15. *Federalist* 84:580.

16. Hamilton did comment in a footnote that "it is notorious that the press no where enjoys greater liberty than in" Britain. Ibid., 580 n. *. Leonard Levy has described this as an implicit acceptance of Blackstone's definition. Leonard W. Levy, ed., *Freedom of the Press from Zenger to Jefferson*, repr. ed. (Durham, NC: Carolina Academic Press, 1996), 144. This turns on its head Hamilton's direct argument in the text of *Federalist* 84, and ignores what that argument makes clear, that Hamilton's contention is that no written constitutional guarantee can safeguard the *proper* liberty of the press, so that "its security . . . must altogether depend on public opinion, and on the general spirit of the people and of the government." *Federalist* 84:580. Hamilton's point in the footnote is not that the British enjoy unsurpassed freedom of the press because the British government observes Blackstone's no-prior-restraint rule, but because British opinion in and out of Parliament was libertarian on the matter.

17. Frank W. Grinnell, "Hitherto Unpublished Correspondence Between Chief Justice Cushing and John Adams in 1789," *Massachusetts Law Quarterly* 27 (October 1942): 11–16.

18. U.S. Ministers Elbridge Gerry, John Marshall, and Charles Cotesworthy Pinkney to Charles-Maurice Talleyrand-Perigord, April 3, 1798, in *Papers of John Marshall*, ed. William C. Stinchcombe & Charles T. Cullen, vol. 3, (Chapel Hill: University of North Carolina Press, 1979), 447–48.

19. The editors of the Marshall Papers observe in an editorial note that Marshall was "[w]orking rapidly and without his usual care." Ibid., 427 n.

20. Marshall's assertion that "[n]o regulations exist which enable the government to suppress" libel shows that his reference to an injured individual being free to carry out "a legal prosecution in court" almost certainly refers to the existence of civil actions for the tort of defamation. Marshall's use of the word "prosecution" does not imply a reference to criminal prosecution; earlier in the reply to Talleyrand he used the word twice in a noncriminal context. Ibid., 437.

21. Ibid., 442. However hastily written, this sentence was carefully constructed to repel any suggestion that the freedom of either the individual or of the press is dependent on the value or wisdom of what is published. "Judgment"/"passions" and

"labors of virtue"/"efforts of particular interests" set up parallel dichotomies between "meritorious expression" and its opposite.

22. The quotation is from John Taylor, denouncing the Sedition Act as a violation of the First Amendment in the Virginia legislature in December 1798. Va. Rep. 119. In the original debate over passing the Sedition Act in the U. S. House of Representatives, a leading opponent, Nathaniel Macon, asserted that "[t]his subject has been so well handled by our Envoys in their reply to Mr. Talleyrand, that he wondered if an attempt of this kind [to defend the Constitutionality of the Sedition Act] should have been made. Nothing he could say would be half so well said as were their observations on the subject. They met with his entire approbation." 8 *Annals of Congress* 2106.

23. On this point, see the discussion in Powell, *A Community Built on Words*, 55–66, 78–80.

24. *Federalist* 37:236.

CHAPTER 8

1. *Prize Ship and Crew—How to Be Disposed Of*, 1 Op. Atty. Gen. 85, 86 (1798); *Bas v. Tingy*, 4 U.S. (4 Dall.) 37, 40–41 (1800) (seriatim opinion of Washington, J.); ibid., 45 (Paterson, J.).

2. 1 Stat. 596.

3. Ibid. § 2. In the remainder of section 2, omitted here, Congress criminalized actions intended to "stir up sedition" or "excite any unlawful combinations" to resist the execution of federal law. Neither this provision, nor the first section of the Act, which made it a crime to conspire to oppose or intimidate the officers or operations of the federal government, provoked significant constitutional dispute, although Republicans opposed them as unnecessary and partisan in intention. Henceforth, unless otherwise indicated, references to the Sedition Act are to the seditious libel provision of section 2 quoted in the text.

4. In this period, the Senate's debates were not published; thus, only the House preserves a record of the first debates over the Sedition Act. The quote is from the House debates.

5. 8 *Annals of Congress* 2093.

6. The quotations may be found in 8 *Annals of Congress* 2139, 2145. The House debate over the First Amendment issue is analyzed in H. Jefferson Powell, *A Community Built on Words: The Constitution in History and Politics* (Chicago: University of Chicago Press, 2002), 55–60. The House also fought over the question whether, apart from the Act, the federal courts could punish seditious libel as a common-law crime, a debate that was both fierce and intrinsically interesting but beside the point for present purposes.

7. Otis's speech is in 8 *Annals of Congress* 2145–48. Otis is reported to have quoted Blackstone, presumably the passage in the *Commentaries* which states that "*the liberty of the press*, properly understood . . . consists in laying no *previous* restraints upon publications, and not in freedom from censure for criminal matter when published." William Blackstone, *Commentaries*, vol. 4, (London: A. Strahan and W. Woodfal, 1795), 151–52 (emphasis original to Blackstone).

8. 8 *Annals of Congress*, 2102; 10 ibid., 933; 8 ibid., 2167.

9. Ibid., 2148.

10. The rhetorical distinction the Federalists often drew between liberty and licentiousness is, as the reader knows, also to be found in Blackstone.
11. 8 *Annals of Congress*, 2105.
12. Ibid., 2160.
13. Ibid., 9:3009. The speaker was John Nicholas.
14. See, e.g., ibid., 8:2161.
15. Ibid., 2140–41. The speaker was John Nicholas.
16. "Report on the Virginia Resolutions (Jan. 1800)," in Philip B. Kurland & Ralph Lerner, ed., *The Founders' Constitution*, vol. 3 (Chicago: University of Chicago Press, 1987), 142.
17. 9 *Annals of Congress*, 3008.
18. 8 *Annals of Congress*, 2160. The formulation was Gallatin's.
19. Joseph Story, *Commentaries on the Constitution of the United States*, vol. 5 (Boston: Hilliard, Gray, 1833), § 1885.
20. 8 *Annals of Congress*, 2152. The speaker was Nathaniel Macon. Gallatin, the leading Republican constitutional expert in Congress, had remarked earlier in the debate that his "opinion was that an appeal must be made to another tribunal, to the Judiciary." Ibid., 2111. For Federalist invocations of the courts' authority to review the Act's constitutionality, see ibid., 2096 (John Allen), 2136 (James A. Bayard).
21. 10 *Annals of Congress* at 916 (Federalist Jonas Platt), 917 (Republican Thomas T. Davis). For other Federalist comments invoking the actions of the federal courts, see ibid., 407 (Bayard), 417 (Otis), 932 (John Rutledge), 960 (Henry Lee).
22. By its own terms, the Act expired on March 3, 1801, the day before the Republican Thomas Jefferson was inaugurated president.
23. An Impartial Citizen [pseud.], *A Dissertation Upon the Constitutional Freedom of the Press* (1801), reprinted in *American Political Writing during the Founding Era 1760–1805*, ed. Charles S. Hyneman & Donald S. Lutz (Indianapolis, IN: Liberty Press, 1983), 2:1126, 1169, 1128.
24. Report of a select committee on petitions for a repeal of the Alien and Sedition Acts (Feb. 25, 1799), in 9 *Annals of Congress*, 2989.
25. Ibid.
26. Ibid.

CHAPTER 9

1. *Schenck v. United States*, 249 U.S. 47, 52 (1919).
2. *Schenck*, 249 U.S 47 at 52. This comment arguably had as much to do with the law of criminal attempts as with the interpretation of the First Amendment. See H. L. Pohlman, *Justice Oliver Wendell Holmes: Free Speech and the Living Constitution* (New York: New York University Press, 1991), 68–70.
3. *Abrams v. United States*, 250 U.S. 616, 630–31 (1919). At other points in his opinion, Holmes made it clear that he did not regard the clear and present danger test as applicable to situations "where private rights are . . . concerned," ibid., 628, or where something more than "expressions of opinion and exhortations" are at issue, ibid., 631. Holmes presumably had individual actions for defamation primarily in mind in his reference to "private rights."
4. "I never have seen any reason to doubt that the questions of law that alone were

before this Court in the Cases of Schenck, Frohwerk, and Debs, were rightly decided." Ibid., 627 (citations omitted).

5. There is no point in attempting an exhaustive list of the tellings. For one account, see G. Edward White, *Justice Oliver Wendell Holmes: Law and the Inner Self* (New York: Oxford University Press, 1993), 412–54.

6. *Curtis Publ'g Co. v. Butts*, 388 U.S. 130, 148 (1967).

7. The quoted language is from the annual report of the United States Attorney General for the year 1918. We quote it from Professor Geoffrey R. Stone's excellent article on the Act, which provides a succinct discussion of the Act's origins. See Stone, "Judge Learned Hand and the Espionage Act of 1917: A Mystery Unraveled," *University of Chicago Law Review* 70 (2003): 335, 336.

8. Act of June 15, 1917, c. 30, Title I, § 3, 40 Stat. 219.

9. Ibid. Largely on the basis of the Act's legislative history, Professor Stone's recent article argues vigorously that Congress did not in fact intend the Act to have "the severely repressive effect attributed to it during World War I" by the federal courts. See Stone, "Judge Learned Hand and the Espionage Act," 335. In May 1918, Congress amended the Espionage Act by adding a considerably more draconian statute sometimes called the Sedition Act of 1918. See Act of May 16, 1918, ch. 75, 40 Stat. 553, repealed by Act of Mar. 3, 1921, ch. 136, 41 Stat. 1359. The 1918 Act was not before the Supreme Court during *Schenck* and *Abrams*, which are conventionally understood as the seminal First Amendment decisions.

10. The reader will recall that we are now speaking of the G.O.P., not the 1798 allies of Madison and Jefferson.

11. Zechariah Chafee, Jr., "Freedom of Speech in War Time," *Harvard Law Review* 32 (1919): 932, 932.

12. As the great states' rights jurist Spencer Roane put it in 1819, "the memorable and unconstitutional alien and sedition laws . . . were put down by the general rising of the people," a judgment shared by nationalists such as Henry St. George Tucker, who described the Alien and Sedition Acts as "measures which were received with the deep-toned murmurs of national disapprobation" because they violated the Constitution. Roane's comment is from one of the essays he published in 1819 under the name "Hampden" attacking the Supreme Court's decision of that year upholding the constitutionality of the Bank of the United States. See Gerald Gunther, ed., *John Marshall's Defense of* McCulloch v. Maryland (Stanford, CA: Stanford University Press, 1969), 109 n. 5. Tucker, one of the leading congressional nationalists in the same period, referred to the Sedition Act in a speech in the House of Representatives in March 1818. See 32 *Annals of Congress*, 1318.

13. There were dissenters, of course: a small group of unreconciled Federalists refused to concede that the Act was invalid, although even they generally came to agree that it was unwise, and the great constitutional scholar Joseph Story (a Republican by origin but in his maturity a harsh critic of anything he associated with Jefferson) insisted that popular opinion could not settle a question of constitutional law. But even Story conceded that in fact the Act's invalidity was a basic assumption of American political culture.

14. See David M. Rabban, *Free Speech in its Forgotten Years* (Cambridge: Cambridge University Press, 1997); Michael Kent Curtis, *Free Speech, "The People's Darling*

Privilege": Struggles for Freedom of Expression in American History (Durham, NC: Duke University Press (2000). The quoted words are from White, *Holmes*, 415.

15. *Patterson v. Colorado,* 205 U.S. 407 (1907).

16. Ibid. Patterson's claim raised a distinct and important constitutional question that had not been posed during the fight over the Sedition Act: does the Constitution impose on the states the same (or a similar) prohibition on interference with freedom of expression to that imposed on the federal government by the First Amendment? In 1789, Madison had proposed, along with what became the First Amendment, a provision that would have banned state abridgments of freedom of conscience and liberty of the press, but the Senate refused to concur in this curtailment of state autonomy. Leading proponents of the Fourteenth Amendment, which was adopted in 1868, insisted that the amendment would achieve Madison's goal belatedly, and impose the First Amendment's requirements on the states. While the Supreme Court did not endorse this view of the Fourteenth Amendment until 1925 (and did so then only tangentially and for the sake of argument), the contention that the federal Constitution protected free expression against state interference was at least a plausible one after 1868. In *Patterson* the Court avoided ruling on this issue, assuming for the sake of argument that "there is to be found in the Fourteenth Amendment a prohibition similar to that in the First." 205 U.S. at 462. Justice John Marshall Harlan's brief dissent in *Patterson* was devoted mostly to arguing that the Fourteenth Amendment protected the First Amendment freedoms of speech and press against state interference, although in a single sentence Harlan went on to express his disagreement with the Court's Blackstonian understanding of the scope of those freedoms.

17. Holmes was quoting *Commonwealth v. Blanding,* 20 Mass. 304, 313–14 (1825).

18. "The preliminary freedom extends as well to the false as to the true; the subsequent punishment may extend as well to the true as to the false." 205 U.S. at 462.

19. *Schenck,* 249 U.S. at 51–52.

20. Quotations from the briefs in *Schenck* and *Abrams* are from Philip B. Kurland & Gerhard Casper, ed., *Landmark Briefs and Arguments of the Supreme Court of the United States: Constitutional Law,* vols. 18–19 (Washington, DC: University Publications of America, 1975). See Brief for the United States in *Schenck v. United States, Landmark Briefs,* 18:1043–45 (quoting Department of Justice pattern jury instruction).

21. *Abrams,* 250 U.S. at 630 (Holmes, J., dissenting).

22. See Brief for the United States in *Abrams v. United States, Landmark Briefs,* 19:851–57.

23. Roscoe Pound, "Equitable Relief Against Defamation and Injuries to Personality," *Harvard Law Review* 29 (1916):640, 650.

24. Ibid.

25. Ibid., 650–51. Pound misread Story. See Chafee, "Freedom of Speech in War Time," 932, 938, 938 n. 13.

26. Pound, "Equitable Relief," 654.

27. Ibid. Pound noted that notwithstanding the endorsement of Blackstone in *Patterson v. Colorado,* the federal Supreme Court had upheld a prior restraint upon publication as an incident to enjoining an illegal boycott. Ibid., 652 n. 29.

28. Chafee, "Freedom of Speech in War Time."

29. See, e.g., White, *Holmes*, 427–30.
30. Chafee, "Freedom of Speech in War Time," 957.
31. Ibid., 937.
32. Ibid.
33. Ibid., 938, 939, 940.
34. Ibid., 942.
35. Ibid, 957.
36. Ibid., 957.
37. Ibid., 958.
38. Ibid., 958–59.
39. Ibid., 960.
40. *Springer v. Government of Philippine Islands*, 277 U.S. 189, 209–10 (1928).
41. Oliver Wendell Holmes, Jr., "The Path of the Law," *Harvard Law Review* 10 (1897): 457, 467. Chafee quoted Holmes's observation about judges' neglecting this duty in "Freedom of Speech," 959. The balancing of interests that lay at the core of the *Abrams* dissent (and Holmes's approach to First Amendment doctrine overall) was not universally praised by Holmes's peers. The great Learned Hand, for one, famously disapproved of what he viewed as Holmes's excessive willingness to trust federal judges, particularly the Supreme Court justices, to apply the clear and present danger test in a consistent way:

> I am not wholly in love with Holmesy's test and the reason is this. Once you admit that the matter is one of degree, while you may put it where it genuinely belongs, you so obviously make it a matter of administration, i.e. you give to Tomdickandharry, D.J., so much latitude [here Learned Hand wrote and struck out "as his own fears may require," and continued] that the jig is at once up. Besides their ineffabilities, the Nine Elder Statesmen, have not shown themselves wholly immune from the "herd instinct" and what seems "immediate and direct" to-day may seem very remote next year even though the circumstances surrounding the utterance be unchanged. I own I should prefer a qualitative formula, hard, conventional, difficult to evade.

Gerald Gunther, "Learned Hand and the Origins of Modern First Amendment Doctrine: Some Fragments of History," *Stanford Law Review* 27 (1975): 719, 769–70.
42. See Brief for the Plaintiffs-in-Error in *Abrams v. United States*, *Landmark Briefs*, 19:819–28.
43. *Abrams*, 250 U.S at 627 (Holmes, J., dissenting).
44. Ibid., 630–31.
45. Richard A. Posner, ed., *The Essential Holmes* (Chicago: University of Chicago Press, 1992), xii.
46. In a 1963 lecture, Dean Erwin Griswold contrasted the approach of the "absolutist or 'Fundamentalist'" judge, who "focus[es] on a few words, and ignor[es] all else," with that of a "comprehensive or integral approach [which] accepts the task of the judge as one which involves the effect of all the provisions of the Constitution, not merely in a narrow literalist sense, but in a living, organic sense, including the elaborate and complex governmental structure which the Constitution, through its words, has erected." The lecture is quoted in Tinsley E. Yarbrough, *Mr. Justice Black and his Critics* (Durham, NC: Duke University Press, 1988), 127–28.

CHAPTER 10

1. *Home Building & Loan Assoc. v. Blaisdell*, 290 U.S. 398 (1934).
2. Ibid., 453.
3. Ibid., 442 (Sutherland, J., dissenting).
4. Ibid., 428 (opinion of the Court).
5. *West Virginia State Board of Education v. Barnette*, 319 U.S. 624 (1943).
6. *Barnette*, 319 U.S. 624, 642. Immediately after the quoted language, the opinion of the Court stated that "[i]f there are any circumstances which permit an exception, they do not now occur to us." See T. Alexander Aleinikoff, "Constitutional Law in the Age of Balancing," *Yale Law Journal* 96 (1987): 943, 964.
7. *Barnette*, 319 U.S. at 643–44 (Black & Douglas, JJ., concurring); ibid., 645–46 (Murphy, J., concurring). The irony that Justice Black was one of the concurring justices distancing themselves from the apparent absolutism of the official opinion of the Court will be apparent momentarily.
8. *Schneider v. State*, 308 U.S. 147, 161 (1939).
9. *Bridges v. California*, 314 U.S. 252, 263 (1941).
10. Black acknowledged that Holmes and Brandeis had "forcefully used" the clear and present danger test "not to narrow but to broaden the then prevailing interpretation of First Amendment freedoms" and that in its historical context, the test was "a great advance toward individual liberty," but after he clearly formulated his absolutist position he consistently insisted that even in its strong form, the test failed to "enforc[e] the First Amendment according to its terms." *Konigsberg v. State Bar of California*, 366 U.S. 36, 62–64 (1961) (Black, J., dissenting).
11. See *Barron v. Baltimore*, 32 U.S. 243 (1833). This conclusion, to be sure, was not universal. Only certain of the amendments are facially limited by their language to federal authority (the First Amendment being one of these), and there were eminent antebellum authorities who believed that the generally worded amendments ought to be construed as limitations on state government as well. See, e.g., William Rawle, *A View of the Constitution of the United States of America*, 2nd ed. (Philadelphia: P. H. Nicklin, 1829), 120–21.
12. *Whitney v. California*, 274 U.S. 357, 373 (1927) (Brandeis, J., concurring).
13. Ibid. Holmes was equally aware of the apparent inconsistency. See *Gitlow v. New York*, 268 U.S. 652, 672 (1925) (Holmes, J., dissenting). The *Gitlow* majority stated that "[f]or present purposes we may and do assume that freedom of speech and of the press" are protected by the Fourteenth Amendment. Ibid., 666. By the time *Whitney* was decided, two years later, the majority took the proposition for granted. 274 U.S. at 371.
14. *Palko v. Connecticut*, 302 U.S. 319, 326 (1937). Black, who had been on the Court only a few months, joined the opinion, an action he subsequently regretted.
15. See *Gitlow*, 268 U.S. at 672 (Holmes, J., dissenting):

The general principle of free speech, it seems to me, must be taken to be included in the Fourteenth Amendment, in view of the scope that has been given to the word "liberty" as there used, although perhaps it may be accepted with a somewhat larger latitude of interpretation than is allowed to Congress by the sweeping language that governs or ought to govern the laws of the United States.

16. *Federal Power Commission v. Natural Gas Pipeline Co*, 315 U.S. 575, 601 n. 4 (1942) (Black, Douglas & Murphy, JJ., concurring).
17. *Adamson v. California*, 332 U.S. 46, 89 (1947) (Black, J., dissenting).
18. Ibid., 75 (Black, J., dissenting).
19. See *Rochin v. California*, 342 U.S. 165, 175, 177 (1952) (Black, J., concurring): "I believe that faithful adherence to the specific guarantees in the Bill of Rights insures a more permanent protection of individual liberty than that which can be afforded by the nebulous standards stated by the majority . . . I long ago concluded that the accordion-like qualities of this philosophy must inevitably imperil all the individual liberty safeguards specifically enumerated in the Bill of Rights."
20. *Adamson*, 332 U.S. at 89 (Black, J., dissenting) (summary of historical claim).
21. Ibid. The elaborate care with which Black presented his historical argument should not obscure the fact that he chose to end the main body of his opinion with a careful restatement of his general objections to the exercise of judicial review on the basis of judicial views about liberty and justice instead of "by looking to the particular standards enumerated in the Bill of Rights and other parts of the Constitution," ibid., 91.
22. Justice Douglas joined Black's dissent. Justices Murphy and Rutledge agreed with Black's assertion that all of the Bill of Rights ought to be treated as enforceable against the states but were unwilling to renounce the possibility that a state proceeding might be so procedurally objectionable that it would "warrant constitutional condemnation in terms of a lack of due process despite the absence of a specific provision in the Bill of Rights" to that effect. Ibid., 124 (Murphy, J., dissenting).
23. From Black's perspective, as he stated already in *Adamson*, this outcome, if untidy, was preferable to a continuation of the "natural law" approach he abhorred since it avoided judicial imperialism by linking the Court's review of state action (in general) to specific textual provisions. Ibid., 89.
24. *Rochin*, 342 U.S. at 176 (Black, J., concurring).
25. Ibid.
26. *Beauharnais v. Illinois*, 343 U.S. 250, 266, 256–57 (1952).
27. Ibid., 256–57.
28. Ibid., 261, 263–64.
29. Ibid.
30. In part, therefore, Frankfurter's opinion confirmed the problem with treating Fourteenth Amendment free expression as subject to a different standard than claims against federal action premised on the First Amendment, a problem Black would solve through total incorporation of the Bill of Rights into the Fourteenth Amendment. Frankfurter, indeed, had studiously avoided any direct mention of the First Amendment or of the cases, which Black listed in a footnote, in which the Court had treated the scope of constitutional free expression as identical under both amendments. In a separate opinion, Justice Robert H. Jackson vigorously attacked the idea of incorporation as a means of interpreting the Fourteenth Amendment's protection of free speech, a challenge that Black in his turn studiously ignored. See ibid., 287–88 (Jackson, J., dissenting).
31. Ibid., 265, n. 19 (Black, J., dissenting).
32. Ibid., 268 (Black, J., dissenting).
33. Ibid., 274–75 (Black, J., dissenting).

34. "Justice Black and First Amendment 'Absolutes': A Public Interview," *New York University Law Review* 37 (1962): 549, 553–54.

35. Black also supported his absolutist reading of the First Amendment with a historical claim: the intended purpose of the amendment, he repeatedly asserted, was to deny entirely any power over religion, expression, or assembly to the federal government. Black never presented a detailed justification of this claim, and in making it often simply quoted Madison's 1789 congressional speech introducing what became the first ten amendments. See, e.g,. *Konigsberg v. State Bar*, 366 U.S. 36, 61 n. 11 (1961) (Black, J., dissenting); *Barenblatt v. United States*, 360 U.S. 109, 143 (1959) (Black, J., dissenting); Hugo Black, *A Constitutional Faith* (New York: Knopf, 1968), 46. On occasion, Black also quoted Jefferson or the great Jeffersonian jurist St. George Tucker. See, e.g., *New York Times v. Sullivan*, 376 U.S. 254, 296 n. 2, 297 (1964) (Black, J., concurring). Needless to say, as a historical argument this is less than satisfactory, but our sense is that Black's real point was that the founders agreed that the First Amendment's language ("Congress shall make no law") was to be taken seriously and therefore that whatever the First Amendment's scope might be, within that scope "government was not to act at all." Black, *A Constitutional Faith*, 7. As we discussed in an earlier chapter, there is no reason to doubt that this is correct.

36. Hugo Black, "The Bill of Rights," *New York University Law Review* 35 (1960): 865, 871.

37. Black, *A Constitutional Faith*, 10, 20.

38. In *Barenblatt v. United States*, 360 U.S. 109, 143–44 (1959) (Black, J., dissenting), Black expressly identified adherence to the absolute quality of the First Amendment's language as a matter of fidelity to "our judicial function."

39. "I understand that it is rather old-fashioned and shows a slight naiveté to say that 'no law' means no law. It is one of the most amazing things about the ingeniousness of the times that strong arguments are made, which *almost* convince me, that it is very foolish of me to think 'no law' means no law." "Justice Black and First Amendment 'Absolutes,' " 553.

40. See, e.g., Black, "The Bill of Rights," 866–67.

41. "Obviously the way to communicate ideas is through words." Black, *A Constitutional Faith*, 45.

42. Black, "The Bill of Rights," 867.

43. Ibid., 875 (sentence order reversed), 879.

44. *Konigsberg v. State Bar*, 366 U.S. 36, 61 (1961) (Black, J., dissenting).

45. *Barenblatt*, 360 U.S. 109, 143–44. On the threat to political democracy posed by governmental control of expression, see ibid., 150–51.

46. See, e.g., Black, *A Constitutional Faith*, 53–60.

47. Tinsley E. Yarbrough, *Mr. Justice Black and his Critics* (Durham, NC: Duke University Press, 1988), 128.

48. Paul A. Freund, "Mr. Justice Black and the Judicial Function," *UCLA Law Review* 14 (1967): 467, 473.

49. Justice Black concurred in the Court's judgment, but of course would have gone much further. Justice Brennan's opinion for the Court held it constitutional to award damages where the defamatory statement was proven to be the product of "actual malice," but Black insisted that the power of any American government

"to impose damages for merely discussing public affairs and criticizing public officials . . . is, in my judgment, precisely nil." *New York Times v. Sullivan*, 376 U.S. 254, 295–96 (1964) (Black, J., concurring).

50. *Brandenburg v. Ohio*, 395 U.S. 444 (1969). The Court held that such speech can be penalized only if it is intended to, and likely to, incite or produce imminent lawless action. Black actually joined the opinion of the Court, although it is unclear that Black fully accepted the Court's position. See ibid., 449–50 (Black, J., concurring) (stating his agreement with Justice Douglas's concurrence, which would have permitted liability only for "overt acts").

51. *New York Times v. United States,* Transcript of Oral Argument quoted at 403 U.S. 713, 718 (1971) (Black, J., concurring).

52. Ibid., 714. The per curiam opinion was drafted by Justice Brennan. See Roger K. Newman, *Hugo Black: A Biography*, 2nd ed. (New York: Fordham University Press, 1997), 617.

53. Ibid., 714–17 (Black, J., concurring).

54. The quotation from Madison's speech, which he delivered on June 8, 1789, can be found in Philip B. Kurland & Ralph Lerner, ed., *The Founders' Constitution*, vol. 5 (Chicago: University of Chicago Press, 1987), 24–29.

55. Ibid., 719 n. 5, 718 (Black, J., concurring).

56. During the conference after oral argument at which the justices discussed the case and announced their conclusions, Justice Potter Stewart (one of the six in the majority) apparently commented that "[t]he First Amendment is not an absolute" and that the Court "as a court of equity, would have the power to enjoin [a] publication" that would "result in immediate, grave and irreparable harm to the United States." Del Dickson, ed., *The Supreme Court in Conference, 1940–1985: The Private Discussions Behind Nearly 300 Supreme Court Decisions* (Oxford: Oxford University Press, 2001), 371. It seems clear from the opinions filed in the case that only Black and Douglas, who joined in each other's concurrences, disagreed with Stewart.

57. In a 1969 case, *Street v. New York*, Black wrote that

It passes my belief that anything in the Federal Constitution bars a State from making the deliberate burning of the American flag an offense. It is immaterial to me that words are spoken in connection with the burning. It is the burning of the flag that the State has set its face against. . . . The talking that was done took place 'as an integral part of conduct in violation of a valid criminal statute' against burning the American flag in public.

394 U.S. 576, 610 (1969) (Black, J., dissenting) (quoting *Giboney v. Empire Storage & Ice Co.*, 336 U.S. 490, 498 (1949). The Court in *Street* overturned the defendant's conviction because a majority of the justices believed that the record did not exclude the possibility that he had in fact been punished for his comments, a rationale with which Black disagreed because he did not think the majority's doubts were justified. Ibid., 609–10 (Black, J., dissenting) (the conviction "rested entirely on the fact that the defendant had publicly burned the American flag—against the law of the State of New York"). But see *Texas v. Johnson*, 491 U.S. 397 (1989) (flag-burning as a protest is expression protected by the First Amendment); *United States v. Eichman*, 496 U.S. 310 (1990) (same).

58. Black was willing to employ a balancing approach to forbid laws that "affect speech indirectly where other means are available to accomplish the desired result without burdening speech or where the need to control the conduct in question is insufficient even to justify an indirect effect on speech." Black, *A Constitutional Faith*, 60. In doing so, he introduced alongside the speech/conduct distinction a second and equally problematic contrast between "direct" and "indirect" burdens on speech.

59. Ibid., 53, quoting Justice Douglas's dissent in *Roth v. United States*, 354 U.S. 476, 514 (1957).

60. Henry J. Abraham, "First Amendment Absolutism," in *The Oxford Companion to the Supreme Court of the United States*, 2nd ed., ed. Kermit. L. Hall et al., 347 (New York: Oxford University Press, 2005).

61. Despite the great confidence with which the critics pronounce Black's absolutism a failure, substantial defenses of his views can be mounted. See Yarbrough, *Justice Black and His Critics*, 126–97; Richard H. Pildes & Elizabeth S. Anderson, "Slinging Arrows at Democracy: Social Choice Theory, Value Pluralism, and Democratic Politics," *Columbia Law Review* 90 (1990): 2121, 2154–58.

62. Perhaps surprisingly, Justice Black's absolutism converges on this point with our former colleague Stanley Fish's critique of First Amendment doctrine. Fish argues that current First Amendment doctrine is empty and indeed deceitful, both because it is manipulable in ways that belie its claim to ideological neutrality and because its intellectual structure—speech may be regulated or even prohibited if a court deems the reasons for doing so weighty enough—is necessarily ideological and political in operation. Fish also believes that "it's a good thing" that First Amendment free speech is in fact a fraud because he is committed to the more general proposition that political disagreements must be fought out as such and that political liberalism's claim to find neutral ground for resolving at least some disagreements is unsustainable. See Stanley Fish, *There's No Such Thing as Free Speech, and It's a Good Thing, Too!* (New York: Oxford University Press, 1994). For our purposes we need take no position on this latter claim, but we actively agree with Fish's criticism of current First Amendment doctrine: as we have argued, at the core of Justice Black's position was the insight—imperfectly realized, it may be, by Black himself—that the sort of balancing natural in a Holmesian jurisprudential world leads to the very regime of governmental regulation of speech the text of the First Amendment appears to forbid. By returning the First Amendment to its original role as a denial of power to government to do a specific thing, we avoid balancing, and therefore the possibility of manipulation, altogether.

63. See, e.g., Black, "The Bill of Rights," 875 (describing the First Amendment as an example of a situation where "the Constitution withdraws from Government all power over subject matter in an area").

64. Black, *A Constitutional Faith*, 7.

65. In our thinking about this issue, we are indebted to the seminal work of Professor Philip Bobbitt. See, e.g., Philip Bobbitt, *Constitutional Interpretation* (Oxford, UK: B. Blackwell, 1991).

CHAPTER 11

1. Charles L. Black, Jr., "Mr. Justice Black, the Supreme Court, and the Bill of Rights," in *The Occasions of Justice* (New York: Macmillan, 1963), 99.

2. This is so even with respect to those areas of constitutional law in which judicial creativity is clearly at its maximum and the role of the text is minimal, or where the primary basis for the court's decision is constitutional structure rather than constitutional text. The early twentieth-century doctrine of freedom of contract and the late twentieth-century privacy doctrine are often criticized as essentially freewheeling inventions of the Supreme Court, but in form both are explications of the implications of the word "liberty" in the due process clauses of the Fifth and Fourteenth Amendments. The Supreme Court's various doctrines concerning federalism and separation of powers are fundamentally about the structure of American constitutional institutions, but that structure is itself tied to and largely derived from many provisions of the text.

3. While this may not be a matter of logical necessity, the Supreme Court has long treated the equal protection clause of the Fourteenth Amendment as safeguarding certain individual liberties against state interference. As a textual matter, the analogous equal protection principle binding the federal government is located in the "liberty" secured by the Fifth Amendment.

4. Similar observations apply to review of action by state governments under the federal Constitution, although as a general matter the internal structure of state government and the existence of an affirmative delegation of power to the state government are not issues of federal constitutional law.

5. Once again, parallel observations can be made about the current understanding of the relationship between federal constitutional rights and state governmental authority, with the difference that the source of state authority is not as a general matter the United States Constitution.

6. There are, to be sure, "political questions"—constitutional issues the resolution of which the courts treat as matters for the legislative and executive branches. The number of modern Supreme Court cases finding an issue to be a political question is extremely small, and the notion has little direct relevance to matters involving individual rights.

7. "Very few," of course, is not the same as "none." We believe, as we suggested above, that individuals have an absolute right not to be punished by government for subscribing (or not subscribing) to a given theological creed.

8. Solicitor General Erwin Griswold quoted in Tinsley E. Yarbrough, *Mr. Justice Black and His Critics* (Durham, NC: Duke University Press, 1988), 128.

9. As Judge Posner puts it:

    [A]t their best, American appellate courts are councils of wise elders meditating on real disputes, and it is not completely insane to entrust them with responsibility for resolving these disputes in a way that will produce the best results in the circumstances rather than resolving them purely on the basis of rules created by other organs of government or by their own previous decisions, although that is what they will be doing most of the time.

    Richard A. Posner, *The Problematics of Moral and Legal Theory* (Cambridge, MA: Harvard University Press, 1999), 257–58. According to Judge Posner, a prop-

erly "pragmatic" appellate court will "tend to treat the Constitution . . . as a kind
of putty that can be used to fill embarrassing holes in the legal and political framework of society." Ibid., 258. Given this view of judging (if that is the word), it is
quite logical, if still a bit startling, to find Posner apparently denying that "the
judge has some kind of moral or even political duty to abide by constitutional or
statutory text." Richard A. Posner, "Pragmatism Versus Purposivism in First
Amendment Analysis," *Stanford Law Review* 54 (2002): 737, 739.

10. *Lunding v. New York Tax Appeals Tribunal*, 522 U.S. 287, 297–99 (1998).
11. Ibid.
12. Ibid.
13. *Planned Parenthood v. Casey*, 505 U.S. 833, 877 (1992) (opinion of O'Connor,
Kennedy & Souter, JJ.).
14. The reader well might ask whether this simply collapses modern constitutional
law into the old and discredited notion that liberty is simply the absence of delegated power.
15. In the same 1963 lecture quoted above, Dean Griswold contrasted the approach of
the "absolutist or 'Fundamentalist'" judge, who "focus[es] on a few words, and
ignor[es] all else," with that of a "comprehensive or integral approach [which] accepts the task of the judge as one which involves the effect of all the provisions of
the Constitution, not merely in a narrow literalist sense, but in a living, organic
sense, including the elaborate and complex governmental structure which the
Constitution, through its words, has erected." Griswold, quoted in Yarbrough,
Mr. Justice Black and his Critics, 128.
16. The example is borrowed from the Court's cases applying the privileges and immunities clause of Article IV. See, e.g., *Lunding*, 522 U.S. 287, 297–99 (1998).
17. See, e.g., John Hart Ely, *Democracy and Distrust* (Cambridge, MA: Harvard University Press, 1980), 109.
18. *Chisholm v. Georgia*, 2 U.S. (2 Dall.) 419 (1793).
19. See Maeva Marcus, ed., *Documentary History of the Supreme Court of the
United States, 1789–1800*, vol. 5, (New York: Columbia University Press, 1994),
627, 637–38.
20. *Hans v. Louisiana*, 134 U.S. 1 (1890).
21. Ibid., 10.
22. As the *Hans* Court explained at length:

This amendment, expressing the will of the ultimate sovereignty of the whole country,
superior to all legislatures and all courts, actually reversed the decision of the supreme
court. It did not in terms prohibit suits by individuals against the states, but declared
that the constitution should not be construed to import any power to authorize the
bringing of such suits. The language of the amendment is that "the judicial power of
the United States shall not be construed to extend to any suit, in law or equity, commenced or prosecuted against one of the United States by citizens of another state,
or by citizens or subjects of any foreign state." The supreme court had construed the
judicial power as extending to such a suit, and its decision was thus overruled.

Ibid., 11.
23. "In view of the manner in which that decision was received by the country, the
adoption of the Eleventh Amendment, the light of history, and the reason of the

thing, we think we are at liberty to prefer [the dissenting view in *Chisholm*] in this regard." Ibid., 18–19.

24. 209 U.S. 123 (1908). Fortunately for the reader, we need not pause over the various oddities and (some argue) absurdities of a doctrine of federal-court jurisdiction that includes both *Hans* and *Young*.

25. *Fitzpatrick v. Bitzer,* 427 U.S. 445 (1976).

26. Ibid. The *Ex parte Young* principle that a state official may be enjoined from enforcing a state statute that violates the federal Constitution also applies to state laws that contradict a valid federal statute, since the supremacy clause of Article VI of the Constitution makes not only the Constitution but also "the Laws of the United States which shall be made in Pursuance thereof . . . the supreme Law of the Land."

27. 427 U.S. at 452–53, 456.

28. 491 U.S. 1 (1989) (plurality opinion by Brennan, J.). The fifth vote sustaining the particular congressional statutory provision at issue was supplied by Justice White, who cryptically noted that he "agree[d] with the conclusion reached by Justice Brennan . . . that Congress has the authority under Article I to abrogate the Eleventh Amendment immunity of the States, although [White did] not agree with much of his reasoning." Ibid., 57 (White, J., concurring in the judgment).

29. Ibid., 17 (Brennan, J.).

30. Ibid., 42 (Scalia, J., concurring in part and dissenting in part).

31. *Seminole Tribe v. Florida,* 517 U.S. 44 (1996).

32. Ibid., 65–66.

33. Ibid., 72. The Supreme Court's decision in *Central Virginia Community College v. Katz,* 546 U.S. 356 (2006), holding that Congress's power under the bankruptcy clause to enact "uniform" laws on that subject is not subject to state sovereign immunity, rests on the "unique history" and function of the clause. Ibid. at 369 n.9. The decision confirms the binary nature of the immunity doctrine. As with the other Article I powers that are subject to the doctrine, there is no judicial balancing: state sovereign immunity either appertains and limits Congress's power or it does not.

34. This point is implicit in *Seminole Tribe.* See especially the Court's discussion of the irrelevance of the fact that, unlike its power over interstate commerce, Congress's power under the Indian commerce clause is virtually exclusive, 517 U.S. at 62. In a later case involving state amenability to suit under the federal Shipping Act of 1984, the Court expressly rejected the argument that it could create an exception to the *Seminole Tribe* prohibition because of the weightiness of the federal government's interest in regulating maritime commerce. See *Federal Maritime Comm'n v. S.C. State Ports Auth'y,* 535 U.S. 743, 767–68 (2002).

35. *Seminole Tribe,* 517 U.S. at 72–73.

36. See, e.g., *Seminole Tribe,* 517 U.S. at 101–68 (Souter, J., dissenting); *Alden v. Maine,* 527 U.S. 706, 781–94 (1999) (Souter, J., dissenting).

37. See *Seminole Tribe,* 517 U.S. at 109 (Souter, J., dissenting). ("The Eleventh Amendment, of course, repudiated *Chisholm* and clearly divested federal courts of some jurisdiction as to cases against state parties.")

38. To be sure, Justice Clarence Thomas has suggested a willingness to consider doing just that, but there is no indication that anyone else on the Court, or likely to

be on the Court, is willing to accept his invitation. Compare Thomas's opinion in *United States v. Lopez*, 514 U.S. 549, 585–603 (1995) (Thomas, J., concurring) with the opinion of the Court, and especially with the concurrence written by Justice Anthony Kennedy and joined by Sandra Day O'Connor, ibid., 569–85 (Kennedy, J.).

39. Because it turned out not to be determinative for the shape of subsequent First Amendment thought, we ourselves have slighted the historically important opinion of Judge Learned Hand in *Masses Publishing Co. v. Patten*, 244 F. 535 (S.D.N.Y. 1917), *rev'd*, 246 F. 24 (2d Cir. 1917), which does receive attention in the standard account of the First Amendment's history. But the existence of Hand's opinion only reinforces our point that (as the reader will see in a moment) the history of the First Amendment is a history of deliberate and creative choice.

CHAPTER 12

1. Jacob E. Cooke, ed., *The Federalist* (Middletown, CT: Wesleyan University Press, 1961), 84:579.

2. See Chase J. Sanders, "Ninth Life: An Interpretive Theory of the Ninth Amendment," *Indiana Law Journal* 69 (1994), 759, 791 (quoting Bork). (Sanders cites to Robert H. Bork, "The Bork Disinformers," *Wall Street Journal*, October 5, 1987, at 22.)

3. William Blackstone, *Commentaries*, vol. 4, (London: A. Strahan and W. Woodfall, 1795), 151–52.

4. Madison, "Report on the Virginia Resolutions (Jan. 1800)," in Philip B. Kurland & Ralph Lerner, ed., vol. 5, *The Founders' Constitution* (Chicago: University of Chicago Press, 1987), 142.

5. See H. Jefferson Powell, *A Community Built on Words: The Constitution in History and Politics* (Chicago: University of Chicago Press, 2002), 59–60.

6. There was more to Holmes's mature thought, to be sure, chiefly his rejection of the "bad tendency" interpretation of constitutional free expression which American courts had evolved in the nineteenth century. See G. Edward White, *Justice Oliver Wendell Holmes: Law and the Inner Self* (New York: Oxford University Press, 1993), 413–14, 417; H. L. Pohlman, *Justice Oliver Wendell Holmes: Free Speech and the Living Constitution* (New York: New York University Press, 1991), 180–84, 222–28. But Blackstone was not taxed with special responsibility for this aspect of pre-1919 free speech law, and the matter is irrelevant to our present discussion.

7. Blackstone, *Commentaries*, 4:150–53.

8. Ibid.

9. Samuel Johnson, *A Dictionary of the English Language*, vol. 2, (London: 1755).

10. Blackstone, *Commentaries*, 4:150–53 (referring to Tacitus, *Histories*, book 1, chap. 1).

11. Ibid.

12. Ibid.

13. Blackstone, *Commentaries*, 4:152 & n. (a).

14. See, e.g., *Alexander v. United States*: "The term prior restraint is used 'to describe administrative and judicial orders forbidding certain communications when issued in advance of the time that such communications are to occur.'" 509 U.S. 544, 550 (1993), quoting Melville B. Nimmer, *Nimmer on Freedom of Speech: A*

Treatise on the Theory of the First Amendment (New York: M. Bender, 1984), §
4.03, p. 4–14. Despite disagreement over the scope and importance of the prior
restraint doctrine, the *Alexander* Court's endorsement of Professor Nimmer's
definition appears to be the mainstream approach.

15. Blackstone viewed monopolies generally as a public wrong, see *Commentaries*
    4:159, picking up on a theme going back to the legendary Lord Coke in the era of
    James I.

16. On Blackstone's familiarity with Milton, see David A. Lockmiller, *Sir William
    Blackstone* (Chapel Hill: University of North Carolina Press, 1938), 192 (quoting
    a poem by Blackstone complaining that legal studies require him to bid farewell to
    his favorite poets, including "*Milton's* mighty self").

17. Vincent Blasi, "Milton's *Areopagitica* and the Modern First Amendment," *Yale
    Law School Occasional Papers*, 2nd ser., 1 (1995): 8, 3.

18. Ibid.

19. Quotes from John Milton, *Areopagitica* as quoted in Blasi, "Milton's
    Areopagitica."

20. John Milton, *Paradise Lost*, bk. 3, lines 94, 95, 98–99 (1667). The relationship
    between *Paradise Lost* and mainstream Christianity is notoriously complicated—
    Blake famously remarked that Milton was "of the Devil's party without knowing
    it," William Blake, "The Marriage of Heaven and Hell," in *The Complete Poetry
    and Prose of William Blake*, ed. David V. Erdman (rev. ed. 1988), 35, but on this
    matter Milton was only restating the official Protestant orthodoxy still common
    to British society in Blackstone's time: God is not responsible for humanity's
    original fall into sin because humanity was created with the ability to stand. The
    consequences of sin, subsequent to the Fall, are therefore not to be ascribed to di-
    vine authority but to human error.

21. See, e.g., *Paul v. Davis*, 424 U.S. 693, 708 (1976) (property interests that are pro-
    tected by the due process clauses are created by independent sources such as state
    law rules).

22. Blackstone, *Commentaries*, vol. 2., "Of the Rights of Things" deals with a num-
    ber of matters that a contemporary American lawyer would not immediately in-
    clude under the heading of property law, including the law of contracts and of
    estates. It was published in 1766, three years before the appearance of volume four
    ("Of Public Wrongs"), where Blackstone discussed libel and liberty of the press.

23. Ibid.

24. Ibid.

25. Ibid.

26. Ibid.

27. See the discussion in the seminal copyright case of *Wheaton v. Peters* where the
    Supreme Court concluded that in passing the first Copyright Act Congress "in-
    stead of sanctioning an existing right . . . created it." 33 U.S. 591, 661 (1834).

28. Perhaps the clearest acknowledgement of the nature of *Sullivan's* innovation is to
    be found in an opinion written by Judge Robert Bork, a well-known critic of judi-
    cial "activism":

    We know very little of the precise intentions of the framers and ratifiers of the speech
    and press clauses of the First Amendment. But we do know that they gave into
    our keeping the value of preserving free expression. . . . Perhaps the framers did not

envision libel actions as a major threat to that freedom. . . . But if, over time, the libel action becomes a threat to the central meaning of the First Amendment, why should not judges adapt their doctrines? Why is it different to refine and evolve doctrine here, so long as one is faithful to the basic meaning of the amendment, than it is to adapt the fourth amendment to take account of electronic surveillance, the commerce clause to adjust to interstate motor carriage, or the first amendment to encompass the electronic media? I do not believe there is a difference. To say that such matters must be left to the legislature is to say that changes in circumstances must be permitted to render constitutional guarantees meaningless.

Ollman v. Evans, 750 F.2d 970, 996 (D.C. Cir. 1984) (en banc) (Bork, Cir. J., concurring), *cert. denied*, 471 U.S. 1127 (1985).

29. Professor Jed Rubenfeld has argued that all of federal constitutional law is shaped by the distinction between the original understanding of what powers or rights a given constitutional provision applied to (the "application understanding"), and original expectations about those matters that the provision was not believed to address. The courts almost invariably respect application understandings while freely disregarding other original views about constitutional meaning. See Rubenfeld, *Revolution by Judiciary: The Structure of American Constitutional Law* (Cambridge, MA: Harvard University Press, 2005). In Rubenfeld's terms, Blackstone's understanding of liberty of the press is the application understanding of the speech and press clauses. While we do not rely on Rubenfeld's account of constitutional interpretation, we think it broadly supports the approach to the First Amendment we take in this book.

30. See Roger K. Newman, *Hugo Black: A Biography* (New York: Fordham University Press, 1997), 499 (quoting correspondence by Justice Black).

31. We substantially agree with Dean John C. Jeffries, Jr., who argued years ago that the prior restraint doctrine as it exists in the context of modern free speech law is conceptually empty. See Jeffries's classic article, "Rethinking Prior Restraint," *Yale Law Journal* 92 (1983): 409.

32. "No one would question but that a government might prevent actual obstruction to its recruiting service or the publication of the sailing dates of transports or the number and location of troops." *Near v. Minnesota*, 283 U.S. 697, 716 (1931).

33. 100 U.S. 303, 307–8 (1880). ("The words of the amendment, it is true, are prohibitory, but they contain a necessary implication of a positive immunity, or right.")

34. *W. Va. State Bd. of Education v. Barnette*, 319 U.S. 624, 642 (1943).

35. Founding-era constitutional thought generally treated the powers of the executive and judicial branches as circumscribed by the limits on the authority of the legislature which would create the laws which the president and the courts would enforce. See G. Edward White, "Recovering the Coterminous Power Theory," *Nova Law Review* 14 (1989): 155. Whatever the status of this concept today, we do not believe that many modern constitutional lawyers would argue that the executive or judiciary can lawfully take actions apart from congressional authorization, which if so authorized would enforce a statute that violates the First Amendment.

36. Justice Clarence Thomas has recently endorsed this view of the establishment clause. See *Elk Grove Unified School Dist. v. Newdow*, 542 U.S. 1, 49 (2004) (Thomas, J., concurring in the judgment).

CHAPTER 13

1. We are entirely comfortable with implications in an absolute First Amendment that go well beyond the focus of our book. We do set to one side a number of categories of expression that we think fall outside likely (or plausible) definitions of "speech" or "press": these would include deception and perjury, for example—neither of which has ever been seen as falling within the protection of the First Amendment under any serious theoretical approach to the subject; we would also exclude many acts that may be "expressive" (the murder of abortion clinic workers, for example, or terrorist assaults by religious fanatics), but which again do not fit within likely or plausible definitions of "speech" or "press." On the other hand, we would not necessarily exclude obscene or defamatory speech, both of which we are quite prepared to suppose are fully protected by an absolute First Amendment—just as we understand Justice Black to have supposed. We offer an explanatory note to this general effect at the beginning of Chapter 4 of our book; and we mean to say essentially the same things again in this concluding chapter. In every instance, the challenge is to define, rather than to balance. It is true, of course, that we cannot elaborate upon all of the possibilities that may follow from our development of our thesis in the context of expressive works currently protected under intellectual property regimes; time and space simply will not allow that. But by no means do we intend to suggest that an absolute First Amendment should be limited to the particular objects of our study.

2. Perhaps we should also make it clear that we do not claim or subscribe to any particular theory of property, though of course we do note that various forms of exclusivity characteristic of many theories of property appear recurrently in contemporary intellectual property regimes. But our objections to exclusivity are not grounded in any theory of property (whether as public goods or otherwise). Instead, they are centered in the particular conflict that arises when congressionally authorized claims of exclusivity in works of expression (as in copyright, for example) are juxtaposed against limitations upon Congressional power to abridge freedom of speech and press imposed by the First Amendment. In our view, the First Amendment's limitation on Congressional power is absolute. Our thesis is that Congress may not grant exclusive rights in expression that otherwise would belong to a universe of discourses. It follows, then, that property of such a nature simply cannot be created or recognized. No theory of property can prevail against this understanding of the First Amendment. We have made this point more than once in the book, and no doubt we could make it more explicit still, but we think it would be a mistake to suggest that property theories (of whatever sort) are relevant beyond this point.

3. *Whitney v. California*, 274 U.S. 357, 375 (1927).

4. L. Ray Patterson & Craig Joyce, "Copyright In 1791: An Essay Concerning the Founders' View of the Copyright Power Granted to Congress in Article I, Section 8, Clause 8 of the U.S. Constitution," *Emory Law Journal* 52 (2003): 909, 945–50.

5. The reader who is familiar with the usual equivalence between "speech" and "expression" in First Amendment discourse will understand, again, that we are using them interchangeably. Of course it is "speech" that is protected by the First Amendment. If an important distinction can be drawn between speech and "expression" in other contexts, so be it. For our purposes none is plausible.

6. 17 U.S.C. § 102(a).

7. On the need to reconcile copyright and the First Amendment, Nimmer wrote:

> Before the task of reconciliation can be attempted, it is necessary in the law, as else-where, to first identify the conflict or paradox which gives rise to the need for reconcili-ation. Jerome Frank has suggested that we often conceal from ourselves the fact that we "maintain, side by side as it were, beliefs which are inherently in-compatible .... We seem to keep these antagonistic beliefs apart by putting them in 'logic-tight compart-ments.'" Nowhere is this phenomenon better illustrated than in the 'logic-tight com-partments' of those devoted to copyright maintaining, on the one hand, their attitude toward copyright, and on the other, their views on freedom of expression under the First Amendment. Not only is there generally a failure to relate the one to the other, but there is, moreover, a failure to perceive that views of copyright and the First Amend-ment, held 'side by side,' may, in fact, be contradictory.

> Melville B. Nimmer, "Does Copyright Abridge the First Amendment Guarantees of Free Speech and Press?" *UCLA Law Review* 17 (1970): 1180 (citations omitted).

8. See Melville B. Nimmer & David Nimmer, *Nimmer on Copyright* § 2.19 (New York: Matthew Bender & Co., 2006); 35 U.S.C. § 171 (a copyrightlike patent en-abling exclusivity for new, original, and ornamental designs); *State Street Bank & Trust Co. v. Signature Fin. Group, Inc.*, 149 F.3d 1368 (Fed. Cir. 1998) (upholding a patent on a data processing system that, as a whole, constituted a patentable method of doing business).

9. Nimmer, "Does Copyright Abridge First Amendment Guarantees?" 1189.

10. As the First Circuit noted:

> Famous trademarks offer a particularly powerful means of conjuring up the image of their owners, and thus become an important, perhaps at times indispensable, part of the public vocabulary. Rules restricting the use of well-known trademarks may therefore restrict the communication of ideas. ... If the defendant's speech is particularly unflattering, it is also possible to argue that the trademark has been tarnished by the defendant's use. The Constitutional implications of extending the misappropriation or tarnishment rationales to such cases, however, may often be in-tolerable. Since a trademark may frequently be the most effective means of focusing attention on the trademark owner or its product, the recognition of exclusive rights encompassing such use would permit the stifling of unwelcome discussion.

> *L.L. Bean, Inc. v. Drake Publishers, Inc.*, 811 F.2d 26, 30–31 (1st Cir. 1987), cit-ing Robert Denicola, "Trademarks as Speech: Constitutional Implications of the Emerging Rationales for the Protection of Trade Symbols," *Wisconsin Law Review* 1982: 158, 195–96; see ibid. at 207 (arguing also that extending the "trademark monopoly must be tempered by the realization that unlimited control over the use of trade symbols will at times interfere with the exercise of basic First Amendment rights"; cited by the First Circuit in *L.L. Bean*).

11. *Restatement (Third) of Unfair Competition* § 39 et. seq; Roger Milgrim, *Milgrim on Trade Secrets* § 1.01 (New York: Matthew Bender & Co., 2006). (" 'Trade se-cret' means information, including a formula, pattern, compilation, program, de-vice, method, technique, or process, that: [i] derives independent economic value,

actual or potential, from not being generally known to, and not being readily ascertainable by proper means by, other persons who can obtain economic value from its disclosure or use, and [ii] is the subject of efforts that are reasonable under the circumstances to maintain its secrecy.")

12. *Restatement (Third) of Unfair Competition*, § 43 cmt. (b) (allowing for persons "to exploit any information acquired through such 'reverse engineering'"); *International News Service v. Associated Press*, 248 U.S. 215, 250 (1918) (Brandeis, J., dissenting).

13. See *Restatement (Third) of Unfair Competition* § 38 et seq.

14. The *Restatement (Third) of Unfair Competition* suggests that the justification for trade secrets is to be seen in the concept of misappropriation. To the extent that misappropriation is about conduct rather than recognition of a property-like exclusivity in expression (as Justice Pitney tried, not altogether unsuccessfully, to maintain in *INS*), protection for trade secrets presumably would raise no issue as against an absolute First Amendment.

15. *Restatement (Third) of Unfair Competition*, §§ 38 cmt. d (common law copyright) and 46 (right of publicity).

16. For more on common law rights and the effect of publication, see *Nimmer on Copyright* §§ 4.01–04.

17. U.S. Const. art. I, § 8, cl. 8.

18. A sampling of compulsory licenses includes: (1) mechanical reproduction (17 U.S.C. § 115); (2) jukebox (17 U.S.C. § 116); (3) and digital audio home recording (17 U.S.C.§ 114). Video compulsory licenses include: (1) cable (17 U.S.C.111); (2) public broadcasting (17 U.S.C.§ 118); (3) satellite retransmission (17 U.S.C.§ 119); (4) and local market retransmission (17 U.S.C. § 122). Compulsory licenses are discussed in *Nimmer on Copyright*, § 8.18, and William Fisher, *Promises to Keep* (Stanford, CA: Stanford University Press, 2004): 41–49.

19. Jefferson to Isaac McPherson, Monticello, August 13, 1813, in Albert Ellery Bergh, ed., *The Writings of Thomas Jefferson* (Washington, DC: Thomas Jefferson Memorial Association, 1903), 330, 333–34.

20. This is easier to prescribe than to achieve. See, e.g., *ProCD, Inc. v. Zeidenberg*, 86 F.3d 1447, 1455 (7th Cir. 1996) (holding that 17 U.S.C. § 301[a] did not prevent enforcement of a "shrinkwrap license" even though the plaintiff's software was within the scope of copyright; in short, the court thought "it prudent to refrain from adopting a rule that anything with the label 'contract' is necessarily outside the preemption clause . . . . [Consequently,] whether a particular license is generous or restrictive, a simple two-party contract is not 'equivalent to any of the exclusive rights within the general scope of copyright' and therefore may be enforced"). The formal reasoning is plausible; the actual outcome on the facts is odious. See generally Mark Lemley, "Terms of Use," *University of Minnesota Law Review* 91 (2006): 459.

21. This is a point we have been stressing for years. See, e.g., David Lange, "Recognizing the Public Domain," *Law & Contemporary Problems* 44 (1981): 147, 170–75; David Lange, "Reimagining the Public Domain," *Law & Contemporary Problems* 66 (2003): 463, 470–71, 482.

22. "No person shall circumvent a technological measure that effectively controls access to a work protected under this title." 17 U.S.C. § 1201(a)(1)(A).

23. 17 U.S.C. § 1201 et seq.

24. See *Universal City Studios v. Corley*, 273 F.3d 429 (2d Cir. 2002). We are referring here to the antitrafficking provisions of the DMCA as interpreted by the court in *Corley*. Under that interpretation, liability will attach to one who cracks the copy control on a DVD and then posts the resulting code on a web site so that others may copy DVDs. In our view, this is plainly an impermissible constraint upon expression despite the Second Circuit's holding to the contrary.

25. The metaphor of the virtual venue seems obvious; we do not recall encountering it elsewhere, but claim no originality in the insight. The challenge will be to constrain it. Cf. Raymond Nimmer, *Information Law* § 4:41 (Eagan, MN: West, 2005) (discussing the constitutionality of DMCA's trafficking rules and the First Amendment, and noting that when "grey areas exist, courts are charged with interpreting a statute to effectuate its purpose within proper Constitutional limits.").

26. Cf. Lawrence Lessig, *Free Culture* (New York: Penguin Press, 2004): 128

    Thus, while it is understandable for industries threatened with new technologies that change the way they do business to look to the government for protection, it is the special duty of policy makers to guarantee that protection not become a deterrent to progress. It is the duty of policy makers, in other words, to assure that the changes they create, in response to the request of those hurt by changing technology, are changes that preserve the incentives and opportunities for innovation and change. In the context of laws regulating speech—which include, obviously, copyright law—that duty is even stronger. When the industry complaining about changing technologies is asking Congress to respond in a way that burdens speech and creativity, policy makers should be especially wary of the request. It is always a bad deal for the government to get into the business of regulating speech markets. The risks and dangers of that game are precisely why our Framers created the First Amendment to our Constitution: "Congress shall make no law . . . abridging the freedom of speech." So when Congress is being asked to pass laws that would "abridge" the freedom of speech, it should ask—carefully—whether such regulation is justified.

27. Nimmer, "Does Copyright Abridge First Amendment Guarantees?" 1196–200 (discussing "The Wedding of Expression and Idea"). See generally Jedediah Purdy, "A Freedom-Promoting Approach to Property: A Renewed Tradition for New Debates," *University of Chicago Law Review* 72 (2005): 1237.

28. Nimmer, "Does Copyright Abridge First Amendment Guarantees?" 1196–200.

29. Nimmer, "Does Copyright Abridge First Amendment Guarantees?" 1203:

    One who wished to fully convey the "idea" of the My Lai massacre photographs could do so only by copying the expression as well as the idea of the photographs. To attempt a simulated photograph with models posing as dead bodies in order to express the idea of the original My Lai photographs would be ludicrous. The expression must be copied along with the idea not because it is onerous for an idea copier to create his own expression, but rather because the idea cannot be conveyed unless the expression as well is copied.

    In our own view, the important issue in this setting is authenticity, rather than expression.

30. Rodney A. Smolla & Melville B. Nimmer, *Smolla & Nimmer on Free Speech: A Treatise on the First Amendment* (New York: Mathew Bender, 1994), § 2:11.

31. Nimmer, "Does Copyright Abridge First Amendment Guarantees?" 1196–200.

32. See Fisher, *Promises to Keep,* 41–49.

33. Stephen Breyer, "The Uneasy Case for Copyright: A Study of Copyright in Books, Photocopies, and Computer Programs," *Harvard Law Review* 84 (1970): 281. See also Rubenfeld, "Freedom of Imagination."

34. Public Law 92–140, (establishing a limited reproduction right in sound recordings); now codified at 17 U.S.C. § 102(a)(7), 14.

35. *Digital Performance Right in Sound Recordings Act of 1995,* Public Law 104–39, 104th Cong., 1st Sess. (Nov. 1, 1995).

36. Copyright Act of 1909, ch. 1, § 1(e) (mechanical copies subject to compulsory license). See also *White-Smith Publishing Co. v. Apollo Co.,* 209 U.S. 1 (1908) (holding that performers and producers of sound recordings did not have exclusive rights in their works under the 1909 Act).

37. See, e.g., Don Henley, "Killing the Music," *Washington Post,* February 17, 2004; Rob Glaser, "Time to Face the (Digital) Music," *Washington Post,* August 24, 2000.

38. It is worth noting that in 2005 "worldwide digital music sales more than doubled to $1.1 billion" as a result of new delivery mediums (e.g., Rhapsody or iTunes) and sales of computer gadgets (e.g., the iPod). See Charles Duhigg, "Apple Renews 99-Cent Song Deals," *Los Angeles Times,* May 3, 2006.

39. *Tombstone* (released December 25, 1993) had a mere six-month jump on *Wyatt Earp* (released June 24, 1994). *Tombstone* grossed $56,505,000; *Wyatt Earp* grossed $25,052,000. See "The Numbers," *The Numbers—Movie Box Office Data, Film Stars, Idle Speculation,* available at www.the-numbers.com (last visited October 2006). (We shall not pause here to give credit to Val Kilmer's transcendent portrayal of Doc Holliday in the first film. We are not film critics, after all.)

40. In fact, most artists prefer to negotiate their licenses through a clearinghouse. The most notable example is the Harry Fox Agency, which in practice represents nearly every copyright holder and publisher in the music industry. The Harry Fox Agency licenses mechanical rights but also represents artists in negotiating reproductive uses not covered by Title 17's compulsory licenses. See Ralph Oman, "Source Licensing: The Latest Skirmish in an Old Battle," *Columbia Journal of Law & the Arts* 11 (1987): 251; see also Alexander Lindey & Michael Landau, *Lindey on Entertainment, Publishing and the Arts* §§ 1:32.70, 8:8 (St. Paul, MN: West, 2004).

41. We have made this point repeatedly in the text. It is a commonplace proposition, well known to all who specialize in copyright, and no less well recognized in the wider precincts of intellectual property at large. See, e.g., Robert Merges, "Contracting into Liability Rules: Intellectual Property Rights and Collective Rights Organizations," *California Law Review* 84 (1996): 1293. Professor Rubenfeld takes it as a likely scenario in the more immediate aftermath of changes in copyright exclusivity under an altered view of the first amendment that emphasizes an apportionment of net profits. We concur.

Bibliographic Note

IN THE INTEREST OF ECONOMY and flexibility alike we have elected to make the bibliography available on-line. A detailed bibliography for *No Law* can be found at the Stanford University Press website, www.sup.org.

As we suggest in the Preface, we have written this work mainly from the perspective of knowledge, understanding, and opinions we had already formed as a consequence of our rather long prior familiarity with the subject matter. The bibliography is meant to include all of the materials we have cited in the notes to the book. We have included some items that were cited at one time or another, but that were eliminated as text or interpretation changed along the way. Finally we have included some citations to materials that we have thought worthy of notice, but not appropriate for citation; generally these materials are in the nature of relevant background reading that did not seem closely related enough to our work to justify inclusion in the notes. In a few instances we have included materials that came to our notice too late for citation.

Errata And Apocrypha

NO DOUBT SOME MISTAKES have crept into our book. No doubt we
have failed to note some works that might have merited acknowledgment. No doubt we have cited some in error. In a project of such length,
and one that has taken several years to complete, it would be remarkable
were it otherwise. For such errors and omissions as there may be, we
apologize. We will welcome corrections from readers.

As we go to press, meanwhile, we note two instances in which we
have boldly stated as fact what may well be merely apocryphal. One is
the suggestion (in Chapter 2) that Judge Hand's manuscripts in *Nichols*
and *Sheldon* "are preserved under glass in the Copyright Office." We
were told as much some years ago, and believe that there is probably at
least some truth to the story. But the Copyright Office is currently undergoing renovation, with considerable resulting disarray. We have been
able neither to confirm our claim, nor to discount it altogether. It is a
charming story, and we have decided to leave it as is.

For similar reasons we have decided not to delete the anecdote involving the nineteenth-century patent commissioner whose supposed
observations about coming to the end of patentable subject matter have
been retailed frequently over a rather long period of time. We have actually discovered a web site that seeks to debunk the tale as myth; we
imagine that myth it probably is. But it is still well-embedded in the lore
and culture of patent law, and we like it. In fact we like it enough to have
included it twice. An old friend used to recite a bit of doggerel that seems
suited to the occasion: "A little nonsense now and then is relished by the
wisest men." We do not claim to be wise, but we beg the reader's indul-
gence in this small matter nevertheless.

Index